Translating Ancient Greek Drama in Early Modern Europe

Trends in Classics –
Pathways of Reception

General Editors
Franco Montanari and Antonios Rengakos

Editorial Board
Lorna Hardwick, Fiona Macintosh, Miltos Pechlivanos

Associate Editors
Anastasia Bakogianni and Rosanna Lauriola

Volume 5

Translating Ancient Greek Drama in Early Modern Europe

―

Theory and Practice (15th–16th Centuries)

Edited by
Malika Bastin-Hammou, Giovanna Di Martino,
Cécile Dudouyt and Lucy C. M. M. Jackson

DE GRUYTER

ISBN 978-3-11-161978-1
e-ISBN (PDF) 978-3-11-071918-5
e-ISBN (EPUB) 978-3-11-071931-4
ISSN 2629-2556

Library of Congress Control Number: 2023933759

Bibliographic information published by the Deutsche Nationalbibliothek
The Deutsche Nationalbibliothek lists this publication in the Deutsche Nationalbibliografie; detailed bibliographic data are available on the Internet at http://dnb.dnb.de.

© 2024 Walter de Gruyter GmbH, Berlin/Boston
This volume is text- and page-identical with the hardback published in 2023.
Cover image: Paul Klee, Hauptweg und Nebenwege

www.degruyter.com

Acknowledgements

This volume draws on the expertise of scholars from across the European continent and largely emerges from two conferences in particular: the first on *Translating Greek Tragedy in 16th-century Europe*, held at St Hilda's College (Oxford) on 14th December 2018; the second on *Translating Greek Drama in 15th–16th century Europe*, held at the Maison Française d'Oxford on 29th November 2019. Thanks go to both of these institutions and the other organisers' institutions for their sponsorship of both events.[1]

But the partnership between, initially, Giovanna Di Martino and Cécile Dudouyt, then broadened to include Malika Bastin-Hammou, and later Lucy Jackson, began at Oxford's Archive of Performances of Greek and Roman Drama (APGRD), with which the editors of this volume are all affiliated. The APGRD's research project *Translating Ancient Drama* soon became the conceptual 'home' for the two conferences just mentioned and those which followed as we moved forward in time.[2] This volume is thus fundamentally grounded in the work conducted for more than three decades on the reception history of ancient Greek and Roman drama by the APGRD, to which we are extremely grateful, both for its support and its ongoing role in pushing the boundaries of translation and reception studies.[3]

We would also like to thank Franco Montanari and Antonios Rengakos, the General Editors of Trends in Classics, for accepting this book for the series, and all those at De Gruyter who have made the volume possible.

---

1 We gratefully acknowledge funding provided by St Hilda's College and the Classics Faculty at the University of Oxford, Pléiade (Université Sorbonne Paris Nord) and Université de la Réunion for the 2018 conference, and Université Grenoble-Alpes for the 2019 conference. We would also like to thank Tristan Alonge, who was part of the organising committee of the first conference.

2 For more information on the APGRD's research project, see http://www.apgrd.ox.ac.uk/about/research/translating-ancient-drama (last accessed 01/09/2022); Macintosh and Di Martino 2021; and Gillespie in this volume. Since 2019, we have moved forward in time, organising two more conferences on the translation of ancient Greek drama from the beginning of the 17th to the end of the 18th centuries: *Translating Ancient Greek Drama in Europe 1600–1750*, online, on 11 December 2020, which was supported by Pléiade (Université Sorbonne Paris Nord), Université Grenoble Alpes, the APGRD, and University College London; and *Translating Ancient Greek Drama (1600–1800)*, at University College London, on 24 June 2022, which was supported by the Leventis Foundation, Pléiade (Université Sorbonne Paris Nord), the APGRD, UCL's Centre for Early Modern Exchanges, and Université Grenoble-Alpes. See https://www.earlymoderntranslation.com (last accessed 01/09/2022) for further details.

3 See http://www.apgrd.ox.ac.uk/about/publications (last accessed 01/09/2022).

Foreword

Every translation manifests an act of reception, a negotiation between difference and repetition, the self and the other. In the case of translation of ancient Greek drama, because of the very antiquity of the material, this *other* is not only set out as a rival, a geographical and cultural other, but also appropriated as an origin. When ancient Greek drama re-emerged in early modern Europe, at the rise of the printing press and of nation states, the relationship between 'ancient' and 'modern', 'old' and 'new' was multifaceted. Although the reception of ancient Greek drama in Italy shaped and informed its receptions in other countries, in a movement that went roughly from east to west, this chronological description hides a far less linear process. The reception engine did not ignite in isolation. It started in urban centres, and was produced and theorised by multilingual scholars, authors and printers who were reading each other's work and travelling from one such centre to another; the life of ancient Greek drama in Italian, Portuguese, French or English is thus also impossible to dissociate from its life in Latin.

This process of reception, appropriation, translation, *translatio studii*, took many forms and was given many names. Here we begin with a visual introduction illustrating the type of aspirations and the enthusiasm underlying the reception of ancient Greek drama from the last decades of the 15th century to the end of the 16th century.

This printer's device adorning the title page of Jean de Lapéruse's *Médée* (1556) depicts the process of giving old texts new life.[1] The publishers, Guillaume and Jacques Bouchet, were both printers and poets, manufacturing the book but also writing dedicatory letters and poems as paratexts, glorying in the power of the press over death and time. Printers' devices were often emblems playing on the printer's name, such as Etienne Dolet's axe ('doloire') for example; but in this mark, the printer-poets chose to depict the man operating the press; in this image the printer is not signified but has himself become the signifier — his body a cypher for the wider spiritual implications of his work. The translinguistic nature of this mission is underlined by the bilingual moto, in Latin above the picture, and in French beneath it.

---

[1] This is the first tragedy in French which reworks ancient plays (primarily Seneca's *Medea*, with elements coming from Euripides' play).

Fig. 1: Jean de La Péruse, *La Médée, tragédie, et autres diverses poésies*, Bibliothèque nationale de France, http://catalogue.bnf.fr/ark:/12148/cb30738384t (last accessed 06/09/2022).

In its tripartite retable-like structure, the image closely resembles other depictions of printers' workshops presenting the tools of the trade: the ink, the paper in the press, and the types.[2] There is on the left, in the background, a worker rubbing dabbers or inking balls; front and centre, the printer operating the press; and on the right-hand side, near a window, the typesetters' station. The viewer's gaze is drawn towards the light on the right-hand side, encouraged by the movement of the printer's arm and by the handle of the printing press, which point towards the two typesetters sitting behind their slanted desk. There, an older bearded man with a plumed hat is supervising the work of a young apprentice. We are not shown the types; the two figures are abstracted from their occupation. They offer a picture of transgenerational transmission, a continuity further symbolised by the older man's foot touching the young man's. Along this horizontal axis the printing press is not only celebrated in its technological materiality, but also in its spiritual powers: printing brings to

---

[2] It closely resembles in its composition the device of Josse Bade, Parisian bookseller and printer (1462–1535). See Budé 1528.

light (a common periphrasis for publication), and that light is also the promise of enduring literary life: the promise of generation after generation of readers.

The vertical axis gives that claim metaphysical dimension. The bilingual motto spells out the particular power of publishing texts translated into vernacular languages as the ultimate literary victory over time. The printers, Guillaume and Jacques Bouchet, triumphantly claim in Latin above the picture: *uitam mortuo reddo* (word for word: 'life to the dead I give back'); and in French at the bottom of the picture 'je ravie le mort' ('I revive the dead'). The striking bodily presence of the printer — barefoot with his sleeves rolled up, and his hand lingering on the lever of the press — joins the two sentences together. The position of his body sets him both in the depth of the depicted workshop and at the surface of the page, with the printed words, his foot firmly on the French syllable 'vie' and his eyes looking straight up at the Latin *reddo*. He does not seem to be in the act of pulling the lever, so much as silently pondering the printed sentence. The horizontal axis showed collaboration, work in common and transgenerational transmission. But the vertical axis, the multilingual intellectuality of the printer-poets-translators, makes an almost blasphemous boast: my work today resurrects the author in his works, in a literary and secular prefiguration of the promised resurrection of the body at the end of time.

Beyond Euripides, the dead who finds new life in this book is Jean de La Péruse, author of the first tragedy written in French that was explicitly drawn from an ancient argument. Earlier published plays in French were either complete verse-to-verse translations such as Lazare de Baïf's *Electra* (1537), Bochetel's *Hécuba* (1544), or Sébillet's *Iphigène* (1549), or imitations of ancient tragedies with the fabulae drawn from the Bible or Roman history, like Théodore de Bèze's, *Abraham Sacrifiant* (1550) or Jodelle's *Cléopatre Captive* (1553). The book belongs to the publishing category of the 'Tombeau poétique' or poetic tomb, texts collected by an author's friends after his death to celebrate his memory and talent.[3] But these 'flying tombs' ('tombeaux volants') were first and foremost celebrations of a victory over death and the means of a resurrection, granting immortality in print. In a poem featured on the back of the image described above, Marc-Antoine Muret, a Latin stylist, uses the verb 'renouveler' ('to renew'): '[Médée] par les vers Pérusins ores *renouvelée*'. Although La Péruse did not translate Euripides *Medea* the echoes of Seneca's and Euripides' texts placed ancient 'intertextuality' at the heart of the artistic ambitions of the playwright; beyond him, his friends, the poets and playwrights who produced this triumphant memorial of a book, were participating in the reinvention of cultural

---

3 See Flegès (2000).

hierarchies within a national context, but in a purely decentralised way, outside the strict circle of a royal (or princely, or ducal) court.

The image suggests not only that one needs to broaden the practical and conceptual framework of 'translation' when working on early modern applications of the term, but that translation practice in this period assumes a metaphorical, even transcendental, meaning. It is as much about prolonging the life of the translated author as it is about giving a new one to the modern translator, in an imitative-emulative relationship that characterises most translations of ancient Greek drama in the early modern period.

Cécile Dudouyt

Contents

Acknowledgements —— V
Foreword —— VII
List of Figures and Tables —— XV
Abbreviations —— XVII

Giovanna Di Martino and Cécile Dudouyt
Introduction —— 1

Part I: Translating Comedy

Micol Muttini
Aristophanes' Readers and Translators in 15th-Century Italy: The Latin Plutus of MS Matrit. Gr. 4697 —— 19

Malika Bastin-Hammou
From Translating Aristophanes to Composing a Greek Comedy in 16th c. Europe: The Case of Alciato —— 37

Simone Beta
The Sausage-Seller Suddenly Speaks Vernacular: The First Italian Translation of Aristophanes' *Knights* —— 53

Part II: Translating Tragedy

II.1: Scholarly Networks: Translation Models and Functions

Alexia Dedieu
An 'Origin' of Translation: Erasmus's Influence on Early Modern Translations of Greek Tragedy into Latin —— 73

Angelica Vedelago
Imitation, Collaboration, Competition Between English and Continental Translators of Greek Tragedy —— 91

Thomas Baier
Why Translate Greek Tragedy? Melanchthon, Winsheim, Camerarius, and Naogeorgus —— 115

II.2: Proto-National Dynamics and Vernacular Translating

Giovanna Di Martino
Translating Ancient Greek Tragedy in 16th-Century Italy —— 137

Claudia Cuzzotti
The Italian Translation of Euripides' *Hecuba* **by Michelangelo Buonarroti the Younger (1568–1647)** —— 159

Maria Luísa Resende
Sophocles in 16th-Century Portugal: Aires Vitória's *Tragédia del Rei Agaménom* —— 175

Cécile Dudouyt
Translating Ancient Greek Drama into French, 1537–1580 —— 189

Part III: Beyond Translation

Lucy Jackson
Translation *Ad Spiritum*: **Euripides'** *Orestes* **and Nicholas Grimald's** *Archipropheta* **(1548)** —— 209

Giulia Fiore
Interpreting Oedipus' *Hamartia* **in the Italian Cinquecento: Theory and Practice (1526–1570)** —— 227

Coda: Dramaturgy and Translation

Giovanna Di Martino and Estelle Baudou
Early Modern Iphigenias and Practice Research —— 255

Stuart Gillespie
Afterword: Prospects for Pan-European Translation History —— 293

List of Contributors —— 305
Bibliography —— 307
Index Nominum et Rerum —— 335
Index Locorum —— 341

List of Figures and Tables

Fig. 1: Jean de La Péruse, *La Médée, tragédie, et autres diverses poésies*, Bibliothèque nationale de France, http://catalogue.bnf.fr/ark:/12148/cb30738384t (last accessed 06/09/2022). —— **VIII**
Fig. 2: Aristophanis *Plutus*, *Matrit. gr.* 4697, National Library of Spain, Madrid, ff. 205v-206r. —— **21**
Tab. 1: Table of French plays drawn from an ancient Greek argument. —— **191**
Figs. 3 and 4: Agamemnon isolated in corners. Lumley's translation (4th episode). Iphigenia Workshop: 21/05/2021. —— **269**
Fig. 5: Agamemnon's peak point. Lumley's translation (4th episode). Iphigenia Workshop: 21/05/2021. —— **270**
Fig. 6: Clytemnestra's peak point. Lumley's translation (4th episode). Iphigenia Workshop: 21/05/2021. —— **271**
Fig. 7: Power balance between the characters. Lumley's translation (4th episode). Iphigenia Workshop: 21/05/2021. —— **272**
Fig. 8: Power balance between the characters. Sébillet's translation (4th episode). Iphigenia Workshop: 21/05/2021. —— **273**
Fig. 9: Agamemnon's lowest point and Clytemnestra's peak point. Sébillet's translation (4th episode). Iphigenia Workshop: 21/05/2021. —— **275**
Figs. 10 and 11: Peripheral position of Iphigenia and the chorus. Sébillet's translation (4th episode). Iphigenia Workshop: 21/05/2021. —— **276 and 277**
Figs. 12 and 13: Chorus members siding with Clytemnestra. Dolce's translation (4th episode). Iphigenia Workshop: 21/05/2021. —— **280**
Fig. 14: Power balance between the characters. Dolce's translation (4th episode). Iphigenia Workshop: 21/05/2021. —— **282**
Fig. 15: Chorus members after Iphigenia's departure. Sébillet's translation (last stasimon). Iphigenia Workshop: 21/05/2021. —— **286**
Fig. 16: Chorus members around Iphigenia. Lumley's translation (last stasimon). Iphigenia Workshop: 21/05/2021. —— **289**
Fig. 17: A random page from *Ilias & Odyssea … cum Latina versione accuratissima: et in easdem scholia, sive interpretatio Didymi: cum Latina versione accuratissima, indiceque Graeco locupletissimo rerum ac variantium lection / accurante Corn. Schrevelio* (Lugduni Batavorum, 1656). —— **296**

Abbreviations

BI: *Biblioteca Italiana* (www.bibliotecaitaliana.it last accessed 06/09/2022)
LCR: *Lessicografia della Crusca in Rete* (www.lessicografia.it last accessed 06/09/2022)
OED: *Oxford English Dictionary* (https://www.oed.com/ last accessed 06/09/2022)
OVI: *Corpus OVI dell'Italiano antico Opera* (www.ovi.cnr.it last accessed 06/09/2022)
TLG: *Thesaurus Linguae Graecae* (http://stephanus.tlg.uci.edu/ last accessed 06/09/2022)
TLIO: *Tesoro della Lingua Italiana delle Origini* (http://tlio.ovi.cnr.it/TLIO/ last accessed 06/09/2022)

Giovanna Di Martino and Cécile Dudouyt
Introduction

The present volume explores the translation of ancient Greek drama into Latin and the vernacular languages from the last decades of the 15th century to the end of the 16th century, in some of the most significant centres of learning in Europe at the time. It combines and integrates the findings of recent publications and conferences on early modern translations of ancient Greek tragedy in Europe[1] with the expanding scholarship on early modern theories of translation. In laying out this rich and colourful mosaic of literary, dramatic, and scholarly activity, this volume also adds an important tile by devoting its entire first section to the translation of ancient Greek comedy. This was a strand of translation that is often forgotten and overlooked, even though it is essential for gaining a full understanding of the literary, dramatic, and scholarly picture.[2]

By combining the scholarship on early modern translation theories with studies of the reception of ancient Greek and Roman texts ('the classics') in this period, the volume inserts itself into both the fields of classical reception and translation studies; it is, in fact, inscribed within the growing interest in translation within classical reception studies, which, as Alexandra Lianeri has recently argued, still lacks 'a book-length survey of debates on translation seen from

---

The introduction and section 1 are by Giovanna Di Martino; section 2 is by Cécile Dudouyt. We would like to thank the other editors of this volume for making additions to, suggestions, and comments on, earlier drafts of this introduction.

---

1 Cf., amongst others, Bastin-Hammou 2015; Demetriou and Pollard 2017; Heavey 2020; and the following conferences: *Greek Drama in Latin 1506-1590. Readership, Translation, and Circulation* (King's College London, 2018); *Translating Greek Tragedy in 16th-century Europe* (Oxford, 2018); *Translating Greek Drama in 15th-16th century Europe* (Oxford, 2019); *Renaissance Academic Drama and the Popular Stage* (St Andrews, 2020); *Classical Receptions in Early Modern English Drama* (Verona, 2022).
2 Cf., amongst others, McLaughlin 1996; Botley 2004 and 2010; Gillespie 2011; Furno 2017; Deligiannis 2017; Petrina and Masiero 2020; for further bibliography on translation theories and practices in the Italian context, see Beta, Cuzzotti, Di Martino, Fiore, and Muttini in this volume; on translation theories and practices relevant to translations into Latin, see Baier, Bastin-Hammou, Dedieu, Jackson, and Muttini in this volume; on translation theories and practices in the English context, see Vedelago and Jackson; on translation theories and practices in the French context, see Bastin-Hammou and Dudouyt in this volume; and on translation theories and practices in the Portuguese context, see Resende in this volume.

[this] viewpoint'.³ Not only does the volume aim at responding to Charles Martindale's call that the reception of an ancient work be at the heart of the study of classics,⁴ it also heeds the exhortation of modern literary specialists like Stuart Gillespie that translation needs to become part of literary history.⁵

As is well-documented throughout the various chapters, translation in the period considered here is at the centre of important cultural and linguistic decisions, some of which heavily contribute to the formation of canons as well as the establishment of, or pushback against, literary, linguistic, and translational norms. Thus, a thorough exploration of the different types, aims, and objects of translation in this period is not just tangential to the study of ancient Greek drama, and the classics more generally, but rather forms an essential part of how we read and receive this rich and ancient dramatic corpus today. This volume represents a timely and important step forward into mapping the multiple ways in which early modern cultures, literatures, and languages interacted with, studied, appropriated, and recreated ancient Greek drama.

1 Early Modern Translation Theories and Practices

Whilst it is usually acknowledged that the first half of the 16th century was a time of intense and prolific translation activity from ancient Greek (and Roman) sources, which occurred in step with the increased distribution of printed books, rarely brought to the fore is the fact that this was also a time of intense reflection on, and formalisation of, translation as a practice, coeval with the emergence of proto-national dynamics and the growth of scientific and literary networks throughout Europe. The contributions gathered in this volume describe a wide variety of translation practices, and comment on many methodological treatises which influence translators, shape discourses around translation, and build on landmark translations from ancient Greek drama, such as Erasmus's *Hecuba* and *Iphigenia at Aulis*.

Beyond the varied picture that they paint of the *translated* reception of ancient Greek drama in the late 15th and 16th centuries, the texts and theories commented upon and analysed in the chapters of this volume also pose a terminological challenge. Many contributors (Bastin-Hammou, Di Martino, Dudouyt,

---

3 Lianeri 2019. For scholarship on the translation of ancient Greek tragedy, see Barbsy 2002; Hardwick 2007, 2010, and 2021; and Macintosh 2013.
4 Martindale 1993, 7.
5 Gillespie 2011, vii.

Jackson, Vedelago) argue that, faced with a continuum of translational practices, it is difficult and even counterproductive to try and draw a clear conceptual line between 'translation proper' and 'not quite translation', even when using terms like 'adaptation'. The various translational choices (verse or prose, Latin or vernacular languages, *ad uerbum*, *ad sententiam*, *ad uersum*, and even *ad spiritum*) deployed by early modern translators and discussed in the paratexts to their translations or in treatises, constitute a rich ecosystem in which there coexists a variety of cumulative functions (emulative, literary, didactic, scholarly, dramatic). Faced with such complexity, sorting out good or bad, 'faithful' or creative translations, misses the mark, whilst also running the risk of projecting conceptions of translation inherited from as early as the 19th century, when translation was (re)defined as the polar opposite of literary creation.

In his chapter 'Cultures of translation in early modern Europe', Peter Burke dates this pivotal shift in translation theories and practices to 1800, which demarcates a clear boundary between early modern and modern practices. The year 1800 is indeed just before Friedrich Schleiermacher's ground-breaking essay *On the Different Methods of Translating* (1813) and Wilhelm Humboldt's preface to his own translation of Aeschylus' *Agamemnon* (1816); that is, before *Verfremdung* as a translational choice and paradigm, but also before the (post)Romantic idea(l) of originality and the genius.[6] Indeed, early modern engagements with ancient Greek dramatic sources eschew contemporary (and, now, rather outdated) oppositions between 'foreignisation' and 'domestication' in translation, to employ Lawrence Venuti's terms,[7] and show that translational processes *are* also at work in the production of new plays. Translation proves, in fact, pivotal in the appropriation of the ancient theatrical genres, and functions as the cornerstone of early modern reinventions of theatre.

As Even Zohar has argued, definitions of translation, translational norms, questions of canon formation, and the very function of a text are all contingent on the timeframe of the translations being considered. Thus, identifying what translation and translating might mean in this period is necessarily 'dependent on the relations within' the early modern 'cultural system';[8] i.e., any definition relies on a collective set of processes and judgments that assign value to the status of the source and target texts. The status of the translated texts thus reflects the makeup of cultural power and highlights the role of translation in the

---

6 Burke 2006, 34–35.
7 Venuti 1995, 20. The validity of such terms has now started to be questioned, particularly from the perspective of Comparative Literature and Global/World Literature.
8 Even Zohar 1990, 51.

creation of literature, and — if it is drama translation — the establishment of a theatrical genre along with its repertoire.

The absence of an all-pervasive conceptualisation of translation, and the relative freedom with which early modern scholars, playwrights, and translators dealt with ancient Greek drama, both call for the otherwise seemingly jarring choice of including texts in this volume that were neither born as translations nor considered as such by later scholarship. The volume therefore calls for a widening of the functions, applications, and definitions of translation in this period. The principal criterion for the inclusion of a text in this volume is based on Gérard Genette's visual metaphor of the palimpsest: if a reader can *see* a source text through or within another text, then the text is considered to be a target text and included in the corpus, regardless of how it would be labelled in the 21st century or indeed was labelled in the 15th or 16th century.[9] This distinction is useful on a conceptual plane, according to which translation is meant in the abstract rather than as a label for a given text. It goes without saying that not every work in which one can occasionally see a prior text will be, in its totality, a translation.

Indeed, acts of *translating* can be found in texts that are not necessarily conceived of as translations nor as explicitly drawing on ancient Greek material. This is the case, for example, with Andrea Alciato's *Philargyrus* (1523), analysed here by Bastin-Hammou; Nicholas Grimald's *Archipropheta* (1548), analysed by Jackson; Pierre Le Loyer's *La Néphélococugie* (1578), Robert Garnier's *La Troade* (1579) and *Antigone* (1580), analysed by Dudouyt; Aires Vitória's *Tragédia del Rei Agamémnom*, analysed by Resende; and the many Italian tragedies examined by Di Martino, Fiore, and Cuzzotti, in which there is indeed much *translating*, even though these may not have been published or considered as such. *Translating*, in this sense, represents the intertextual reworking of one source, or the fragmentary combination of different ancient Greek and early modern sources, in a dynamic and creative way, typically, though not exclusively, by a playwright or poet. *Translation*, on the other hand, usually features as the production of a full-length target text, often (but not necessarily) the work of a scholar. As acts of norm-creation and opposition, both *translation* and *translating* as practices can become new sites of imitation, as is the case, for example, of Erasmus's ground-breaking translations of Euripides' *Hecuba* and *Iphigenia at Aulis*.[10]

---

9 Genette 1997.
10 See Dedieu in this volume.

In one of its many applications, as we have heard, *translating* was at the heart of the creation of national theatrical repertoires, a project that went hand-in-hand with 'vernacularization' and the rise of nation-states.[11] It combined translating ancient plays with the creation of treatises setting forth rules that could support, as well as inform, the production of drama. Aristotle was certainly amongst the primary sources chosen and reinterpreted in order to nurture such projects for the tragic genre, whilst the Roman scholar and grammarian Aelius Donatus and his *Commentary on Terence* was pivotal in the development of the comic genre. In addition, Aristotle was also particularly useful in claiming that a literary creation recast previous literature and in justifying imitation aesthetically and ethically.[12]

Translating was also part of a wider programme of establishing the study of Greek and Latin texts as a practice: translation of ancient Greek drama was pivotal in furthering knowledge of the ancient Greek world and a useful tool for exploring the mechanisms and vocabulary of the ancient Greek poetic language, metre *in primis*. Quite uniquely, *translation* and *translating* of ancient Greek drama in this period stand within the realms of philology, pedagogy, and theatre.

A challenge that was unavoidable for early modern translators of drama was how to deal with the plays' varied metres (iambic trimeter, trochaic tetrameter, anapaests, etc.) and complex lyric choral odes. Here, too, we see how practice varies amongst different authors and target cultures. Most translators opted for a pragmatic approach and either ignored the metre or chose iambic trimeter or the more familiar Latin iambic senarius. A few seem to have relished the opportunity to experiment, even drawing on the contemporary song cultures of their own time.[13] What the challenge of dramatic metres offered to all was the opportunity to engage competitively with other translators. The gauntlet was most clearly thrown down by Erasmus, as Dedieu and Vedelago discuss in this volume, and it was clearly a challenge which some wished to tackle head on, as we can see from the paratexts of many subsequent translations, such as those of Naogeorgus.[14] Personal preference and inclination seem to have been para-

---

11 Cf. Pollock 2000, 592.
12 On the influence of Aristotle on playwriting, see Di Martino, Dudouyt, and Fiore in this volume.
13 Cuzzotti in this volume.
14 Baier in volume. For a less explicit translation of lyric Greek metre into stichic lyric metre (the hendecasyllable), see Jackson in this volume.

mount here, but the aural experience and expectations of the readers of the translations must surely have also played a part.

Similarly, translation theories of the time depend upon the ideological realm in which they were produced and circulated. Theories about translation in the period were as heterogeneous as the various ways of translating in practice, hence the use of 'theories' rather than 'theory' throughout the volume.[15] By the second half of the 16th century, and as part of the general systematisation that was also connected to the (re)creation of national dramatic repertoires, translation was transitioning towards stricter and more limiting definitions. The famous Ciceronian passage, 'and I did not translate as an interpreter, but as an orator' (*nec converti ut interpres, sed ut orator*), was understood to suggest that whilst the task of the translator was simply to stay within the same 'ideas, forms, and figures of thought' (*sententiis isdem, earum formis, tamquam figuris*) of the original text, the orator was more concerned with preserving the 'general style' (*genus*) and 'force' (*vim*) of these thoughts and ideas, and 'weighing' words (*appendere*). The translator was charged with reproducing them 'word for word' (*uerbum pro uerbo*) and 'counting' (*adnumerare*) each word (Cic. De opt. 14).[16] And if the translator was in no way an imitator or an orator, but rather, a faithful transposer, the rules by which one was to interpret the translator's task belonged to rhetoric, as is evident in some of the translation treatises which had currency at the time.[17]

---

15 The editors firmly believe that labels such as 'Renaissance' and 'Humanism', often applied liberally at this time, are equally geographically determined: in Italy the 'Renaissance' occurred a full century (at least) before its cultural counterpart in, e.g., England. Likewise 'Humanism' with its secular overtones for modern readers can be confusing when used without further temporal or pedagogical definition. For this reason, we have eschewed both terms throughout this volume and opted instead for 'early modern', a descriptor that is obligingly capacious to encompass the 16th-century translation and scholarly activities.

16 Cf., amongst others, Fausto da Longiano 1556, 77; Toscanella 1575, 34–35; Piccolomini 1575, 213, 216; Catena 1581, 5–6 (and Pierre Daniel Huet 1683, 157 for a reading of this passage influenced by Catena); Castelvetro 1570, 10–11; and Humphrey 1559, 245–246; on the concept of *adnumerare* (*numerositas*) in early modern translation theory, see, for example, Dolet's precept to respect the 'nombres oratoires' (1540, 17ff.). Likewise, Horace's 'and do not render word for word, faithful interpreter' (Hor. Ars Poet. 133–134: *nec uerbo uerbum curabis reddere fidus / interpres*) again implied (*a contrario*) that the interpreter/translator's task was in fact to render word for word; Horace was concerned with imitation in this passage, not translation. On the widespread use of Hor. Ars Poet. 133–134 for translation matters in the Middle Ages and beyond, see Copeland 2013.

17 Cf., amongst others, Leonardo Bruni's *De interpretatione recta*; Juan Luis Vives' *Versiones seu Interpretationes* (1532); Etienne Dolet's *La manière de bien traduire d'une langue en aultre* (1540); and Fausto Da Longiano's *Dialogo del modo de lo tradurre d'una in altra lingua secondo*

Yet, there co-existed other and opposite visions of translation, which saw it as a creative enterprise grafted onto the imitative nature of literature as well as the 'bettering' nature of imitation itself; i.e., the idea of emulation as inevitably engineered into the imitation process itself. If the French scholar Thomas Sébillet's *Art poétique françois* (1548) openly equated 'translation' with 'poem', with a new literary creation, he also afforded translation the ability to emulate the source in the new language.[18] There are a number of paratexts belonging to treatises on imitation, poetic art, poetics more generally, notwithstanding the translations examined throughout this volume, which can testify to the currency of such an assertion.[19]

Indeed, not only did translation concepts change from one place to another at this time, but they also heavily depended on the genre they were translating and/or writing within. The traditions of translating comedy and tragedy chart overlapping, but separate, courses in literary history. Ancient Greek comedy, for example, had been used to teach Greek to beginners since antiquity, a practice that continued from a very early date in Italy with Aristophanes (Bastin-Hammou, Muttini). The comic playwright was one of the most widely used authors by teachers and students of Greek. The *editio princeps* of the first nine surviving plays was printed by Aldo Manuzio in Venice in 1498, before those of Sophocles (1502), Euripides (1503), and Aeschylus (1518). But the history of the plays' translations had begun almost a century earlier, at a time when reflections upon translation were only just starting to emerge. Translators of Greek comedy were, and still are, faced with issues specific to comedy, such as the presence of obscene language, political attacks, religious disrespect, and, more broadly, the fact that they did not have access to a range of ancient Greek comic texts beyond those of Aristophanes, or a treatise equivalent to Aristotle's *Poetics* that discussed the genre of ancient Greek comedy as a whole.

A final note to add to a volume on the translation of ancient Greek drama concerns the very nature of drama translation. Indeed, translating dramatic texts

---

le regole mostrate da Cicerone (1556). On Bruni and the rhetorical tradition, see Bertolio 2020, 9–60; on the evident influence of the rhetorical tradition on Dolet's treatise, see Norton 1974; see also Juan Luis Vives' section on 'translation' (*Versiones seu interpretationes*) in his 1532 treatise *De ratione dicendi*, which contained an understanding of translation that was wholly grafted onto rhetorical theory (Vives 2018; cf. Bertolio 2020, 45).

18 'la Version ou Traduction est aujourd'huy le Poème plus fréquent et mieus receu dés estimés Poètes et dés doctes lecteurs, à cause que chacun d'eus estime grand oeuvre et de grand pris, rendre la pure et argentine invention dés Poètes dorée et enrichie de notre langue'; Sébillet 1548, 21.

19 See, in particular, Di Martino, Dudouyt, Fiore, Vedelago, in this volume.

inevitably involves a negotiation of the source's cultural and theatrical conventions with new ones. Such negotiation, which is inherent to this type of translation, renders its process distinctive, regardless of whether a *mise-en-scène* of a translated text actually occurred or not. In other words, there is a dramaturgy of the translated text that is scripted into the process of translation itself because the source is dramatic (and dramaturgical) to begin with. Whether translation is conceived of as a philological endeavour or in view of an actual performance, it implies and includes considerations and problems relating to dramaturgy, which can be consciously addressed or lie dormant, but which inevitably put translation into dialogue with the theatrical and performance culture of the time period into which the source text is being adapted.[20] This is why the volume ends with an exploration of the various dramaturgies contained in three 16th-century translations of Euripides' *Iphigenia at Aulis* through the lens of performance practice (Di Martino-Baudou).

2 Description of the volume

Section One: Translating Comedy

The first section of this volume focuses on the translation of Aristophanes' plays and shows just how prolific and wide-ranging this activity was. Until the late 15th century, these target texts were mostly in Latin and aimed at didactic purposes, but 16th-century translations as well as Aristophanes-inspired comedies document a dynamic interplay between translating ancient Greek comedy and recreating the comic genre.

In Chapter One, Micol Muttini addresses the earliest translation analysed in the volume, undertaken just before the first edition of Aristophanes' plays: Lodovico da Poppi's translation of Aristophanes' *Plutus* in Latin verse, dating from the last quarter of the 15th century. Muttini analyses the strategies chosen by the translator in order to reconstruct his implicit norms, showing that this (mostly linear) translation strives to reproduce syntactical as well as stylistic features of the source text, whilst also opting for verse over prose. Finally, compared to the first partial translation of the same play by Leonardo Bruni (ca. 1440), who downplayed scatological or sexual references, Lodovico's text is a remarkably

---

20 Dramaturgy and translation have often been seen as comparable activities that rest on similar presuppositions; recent contributions to the topic are Versényi 2014 and Trencsényi 2015, 51–66.

frank rendition of Aristophanic obscenity. Beyond oppositions between faithful and free, or *ad uerbum* and *ad sententiam* translation, this close, linear translation also represents a cultural translation, mobilising linguistic and comedic references to Plautus and Terence as target linguistic models, as well as providing relevant information about, and a commentary on, ancient Greek political and religious institutions through marginal glosses. From these translation choices, Muttini derives the implicit functions of the translation: both didactic and poetic, this text gives access to the original Greek both linguistically and culturally, but also produces a valid comedy in Latin following Latin comedic standards.

In Chapter Two, Malika Bastin-Hammou explores the impact of translating ancient Greek comedy on the production of original Latin comedies in the 16th century. The dynamic whereby translation contributes to setting generic, rhetorical, and dramatic standards is often ignored if translations are considered separately from literary and/or dramatic productions. Bastin-Hammou's survey of the Latin translations of Aristophanes' *Plutus* in the early 16th century shows a continuum of translation practices ranging from *ad uerbum*, interlinear translations for students of ancient Greek, to rewritings of the ancient Greek comic material with additions and omissions. She identifies a turning point in the translation of Aristophanic plays in the 1530s, changing from being mostly didactic, meant for students learning the language, to becoming a literary endeavour for an educated audience. She shows that this evolution from *ad uerbum* to *ad uersum* practices produces translations that are at the same time creative and often more complete, with fewer digressions or omissions. Through the case study of the poet and jurist Andrea Alciato's Latin verse translation of *Clouds* (1517) and his later production of an original Latin comedy entitled *Philargyrus* (1523), Bastin-Hammou explores the translation of textual and generic features in the creation of a new comedy, demonstrating that translational practices are at work in the production of early modern Latin drama.

In Chapter Three, Simone Beta analyses and re-evaluates the first Italian translation of Aristophanes' eleven comedies, co-translated by two brothers, the physicians Bartolomeo and Pietro Rostini, and published in 1545. This prose translation has often been decried as a mediocre retranslation of Andreas Divus's Latin complete Aristophanes (1538). However, Beta demonstrates through close analysis of the Rostinis' translation of *Knights* that the translators were in fact familiar with the marginal scholia published in the Aldine edition of Aristophanes' plays (1498), and referred to the Greek text itself to rework and at times improve upon Divus. Beta shows that in spite of their reliance on Divus's Latin version and the heterogeneity of the translation (perhaps to be attributed to the differences in skill and training between the two brothers), this first translation of Aristophanes' complete plays into the Italian vernacular is often livelier and more accurate than its more 'correct' Latin predecessor.

Section Two: Translating Tragedy

Part One: Scholarly Networks: Translation Models and Functions

The second section of this volume focuses on the different modes of reception of ancient Greek tragedy in early modern Europe. In the first part, contributors explore the European network of scholars that first translated Euripides' and Sophocles' tragedies, as well as their methodologies and reflections of the function(s) of translation. Erasmus's Latin verse translations of Euripides' *Hecuba* and *Iphigenia at Aulis* (1506) stand out as a powerful translational model, which translators across Europe inevitably grappled with and situated their own translations against.

In Chapter Four, Alexia Dedieu highlights the importance of Erasmus's Latin verse translation of *Hecuba* and *Iphigenia at Aulis* which was first published in 1506 by Josse Bade in Paris, then published again in 1507 by Aldo Manuzio in Venice, where it was reprinted over twenty times until 1567. Dedieu uses Antoine Berman's concept of an 'origin of translation' to describe the influence of Erasmus's translation practice, in between *ad uerbum* and *ad sensum* translation: later translators of the same plays especially position themselves as either followers or rivals of his method. Erasmus anticipated the flush of translations of ancient Greek tragedies in the 1540s by over 30 years, but Dedieu shows that even decades later, he is an explicit model for George Buchanan in the paratexts to his Latin verse translations of Euripides' *Medea* (1544) and *Alcestis* (1556), as well as for Sigismond Gelous's *Orestes* (1551), which openly comments on Erasmus's translation technique and dismissive views on the tragic chorus. Dedieu adds that Erasmus as an 'origin' is not an uncontested model, but that the political, religious, and literary themes he outlines had a long-lasting impact: his influence receded only in the 1560s, when the authority of German scholarship in the persons of Joachim Camerarius and Philip Melanchthon imposed itself on the European context.

In Chapter Five, Angelica Vedelago begins with a survey of early modern treatises on translation and imitation. She shows that, beyond the emulation of a source text, there exists emulation between translations, stressing that translators and imitators do not only compete with the source author but also with each other. Vedelago traces the formulation of this type of emulation back to

Erasmus's paratexts and his biography, but finds its clearest formulation in Laurence Humphrey's *Interpretatio linguarum* (1559). Humphrey contrasts the imitator's emulation of the author of the source text on the one hand, and the translator's emulation of previous translators on the other, thus distinguishing between author and translator. Vedelago argues for the existence of two emulative stances in translators and imitators, defining the first as collaborative and heuristic, that is, following in the footsteps of already established translating norms; and the second as challenging and emulative of such norms. Jane Lumley's English prose translation of *Iphigenia at Aulis* (ca. 1557) provides an illustration of the collaborative and heuristic mode of emulation with regards to Erasmus's Latin verse translation and his methodology, whilst Thomas Watson's Latin verse translation of *Antigone* (1581) is presented as a case of eristic emulation with regards to Thomas Naogeorgus's Latin verse translation of *Antigone* (1558).

In Chapter Six, Thomas Baier explores the conceptions of translation developed by the school of Wittenberg, stressing the strictly ancillary and didactic role they afforded to translation in the teaching of ancient Greek. This position explains Philip Melanchthon's and his disciple Veit Winsheim silence on translation in spite of the latter publishing a complete prose translation of Sophocles into Latin in 1546. Baier demonstrates the collaborative nature of this network of scholars: Winsheim publishing Camerarius's *De autoribus tragoediae* (1534) as a paratext to his translations, and Camerarius postponing his translation of Sophocles' tragedies after the publication of Winsheim's complete plays are presented as examples of this. Through the analysis of the paratexts to Camerarius's commentary on, edition, and translation of Sophocles' plays, Baier delineates the scholar's two methods of translating. The first is exemplified in his interlinear rendition of *Ajax*, which follows the syntax of the source text and is propaedeutic to reading the play in ancient Greek; the second, manifested in his *Electra*, whilst providing a close translation of the content in prose, is intent on adapting it to the rhetorical features of the target language and to the target culture, i.e., to Christian moral values, as a way of rendering the text more accessible to students. Baier then goes on to contrast these two methods of translating developed by Camerarius with Thomas Naogeorgus's Latin verse translation of Sophocles' complete plays (1558), which follows in the footsteps of Erasmus's *Hecuba* and *Iphigenia* (1506).

Section Two, Part Two: Proto-National Dynamics and Vernacular Translating

Part One focuses on the networks of scholars translating ancient Greek tragedies, mostly into Latin, outlining methodologies and defining the function(s) of translation. Part Two questions the distinction between derivative translation and original tragedies in the context of the massive appropriation of the ancient material, which contributes to the development of vernacular literatures, languages, and theatre, and in turn to the construction of national dynamics.

In Chapter Seven, Giovanna Di Martino provides an analysis of the interplay and overlap between translations of ancient Greek tragedy and the creation of new tragedies aimed at establishing the tragic genre in 16th-century Italy. Di Martino first identifies the theoretical roots of imitation in the early modern Italian reception of Aristotle's' *Poetics*, which justifies and grounds the generally free and emulative approach to ancient Greek tragedy. As Di Martino demonstrates in her analysis of the paratexts to the translations and tragedies considered, the playwrights and translators — amongst whom Alessandro Pazzi de' Medici, Lodovico Dolce, Marcantonio Cinuzzi, and Luigi Alamanni — were not only aware of their imitative approach but framed the very freedom with which they imitated the ancients as itself an imitation of how the Romans appropriated Greek literature, thus artfully combining the prestige of imitating the newly 'rediscovered' ancient Greek sources with the celebration of their own invention. Di Martino goes on to uncover the hybridity of these works by examining the very labels attached to them by later scholarship. She focuses on 'volgarizzamento', in particular, in order to question its validity for 16th-century translations of ancient Greek tragedy.

In Chapter Eight, Claudia Cuzzotti focuses on Michelangelo Buonarroti the Younger's translation of Euripides' *Hecuba*. She first puts this target text in the context of the other *Hecubas* translated in Italy, from Leonzio Pilato's Latin partial translation of the play in 1362 to Buonarroti's last version of his translation at the end of the 16th century. Cuzzotti identifies six other important engagements with the same play in Italy and by the most prominent translators and tragedians of the time, Lodovico Dolce, Giovan Battista Gelli, Giovanni da Falgano, Giovanni Balcianelli, Matteo Bandello. It is against the translation practices emerging from these target texts that Cuzzotti evaluates and analyses Buonarrotti's own translation technique. She pinpoints some general trends in the translation of Euripides' plays in 16th-century Italy, amongst which the wide use of *amplificatio*, the simplification of mythological and topographical references in the target text, the adoption of unrhymed hendecasyllables and the 'canzone' structure inherited from Petrarch for episodes and choral odes respectively, and the numerous linguistic echoes with the Italian literary tradition, namely Dante and Petrarch. Cuzzotti's analysis of Buonarroti's translation also includes evaluation of the differences between the two most important 'drafts' of his *Ecuba*: the version sent to Maffeo Barberini (the future Pope Urban VIII) in 1599 and the last version of this translation.

In Chapter Nine, Maria Luísa Resende explores the mutual influence between the translation of ancient Greek tragedy and the Portuguese theatrical tradition through her analysis of Aires Vitória's *Tragédia del Rei Agaménom* (1555, though the first edition was probably issued in 1536). Vitória's tragedy does not directly translate an ancient Greek source; it is in fact a verse translation of Fernán Pérez de Oliva's Castilian prose translation of Sophocles' *Electra* (1528). Through a comparison between the two, Resende shows that Vitória's additions to and transformations of his Spanish source can be interpreted as a desire to meet the expectations of his Portuguese audience and, more generally, make ancient Greek tragedy more accessible and known. Pérez de Oliva had already adapted the original structure of the play to the more widely used division into acts and scenes, and had already drastically reduced the importance of the chorus by eliminating most of the lyrical parts. Vitória's further reduction of the chorus to two female confidents, adoption of scenes and acts, and use of rhyming and traditional heptasyllabes (*redondilha maior*), are all choices aimed at inserting his version of the play into the tradition of other contemporary Portuguese plays. Resende also demonstrates that, though Vitória adopts the main cultural and Christianising changes present in his Spanish source, he also deliberately presents the tragedy as Greek, restoring the many mythological references to the pagan gods present in the original, for whom Pérez de Oliva had instead used the monotheistic singular, and adding a layer of mythological references not found in the Greek source text, but familiar to Portuguese readers and spectators through contemporary plays, such as Gil Vincente's.

In Chapter Ten, Cécile Dudouyt explores how translation practices towards ancient Greek drama undergo a patent change in France halfway through the century. The reason for such change is to be identified with a reconceptualization of translation in poetics treatises. Through a detailed analysis of two important treatises on French poetry, one by Thomas Sébillet (1549, *Art Poétique françoys*), and the other one by Joachim du Bellay (1549, *Deffense et illustration de la langue françoyse*), Dudouyt argues that translation shifts from being thought of as a highly creative enterprise, much like writing a poem, to becoming the polar opposite of new literary creation. Such a shift, she argues, is cause for a change in approach to the translation of ancient Greek drama, which, from the 1550s onwards, becomes a much more covert and fragmentary endeavour, aimed at recasting the (hidden) sources into new 'original' texts so as to contribute to the creation of France's national literature. Stripped of its creative powers and linguistic function as a tool to enrich and widen the French language, *traduction* becomes an ancillary and constrained exercise. However, *translating* still seems to be at play in many post-mid-16th-century target texts, such as Pierre Le Loyer's *La Néphélococugie* (1578), and Robert Garnier's *Antigone ou la piété* (1580) and *La Troade* (published in 1579 and probably performed in 1581). These plays are brought as examples to illustrate the new trend in translation practices, from *translations* to *translating*.

Section Two, Part Three: Beyond Translation

Part Three moves beyond translation and explores the liminal translational practices through which ancient Greek tragedy fuses with early modern scholarship and the writing of new plays.

In Chapter Eleven, Lucy Jackson explores a particular mode of translation of ancient Greek tragedy, one that she defines *ad spiritum*. Building on Marvin Carlson's use of the metaphor of 'haunting' for theatrical allusion, Jackson argues for the presence of Greek tragic 'ghosts' haunting Nicholas Grimald's Latin play *Archipropheta*, on the last days of John the Baptist, published in Cologne in 1548 by Martin Gymnicus and probably performed in Cambridge, where Grimald studied. Jackson first puts Grimald's work into the wider context of the study of the ancient Greek language and the prolific writing of biblical Latin plays in 16th-century England, and Oxford and Cambridge in particular. She then moves on to analyse the lurking presence of Euripides' *Orestes* and Aeschlylus' *Agamemnon* in Grimald's play. Whilst Orestes may be behind the representation of Herod in a scene dramatising a banquet in Herod's palace, the messenger figure of the enslaved Phrygian attendant of Helen's may be haunting the Syrian ancilla attending to Herod and embodying the messenger's function in Grimald's play. But, Jackson argues, the Syrian attendant also resonates with another famous female character in the Greek tragedy tradition, that of Cassandra in Aeschylus' *Agamemnon*. Jackson's contribution is an important step forward into charting the subterranean presence of Greek tragedy in the early Latin dramas of the 16th century.

In Chapter Twelve, Giulia Fiore explores the impact of the reception of Aristotle's *Poetics* on tragedies and theoretical debates in 16th-century Italy through analysis of a selection of translations of the term *hamartia*. Building on Hartmut Böhme and Johannes Helmrath's concept of 'mutual transformation' as reception, which emphasises the interdependency and reciprocity between the ancient and early modern cultures, Fiore's chapter contributes to exploring the mutual influence between ancient Greek tragedy, Aristotle's *Poetics* and 16th-century tragedies and theoretical treatises. Beyond stark oppositions between domestication and foreignisation, Fiore analyses the increasing tendency to translate the term *hamartia* as *peccatum/peccato* ('sin') in the mid-16th century. Her analysis ranges from Alessandro Pazzi de' Medici's influential Latin translation of the *Poetics* (1536), where he translates δι'ἁμαρτίαν τινά ('because of a certain fallibility'; Arist. *Poet*. 13, 1453a7–14) as *humano quodam errore* (stressing the protagonist's agency), to Francesco Robortello's commentary (1548), where the protagonist's sin is presented as necessary to validate providential punishment, to Lodovico Castelvetro's first Italian commentary of the *Poetics* (1570), where *hamartia* is explicitly linked to the Christian sin for the first time. Beyond translations of, and commentaries on, the *Poetics*, Fiore also shows the varied facets of this ideological syncretism not only in debates about vernacular tragedies, such as the literary quarrel around Sperone Speroni's *Canace*, but also in early modern *Oedipus* plays, such as Alessandro Pazzi de' Medici's *Edipo Principe* (1525–1526) and Giovanni Andrea dell'Anguillara's *Edippo* (1565).

Section Two, Coda: Dramaturgy and Translation

At the intersection between performance and translation studies, Chapter Thirteen describes and theorises a new methodology which unpacks the latent dramaturgy of drama translation through practice research. In this last chapter, Giovanna Di Martino and Estelle Baudou present the results of two workshops (28th–29th November 2019 and 21st May 2021) which explore lines 1098–1208 (fourth episode) and 1510–1531 (last stasimon) of Euripides' *Iphigenia at Aulis* in three translations of the play: Thomas Sébillet's *Iphigénie* (1549), Lodovico Dolce's *Ifigenia* (1551), and Lady Jane Lumley's *The Tragedie of Euripides called Iphigeneia* (ca. 1557). The performing process designed by Baudou and Di Martino relies on actors selecting turning points in the texts and matching words with bodily movements. The theatrical exercises proposed each time serve to investigate the power dynamics between the characters and its evolution within the scene, the place and function of the chorus, and the situation — whether intimate or public — envisaged in the dramaturgy of each translation. As a term emerging in the course of developing their methodology and resting on Derrida's conceptualisation of it, 'contamination' is employed throughout the chapter to capture the complex and mutual influence between the multiple stages and 'bodies' involved in translating for the stage. Not only does the chapter chart new possible ways of investigating drama translation through performance practice; in line with the rest of the chapters in this volume, it also contributes to widening the very meaning of translation, and drama translation in particular, proving that it is necessarily part of, and heavily relies on, a wider dramaturgical process.

Overall, it is the translator's 'dancing back and forth between cultural and theatrical languages', as Adam Versényi so eloquently puts it, that is at the heart of this volume.[21] By exploring translation of the ancient Greek dramatic corpus in important European centres from the last decades of the 15th century to the end of the 16th century, this volume inevitably rewrites an important chapter in the history of the reception of these ancient plays. It strategically puts translation in dialogue with early modern drama, theatre culture, and performance practice. But it also grants translation the importance it deserves: as part of literary history more generally and of the very texture of the plays that we read today.

---

[21] Versényi 2014, 289.

Part I: **Translating Comedy**

Micol Muttini
Aristophanes' Readers and Translators in 15th-Century Italy: The Latin *Plutus* of MS Matrit. Gr. 4697

Abstract: This study will focus on an unedited and little-known Latin version of Aristophanes' *Plutus*, which is preserved in the manuscript Matrit. gr. 4697 at the National Library of Spain. It is a paper codex, which dates back to the last quarter of the 15th century and was copied by the Italian humanist Lodovico da Poppi. The Greek text of the *Plutus* is accompanied by an interlinear translation into Latin, almost unknown until now. This hitherto neglected codex is especially interesting because of the Latin version it contains, since it appears to be amongst the first ever made of Aristophanes' *Plutus*. In this chapter, I will examine and discuss the various translational strategies employed by Lodovico to move Aristophanes' 4th-century Greek text to a 15th-century Latin-reading community. The analysis ultimately sheds light on the history of the transmission of Aristophanes' text and the scholarly activities around during this period.

During the early modern period, there was a general rebirth of interest in all things classical, so it was natural that the Greek playwright Aristophanes should figure prominently in that rebirth. At the dawn of the 15th century, a rapid increase in efforts to make Aristophanes available to a Latin readership was driven almost exclusively by Italian scholars. Latin versions of texts and related commentaries were principally responsible for introducing Aristophanes into the high Latin culture of western Europe, and Aristophanic works were recovered and studied with new intensity.[1] The circulation of Old Comedy texts took place at an immense scale in Italy: the Byzantine triad (*Plut. Nub. Ran.*) played a decisive role in the education system. In particular, Aristophanes' *Plutus*

---

[1] On the rediscovery in the 15th century of Aristophanes' text see Süß 1911; Bolgar 1954, 495–496; Botley 2010, 88–91; Sommerstein 2010; Wilson 2014. On early modern translations of classical authors see Sabbadini 1922, 17–27; Bertalot 1929–30; De Petris 1975; Gualdo Rosa 1985; Chiesa 1987; Berti 1988; Berschin 1989; Folena 1991; Nicosia 1991; Cortesi 1995a; Baldassarri 2003; Morani 2003; Botley 2004; Cortesi 2007; Deligiannis 2017.

https://doi.org/10.1515/9783110719185-002

became a central schoolbook and the most popular play in the early modern period (notably, it was the first to appear in Latin translation).[2]

In this chapter, I focus on an unedited and unknown Latin translation of Aristophanes' *Plutus*, which is preserved in the manuscript *Matrit. gr.* 4697 in the National Library of Spain. This hitherto neglected codex is especially interesting because of its significance for the reception and interpretation of ancient comedy in 15th-century Italy.

1 On Translating Aristophanes' *Plutus*

Matrit. gr. 4697 is a paper manuscript (foll. IV + 292; mm 218 x 148; 10 ll./p.), datable to the last quarter of the 15th century, containing the comedies *Plutus* (ff. 166r–225v) and *Clouds* (ff. 226r–292v).[3]

This section was copied by the Italian scholar Lodovico da Poppi, as can be seen in the *subscriptio* written in red ink at the end of the codex (f. 292v): *Ludovici Presbyteri de Puppio manu propria scriptus*.[4] Lodovico was a professor of Latin grammar who lived in a number of cities in Italy, including Florence, Siena, Pisa, and Rome.[5] He is known as the editor of the only 15th-century commentary on the very influential *Carmina differentialia* by Guarino Guarini, *In differentias Guarini Veronensis interpretatio* (Pisa 1485), probably the result of notes taken in his classes.[6] Lodovico is also the author of one of the best com-

---

[2] The reasons for the revival of Aristophanes' *Plutus* have been accounted for sufficiently in the secondary literature: Chirico 1991; Pincelli 1993; Wilson 2007, 1–14; Cisterna 2012; Radif 2014; Bevegni 2017; Totaro 2017; Bastin-Hammou 2019; Beta 2019. Almost 170 manuscripts are witness to the enormous popularity of this comedy in the 15th century: on the early modern manuscript tradition of the *Plutus* see Muttini 2019a; Muttini 2019b.

[3] This manuscript is not mentioned in White 1906 and appears to be unknown to the editors of these texts. For a palaeographical and codicological description of the MS see De Andrés 1987, 258–260; Vieillefond 1935, 201–202. For its value and position in the textual tradition of Aristophanes see Muttini 2019a, 10, 16, 28–31.

[4] The section of the codex that extends from f. 12r to f. 292v was copied by Lodovico. This part contains a selection of 144 fables of Aesop (ff. 12r–58r), *Batrachomyomachia Homeri* (ff. 59r–65r), Theocritus' first 17 *Idylls* with an interlinear Latin translation of the first three *Idyllia* (ff. 69r–161v), *Aristophanis Plutus*, with a Latin version, and *Nubes* (ff. 166r–292v). *Folia* 1r–11v are ascribed by Eleuteri/Canart 1991, 140–142, to the hand of Carlo Antinori, a pupil of Poliziano.

[5] The most complete biography is to be found in Hausmann 1980, 441–442; Vioque 2011.

[6] In the preface, Lodovico states that he wrote it in response to the demand from his young students (*plerique et generosi adolescentuli*). The prologue is published in Garin 1958, 499–500.

mentaries on the *Carmina Priapea*, his *Commentarius in Priapea Virgilii aliaque opuscula critica* (Rome 1500).[7]

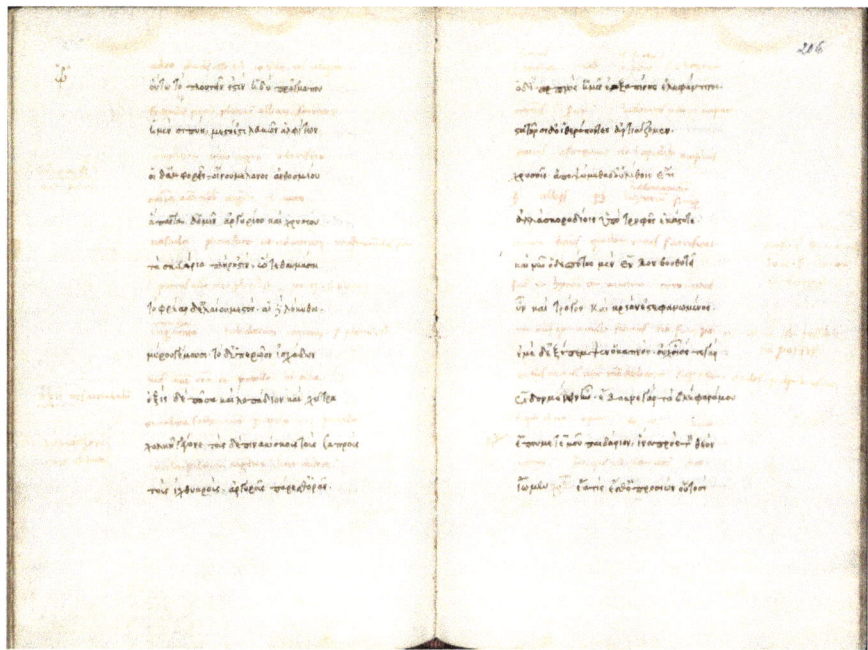

Fig. 2: Aristophanis *Plutus*, *Matrit. gr.* 4697, National Library of Spain, Madrid, ff. 205v–206r.

The manuscript *Matrit. gr.* 4697 is the only testimony of his Greek writing. It seems to be a 15th-century Italian scholarly textbook for the study of Greek since it focuses on the text of Aristophanes used in schools, where the practice of interlinear translation into Latin was highly recommended to improve students' command of both Greek and Latin.[8] The Latin interlinear translation it contains

---

[7] Lodovico must have given university lectures on this subject as he calls his commentary *oratio*: Hausmann 1980, 428, 439–442.

[8] The codex was probably copied in Tuscany. The watermark is similar to Briquet n. 89 (Florence, 1501). It is rather difficult to determine the genesis of Lodovico's Aristophanic translation since precise facts about his life and teaching are lacking. It appears to be an erudite exegetical work along the lines of those habitually done for didactic purposes by early modern educators. On the use of Latin in teaching Greek during the 15th century see Rizzo 1996; Black 2001; Maisano/Rollo 2002; Rollo 2016; Ciccolella 2017; Ciccolella/Silvano 2017; Rollo 2019; Silvano 2019.

appears to be among the first-ever versions of Aristophanes' *Plutus*. Lodovico's word-for-word translation is one of the first complete versions of this play, following those made by Pietro de Montagnana (mid. 15th c.) and Alexander of Otranto (1458).[9] Further, Lodovico's translation is not indebted to the few predecessors that had made some kind of translation of the play.

In this study, I shall discuss the various translational strategies employed by Lodovico to move Aristophanes' fourth-century Greek text to a 15th-century Latin-reading community. Lodovico's translation is, in many ways, a product of the late Quattrocento. The translation is an historical artefact of a particular scholar, time and place: the translator crafts a text that reflects their particular values, linguistic skills and techniques. In a translation, a source text is not merely transferred linguistically into another language like a code sequence.[10] Instead, it is mediated through a translator who leaves their marks throughout the translation. The Latin *Plutus* of the codex *Matrit. gr.* 4697 thus clearly constitutes a cultural translation, not just of words and sentences.[11]

For the purposes of this analysis, I understand the translator's goal as to produce a target text that is in some way semantically equivalent to a pre-existing source text, which was written in a different language and for a different culture. Consequently, how far does Lodovico succeed in translating the troublesome Greek text of Aristophanes? To address this question, I make a close comparison between the Greek original, in the form that was read in the manuscript, and Lodovico's rendering.[12] From this, it is clear that Lodovico never changes the content substantially: he offers the reader a correct and fluent

---

Early modern education in Italy is examined in Grendler 1989; Grendler 2002; Garin 1949; Garin 1957; Marrou 1965, 369–389; Grafton/Jardine 1986; Del Corso/Pecere 2010.

9 Previously, Rinuccio Aretino and Bruni, the latter probably in collaboration with Giovanni Tortelli, had made partial translations of the comedy. The *Quattrocento* translations into Latin of the *Plutus* have been studied by, among others, Lockwood 1913; Lockwood 1931; Cecchini 1965; Cecchini/Cassio 1972; Cortesi 1979; Chirico 1991; De Cesare 2005; Radif 2011; Gamba 2016, 133–136, 174–184. After Lodovico several others also ventured upon a Latin translation of this play before the end of the 16th century: for a list see Van Kerchove 1974; Giannopoulou 2007; Bastin-Hammou 2015.

10 On the theory and practice of translation, see Mounin 1965; Steiner 1998; Derrida 1985; Nergaard 1995; Venuti 1995; Benjamin 2000; Nergaard 2002; Eco 2003; Burke 2007; Bettini 2012.

11 For the concept of 'cultural translation', I refer to the introduction of this volume.

12 A full collation reveals that the Greek text of Aristophanes' *Plutus* copied by Lodovico follows all the readings pointed to by Di Blasi 1997, 371–373, as characteristic of the *recentiores* manuscripts Ambr. L 39 sup., Par. gr. 2718 and Laur. Plut. 31.16. It is more closely related to Laur. Plut. 31.16, transcribed by Iohannes Skutariotes. In addition, Matrit. gr. 4697 has been influenced by the Thoman-Triclinian recension: Muttini 2019a, 28–31.

translation, meeting the requirement to remain faithful to the Greek original. The Latin version reveals Lodovico's attitude towards classical literature as he treats his source with respect.

The first 7 lines run as follows:

> CAR. *Quam molesta res est, o Iupiter et dii,*
> *servum fieri insani heri.*
> *Si enim optima servus dicens fuerit, vel dicens contigit,*
> *appareat autem non agere hec possidenti,*
> *participem esse necesse est famulum malorum.*
> *Sui corporis nam non sinit dominum*
> *dominari fortuna, sed eum qui illum emit.*

The corresponding Greek lines run:

> ΚΑ. ὡς ἀργαλέον πρᾶγμ' ἐστὶν, ὦ Ζεῦ καὶ θεοὶ,
> δοῦλον γενέσθαι παραφρονοῦντος δεσπότου.
> ἢν γὰρ τὰ βέλτισθ' ὁ θεράπων λέξας τύχῃ,
> δόξῃ δὲ μὴ δρᾶν ταῦτα τῷ κεκτημένῳ,
> μετέχειν ἀνάγκη τὸν θεράποντα τῶν κακῶν.
> τοῦ σώματος γὰρ οὐκ ἐᾷ τὸν κύριον
> κρατεῖν ὁ δαίμων, ἀλλὰ τὸν ἐωνημένον.

> *Carion*: Zeus and all you gods, what a ghastly thing it is to be the slave of a master who's out of his mind! It may happen that the servant is the one who makes the best recommendation, but if his owner decides not to follow it, then the servant's forced to take the evil consequences together with him: the deity won't let a man be in charge of his own body, but puts it in the power of his purchaser.[13]

Lodovico's rendering of the Greek thus illustrates his commitment to producing a version that closely mirrors the morphology and syntax of the original. Indeed, the translation reads like a well-constructed aid for the studious readers whose knowledge of the language does not allow them to fully comprehend the ancient text without the supplementary guidance of a linear, literal Latin version. The Greek is rendered word-for-word, and the position of the keywords is preserved, with each Latin line beginning in a manner corresponding to the original. Lodovico is content to produce an accurate and scanning version of Aristophanes' *Plutus*, and he usually succeeds in transferring the general meaning of the Greek text.

---

13 All English translations are quoted, with some minor changes, from Sommerstein 2001.

In Lodovico's view, then, the essence of the translation is to transfer correctly what is written in one language into another. As a consequence, a Latin translation is wholly correct if it corresponds to the Greek original. To perform this kind of translation requires certain abilities from the translator. No one can perform this task correctly if they lack a wide vocabulary and extensive knowledge of both languages, and part of the task of the translator is to enter into the author to be translated.[14]

At times, the comedy of Aristophanes is rather coarse in its wording or content, but our translator does not hesitate to insert the cruder expressions.

His rendering of *Plut.* 149–156, for instance, runs as follows:

CHR. Etiam meretrices aiunt Corinthias,
quando quidem ipsas aliquis puer (pauper exspectes) innuens fuerit,
nec autem adhibere mentem; si autem dives,
clunem ipsas continuo in hunc vertere.
CAR. Et pueros aiunt hoc idem agere,
non amatorum, sed argenti gratia.
CHR. Non bonos, sed scorta: quoniam
petunt non argentum boni. CAR. Quid vero, scilicet petunt?

Aristophanes' corresponding lines read:

ΧΡ. καὶ τάς γ' ἑταίρας φασὶ τὰς Κορινθίας,
ὅταν μὲν αὐτάς τις πένης πειρῶν τύχῃ,
οὐδὲ προσέχειν τὸν νοῦν, ἢν δὲ πλούσιος,
τὸν πρωκτὸν αὐτὰς εὐθὺς ὡς τοῦτον τρέπειν.
<ΚΑ.> καὶ τούς γε παῖδας φασι ταὐτὸ τοῦτο δρᾶν
οὐ τῶν ἐραστῶν ἀλλὰ τἀργυρίου χάριν.
ΧΡ. οὐ τούς γε χρηστούς, ἀλλὰ τοὺς πόρνους· ἐπεὶ
αἰτοῦσιν οὐκ ἀργύριον οἱ χρηστοί. Κα. τί δαί;

Chremylus: And they say, too, about the courtesans in Corinth, that when the man who's propositioning them happens to be poor, they don't take the least notice of him, but when he's rich, they turn their backside at him instantly. *Carion*: And people say that when the young lads do the same thing, it's not for the sake of their lovers but for the sake of money. *Chremylus*: The young gentlemen don't do that, it's only the young professionals. Decent lads don't ask for money. *Carion*: Oh, what do they ask for?

---

14 As Leonardo Bruni expressed it in his treatise *De recta interpretatione*: *Rapitur enim interpres vi ipsa in genus dicendi illius, de quo transfert*. According to Bruni, a worthy translator must enter into a condition of empathy with their source and be seized by the power of their subject's style. See Viti 2004, 84–86; Bertolio 2020, 49.

These verses exemplify Lodovico's fidelity to the author: his rendition of Aristophanes' humorous and obscene passage is faithful to the Greek original and suggests some effort to recreate the dynamic playfulness of the Aristophanic text. Obscene language is here used to vivify the rather heavy-handed moralising of Chremylus and Carion regarding the influence of wealth on the price of prostitutes and the willingness of young boys to succumb to the advances of lovers.[15]

Corinth was the capital of commercial sex in mainland Greece and home to more famous and expensive courtesans than any other city. The two most common words for 'prostitute' in Latin were *scortum* and *meretrix*. Lodovico, in his translation, uses the Latin expression *meretrices* as an equivalent to ἑταίρας ('female Corinthian prostitutes'); he renders the Greek word πόρνους ('male whores') in Latin by using the substantive *scorta*. In classical antiquity, *scortum* was the more pejorative word, as can be deduced from the collocations in which the two terms *meretrix* and *scortum* were used in Plautine Comedy.[16] The thoroughly vulgar word πρωκτός is used to refer to women only three times in Aristophanes; indeed, it was very common in the humour of homosexuality. In Lodovico's version, the Greek expression πρωκτός ('asshole') is rendered by the Latin term *clunis* (= *-es*), which frequently appears in Horace (e.g., *Sat.* II, 8, 91).[17]

I have already mentioned the existence of a partial Latin translation of *Plutus* by Leonardo Bruni, the earliest version of the comedy (ca. 1440). It may not be out of place to put Lodovico's achievements into perspective by comparing the two translations. Bruni has an interventionist approach to translation, which frees him from the Greek text: the translation is sometimes so distant from the Greek that it hardly represents the Aristophanic text at all. The Florentine scholar makes numerous blatant changes in translating from Greek to Latin. He transforms, for example, the sexually explicit expression τὸν πρωκτὸν τρέπειν ('they turn their backside to him', i.e., 'submit to anal penetration') into *obsequi* (152); moreover, he omits any mentioning of pederasty, a regular feature of Greek erotic life, cutting passages such as verses 153–154.[18] Furthermore,

---
15 Henderson 1975; Sommerstein 2001, 143–144; Chantry 2009, 352–354, 362–363.
16 Adams 1982, 321–325.
17 Adams 1981. Indeed, Alexander of Otranto uses *culum* for the Greek πρωκτόν: *culus* and related forms occur six times across four poems by Catullus. See Lateiner 2007.
18 Similarly, in his printed Latin version of the *Plutus* (Napoli 1556), Coriolano Martirano performs extensive censorship: he could not stomach the passages about homosexuality and in the end expurgated about eight lines of the comedy (149–156). Anal sex was commonly considered sinful in the socio-historical context of this period; on another level, however, one might

Bruni transforms both the words and the sense of the same-sex sexuality of the *Plutus*: the most widespread semantic change may be that throughout his version Bruni uses the female noun *meretrices* instead of τοὺς πόρνους (155) to conceal the homosexuality of the lovers;[19] in addition, he renders χρηστούς as *probae* (155) and αἰσχυνόμενοι as *veritae* (158), an attempt to render the text comprehensible in a early modern context, in which explicit same-sex seduction was deemed unacceptable.[20]

In contrast, Lodovico attempts to imitate Aristophanes' verbal inventions: in translating *Plut.* 176, he aptly approximates the comic brusqueness of the dialogue, proposing *pedit* as an equivalent of πέρδεται ('fart').[21] Similarly, he offers a translation of line 706 that neatly approximates the Aristophanic term of abuse with which Carion shockingly calls the god Asclepius: the Latin expression *stercum comedentem* is a literal translation of the Greek word σκατοφάγον ('shit-eater'). Sexual and scatological language is also contained in the scene (959–1096) between a wealthy Old Woman and her former gigolo. The Young Man, newly enriched thanks to Plutus' renewed sight, has lost the only motivation (financial) he ever had for satisfying her sexual desires. Consider, for instance, lines 1082–1083:[22]

---

assume that pederasty, or ancient Greek culture in a broader sense, had to be transformed to fit into the new context.

19 The most common obscenities in Catullus concern male sexuality and penetration. The three used most frequently are *mentula*, *cinaedus* and *irrumare*. Each term, along with its related forms, occurs eight times throughout the *corpus*, appearing in six different poems. Andrea Divo, in his Latin translation of Aristophanes' *Plutus* (Venezia 1538), chooses to render τοὺς πόρνους by the Latin equivalent *cinaedos*. The ThLL defines a *cinaedus* as a *scortum masculum*, *vir obscaenus* and includes references from Plautus, Lucilius, the *Corpus Priapeorum* and Petronius.

20 Bruni was simply unable to accept Aristophanes' explicit treatment of homosexual acts. For an early modern audience, male-male anal sex was unmentionable. See Canosa 1991; Rocke 1996.

21 Cf. *pepedi* (699 ἀπέπαρδον), *pedo* (703 βδέω). The verb *pedo* frequently occurs in Horace (e.g., *Sat.* I, 8, 46). The language of Bruni's translation of the *Plutus* makes the obscenity less shocking: Bruni renders πέρδεται (176) as *est prodigus*, which is not borne out by the Greek.

22 Another moment of inventive wordplay comes at verse 1061: πλυνόν με ποιῶν ἐν τοσούτοις ἀνδράσιν] *nullius pretii me faciens inter tot viros*. Πλυνός means either 'washing-tub or -trough' or 'item to be washed' (lit. 'making me a washing', i.e., 'abusing me', 'humiliating me utterly'). Lodovico opts for the translation *ad sensum*, at times relaxing the exigencies of literal precision. The translation distances itself from the literal meaning of Aristophanes' words, but it also seems to reflect an attempt on Lodovico's part to re-establish the playful, ironic tone of the passage.

Iᴜᴠ. *Nequaquam colloquerer te subagitata*
decem milibus civium et ter mille.

Νε. οὐκ ἂν διαλεχθείην διεσπλεκωμένῃ
ὑπὸ μυρίων ἐτῶν γε καὶ τρισχιλίων.

Young Man: I'm not having anything to do with a woman who's been shagged to pieces by thirteen thousand…years.

The Greek διαλέγεσθαι (lit. 'converse with') and σπλεκόω bear the sense of 'have sexual relations with' or 'screw', and Lodovico's rendering yields the complete import of the Greek words in Aristophanes.[23]

Translation of comedy has many challenges, one of which is the problem of translating personal names. Rendering proper nouns is certainly no simple task, and translators must be familiar with the culture of both the source and target languages since awareness of culture-bound names will lead to the most appropriate translation. I quote *Plut.* 174–180 with Lodovico's translation:

Cᴀʀ. *Pamphilus autem nonne propter hunc flebit?*
Cʜʀ. *Venditor velorum autem nonne cum Pamphilo* κλαύσετε?
Cᴀʀ. *Argirius autem nonne propter hunc pedit?*
Cʜʀ. *Philepsius autem nonne gratia tui fabulas dicit?*
Cᴀʀ. *Societas vero nonne propter te*[scilicet fuit] *Egiptiis?*
Cʜʀ. *Amat autem Lais nonne propter te Philonidem?*
Cᴀʀ. *Timoteus vero turris.* Cʜʀ. *Cadat in te!*

Κα. ὁ Πάμφιλος δὲ οὐχὶ διὰ τοῦτον κλαύσεται;
Χρ. ὁ βελονοπώλης δὲ οὐχὶ μετὰ τοῦ Παμφίλου;
Κα. Ἀργύριος δὲ οὐχὶ διὰ τοῦτον πέρδεται;
Χρ. Φιλέψιος δὲ οὐχ' ἕνεκα σοῦ μύθους λέγει;
Κα. ἡ ξυμμαχία δὲ οὐχὶ διὰ σὲ τοῖς Αἰγυπτίοις;
Χρ. ἐρᾷ δὲ Λαῒς οὐχὶ διὰ σὲ Φιλωνίδου;
Κα. ὁ Τιμοθέου δὲ πύργος. Χρ. ἐμπέσοι γέ σοι.

Carion: Isn't it because of him that Pamphilus…will cop it? *Chremylus*: And that needle-seller as well along with Pamphilus? *Carion*: Isn't it because of him that Agyrrhius is in clover? *Chremylus*: Isn't it for your sake that Philepsius tells stories? *Carion*: Isn't it because of you that we've an alliance with the Egyptians? *Chremylus*: Isn't it because of you

---

23 Aristophanes here plays on the ambivalence of ἐτῶν = *annorum* (ἔτος)/*civium* (ἔτης): see Chantry 2009, 216; Sommerstein 2001, 207–208. Cf. *non loquerer supposita a mille annis et tribus milibus* (Pietro de Montagnana); *numquam diligam strupizatam a mille civibus tribus milibus* (Alexander of Otranto).

that Lais loves Philonides? *Carion*: And Timotheus' tower... *Chremylus*: I wish it would fall on your head!

This passage demonstrates that Lodovico is careful when translating proper nouns.[24] In particular, he uses the translation strategy of transference, a method where the translator makes use of the proper noun from the source text without applying any changes derived from the target language.[25] For example, the name Πάμφιλος — an Athenian general put on trial in 388 for embezzlement, whose name ironically means 'beloved by all' — is expressed in Latin as *Pamphilus*, without any changes.[26] In the very same section, Lodovico provides a literal semantic rendering of Aristophanes' substantive βελονοπώλης (*schol. vet. Plut.* 175a–b; *schol. rec. Plut.* 174–175): *venditor velorum* ('the needle-seller') — perhaps another Athenian politician, about whom Aristophanes regularly sneers by calling them 'sellers' of one thing or another (a marginal gloss explicates the lemma: *venditor acorum vel velorum*). Further, translation of the *realia* (i.e., objects of material culture) demands the translator be especially careful: the main feature of the *realia* is their tone, and to convey this colouring is the most challenging task for any translator.

There exist two ways to render the *realia* into the target language in Lodovico's Latin version: transliteration from the Greek (to be avoided, according to Bruni), or approximate translation (generalisation, functional analogue, description, explanation, interpretation).

Examples of transliteration would be the Latin renderings *amitum* (999 ἄμητα, 'milk-cake') and *baratrum* (431 βάραθρον, 'the Pit', i.e., a cleft in the rock behind the Acropolis into which the bodies of criminals were thrown). For Lodovico, approximate translations of *realia* are more common. This approach allows him to translate the material content of an expression at least in a vague way, but the semantic colouring of words is nearly always lost. Misinterpretations in the *Plutus* account for the translation of τύμπανα ('pillories') as *virge*

---

24 Alexander of Otranto declines to translate personal names in his Latin *Plutus*: proper nouns are often glossed with the expressions *ille vir/illa mulier* and *nomen proprium*.
25 E.g., *Plut.* 84–85: Πλ. ἐκ Πατροκλέους ἔρχομαι, / ὃς οὐκ ἐλούσατ' ἐξ ὅτουπερ ἐγένετο] *Ex Patroclis (scilicet domo s.l.) venio, / qui non lavit, ex eo tempore quo ortus est*. For ἐξ ὅτουπερ ἐγένετο, at the end of verse 85, Lodovico employs *ex eo tempore quo ortus est*; his choice represents a considerable improvement of the interpretation of this passage: cf. *qui numquam lavit postquam secum fui* (Bruni), *qui non lotus est ex quo factus est, scilicet dives* (Pietro de Montagnana), *qui non lavit ex quo factus est, scilicet dives* (Alexander of Otranto); on this misinterpretation of Aristophanes see Cecchini/Cassio 1972, 480; Chirico 1991, 86–87, 187; Chantry 2009, 298–300.
26 Chantry 2009, 298–299. Cf. Holmes 1990; Olson 1992.

(glossed in the margin as *strumenta erant quibus servi vapulabant*) and κύφωνες ('execution-boards') as *strumenta* at verse 476.[27] Despite these quibbles, the translation is readable. It is fluent Latin and avoids clumsy translation *ad uerbum*.

One remarkable feature in Lodovico's version is his knack for rendering interjections and exclamations by an appropriate Latin idiom. The interjection πώμαλα (66) — which is approximately equivalent to οὐδαμῶς or the colloquial address 'why on earth, no way!' — is, for instance, represented by *nequaquam*.[28] In this case, Lodovico's rendering is more felicitous than Bruni's translation: in the first early modern Latin version of this passage, the Florentine scholar fails to render the meaning of πώμαλα, which he fancifully translates as *etiam cessas?*.[29]

One of the difficulties to which Lodovico himself draws attention is the variety of compound adjectives and nouns occurring in Aristophanes. The translator deals with them in more than one fashion; in a considerable number of cases, Lodovico uses the conservative approach of separating Greek compound words into their component parts, rendering them into Latin by a conjunction of verb and object, noun and objective genitive, or similar construction. Examples of this practice can be found in *Plutus* where the phrases *ante sacrificia* and *deum colens* translate προθύματα (660) and θεοσεβής (28). Similarly, we find in the Aristophanic version the expression *male fortunatus* for κακόδαιμον (386) and *bonum filium* for εὔπαιδα (639).

---

27 Lodovico has not found the exact Latin equivalent of τύμπανον (lit. 'drum', i.e., 'stretching-frame'), the instrument used in ancient Greece to inflict the form of execution known as *apotumpanismos*. A misunderstanding is also at the root of the translation given at verse 1128: *propter erniam*, where the Greek text says κωλῆς ('legs', strictly 'thigh, ham', i.e., the most important of those portions of a sacrificial animal that were not consumed by the worshippers but were burnt on the altar for the god). In another passage, Lodovico's translation is perhaps not entirely wrong, but at any rate misleading: *nittarium an et batium* (1011 νιττάριον ἂν καὶ βάτιον); his commentary *ad locum* — *amatores lascivi* (mg. sin.) — suggests that he mistakes the Greek words (diminutives of duck and ringdove/little skate) for personal names. In addition to these passages, see *Plut.* 661 πέλανος ('a sacrificial mixture')] *legumen*; 1206 γραῦς ('wrinkly skin')] *vetula*. Such divergences and misinterpretations will seem negligible, however, if we consider that Lodovico composed the translation without anyone to provide him with explanations, without the aid of any commentaries and relying on his own knowledge of the ancient culture.
28 Willi 2003, 59; Chantry 2009, 398–399.
29 One suspects that his free translation stems from a lack of resourcefulness rather than an active purpose. See Cecchini/Cassio 1972, 479.

Lodovico's Latin lexicon in *Plutus* does not always conform to the ideals expressed by Bruni who, in his *De recta interpretatione*, stresses that the Latin used by translators should imitate *auctores*, not borrow words from the Greek nor contain new words, especially if clumsy.[30] In fact, he uses a number of classical and late Latin words which, according to the *Thesaurus linguae Latinae*, were extremely rare in Antiquity.[31] Some of these terms grew into common usage in Medieval Latin; others did not. This taste for rare classical or late Latin terms is quite common among Latin writers.[32] Lodovico's *Plutus* also contains examples of Ecclesiastical Latin and several vocabularies so far attested only in Medieval texts.[33] Moreover, some of the words used in the translation are found in later Latin texts.[34]

Latinization is also a common device in Lodovico's version: in the *Plutus* we find, for instance, *zelotypus* ('jealous'), which was introduced into Latin in classical times (1016 ζηλότυπος), and *sicofantam* (937 συκοφάντην). In his choice of words, Lodovico draws on the resources of the whole of Latinity, though of course there is naturally a marked influence of Plautus and Terence.[35] It may be noticed in forms and typical expressions such as the following: 29 κακῶς ἔπραττον] *infortunatus eram* (Plaut. *Bacch.* 1006, Ter. *Eun.* 298); 266 νωδόν] *edentulum* (Plaut. *Rud.* 662); 293 βληχώμενοι] *balantes* (Plaut. *Bacch.* 1138a); 560 παχύκνημοι] *suras crassas* (Plaut. *Pseud.* 1118); 529 νύμφην] *sponsam* (Ter. *An.* 324); 674, 688, 1095 γρᾴδιον, 1024 γραός] *vetula* (Plaut. *Mostell.* 275); 1067 τιτθίων] *mamillas* (Plaut. *Pseud.* 180); and 1139 σκευάριον] *vasculum* (Plaut. *Aul.* 270). Also,

---

30 Viti 2004. Cf. Hankins 1994; Cortesi 1995b; Berti 1998.
31 E.g., *lippitudine* (115 ὀφθαλμίας); *percupit* (195 ἐπιθυμεῖ); *vinolentum* (298 κραιπαλῶντα), *pruriginem* (974 κνισμόν). Words such as *concives* (254 δημόται) and *comistiones* (989 μισγητίας) belong to post-Classical usage.
32 Rizzo 2002; Bernardi Perini 2004; Tateo 2006.
33 Terms that our dictionaries record as Ecclesiastical Latin are *eclesia* (171, 330, 725 ἐκκλησία); *clarificatus est* (635 λελάμπρυνται); *insensatum* (705 ἄγροικον); *decimas* (1185 τὰ νομιζόμενα). Words known from mediaeval sources are *cottum* (138 ψαιστόν); *erniam* (267 ψωλόν); *masticans* (321 μασώμενος); *gatta* (693 γαλῆς); *cassulam* (711 κιβώτιον); *delatrix* (970 συκοφάντρια); *frittellam* (1115 ψαιστόν); *servitialis* (1170 διακονικός); and *superficialiter* (1206 ἀνωτάτω). Du Cange 1883–1887.
34 E.g., *obtemperantia* (146 ὑπήκοα); *maxillatus* (690 παρείας). See the *Neulateinische Wortliste* by Johann Ramminger (http://www.neulatein.de — last accessed 01/09/2022). The Latin version proposes the vernacular word *impegolabam* as an equivalent to Aristophanes' inventive ὑπεπίττουν (1093) — 'working on the underside of that old boat', lit. 'pitching her underneath', with reference to the practice of covering the outside of a ship's hull with a coat of pitch.
35 On early modern imitation of Plautus see Pillola 1994; Beta 2017.

scurra (279 μόθων and κόβαλος, 'rogue') may be considered, I argue, as a reminiscence of the Plautinian verses 199–202 of the *Trinummus*.[36]

During the 15th century we increasingly see that, in an attempt to render the style of the Greek originals in Latin, the translator would not only use classical Latin idioms and syntax but also imitate an existing Latin text, written in the same genre as the Greek original. Aristophanic comedy and Plautus or Terence will often figure side by side, overlap and interact even within the same modern text as reflections of the Greco-Roman literary past. Thus, Lodovico renders Aristophanes in Plautinian verses or using Terentian phrases. In so doing, he transports the *Plutus* into a Roman universe, not just with regard to the content, but also in terms of style and poetics. Lodovico attempts to make Aristophanes into a Latin poet; he aims at a translation which would effectively import the Greek original into Latin early modern culture, producing a text adapted to the linguistic, literary and stylistic decorum of that culture.[37]

Moreover, we find the Italian teacher explaining the original instead of mechanically translating it; in so doing, he behaves more like a commentator than a translator. There are many instances where Lodovico feels the need to explain the original, to make it more easily accessible through its translation. Sometimes he gives a paraphrase of the Greek text, and, in most cases, he evidently understood quite well what Aristophanes meant.

For example, at times, Lodovico substitutes the Greek with Latin expressions which to some extent render the factual content of Aristophanes' sentences, but do not constitute a translation as much as an explanation. He does so in the *Plutus* to clarify the meaning of στιβάδα ('mattress'): *vimina ex papiro* (541) and to show the meaning of ἱκετηρίαν ('suppliant-branch'): *ramum olivae* (383).

In some instances, he does not substitute the Greek with a Latin explanation; instead, he adds the explanation after the close rendering or transliteration of the Greek, almost as a gloss.[38] Thus, we find *ex insula, scilicet Sfiti* (720 Σφηττίῳ) and *spargimina* (768 καταχύσματα, 'sweetmeats') with the added explanation *scilicet ut nuces, carice*.

---

36 Corbett 1986; Cesarini Martinelli 2016, 555–562. Cf. Chantry 2009, 388–389, 394–395.
37 The tendency to transform not only words and phrases but also style and literary form into the idioms of the 'host' culture is a hallmark of early modern translation, both in theory and in practice. See McLaughlin 1995.
38 Lodovico sometimes acts as an interpreter, adding interlinear explanatory phrases for the reader's benefit: 925 σίλφιον] *pretiosissimum, scilicet amulum unguentatum*; 1021 Θάσιον] *taxium, scilicet vinum*; 1087 τρύγοιπος] *colatorium, scilicet vini*; 1121 οἰνοῦτταν] *polentam, scilicet cum vino*.

An examination of Lodovico's work shows the addition of explanatory glosses such as possessive pronouns and adjectives in the interest of clarity (e.g., the addition of *sui* to *corporis* at verse 6 and of *mei* to *filii* at verse 292). The deployment of additional pronouns and adjectives is a standard early modern technique.

Innumerable times, Lodovico adds adjectives to nouns, adverbs to verbs, or renders one Greek noun with two Latin ones (semantic doubling). He allows himself certain liberties, adding the noun *ovis* to *lavat pellem* (166 πλύνει κῴδια, 'washes fleeces') and the adjective *parvi* to *solii* (546 πιθάκνης, 'cask'), the sense of which remained implicit in Aristophanes. Elsewhere he translates a simple Greek word in a rather long-winded fashion as *posteriorem partem templi* (1193 ὀπισθόδομον, 'inner chamber'), *concutis alas* (575 πτερυγίζεις, 'flap the wings'), *ostendentes pudibunda* (295 ἀπεψωλημένοι, 'cocks skinned'); in some cases, he doubles nouns, such as *cum delitiis vel pigritia* (325 καταβεβλακευμένως, 'slothfully'), *ianua vel portella* (1097 θύραν, 'door'), *magistro scilicet vel mihi poete vel Plutoni* (797 διδασκάλῳ, 'producer'), and *cribrum vel circulus cribri* (1037 τηλία, 'hoop of a corn-sieve').[39]

Some Aristophanic words receive the interpreter's special attention. Lodovico successfully captures the sense of the Greek adverb ἀναβάδην ('with one's feet up') at verse 1123, that is rendered *superposito crure* and subsequently explained in a marginal gloss (*ociose vivere*).[40] Similarly, Lodovico produces a full and satisfying translation of Aristophanes' wordplay ἀσκωλίαζ' in *Plut.* 1129 (lit. 'play the bladder game', i.e., 'bounce off'), paraphrasing it as *sali per utrem*.[41]

---

39 The normal meaning of τηλία is 'board with a raised rim'; more specifically, it is applied to 'hoop of a sieve' (*schol. vet. Plut.* 1037m) and later just 'sieve', or to trays used by itinerant sellers of bread and barley meals for displaying their wares (*schol. vet. Plut.* 1037a–d–e–f–g–h). See Chantry 1994, 77–86; Sommerstein 2001, 204–205; Chantry 2009, 402–403. The Aristophanic context requires that the reference be to some 'ring' that would be big enough to accommodate the Old Woman's fat bodily circumference. Translators and commentators of Aristophanes in the Italian 15th to 16th centuries have variously rendered the reading τηλία at the end of the verse 1037 as *circulus cribri* (Guarino Veronese), *cribri circulus* (Pietro de Montagnana), *tina* (Alexander of Otranto), *cribri magni* (Francesco Passi), *circulus cribri* (Andrea Divo), *vanni aut dolii cyclus* (Coriolano Martirano) and *cerchio di crivello* (Bartolomeo and Pietro Rositini).
40 Mastromarco 1983; Chantry 2009, 274–275.
41 Pietro de Montagnana's lexical choice remains less precise (*salta*) and Alexander of Otranto is not successful in rendering the full impact of Aristophanes' wordplay (*tarda*). In the very first Italian translation of the *Plutus*, Bartolomeo and Pietro Rositini propose *salta quà à lo aere per di sopra le pelli* as an equivalent to Aristophanes' inventive ἀσκωλίαζ'. Carion is alluding to a game that certainly existed in classical Athens: Sommerstein 2001, 210–211.

Such use of explanatory glosses and periphrasis again illustrates the translator's preference for literal equivalents that resemble the kind of explanatory amplification likely to appear in philological commentaries.

Lodovico shares with contemporary translators the dilemma of choosing between a literal and a liberal translation, or rather the difficulty of steering a middle course between these extreme forms.[42] He embraces his role as an intermediary between Greek source and Latin readership, drawing the line between his responsibility towards the Greek author — which obliges him to convey the meaning of the original faithfully and accurately — and his considerations for the needs of the reader, which prompts him to adopt the role of a commentator. Moreover, we are able to observe the skilful translator at work: we recognise Lodovico's creativity and resourcefulness in his choice of words, and his mastery of translation techniques (such as the addition of explanatory glosses and the emphasis of the verse by rhetorical *imitatio auctorum*). All this indicates that Lodovico was a gifted translator of Aristophanes and that he possessed a very fair knowledge of both Greek and Latin.

2 Glossing Aristophanes' *Plutus*

The manuscript *Matrit. gr.* 4697 also contains a series of interesting annotations autograph of Lodovico: most are tags to assist with the Latin version, and they offer a fascinating insight into the way 15th-century readers addressed the *Plutus*. *Matrit. gr.* 4697 is glossed by Lodovico both in the margins and interlineally in the principal text.[43] These glosses are mostly Latin, and the vernacular glossing represents no more than a tiny portion of the overall paratext. The careful execution of the volume together with the annotations, which are beautifully written in red ink in the generous margins, convey the impression that the book

---

[42] For the general topic of early modern methods of translation — the literal, the semantic and the free method — see Sabbadini 1922, 24; De Petris 1975, 15–32; Gualdo Rosa 1985, 178; Berti 1988, 245–266; Berschin 1989, 336; Cortesi 1995a; Cortesi 2007.

[43] A number of the glosses are *notabilia* or index notes that draw the reader's attention to interesting passages by repeating either a name or some words from the text. Though not exactly a full commentary, most of them go far beyond the mere repetition of the information contained in the text to which they refer; instead, they explain Aristophanes' text using information found in the Greek *scholia* to *Plutus*. Many of Lodovico's exegetical glosses are a mixture of Thoman and Triclinian material translated into Latin (*thPstr* in Chantry 1996).

is planned as a whole, and a closer examination of the *marginalia* strengthens this impression.

The process of glossing is a highly common, and perhaps even universal, activity in written cultures all over the world.⁴⁴ Glosses have various functions and manifestations, all of which are in some way intended to facilitate the needs and requirements of the reader. As an example, a significant number of postils in the manuscript *Matrit. gr.* 4697 elucidate the morphology and syntax of the Aristophanic text: the grammatical glosses, explaining the parts of speech and the grammatical properties of words, also help establish the literal meaning of the text; syntactical annotations help construe the word order of the Greek text.⁴⁵ The syntactical, lexical and grammatical notes are seen as pedagogical devices as lexical and grammatical instruction is essential for understanding a work of such antiquity.

Lexical glosses abound in the Aristophanic manuscript under consideration. They provide lexical equivalents or near-equivalents of a word or group of words through a variety of devices: synonyms, hypernyms, an explanatory sentence or paraphrase. Lexical notes are often introduced by such words as *id est*, *vel* or *scilicet*.⁴⁶ The most important category of lexical annotations is the synonym or near-synonym, of which the glossator seems to be particularly fond. In the marginal glosses to Aristophanes' *Plutus*, for example, one finds *vendentem ova* (427 λεκιθόπωλιν, 'porridge-vendor'): *vendentem vel olera vel legumina* (f. 187r, mg. dext.), *sicariis* (521 ἀνδραποδιστῶν, 'kidnappers'): *predonibus, latronibus, ligatoribus pedum* (f. 191v, mg. sin.) and *velum* (729 ἡμιτύβιον, 'napkin'): *nasitergium, manipulum* (f. 201v, mg. sin.).⁴⁷

---

44 Only recently has the study of glosses and *marginalia* started to focus on broader issues such as their value as witnesses to literary and textual culture, the history of reading and the early modern transfer of learning. See Fera/Ferraù/Rizzo 2002, with its rich bibliography. Research on glosses generally emphasises their importance as teaching tools: see Dionisotti 1984–1985; Holtz 1995; Holtz 1996; Blair 2008; Black 2010. On the early modern attitude toward the classics, see Buck/Herding 1975, 7–19; Grafton 1985; Lo Monaco 1992; Grafton 1997; Campanelli/Pincelli 2000; Avezzù/Scattolin 2006; Pincelli 2008; Enenkel/Nellen 2013; Kraus/Stray 2016.

45 The most numerous of all are the suppletive glosses, which supply omitted words. Suppletive nouns and pronouns in the nominative usually provide the subject of the sentence: 704 αὐτὸς δ' ἐκεῖνος] *ipse autem ille, scilicet Esculapius* s.l.

46 Here I offer some examples of marginal notes: 109 ἀτεχνῶς] *sine arte, id est manifestissime*; 192 μάζης] *sicci panis, scilicet biscotti*; 243 κύβοισι] *significat taxillos vel cubos*; 694 ἔφλων] *tundebam, scilicet dentibus*.

47 Synonyms are amongst the most numerous of all the glosses in the margins. A list of them follows: 45 ἐπίνοιαν] *sententiam, consilium, conceptum, diffinitionem, intentionem*; 165 τοιχω-

Hypernyms are also used to convey lexical equivalence by giving the *genus* of a word for its *species*, glossing *patula* (1096 λεπάς, 'limpet'), for example, with its hypernym *piscis genus adherens lapidibus* (f. 219v, mg. sin.). In the same spirit are the many postils that elucidate the literal meaning of a word or phrase, as in *lectum* (663 στιβάδα, 'bed of straw'): *lectum ex iugis factum* (f. 198r, mg. dext.).

In certain cases, the gloss specifies the meaning of the lemma, or attempts to clarify and even interpret it, as in the following example: f. 219r, mg. dext., *rugas*] *vestis lacerata, sed non hic* (1065 τὰ ῥάκη). Its function should be to resolve potential ambiguity in the poetic text, where Aristophanes employs the term ῥάκη (lit. 'rags') in the sense of 'wrinkles', with reference to the face/mask of the Old Woman. As this last example suggests, vernacular words also appear in the glosses to Aristophanes' *Plutus*: *mattera* (545 μάκτρας): *mattera strumentum in quo fit panis, que madia vulgo dicitur* (f. 192v, mg. sin.). It is interesting to underline the fact that the use of the vernacular mostly concerns terms belonging to the familiar and everyday vocabulary, such as μάκτρα ('kneading-trough'), for which the use of the maternal language could take on a particularly connotative meaning.[48]

In all of the above cases, it seems that the primary aim is to enrich the vocabulary and make the text of Aristophanes comprehensible, adding the knowledge of the Greek language and culture that is necessary for a proper understanding of the play. Moreover, the greater part of the Latin paratext added by Lodovico consists of commentary glosses.[49] Notes give explicative commentary, for example on exegesis or historical background. A typical example of explicative gloss is the marginal gloss on *Plut.* 606 (ἐς τὸν κύφων'), *chifona* ('to the pillory'): *locus noxiorum* (f. 195v, mg. sin.). This note provides historical information about a device used to punish criminals: κύφων (lit. 'stooper') was a frame in which lesser criminals were made to stand or sit with their necks clamped.

ρυχεῖ] *parietem perforat, ingreditur domum*; 561 σφηκώδεις] *vespositatem, gracilitatem*; 571 βάσκανος] *fascinatrix, insana, invida*; 758 εὐφημοῦντες] *canentes innos, benedicentes*; 1063 καπηλικῶς] *cauponice, fucate, meritorie*; 1150 ἀστεῖον] *urbanum, generosum*.
48 On the developing role for the vernaculars in early modern Humanism see Vitale 1953; Fubini 1961; Dionisotti 1968; Tavoni 1984; Black 1996.
49 These *marginalia* provide new information to and elucidate a given lemma: 602 Παύσωνα] *Passonem: virum pictorem*; 604 ἐς κόρακας] *corvos: locus condemnatorum*; 884 Εὐδάμου] *Edamus artifex vel orifex*; 925 Βάττου] *viri conditoris Cirenis civitatis*; 1054 εἰρεσιώνην] *ramus olive cum lana qui appendebatur hostiis*.

The religious institutions of the Greeks appear to have been of particular interest to Lodovico, such as the Greater Mysteries celebrated at Eleusis (f. 215v, mg. sin., 1013 μυστηρίοις δὲ τοῖς μεγάλοις] *arcanis misteriis*). Likewise, information about Greek history and political institutions are carefully culled from the text: e.g., f. 222r, mg. dext., 1146 Φυλὴν] *mons erat Athenis, vel mons occupatus a Thrasybulo causa liberatus a triginta tyrannis*. The annotation alludes to events of the year 403: the occupation of Phyle by Thrasybulus was the initial step in the overthrow of the Thirty and the restoration of the democracy at Athens.[50] In many ways, then, the *marginalia* in the manuscript examined definitively reveal an interest in the historical information found in Aristophanes' *Plutus*; in general, they only draw attention to it, and do not in any way comment upon names, customs, institutions *vel sim.*, independently of Aristophanes' account.

The relation between Lodovico, his translation, his marginal commentary, his readership, and the author of the *Plutus* cannot be characterised as sterile. On the contrary, Lodovico frequently intervenes in the text by using various techniques; he guides his reader, reminding them of what he considers important and explaining it when he feels the need.

3 Conclusion

The beginning of the 15th century marked a new stage in the reception of the Aristophanic *corpus*. Aristophanes' works, lost after the fall of Rome and unknown in the early modern period, were reintroduced in the first quarter of the Quattrocento. They gained instant popularity with 15th century readers, and by 1500 a considerable number of translations were in circulation.

The history of Aristophanic translations still needs to be written as many of these texts lie unedited and unexplored in some of the recent manuscripts of Greek Comedy.[51] What is clear, and what I hope to have shown here, is that the analysis of Latin translations and glosses preserved by early modern witnesses will shed light on the history of the revival of Aristophanes and the story of how the writings of the ancient playwright were received and interpreted, some 1800 years after they were written, in an alien language and culture.

---

50 Geographical and historical references need identification, as do mythological figures: 170 μέγας δὲ βασιλεὺς] *Magnus vero rex, scilicet Xerses* s.l.; 702 Πανάκει'] *Panachia significat tota remedio; filie due erant Esculapii, Iaso et Panachia* mg. dext.; 718 Τηνίων] *insula, scilicet Teno* s.l.
51 Wilson 1992, 7: 'In that solemn fifteenth century which can hardly be studied too much'.

Malika Bastin-Hammou
From Translating Aristophanes to Composing a Greek Comedy in 16th c. Europe: The Case of Alciato

Abstract: There is a long-lasting and early tradition of translating Aristophanes in early modern Europe which is to a large extent due to the fact that his comedies were used to teach ancient Greek. Some of those translations come with paratexts written by the translators which give us precious insight on the reasons why they chose to translate Aristophanes, the difficulty they encountered and the choices they made. This paper analyzes the specificities of this discourse on translating comedy and its evolutions, during the beginning of the 16th c. It shows that while the first Latin translations fall roughly into two categories, *ad uerbum* and adaptations, a turn occurs with Alciato, who both translated *Clouds* and wrote an Ancient Comedy in Latin. From them on, especially in the Holy Empire, translators focussed on metre and strived to translate Aristophanes *ad uersum*, and their paratexts stress how difficult this was.

Greek drama has had an important influence on European drama in the 16th century and this was to a large extent due to the circulation of Latin translations of ancient Greek drama, but also of Latin tragedies or comedies inspired by Greek drama, which can be considered as translations in a broader sense: not of texts, but of the genre, structure, themes and main features of the originals.

Much research has been done on tragedies and, to a lesser extent, comedies inspired by Greek drama in the 16th century.[1] Recently, scholars have studied the impact of Latin translations of Greek drama on the invention of European drama,[2] and there have been a few studies on the interactions between translations of Greek tragedy into Latin and Latin tragedies inspired by Greek tragedies.[3] But there has been no study on the interactions between Latin translations of Greek comedy and comedies inspired by Aristophanes and written in

---

[1] See, for a recent overview, Zyl Smit 2016, part II and III.
[2] On the general influence of Ancient Greek comedy on Latin and vernacular comedy in the 16th century, see, for Germany, Best 1971, Holzberg & Brunner 2020, 75–78; for France Le Loyer 2004, Bastin-Hammou 2015, Dudouyt 2016; for Italy, Nogara 2016 and Radif 2014; for England, Steggle 2007 and Miola 2014; and Sommerstein 2019 *passim*.
[3] See, amongst others, Jackson 2020 and in this volume.

https://doi.org/10.1515/9783110719185-003

Latin. The purpose of this chapter is thus to determine the importance of the interactions that occur between Latin translations of Aristophanes and comedies inspired by Aristophanes and composed in Latin.

A focus on *Plutus*, which had been abundantly translated into Latin from very early on and, to a lesser extent, adapted and imitated, may help us better understand the complex relation between Latin translations and Latin creations in early modern Europe. The study of the specific case of Andrea Alciato, who translated *Clouds* into Latin ca. 1517 and wrote *Philargyrus* ca. 1523, a Latin comedy inspired by Aristophanes, should shed new light on the interaction between translation, imitation and creation of ancient Greek comedy in early modern Europe.

Greek comedy did not influence early modern drama as much as Greek tragedy did; 15th- and 16th-century comedy took its main inspiration from Latin comedy and the mediaeval farce. This is not due to the fact that the texts of Greek comedy were less available or known than those of Greek tragedy. It is quite the opposite: the *editio princeps* of nine of Aristophanes' comedies was published in Venice in 1498 by Aldo Manuzio, while the *editio princeps* of Sophocles was published three years later, in 1502, that of Euripides in 1503, and that of Aeschylus in 1518. This lack of interest in Aristophanes from 16th-century dramatists was not due to poor knowledge of the Greek language either, as Aristophanes had been translated into Latin very early on, mostly in Italy.

But these Latin translations did not influence dramatists that much: most were translations of *Plutus* and not intended for dramatists and readers in general but for students of the Greek language, especially beginners. Indeed, students learned to write, read and translate Greek with Aristophanes' *Plutus*.[4] There were, however, a few adaptations, and even creations derived from Aristophanes, but it seems that they generally belonged to the same social and professional world, that of scholars and professors; indeed, texts that would now be considered adaptations written for the stage might well have been translations in a broad sense. The aim of this chapter is to show that there is no line to be drawn between translations and adaptations if we want to understand the general attitude of scholars toward Greek comedy at the beginning of the 16th century; but also that there is a major shift in the third decade of the century, and maybe earlier, as the case of Alciato demonstrates. From then on, most translators quit the habit of adding digressions to, or removing parts of, the translated text, did not translate *ad uerbum* anymore and focused on translating *ad uersum*. Each Greek line was translated into a Latin one and translators re-

---

4 Botley 2010; Bastin-Hammou 2019.

sorted to both fidelity, as they translated the source text in its entirety, and creativity, as they translated into verse.

1 Translating Aristophanes into Latin before 1517

Indeed, Aristophanes seems to have been read in Italy quite early on. We know that in 1406 Guarino bought a manuscript of Aristophanes in Constantinople. In 1443, Theodore Gaza taught Greek in Mantua on Aristophanes, and in 1445 Vittorino da Feltre held a copy of Aristophanes in his library.[5]

As for translations, they started quite early too and we have several manuscript translations of *Plutus* written in the 15th century. In the first half of the 15th century, ca. 1415, Rinuccio di Castiglione wrote a loose adaptation of *Plutus*, *Fabula Penia*; ca. 1440, Leonardo Bruni translated the beginning of this same comedy, and Pietro da Montagnana two parts of it. In the second half of the century, ca. 1458, Alessandro d'Otranto translated it *ad uersum*. In this volume, Micol Muttini analyses another 15th-century translation of *Plutus*, made by Lodovico da Poppi in the last quarter of the quattrocento.[6] These early translations are very different from one another, but were all made in 15th-century Italy.

What characterises these early Italian translations seems to be a *continuum* from translating *ad uerbum* to writing a new comedy, and the fact that they are mostly made by professors or students of Greek.

The *Fabula Penia* composed by Rinucci da Castiglione ca. 1515–16 is, in fact, quite far from Aristophanes' *Plutus*, though clearly inspired by this comedy. It paraphrases the scene featuring Πενία, corresponding to lines 400–426. Πενία demonstrates to the hero that, without poverty, richness cannot exist. This is a short and moralising text, as expected from a *Fabula*. Rinucci never mentions Aristophanes in his three preliminary texts — a letter, a eulogy and a prologue. Besides, the adaptation of the Penia scene is quite loose. But some lines seem to be translated: 403–409, 413–414, 489–610, though with many omissions. Rinucci probably had the Greek text, which he sometimes translated, and most times rewrote.[7]

---

5 Botley 2010.
6 See Muttini in this volume and in her forthcoming Thesis.
7 Ludwig 1975; Radif 2011; Lockwood 1913, 51–109 and 72–76.

Leonardo Bruni, himself a theorist of translation in the *De interpretatione recta*, translated the first 269 lines of this same comedy in ca. 1440.[8] The fact that a theorist of translation chose to translate Aristophanes is in itself interesting for our purpose. Laurence Bernard-Pradelle suggested that this choice of translating *Plutus* was due to the fact that Bruni wanted to test his ideas on translation on different samples of Greek texts. As a matter of fact, the comic poet seems to have been regularly chosen to practise translation, probably because the *Plutus* was traditionally used as a textbook to learn Greek, as this play was considered easy, written in good attic Greek and pleasant for beginners.[9] Bruni is closer to the Greek text than Rinucci; he nevertheless omits some words, adds others and changes their meaning to make the text more understandable, or morally acceptable to 16th-century Italian readers.[10]

At about the same time, ca. 1440, Pietro da Montagnana also translated the beginning of *Plutus*. He focused on two parts of the play, the prologue (l. 1–287) and the lines 403–610, where Chremilos introduces Plutus to Blepsidèmos. This 'translation' is actually an interlinear one, which looks in many regards like a draft. One can read several Latin words for a Greek one and can thus follow the translator at work. Nothing is said by the translator himself about his aims and methods, and we can even doubt he considered himself as a translator: he was just translating – that is, here, trying to understand the Greek text.

The translation made by Alessandro d'Otranto a few years later, ca. 1458, is of the same kind: it is an interlinear one in which obvious words are sometimes omitted. Translating, here, means merely writing down the meaning of difficult words. While Alessandro d'Otranto is the first one to confront the whole text, he does not preface his attempt either, nor calls it a translation.[11]

On the other hand, Lodovico da Poppi, on the other hand, who also produced an interlinear translation of *Plutus* at the end of the century, seems to have translated not only the words but the whole meaning of the play and the features of the genre.[12] Thus, by the end of the 15th century several attempts had been made in Italy to understand Aristophanes' *Plutus* by translating his words and rewriting parts of it. 1501 marks a turning point, with Franciscus Passius' *Plutus*, the first printed translation of an Aristophanic comedy. The fact that this

---

8 Cecchini 1965; Lockwood 1909, lvi–lvii; Lockwood [1931] 1967, 163–172; Bernard-Pradelle 2016.
9 Bastin-Hammou 2019.
10 Cecchini 1965.
11 Chirico 1991.
12 Muttini in this volume.

is the first printed translation of Aristophanes is important, as printed texts circulated much more easily than manuscripts.

This translation belongs to the tradition illustrated by Rinucci and Bruni. As stated above, both Rinucci and Bruni digressed from the text of *Plutus* and this practice of digressing while translating is to be found again in Passius; but while Rinucci mostly invented and only translated a few lines, the balance is here reversed, as Passius mostly translates and only at times digresses. Furthermore, because it was printed, this translation shows a title page which is very instructive: on the front page, one can read that this is 'a translation'. By calling his text a translation, but also by referring to Aristophanes and naming his work *Plutus*, Passius probably wanted to take some distance from those 'translators' who, like Rinucci, did not mention Aristophanes, *Plutus*, or translation. He nevertheless translated quite loosely, introducing digressions and, more interesting, adding a prologue which is completely absent from the Greek original.[13]

Then came adaptations in the vernacular. In 1504, Niccolò Machiavelli wrote a comedy inspired by Aristophanes *Clouds*, *Le Maschere*, now lost, in which he is said to have attacked his contemporaries: he would thus be the first of a long *lignée* of imitators of the satirical Aristophanes.[14] Eufrosino Bonini, ca. 1512, also adapted a Greek comedy in the vernacular, *Comedia di Iustitia*, which was rather close to *Plutus*, performed at the Medici palace; as Machiavelli's comedy, it referred to the political situation in Florence at that time.[15]

All these attempts to translate Aristophanes are very different: some are complete, others are not; some are written in verse, others in prose; some are *ad uerbum*, others claim to be *ad sensum* or *ad sententiam* and others are clearly adaptations, that is, here, mostly translations with digressions, or imitations with bits of translations. These differences from the original are puzzling for a modern reader used to a strict definition of translation, but they all highlight the translator's will to understand and make Aristophanes accessible; the translations mentioned all have in common the fact that they were produced in Italy, incorporated the codes of Latin comedy, and were mainly of one single comedy, *Plutus*.

---

13 Passius 1501. See Beta 2017.
14 Radif 2014.
15 Stefani 1986; Sommerstein 2019, 142, 766. The translation is now held at the National Library of Florence under the shelfmark ms. Magl. Strozz., VII, 1211.

2 Alciato's Choice of the *Clouds*

Alciato probably knew some of these translations — at least the 1501 printed *Plutus*. He, as the others, used the codes of Latin comedy to understand and make readers understand Greek comedy. But he did not choose to translate *Plutus*, as most did before and many did after him. He rather chose *Clouds*, which he translated *ad uersum*; and a few years later, he did not adapt any of these comedies but wrote a new old comedy in Latin, *Philargyrus*, using what he considered to be the main features of the Greek comedy genre. This makes him an interesting case for the study of the different forms of 'translation', in a broad sense, of Greek comedy. It also gives us an insight into the evolution that led him from translating one Greek comedy *ad uersum* to writing a brand new one: he is the only poet who did both, and, at that, in a relatively short period of time. Finally, the fact that he had none of his translations printed could also shed light on the way Greek comedy was considered in 16th-century Europe.

At that time, *Clouds* had been printed with eight other comedies in the Aldine *princeps* of 1498. During the second decade of the 16th century, printers and scholars of the Holy Empire started to rival the Italians: in 1517, Peter Schade, a.k.a. Mosellanus, published an edition of the *Plutus*, and so did Thierry Martens in 1518. But nobody took pains to publish a separate edition — let alone a translation — of *Clouds*, until Melanchthon in 1521.

Yet, *Clouds* had always been an important comedy among Aristophanes' plays. Though it did not win the first prize in 423 B.C., it had been very well transmitted and took place among the Byzantine triad, the choice of three plays used to teach Aristophanes during the Byzantine era, probably because of the presence of Socrates among the characters and, even more, of the responsibility attributed to Aristophanes and to this particular comedy in the death of the philosopher.

But Socrates does not seem to have interested Alciato as much as Strepsiades and what, in his adventures, relates to Athenian law. If Strepsiades decides to go to Socrates' school, it is because he has debts and wants to learn how to plead in order not to pay them. The prologue of the play offers an interesting insight into the details of the Athenian law concerning debtors and creditors. This same interest for Athenian law will be observed in Alciato's *Philargyrus*. The satirical attacks which interested Machiavelli in 1504 seem to have also interested Alciato. This interest in the law and satirical attacks may explain why Alciato chose *Clouds* instead of the moralising and often translated *Plutus*.

Indeed, while Alciato published many works in verse, he is mainly known for being an important jurist, which explains his interest in legal matters in Aristophanes. Most studies on him focus on his work as a jurist and, to a lesser extent, the *Emblemata*. His elegies and comedies, on the other hand, were not mentioned before 1745 and his works relating to Aristophanes have been understudied.[16] Some authors did mention them, but briefly and in a dismissive way. Other scholars studied what, in those works, relates to the study of the law: Vismara, for example, studied the law concerning heirs.[17] The *Philargyrus* has been discussed by Barni, who identified some contemporary events and people with those in the play, and by Nogara. Recently, Thomas Penguilly commented on his *Clouds*.[18] But nobody has studied the relation between these two works from the point of view of the reception of Ancient comedy, that is to say the relation between Alciato's *Clouds* and other contemporary translations of Aristophanes, but also the relation between *Philargyrus* and other creations inspired by Aristophanes, and eventually the relation between those two texts. Yet, these are obviously related to each other, and to the history of the translation and reception of Aristophanes in general.

Furthermore, these works are still considered as some kind of leisure for the serious jurist: Nogara calls them *otia* ('Gli otia di un giurista filologo'); and Alciato himself may have contributed to this tradition by calling them, in his correspondence, *lucubratiuncules*. Even if this is partly a rhetorical posture, the fact he never published them reveals that he did not consider them as major works.

But he did translate *Clouds* and write *Philargyrus*, and his interest in Aristophanes lasted at least ten years, as the last additions to the *Philargyrus* date back to ca. 1527; in addition, he had the *Philargyrus* copied in *bella copia* and dedicated his *Clouds*.[19] This makes them definitely worth studying, not only for themselves but for the complex interaction that is at work between them, and what this interaction reveals of what it meant to 'translate' Greek comedy in the first decades of the 16th century.

The two manuscripts are now in the Biblioteca Trivulziana in Milan; in the same codex (Cod. Triv. 738) one can read the *Interpretatiunculae* on Philargyrus by Albuzzi (in fact, according to Nogara, the *Interpretatiunculae* were written by Alciato himself) and *annotationes* to the *Clouds*, attributed to Gualtierro Cor-

---

16 Nogara 2016; Argelati 1745 first mentioned the manuscripts of the *Philargyrus* and the *Clouds* ('*Quae duo Alciati nostri poemata stylum Plautinum redolent*', 'These two poems from our Alciato smell the style of Plautus').
17 Nogara 2016, 7.
18 Nogara 2016, 6.
19 Penguilly, 2019.

betta.[20] This means that we not only have two very different works inspired by Aristophanes, but also Alciato's own comments on at least one of these works. They are, as well as the prologues he wrote for both works, precious insights into his understanding of Aristophanes.

Adding these paratexts might have been a strategy to show that these works deserved attention; but they were also of help for readers to understand them, all the more so as he had not chosen to translate or imitate the well-known *Plutus*.

Alciato had a strong education in Latin and Greek thanks to the importance of Hellenism in Milan during his childhood. Parrasio was his professor in Milan, from the age of 12 to 14 (1504–1506) and he may have come across Jean Lascaris, too.[21] Indeed, there were many Greek refugees in Milan at that time and it probably made Alciato eager to learn Greek. In 1508, at the age of 15, he went to the University of Pavia to study law and in 1511 he left Pavia for Bologna where, in 1514, he got his doctorate at the age of 22.[22]

He then went back home to Milan to work as a lawyer, not being sure yet whether he wanted to be a lawyer his whole life. When he had no case to work on, he carried on studying civil law; he prepared *Paradoxa*, *Dispunctiones*, *Pratermissa* and *De eo quod interest*, which he published in 1518. During this period, he also translated *Clouds* into Latin, which remained unpublished. Did he ever consider publishing it?

Most scholars, even when they have taken interest in the *Philargyrus*, have regarded his *Clouds* as a mere translation exercise. Yet, this is more than a mere exercise: it contains the seeds that were to be developed in *Philargyrus* and the way Aristophanes was understood and latinized during the 16th century; it also announces a turn in translation practises concerning Greek drama.

Indeed, when translating the Greek text, Alciato keeps the main features of Greek comedy. The translation is written in verse, and Alciato does not make any digression: there are as many trimeters in Greek as there are in the Latin. In this regard, Alciato differs from both Alessandro di Otranto and Pietro da Montagnana with their *ad uerbum* translations, and from Bruni, Rinucci and Passius who added some lines and omitted others, or even completely rewrote the play, in the case of Rinucci. In fact, he is closer to translators like Thomas Venatorius

---

20 There is another manuscript of *Clouds* in Basel; it is a transcription made by Amerbach when he was a student of Alciato in Avignon. See Belloni 2016, 773–774.
21 Penguilly 2014, 178.
22 Penguilly 2014, 178.

or Adrianus Chilius, who translated *Plutus ad uersum* some fifteen years later, respectively in 1531 and 1533.

There are mainly five features of Greek comedy which appear to be problematic to 15th and 16th translators of Aristophanes — and some of them to translators of all times: realia, personal attacks, obscenities, gods and the metre. While the metre and realia are problematic for any translator, personal attacks, obscenities and gods depend on the cultural context in which the translator lives and, eventually, publishes his or her work. Specific to 15th and 16th translators are the extent to which the translation imitates Latin comedy, for instance by changing the names of the characters and picking names characteristic of Latin comedy, and the presence or absence of omissions and digressions.

When one studies the first Latin translations of *Plutus*, it is possible to compare the way translators faced those problems by a word for word analysis, which also reveals to what extent translators copied each other or, to put it in another way, how these translations circulated and which among them became references and contributed to establish a tradition of the way one should translate Aristophanes.

This method cannot be applied here, as Alciato's *Clouds* is the first complete Latin translation of *Clouds*. The next Latin translation of this comedy was printed some twenty years later, in 1538 in Venice; it is a word-for-word translation in prose, to be found in the first complete Latin translation of Aristophanes, made by Andreas Divus, which became the reference for more than a century. To read a new Latin verse translation of *Clouds*, one has to wait until Coriolano Martirano's translation in 1556; and neither Divus nor Martirano seem to have known Alciato's work.

Indeed, one can get an idea of what kind of translator of Aristophanes Alciato is by examining his translation techniques and focusing on the five items mentioned above.

It is clear from the first lines that this is not an *ad uerbum* translation. Alciato translates the genitive singular ἀλεκτρυόνος line 4 with the accusative plural *gallos*; the plural *dispendiis* translates the singular δαπάνης. In this regard, he differs from the notes of Alessandro di Otranto and Pietro da Montagnana, but also from the later Andreas Divus, who kept the case and the number of the words translated, even if they did not fit in Latin.

Furthermore, when a Greek word is not clear, he explains it and elaborates on it, as with the participle ἐγκεκορδυλημένος, translated with the three Latin participles *cubans*, *involutus* and *stratus*:

ἀλλὰ πέρδεται
ἐν πέντε σισύραις ἐγκεκορδυλημένος

But he farts
Wrapped in five blankets

quin magis pedit cubans
Quinque involutus, atque stratus pellibus

There's more, when he sleeps he farts
Wrapped and lying in five blankets

The significance of Pheidippides' haircut, evoked by the phrase ὁ δὲ κόμην ἔχων line 14, characteristic of rich young men who served as cavalry, is judiciously translated with the Latin *comatulus*, diminutive and pejorative of comatus.[23]

The same treatment is applied to the choruses, notoriously hard to translate: not a single line is omitted, some words are added to explain obscure phrases, others are interpreted.

Obscenities do not seem to be a problem to Alciato either, who straightforwardly translates the scene of the farting mosquito.

Alciato also keeps the Greek names of the characters, while Bruni changed them and latinized them, and, though to a lesser extent, Greek realia: *calendaria* translates γραμματεῖον, the book where Strepsiades keeps track of his debts, but everything else concerning the payment of debts relates to the Greek custom as in Aristophanes.

Nevertheless, he, like other translators of his time, quite often uses the filter of Latin comedy to translate Greek comedy: he notably uses archaisms, imitating the style of Plautus, even if there is no archaism in the Greek. For example, he uses *antidhac* rather than the more Ciceronian *antehac*.[24]

Alciato as a translator thus inherits from his predecessors: difficult words and puns are developed and made clearer if needed, realia are kept when clear and, if not, they are transposed into a Latin context; what concerns religion is not omitted either, even when it can be judged disrespectful. But he also innovates. While his Italian fellow predecessors, when they did not translate *ad uerbum*, often added to the text, he did not. In this regard, his translation is closer to those of later translators, from the 1530s: not *ad uerbum*, but without digressions. Another major difference lies in the writing of a prologue, which

---

23 Dover 1970, 70.
24 *Antidhac* is to be found in Plautus *Amphitryon* 711, *Aul.* 396.

translates nothing but can be seen as an introduction to Aristophanes, in the manner of Aristophanes.

3 Alciato Prologus to *Clouds*, between the Tradition of Latin Comedy and Scholarly Paratext

This 181-line prologue gives a very interesting insight into Alciato's understanding of the comic poet. It is partly a *captatio*, in the manner of the prologues of Latin comedy, and in this regard it can be compared to the prologue Passius wrote and added to the beginning of his translation of the *Plutus*; but it is also close to the scholarly paratexts that can be read in editions of the comic poet, in that it reveals the aims of Alciato and his understanding of the play.

Alciato is not the first translator to add a prologue to an Aristophanic comedy. Passius, in his 1501 *Plutus*, also wrote a prologue in the manner of Latin comedy, which came right after four preliminary paratexts, and just before the translation itself. In the first paratext, which is a dedicatory letter, Passius claimed the novelty of his *Plutus*: there is no Ancient comedy in Latin, his will be the first.[25] He also justified his choice of writing it in trimeters, while the Greek text used many different metres.[26]

Then, in his prologue, Passius, through the mouth of Prologus, called himself a poet, and, just like the prologues of Latin comedy, addressed the specta-

---

[25] *Dubitanti quam mihi potissimum scribendi materiam ex multis quae occurebant assumerem : Aristophanis Plutus in primis mihi digna uisa fuit: quam in latino sermone imitaremur. Partim nouitate rei (non est nim apud nos ulla antiqua comedia)* [...] 'As I was wondering on which material I should write preferably, among the many ones that occurred to me, Aristophanes' Plutus appeared to be the most worthy of an imitation in Latin, partly because of the novelty of the project (we do not have any Ancient comedy)...'. Dedicatory letter to Albertus Pius (*Illustrissimo ac eruditissimo Alberto Pio principi Carpensi, ingeniorum fautori, Franciscus Passius Carpensis domino suo felicitatem dicit*).

[26] *Solis trimetris fabula haec continetur: quam dimetris trimetris tetrametris acataleticis & hyper cataleticis fecerat Aristophanes. Ubi illud maxime Quintiliani iudicium sequti sumus adserentis Terentium maiorem laudem assecuturum fuisse si se inter trimetros continuisset.* 'I composed my play in trimeters only, while Aristophanes wrote his play in dimeters, trimeters, tetrameters acatalectic and hypercatalectic. There I followed Quintilian's advice, who says that Terentius would have had more glory if he had written in trimeters only'. Dedicatory letter to Albertus Pius (see above).

tors and criticised an old man who coughs. Just like the Latin prologues too, he referred to his Greek model and stated the literary rivalry, and his efforts to make his play more credible; the Prologus also ended his speech by announcing he would soon be back, but under the costume of a character of the play.[27]

Alciato's *Clouds*, in the Biblioteca Trivulziana manuscript, is devoid of a dedicatory letter and of any kind of the usual paratexts that accompany other 16th-century editions.[28] But the Prologus he writes and adds before his translation is in many ways similar to Passius' preliminary texts and Prologus.

His Prologus first addresses the 'spectators', and refers to his time; he also evokes the main themes of the play and the trial of Socrates; finally, he gives a detailed summary of the comedy, much more detailed than the five-line argument preceding the prologue. At that time, *Clouds* is almost unknown so this long introduction, trying to catch the attention of his readers, is definitely needed.

Right from the beginning, Alciato addresses his fellow citizens of Milan and criticises their laziness and their interest in foreign gods.[29] He also criticises taxes (vv. 50–52), the world of justice, fiercely attacking judges and lawyers (97–106), religion and friars (149–173). The setting is clearly his own world. In these attacks, he sometimes names the people of his time.[30] Indeed, by addressing the spectators and opening the play with a prologue of the kind, Alciato writes a prologue in the manner of Latin comedy, but he also transposes the Aristophanic practice of personal attacks; that is, he gives the names of real people when attacking them – just as Ancient comedy did. The friar he attacks is not named, but his description is so detailed that he was probably easy to identify by Alciato's readers.

This question of naming will be addressed again by Alciato in the *Philargyrus*, as will be the practice of attacking his fellow-citizen in general: in this way,

---

27 Bastin-Hammou 2015, Beta 2017.
28 Thomas Penguilly has shown that he did write a dedicatory letter, to an anonymous high-ranking official French man in Milan. But this letter does not give any new information about Aristophanes' *Clouds*. See Penguilly 2019, 187–188.
29 *Namque, estis odio illis. Manere nesciunt / vestris in aedibus; per Alpes cursitant / sed aut ad Helvetias vel aras Gallicas / clausique bulga visitant Belgas viros* (l. 26–29). 'Indeed, they hate you, do not want to stay in your temples but run away through the Alps towards the altars of Switzerland or France and, inside a purse, pay a visit to the Belgians'. This reference to *dei forensis* can be related to the trial of Socrates, who was accused of neglecting the Greek gods and introducing foreign divinities.
30 *Scepteuchidem cognovi ego et Meleuretem / quam maximi sint ventriones: totius / haud civitatis fiscus hos saturos facit* (l. 50–52). 'I know Scepteuchides and Meleuretes, big stomachs! the money of the whole city is not enough to feed them'.

the prologue of *Clouds* can be considered as a first attempt to escape from the exercise of translating and test the writing 'in the manner of', which in the *Philargyrus* will be fully matured.

Indeed, this prologue is not only a *captatio* but also a synthesis of what Alciato came to consider as the most interesting features of Greek comedy – the ones he will use when composing his *Philargyrus*. In this way, this prologue can be considered as a paratext similar to those that can be found in manuscripts and even more in the printed editions of the comic poet. One very often finds, among those, an *Argumentum,* or *Hypothesis*, which sum up the play in a few lines, and treatises on the genre of comedy. The prologue, which explains both the intrigue and the features of comedy by using them is thus as much an inheritance of Latin comedy as a programmatic paratext.

Finally, it gives a detailed account of the role of the comic poet in the accusation of Socrates, which is very close to Aelianus: how Anytos and Melitos came to the poet and paid him to attack the philosopher.[31] Aelianus' text is very often recalled in the paratexts to Aristophanes' editions, as a way of contextualising the play and introducing it to his readers. This also makes this prologue close to scholarly introductions that commonly precede the comedy.

Thus, this prologus is in between two genres: that of the Prologus of Latin comedy and that of scholarly paratexts introducing both the comic genre and its characteristics and the context of the play. By writing it, Alciato demonstrates both his ability to understand and make readers understand Aristophanes, and to compose in the manner of Aristophanes – something he will do again, and to a much larger extent, with his *Philargyrus*.

This prologus, which thus belongs both to the tradition of the Latin Prologus and to that of scholarly paratexts, can be considered a first step toward *Philargyrus*, which he wrote about six years later, while in Milan, between his two professorships of Law in Avignon: it seems he then had time for what he called his '*lucubrationes*'.[32]

---

31 Ael., *VH*, II, 13.
32 See letter 32 to Amerbach, 10th May 1523, in Hartmann 1943. When he went back to Avignon to teach law, in 1527, he published his legal works, but not those two Aristophanic works, which were of no use for his career as a Jurist, if not dangerous.

4 *Philargyrus* and its Relation to Alciato's *Clouds*: The Role of the Prologus

Indeed *Philargyrus* sounds in many respects like the continuation and realisation of *Clouds*. Composed within the six years following the translation, it was not published either, but Alciato had it copied in *bella copia*. It is followed by *Interpretatiunculae* attributed to Albuzzi but probably written by Alciato.

The history of the manuscript, the play and its interpretations have been studied by Antonio Nogara and so I shall concentrate here on the links between the translation of *Clouds* and *Philargyrus*, that is, the process that led Alciato from translating an Ancient comedy to composing a Latin Ancient comedy, by focusing on how Alciato himself reflected upon this in the prologus of the play.

Again, for his *Pilargyrus*, Alciato composed a prologue told by the character Prologus which combined the features of the Latin comedy prologue and that of scholarly paratexts commenting on the genre of Ancient comedy. This concerns first his attitude towards personal attacks. This characteristic of Ancient comedy had been used by Alciato in the prologus of *Clouds* and it is here theorized in the prologue of *Philargyrus*, where it is presented as the main characteristic of Greek comedy.[33] Alciato underlines comedy's ethical and political virtues, a *topos* of the interpretation of Aristophanes. This was discussed in antiquity by Horace in particular,[34] and in the paratexts of the *editio princeps*.[35] But, though praising

---

[33] *Cum multi Athenis improbi cives forent/Et factiosi et perfidi et siccarii/Aetate quales Flegmylos hac cernimus,/Fuit institutum uti liceret vatibus/Aperte in illos nominatimque invehi/Ut prae pudore iniuriis desisterent/Id Aristophanes, qui solus extat comicus/Liberrime servavit et fel melleis/Libis amarum miscuit* [...] (l. 37–45). 'When there were many dishonest, sectarian, perjured and murderous men in Athens, such as we see nowadays the Flegmili, it was decreed that poets should be allowed to speak openly and by name against them, so that in shame they would renounce their violence. Aristophanes, who is the only comic poet left to us, maintained this rule with great freedom and mixed very bitter gall with honey cakes'.

[34] Hor., *Sat.*, I,4, 1–5.

[35] τοὺς μὲν ἀρετῆς ἀντιποιουμένους εὐλογεῖ, τοὺς δὲ φαύλης τύχοντας ἀγωγῆς, καὶ διὰ τοῦτο τὸν τρόπον ἀποβάντας οὐ μάλα σπουδαίους ὁτὲ μὲν τῇ παρ' ὑπόνοιαν ἐλέγχει δριμύτητι, ὁτὲ δ' ἀπροκαλύπτως ὡς αὐτός φησιν Ἡρακλέους ὀργὴν ἔχων ἔπεσι μεγάλοις καὶ σκώμμασιν οὐκ ἀγοραίοις, μετὰ παρρησίας διαβάλλων οὐδὲ στρατηγοῦ ἀπέχεται ἁμαρτάνοντος, τί μὲν αἱρετὸν καὶ φευκτὸν ταῖς προσεσχηκόσιν αὐτῷ τὸν νοῦν εἰσηγεῖται. 'He praises those who strive after virtue. Those who received a bad education, and as a result turn out not at all honourable in character, he sometimes exposes with subtle acerbity, at other times without disguise, as he himself says, with the spirit of Hercules, in grandiose verse and with jokes that are not vulgar. He criticises freely and does not even spare a military commander who was at fault. To those

Aristophanes after Horace and Mousouros, Alciato also claims in this prologus that he will limit his own freedom of speech: he will not attack people personally, not even under fake names, unless they are dead.[36] The Prologus also explains the choice of keeping a chorus, (87–101) and indeed a choral song ends each act.

Even though some aspects of *Philargyrus* come from Latin comedy — it starts with a Prologus, and it is divided in four acts as Plautus' comedies in the edition of Merula published in 1490 — it is definitely and boldly derived from the genre of Ancient comedy.

The names are Latinized Greek and they have, just as in Aristophanes, a meaning — one of the sons of Philargyrus is called 'Delphax'", which means 'little pork' in Greek. Besides, Alciato refers to his fellow citizens, their faults and the society he is living in, as Aristophanes did. This concerns mainly the friars and the jurists: Gypius and Corax represent the Franciscans and the Dominicans, traditionally attacked since the *Decameron*, and the notary Adigius represents the world of Jurists, with its obscure language.

But what is really new with the *Philargyrus* is that it is not an adaptation of any comedy in particular but a comedy in the manner of Aristophanes. The plot itself is new. Philargyrus, a greedy old man, is about to die: getting close to the Acheron, he meets Charon who rejects him. He then goes back home where he finds his two sons, Delphax 'piggy', and Chimarus 'the young goat', fighting about his heritage. Thanks to his slave Brigantius they find an agreement and the comedy ends with a banquet.

Thus, this composition in the manner of Aristophanes is not a translation nor an imitation and recalls later attempts, like Pierre Le Loyer's *Néphélococcugie*, or, to a lesser extent, Racine's *Les Plaideurs*.

Alciato was probably reading the *princeps*, and had read not only the plays but its many ancient and Byzantine treatises on comedy, which explains his ability not only to translate and imitate, but to reflect upon the genre of Ancient comedy and compose one.

---

willing to listen to him he shows what they should do and not do'. Μάρκος Μουσοῦρος ὁ Κρὴς τοῖς ἐντευξομένοις εὖ πράττειν, *Aristophanis Comoediae Novem*, 1498, Prefatory letter by Markos Mousouros, in Wilson 2016, 277.

36 *Nec clam nec aperte versibus mordacibus/lacerabit ullum neque in honorem saeviet:/de mortuis tantummodo quique amplius/non sunt loquetur, idque tecto nomine/ne possit aliquo offendere viventes modo.* Alciato, Philargyrus, 76–80. 'He will not lash out either secretly or openly at anyone with biting lines and he will not strike at honour. He will only speak of the dead and the departed and he will do so under a fictitious name so as not to offend the living in any way'.

It thus seems that translating *Clouds* combined to other readings made Alciato discover some Aristophanic features — the personal attacks and the comic chorus especially — he used composing his *Philargyrus*, even though this play is much more than a mere adaptation: it is a creation, far from the loose adaptations mixed with translations of the 15th, but more faithful to Aristophanes than them in the spirit, something he probably owes to the deep understanding he had acquired through reading and translating *Clouds*.

5 Conclusions

Beyond a clear interest in Aristophanes that led scholars to translate from quite early on Aristophanes into Latin, in the first decades of the 16th century there occurs a shift, of which Alciatius' work appears emblematic. While *Plutus* had been the most translated comedy, the object of both translations *ad uerbum* and translations indulging in digressions, by 1517, Alciato, with his *Clouds* and a few years later with his *Philargyrus*, had initiated a new attitude towards the comic poet and, more broadly, towards translating and composing Greek drama.

His *Philargyrus* came after and from his translation of *Clouds*, as the study of the paratexts and especially the Prologus showed, revealing the process behind the creation of this Neo-Ancient comedy, which sprang from a deep understanding of the ancient play *through* translation, anticipating later works, such as Le Loyer's *Néphélococugie*.

Yet, this does not relegate his *Clouds* to the past, quite the opposite, since he translates *Clouds* in the same way as Thomas Venatorius or Adrianius Chilius will translate *Plutus* some fifteen years later. In this regard too, Alciato is definitely a pioneer.

His translation of *Clouds* did not circulate, however, and neither did his *Philargyrus* as they were never printed. This decision may be related to a career strategy: after hesitating, he chose to be a professional jurist rather than a philologist or a dramatist. Had the *Philargyrus* been printed and staged, the history of European comedy may have been different.

Simone Beta
The Sausage-Seller Suddenly Speaks Vernacular: The First Italian Translation of Aristophanes' *Knights*

Abstract: In 1545 two Italian physicians published in Venice the first vernacular translation of Aristophanes' eleven comedies. But, in spite of what they write in the prefatory letter addressed to Camillo Gambara, Pietro and Bartolomeo Rositini did not know Greek very well (or, at least, their knowledge of the ancient language was surely not enough for them to understand and translate such a difficult poet), and so they made extensive use of the first complete version of Aristophanes in a language other than Greek — namely, Andrea Divo's Latin translation, first published in 1538 in Venice. Through a detailed analysis of the first Italian translation of Aristophanes' *Knights*, this essay will show not only the undeniable debt of the Rositini brothers toward their predecessor, but also the creativity and imagination displayed by the two amateur translators, especially through the frequent use of comic words or expressions taken from the Venetian vernacular.

In 1545, two Italian physicians, Bartolomeo and Pietro Rositini, published the first vernacular translation of the eleven comedies by Aristophanes in Venice.[1] The quality of this version, published less than half a century after the *editio princeps* printed by Aldo Manuzio in 1498,[2] has been severely questioned by some scholars.

---

[1] The book (*Le comedie del facetissimo Aristofane, tradutte di Greco in lingua commune d'Italia, per Bartolomio & Pietro Rositini de Prat' Alboino, con privilegio de lo Illustrissimo Senato Veneto per anni diece*) was printed 'apresso Vicenzo (sic!) Vaugris, al segno d'Erasmo'. Vincenzo Valgrisi (whose real name was Vincent Vaugris) was born in Lyon at the end of the 15th century; after a short stay in Rome, he moved to Venice, where he established his printing factory, called 'Al segno d'Erasmo' or 'Ex officina erasmiana'. On this translation, see in particular Quaglia 2006 and Beta 2013. The surname of the translators is also attested under other similar forms: 'Rossettini', 'Rosetini', 'Rostinio', 'Rostino'.
[2] The so-called 'Aldine' was edited under the supervision of the Cretan philologist Marcus Musurus. It only contained nine comedies; the *Women at the Thesmophoria* and *Lysistrata* were

Two pieces of criticism stand out. Both brothers show poor familiarity with the ancient Greek language, and their cluelessness comes as unexpected, considering what they state in the prefatory letter, addressed to Camillo Gambara, provost of Pralboino, a little town of the Po Valley, between Brescia and Cremona.³ Moreover, their translation seems to hold a tight relationship with the first complete Latin version of Aristophanes, by an Istrian professor, Andreas Divus, a native of Capodistria, first published in 1538 in Venice 'apud d. Iacob a Burgofrancho Papiensem', and soon reprinted in Basel by Andreas Cratander in 1539 and 1542.⁴

In this chapter, I do not challenge this blunt assessment, whose soundness can indeed be shared by anyone taking the trouble to read even just a couple of pages of the Rositini's translations. By means of a detailed analysis of some passages of their version of *Knights*, however, I intend to show that, behind their undeniable debt towards the work of their 'Iustinopolitanus' predecessor (whose proficiency in Greek was not of the highest quality either),⁵ their struggle against the problematic text of Aristophanes displays some hitherto hidden qualities that might help in softening what I believe was ultimately undeserved blame. After all, at the time, their work was a ground-breaking achievement.⁶

I will begin with the occurrences in which the Rositini provide a better translation than Divus, as surprising as this may sound. Let us start with l. 16 (πῶς ἄν σύ μοι λέξειας ἁμὲ χρὴ λέγειν;), a tragic quotation.⁷ In his translation (*Quomodo tu mihi dixeris, quae oportet dicere?*), Divus forgets to indicate the subject of the infinitive (the ἐμέ hidden in ἁμὲ, a crasis for ἃ ἐμὲ); the transla-

---

printed by another editor, Bernardo Giunta, in Florence, in 1516. On the significance of Manuzio's work as editor of Greek texts, see Sicherl 1997.

3 On this letter, see Beta 2013, 58.

4 On the connection between these two translations (both in prose), see Sonnino 2017, 108–110; n. 382, p. 110, is a long list of all the severe reviews to both versions (some examples are quoted *infra*, n. 35).

5 On the translation of Divus (whose complete title was *Aristophanis, comicorum principis, Comoediae undecim, e Graeco in Latinum, ad uerbum translatae, Andrea Divo Iustinopolitano interprete*), see Nassichuk 2013; on his translation of *Lysistrata*, see in detail Beta 2012; on his silent (and not always acknowledged) improvements of Aristophanes' text, see Wilson 2007, 12.

6 The significance of their endeavor is strengthened by the fact that the second complete translation of Aristophanes' eleven comedies in another modern language (French) was not published until 1784 (*Théâtre d'Aristophane, traduit en français, partie en vers partie en prose, avec les fragments de Ménandre et de Philémon*, par M. Poinsinet de Sivry, Paris, Didot jeune) — that is almost two centuries and a half after the Rositini.

7 Euripides' *Hippolytos* 345. On this quotation, see Lauriola 2016.

tion of the Rositini, although clumsy, includes and unveils the concealed subject ('A che modo tu mi dirai quello, che à me bisogna dire?').

Another example of an improper translation is the Latin rendering of the adverb ἔνδοθεν at l. 110: the accurate 'fuora de là' that we read in the Rositini's text cannot be considered the copycat of the inaccurate *intus* printed by Divus.

Lastly, in a few passages, the Capodistrian professor does not seem to understand the difference between νὴ Δία ('Yes, by Jupiter!') and μὰ Δία ('No, by Jupiter!'): as a result, he omits the negative twice (ll. 85 and 336: *Per Iovem*), unlike the Rositini ('Non per Giove').[8]

The following three cases are different in that they seem to be just lexical choices; however, they might also help to demonstrate that the Rositini did not always follow Divus mechanically.

At l. 45, when the first slave, the one named Demosthenes in the manuscripts, portrays the character of the Paphlagonian (the personification of Cleon), he refers to him as διαβολότατον: the word printed by the Rositini ('calumniosissimo') is more appropriate than Divus's rendition (*criminatorem*). The same is true of the rendering of δημαγωγία at l. 191: Divus's *principatus* is a weak translation, whereas 'la governatione de'l popolo' is much more powerful. Finally, at l. 212, in the same scene (the presentation of the Sausage-seller), the expression τὸν δῆμον [...] ἐπιτροπεύειν is better depicted as 'governare il popolo' than through the vague *populum* [...] *procurare*.

Let us now move to the most meaningful examples showing the Rositini's thoroughness rather than their infamous carelessness. In these instances, they translate better than Divus because, unlike him, they have likely read the scholia printed in the margins of the Aldine edition.

At the beginning of the prologue, the two slaves, Demosthenes and Nicias, make fun of Euripides: it is the same passage mentioned above, where Nicias quotes Phaedra's line. At l. 18, Aristophanes creates the *hapax* κομψευριπικῶς (LSJ: 'with Euripides-quibbles'.) While Divus only translates the allusion to the style of the tragic playwright (*Euripidice*), the Rositini say 'malitiosamente'; however incomplete (the hint at Euripides is indeed missing), such a translation seems to note the scholium, which clarifies that, instead of saying 'Euripides-

---

[8] A similar omission is present at l. 338, where μὰ τὸν Ποσειδῶ becomes *per Neptunum* (cf. 'Non per Nettuno', Rositini). Other possible intentional diversions from Divus's wrong or inaccurate translations are at l. 238 (the rendering of ἀφίστατον as 'fate ribelli a' is clearly independent from Divus's *ardeatis*, likely a typo for *arceatis*), 408 (βακχέβακχον is more 'Bacco Bacco' than simply *Bacchum*) and 422 (the plural ἀκαλήφας is correctly rendered by 'ortiche', and not by the singular *urticam*).

like' (εὐριπιδικῶς) and 'cleverly' (δεινῶς), Aristophanes had meant 'knavishly' (πανούργως).

In the following line, we find another *hapax* by Aristophanes: the imperative μὴ διασκανδικίσῃς contains the noun σκάνδιξ (LSJ: 'wild chervil'), a naughty allusion to the presumed job of Euripides' mother. The scholium is very detailed: first, we read διευριπιδίσῃς· ἡ γὰρ μήτηρ Εὐριπίδου σκάνδικας ἐπίπρασκεν, ὅ ἐστιν ἄγρια λάχανα ('[don't] play the part of Euripides: his mother used to sell wild chervil, that is wild vegetables'), and then μὴ ἀποδειλιάσῃς, μὴ μεταμελήσῃς. σκώπτει δὲ τὸν Εὐριπίδην ὡς λαχανοπώλιδος υἱόν· σκάνδιξ γὰρ εἶδος λαχάνου ('don't be a coward, don't feel repentance: Aristophanes makes fun of Euripides by stating that he was the son of a greengrocer woman: in fact, wild chervil is a kind of vegetables').[9]

Divus's translation (*ne olorizes*) is quite smart because it is in its turn another *hapax*, based on *olus* / *holus* (in Latin, 'vegetable'): either he had read the scholium, or he just knew that the comic poets made fun of the presumed job of Euripides' mother.[10] Nevertheless, *olorizere* only grasps one side (the wordplay) of Aristophanes' creation, without conveying the other meanings expressed by the verb and listed in the second part of the scholium. The three different translations written by the Rositini ('non haver paura, ne timidità, et non volere essere negligente') seem to imply that the Italian translators had looked for help not, as they very often used to do, in Divus's rendering (*olorizere* probably sounded gibberish to them), but in the scholia. In fact, 'avere paura' and 'avere timore' are the correct translation of the Greek verb ἀποδειλιάω; if the correct meaning of μεταμέλει / μεταμέλομαι is 'to repent', the third verb used by the Rositini ('essere negligente') is nonetheless the Italian equivalent of the similar ἀμελέω ('to neglect').

The most conclusive witness that, on at least some occasions, the Italian physicians did try to move beyond the Latin translation, and to take advantage of the precious indications of the ancient scholia, is their rendering of the enigmatic name Κοαλέμος of l. 221. If Divus does not give any help to his readers and simply transliterates the word (*Coalemo*), the Rositini print 'stolido et pazzo' — a clear indication they had read the scholium, because in the margins of the Al-

---

9 On the verb διασκανδικίζω, see also Beta 1999, 230.
10 In two passages of the *Frogs*, the comedy that precedes the *Knights* in Divus's book, Aristophanes alludes again to Euripides' mother (840, with a much-detailed scholium, and 947).

dine the term Divus had not been able to understand is glossed with ἀντὶ τοῦ ἀνοίᾳ.[11]

Therefore, we can be sure that, while working, the Rositini read and checked, in addition to the Latin translation, the Greek text printed by Aldo Manuzio. At any rate, this does not seem to be the only version they had consulted: there is at least one circumstance that may lead to the inference that they have sometimes referred to a different edition.

At l. 1004, for instance, instead of the correct 'Glanide' (Γλάνις, the faked oracle-monger, a name with an assonant echo to Βάκις, who was a real soothsayer known to Aristophanes' audience), the Rositini write 'Planide'. Why? Because Πλάνιδος, instead of the correct reading Γλάνιδος, is the wrong reading we find in two among the editions available at the time, specifically those published by Bartolomeo Zanetti and Giovanni Farri.[12]

It would be interesting to know whether the Rositini, in the process of translating Aristophanes, in addition to checking some of the printed editions and consulting the scholia of the Aldine, were also concerned with the soundness of the Greek text. To answer this question, it would perhaps be more appropriate to study their overall work on Aristophanes' corpus, which is not within the terms of reference of this research, rather focused on the translation, and on one play only.

---

11 For another similar example, see l. 31 (θεῶν ἰόντε προσπεσεῖν του πρὸς βρέτας), translated by Divus *deorum euntes irruere aliquot ad idolum* and by the Rositini 'andando a ingenocchiarsi a qualche luogo a una imagine de dei'. In the scholium printed by Musurus in the margins of the Aldine (which is different from those printed by Mervyn Jones and Wilson 1969, 14), the expression πρὸς βρέτας is illustrated by ἄγαλμα θεῶν, with the addition that the verb προσπεσεῖν is referred to ἱκέτας καθίσαι: it is therefore possible that the use of 'inginocchiarsi' ('to kneel down') by the Rositini is due to the presence, in the text of the scholium, of the words ἱκέτας ('suppliants') and καθίσαι ('sit down').

12 Ἀριστοφάνους εὐτραπελωτάτου κωμῳδίαι ἔνδεκα, *Aristophanis facetissimi comoediae undecim*, *Venetiis in aedibus Bartholomaei Zanetti Casterzagensis, sumptibus vero D. Melchionis* (sic!) *Sessa* (sic!), *anno 1538 mense Septembri*; *Aristophanis facetissimi comoediae undecim*, *Venetiis apud Ioannem Farreum, et fratres, anno à partu Virginis 1542*. I cannot exclude the possibility that yet another edition might have provoked the mistake in the translation of the Rositini: in the book edited by Simon Grynaeus, the first comprising all of the eleven comedies, published in 1532 in Basel '*apud And. Cratandrum et Ioannem Bebelium*' (Ἀριστοφάνους εὐτραπελωτάτου κωμῳδίαι ἔνδεκα, *Aristophanis facetissimi comoediae undecim*), the capital gamma is identical to the capital pi. Nevertheless, considering the location of the publishing houses of the first two books, it looks more probable that the Rositini had used, besides the Aldine, an edition printed near their own town as a reference text (and, incidentally, we cannot rule out the possibility that the mistake in both the Zanetti's and Farri's editions might have been caused by their misreading of the word in Grynaeus' edition).

Some of the strongest critics of the Rositini's work would laugh at this scenario, but even a quick look at their intervention and sensibility (though, again, not systematic) towards the punctuation of some passages suggests a different, less skittish, attitude with regard to their competence.

There are at least three cases, if not more, when Divus, who follows the text of the printed editions on which he bases his own translation closely, does not put the question mark called for by the context. On the contrary, the Rositini do, in the same way as modern editions: see l. 11 ('Che cosa ululeremo altramente?'), 1193 ('Oime, donde haverò io carne di lepore?'), and 1207–1208 ('Che non giudichi o popolo, qual de noi dui è più huomo da bene, per té, et per lo ventre?').[13]

In similar fashion, at ll. 87–88, all the ancient printed editions have a question mark after v. 87 (ἰδού γ' ἄκρατον. περὶ πότου γοῦν ἐστί σοι; / πῶς δ' ἂν μεθύων χρηστόν τι βουλέσαιτ' ἀνήρ;). Furthermore, Divus has a question mark after both lines (*Ecce purum circa potum igitur est tibi? / Quomodo autem inebrians bonum aliquid consultabit vir?*), whereas the Rositini print it only after v. 88 ('Ecco'l puro, à te tocca dunque bevere. Ma à che modo un'huomo embriacandosi potrà consultar cosa buona?'), a choice of punctuation made by all other modern editions, from Coulon to Wilson.[14]

As captivating as this analysis proves to be, however, I shall pursue it elsewhere. Since this volume is concerned with translation theory and practice, I devote the second and last part of this chapter to discussing some interesting features that mark the translation habits of the Rositini.

The most distinctive peculiarity of their rendering is the frequent use of the rhetorical figure called 'dittologia sinonimica', a specific kind of hendiadys.[15] Whilst Divus always translates *uerbum de uerbo*, because his main purpose is to

---

13 Here is the text of Wilson 2007 (all the quotations of Aristophanes' *Knights* come from this edition): τί κινυρόμεθ' ἄλλως; οὐκ ἐχρῆν ζητεῖν τινα [...] (*Quid ululabimus aliter, non oportet quaerere aliquem...*); οἴμοι, πόθεν λαγῴα μοι γενήσεται; (*Hei mihi unde carnes leporinae mihi erunt*); τί οὐ διακρίνεις, Δῆμ', ὁπότερός ἐστι νῷν / ἀνὴρ ἀμείνων περὶ σὲ καὶ τὴν γαστέρα; (*Quid non dijudicas popule uter nostrum / vir melior circa te et ventrem*).
14 Unless I am mistaken, the first editor who prints the question mark after l. 88 only is Green 1870, followed by Zacher 1897, Van Leeuwen 1900 and Neil 1901; the other modern editions mentioned above are Coulon 1923, Cantarella 1949, Sommerstein 2001, Mastromarco 1997, and Henderson 1998. Hall and Geldart 1906 (and, before them, Blaydes 1875, Meineke 1860 and Bergk 1852 — there are even earlier works, but they are irrelevant) print the question marks at the end of both lines, like Divus.
15 A trope studied by the Dutch scholar Gerrit Janszoon Vos, known mainly by the Latin name Gerardus Vossius, in his *Aristarchus, sive de arte grammatica libri septem, accedunt de vitiis sermonis, et glossematis latino-barbaris, libri novem*, published in Amsterdam, in 1695.

help the readers understand the Greek text through his literal rendition, the Rositini, instead, often use two words instead of one, in order to unfold all the nuances of the Greek term.¹⁶

They apply it to nouns: τρόποι (in Divus, *mores*) becomes 'i suoi gesti e usanze' (l. 390); συμφοραί (*calamitates*) becomes 'calamità e disaventure' (l. 406); ὄνυξι (*unguibus*), 'con le unghie, et con le sgraffe' (l. 708); πολλὰ χρήματα (*multas pecunias*), 'molta roba et assai danari' (l. 840).

They employ it to adjectives as well: φαυλότατον ἔργον (*minimum opus*) is translated as 'la più facile, e più vile impresa' (l. 213); Cratinus' loose harmonies (διαχάσκουσαι / *dissolutae*) become 'harmonie disfatte e guaste' (l. 533); a bright idea (σοφόν / *sapiens*) is a 'savio [...] et dotto' scheme (l. 885); a politician who is παχύς (*plenus*) is, for the Rositini, 'pieno, e grasso' (l. 1139).

The same procedure can indeed be seen with verbs: at l. 156, when the two slaves understand that the Sausage-seller is doomed to replace the hateful Paphlagonian, they ask him to kiss the earth and pray the gods ('bascia la terra, et prega i dei': τὴν γῆν πρόσκυσον καὶ τοὺς θεούς, *terram adosculare et Deos*); at l. 646, when the Sausage-seller tells the audience that his good news have reassured the Athenian citizens, he says that their faces are appeased and overjoyed ('si sono pacificati, et alegrati': τὰ πρόσωπα διεγαλήνισαν, *vultus tranquilli facti sunt*); at l. 710, the Paphlagonian threatens to punch and drag away the Sausage-seller ('ti menarò e strascinarò': ἕλξω, *traham*); at l. 827, the Sausage-seller blames the Paphlagonian for eating and devouring the public money ('mangia et divora': μυστιλᾶται, *devorat*); at l. 1148, People of the Pnyx boasts he can make the politicians throw up and come clean ('vomitare et confessare': ἐξεμεῖν, *evomere*).

---

16 This practice will not only be employed by the Sienese scholar Alessandro Piccolomini in his own translation of Aristotle's *Poetics*, published in Siena in 1572, but also theorised in his letter *Ai lettori del modo del tradurre*, attached to the translation: 'Quanto poi alle parole, [...] se ben uno stesso significato non hà nell'una, et nell'altra lingua una sola parola appropriata, può nondimeno l'una d'esse lingue esprimerlo et significarlo, se non con una, almen con due, o con più parole. Et in tal caso, [...] con più parole copulate esprimeremo l'espresso con una sola: il che nella detta traduttione di greco in volgare assai sovente occorre' ('Speaking about words, [...] if the target language does not possess one word that has the same meaning as the word of the source language, it can nonetheless convey and express that same meaning if not with one word, with more than one. And in such a case, [...] we will express with more than one word coupled together what is expressed with one word in the source language: which often happens in said translation from the Greek into the vernacular; Piccolomini 1572, 3). On Piccolomini's translation practice, see Cotugno 2006.

Another peculiarity — a device modern translators often resort to in order to make the construct of the circumstantial participle more fluid — is the use of the parataxis: at ll. 109–111, κλέψας ἔνεγκε becomes 'roba [...] e portale' ('steal and bring'), whereas Divus closely follows the Greek construction (*furans effer*); likewise, at l. 778 ἁρπάζων [...] παραθήσω becomes 'robarò [...] e portarò' ('I will steal and bring'), instead of *rapiens* [...] *apponam*.

In numerous passages, Rositini's Italian is much more expressive and powerful than Divus's Latin. When, in the prologue, one of the slaves tells his fellow that the Paphlagonian is sleeping on his couch, after having drunk a lot of wine, the simple adjective 'supine' (Greek ὕπτιος, Latin *supinus*) is rendered through the periphrasis 'stravaccato con la bocca aperta' (l. 104); at l. 830, when the Sausage-seller makes fun of the Paphlagonian, who is squawking like a bird, by using the verbs θαλαττοκοπεῖν and πλατυγίζειν, Divus trivializes the two metaphors by Aristophanes (*quid vociferaris et clamas?*), whereas the Rositini create, for the second one, the neologism 'smergolare' (from 'smergo', a kind of sea duck).

Some peculiar expressions, often strengthened by the recourse to the dialect of Venice, help make this version more brilliant and less dull than the Latin translation. In those years, Pralboino — as most of today's Lombardia, including Bergamo and Brescia — were part of the mainland territories of the Serenissima.

I quote a few examples here: at l. 448, δορύφοροι (*satellites*) is translated with 'zaffi', a slang word for the policemen; at l. 639, καταπύγων ἀνήρ (*cinaedus vir*) becomes 'bardassa', a derogatory term quite common until the last century, derived from the Arabic 'bardag' (that is, 'young slave');[17] at ll. 662 e 945 for the Greek currency ὄβολος (*obolus*) the Rositini use 'bagattino', a small coin freshly introduced in 1442 in Venice for the small exchanges within the mainland; at ll. 870, 872, and 875, the ἐμβάδες, a type of slippers, either transliterated (*embades*) or Latinized (*crepides*) by Divus, are rendered by the Rositini through a couple of words ('pianelle' and 'pantofole'), which are still the most usual terms used nowadays for indicating the comfortable slippers people wear at home in Italy; at ll. 892 and 1314 the metaphorical 'crows' to which the Greeks would send the rascals they wanted to get rid of (ἐς κόρακας) are not literally (and moronically) translated (*ad corvos*), but more adequately become an invitation to hang oneself ('a le forche!'); at l. 964 the slang term ψωλός, whose precise

---

17 The last occurrence of this abusive word seems to be a passage from the poem *Le città terribili* by Gabriele D'Annunzio, published in 1903 as a part of the *Maia* section of the book *Laudi del cielo del mare della terra e degli eroi* ('*E il bardassa trae per le scale / già buie il soldato che ride, / e la libidine incide / l'enorme priàpo sul muro!*').

meaning is usually translated by Divus with a medical wording (*sine praeputio*), receives a more straightforward rendering by the Rositini ('senza capella').[18]

As for the translation of most references to the empty chattering of the politicians — there are quite a number in this comedy[19] — instead of the trivial verb always used by Divus (*nugari*), the Rositini choose to have recourse to the more colloquial 'zanciare', a Venetian version of the standard-Italian 'cianciare': at l. 536, the verb translates ληρεῖν; at l. 545, φλυαρεῖν; at l. 664, φληναφᾶν.[20]

Furthermore, there is one occurrence that seems to be related to the language of church: at l. 1016, the innermost shrine of the Delphic sanctuary, the so-called ἄδυτος, become a 'sacristia', i.e., a vestry.

Finally, there is another methodology that characterizes their way of translating: since the Rositini do not aim at replicating the verse structure of the original and choose instead to write their translation in prose, they tend sometimes to normalize complicated sentences. This happens especially where Aristophanes makes use of the prolepsis or anticipation, i.e., the 'construction whereby the subject of a subordinate clause occurs by anticipation as an object in the main clause'.[21]

One plain example is ll. 777–785, a long sentence uttered by the Sausage-seller in the second 'agon':

τοῦτο μέν, ὦ Δῆμ', οὐδὲν σεμνόν· κἀγὼ γὰρ τοῦτό σε δράσω.
ἁρπάζων γὰρ τοὺς ἄρτους σοι τοὺς ἀλλοτρίους παραθήσω.
ὡς δ' οὐχὶ φιλεῖ σ' οὐδ' ἔστ' εὔνους, τοῦτ' αὐτό σε πρῶτα διδάξω,
ἀλλ' ἢ διὰ τοῦτ' αὔθ' ὁτιή σου τῆς ἀνθρακιᾶς ἀπολαύει.   780
σὲ γάρ, ὃς Μήδοισι διεξιφίσω περὶ τῆς χώρας Μαραθῶνι,
καὶ νικήσας ἡμῖν μεγάλως ἐγγλωττοτυπεῖν παρέδωκας,
ἐπὶ ταῖσι πέτραις οὐ φροντίζει σκληρῶς σε καθήμενον οὕτως,
οὐχ ὥσπερ ἐγὼ ῥαψάμενός σοι τουτὶ φέρω. ἀλλ' ἐπαναίρου,
κᾆτα καθίζου μαλακῶς, ἵνα μὴ τρίβῃς τὴν ἐν Σαλαμῖνι.[22]   785

---

18 The Italian word 'cappella' is a slang expression for indicating a hard penis with the prepuce drawn back.
19 On this topic, see Beta 2004, 259–263.
20 See also l. 449, 'zanciatore', for the Greek term κόβαλος (in Divus: *dicax*), and at l. 902, 'zancie', for βωμολοχεύματα (in Divus: *nugae*).
21 Panhuis 1984, 26.
22 'Demos, that's nothing to brag about; I'll do the same thing for you. I'll snatch other people's loaves and serve them to you. The first thing I'll prove to you is that he isn't your friend or your partisan, save only that he enjoys sitting by your fire. At Marathon you outdueled the Medes in defense of our country, and your victory bequeathed to our tongues matter for minting great phrases. But he doesn't care if you have to sit like that on the hard rocks, unlike me,

The Rositini translate l. 781, which begins with the accusative σέ, depending from the verb φροντίζει placed after two lines, at l. 783, in order to respect the more logical and less poetical construction: 'Di questo pure ò popolo niente di buono, et anchora io ti farò questo. Per che robarò de'l pane à gli altri, et te ne portarò. Et se non ti ama, ne ti porta amore, questa cosa medesima t'insegnarò per la prima, et per questo proprio che adopera la tua bragia, *perché non si cura di te che così aspramente stai à sedere su le pietre*: che cò i Medi hai combattuto à torno à la cità in Maratone, et vincendo da valente huomo ne hai dato il parlar figurato: non si come io son per essere ti porto questo: ma leva su, et poi senta pianamente, à ciò che non consumi colei ch'è in Salamine'.[23]

I trust that all the examples I have quoted are enough to prove that, for many reasons, the work carried out by Bartolomeo and Pietro Rositini does not deserve the absolute reprobation that has been poured over them — and I am sure that a similar conclusion would come out of a comparable analysis of the other ten comedies.

Be that as it may — I admit this is quite a difficult question — one might ask how the few steps forward in the full comprehension of such a tough text can coexist with the general carelessness of their overall translation, often unintelligible and close-fitting, both in good and evil, to the Latin translation they were surely consulting. Moreover, if we can forgive Divus's rendering for some of his flaws by acknowledging that they were mostly triggered by a very noble purpose (the willingness of publishing a translation that, exactly through its *uerbum de uerbo* matching, could lend a hand to the readers who wanted to get acquainted with the complex Greek of Aristophanes), the same intention was not shared by the Italian physicians.

I put forward a possible explanation as an invitation to investigate the story of this really unique achievement: the work had not been done by one person only, but it has been the result of the efforts of more than one person. And, since the translators named in the front page are two, it might be possible that, in

---

who bring this cushion I've made for you. Here, get up a moment; now sit back down comfortably, so you don't chafe what sat to the oar at Salamis' (Henderson 1998).

23 Here is a fairly close English rendering of the Rositini's translation: 'People, there is nothing good about it, and I'll do this for you as well. I'll steal other people's bread, and bring it to you. And if he does neither like you nor love you, this is the first thing I'll teach you: the reason why he uses your fire lies in the fact that he doesn't care if you have to sit like that on hard rocks: since you have defeated the Medes near the town of Marathon and have won, like a strong man, you have minted great phrases — not like me, who limit myself to bringing you this (cushion): get up instead, and then sit back down comfortably, so you don't wear out the buttock that was at Salamine'.

order to speed up their job, Bartolomeo and Pietro had split the parts to translate into Italian between themselves.

The different quality of the translation might therefore be explained by their different competence in the Greek language: this may explain why the accuracy of the rendering is not the same, and why the result of the work is so strikingly uneven.

Inside this single comedy we find a number of oscillations between the translations of the same word; it would be very difficult to explain this accident in a different or another, more reasonable, way. One example should be enough to illustrate what I mean.

Demos of Pnyx is, together with the two demagogues, the main character of the play. In the great metaphor built by Aristophanes in the *Knights*, the Athenian '*demos*' wears the clothes of the real protagonist, being the one fighting against the politicians who try to deceive him.

Divus always translates Δῆμος with *populus* — and with good reason, because there is no other better way to translate the word in Latin. And how do the Rositini translate it? Often, this is true, with 'popolo' — starting with the *dramatis personae*, where we read 'Popolo'. At l. 42, when Demosthenes introduces him to the audience, he calls him Δῆμος Πυκνίτης, and the Italian rendering is 'populo predicatore' (probably inspired by Divus's *populus concionarius*).

Nevertheless, on occasion we find another translation — admittedly quite bizarre: at l. 710, when the Paphlagonian threatens the Sausage-seller to drag him in presence of the 'people' in the section that follows the parabasis, Demos is translated with 'brigata' (literally 'brigade', or 'party').

Why 'brigata'? What is the sense of this word, here? And the same question can be asked a few lines later, before Demos goes on stage (l. 719–720: 'Et per Giove con la mia destrezza posso far una brigata grande, et stridola'), and even further, when he finally makes its entrance: 'andiamo à la brigata' (l. 723), 'ò brigatella carissima' (l. 726), 'perché ti amo o brigata et ti osservo' (l. 732), 'facio ben io de'l bene à la brigata' (l. 741). For the remainder of the comedy, 'popolo' goes back to being the most used term, with just a couple of exceptions, at ll. 769 and 873, where we meet again this weird 'brigata'.

What other more convincing explanations could we find in order to account for such a conflicting translation? To give one further brief example, how would it be possible for the same person to translate so effectively τὸν δῆμον [...] ἐπιτροπεύειν as 'governare il popolo' (see *supra*, p. 55) and then, two hundred lines later, at l. 426, in the heart of the agon, to prefer a weaker rendering ('avere cura del popolo') for the same expression?

Aristophanes was not the only Greek writer translated by Bartolomeo and Pietro Rositini. In that very 1545, the two brothers published together, with the same editor, another Italian translation, the *Lives and opinions of eminent philosophers* by Diogenes Laertius, dedicated to another member of the Gambara family, the Count Giovanni Francesco — but, as far as I know, no one has yet analysed the quality of that version.[24]

Then, ten years later, in 1555, in Venice, the printer Baldassarre Costantini, a partner of Vincenzo Valgrisi, published ('ad signum Divi Georgii') another version by the Rositini brothers:[25] this time the translated work was the *Aphorisms* of Hippocrates, preceded by a dedicatory letter written to Francesco Venier, who was Doge of Venice from 1554 to 1556.[26]

But there are two significant differences that need to be pointed out: first, the translation is not in Italian, but in Latin; second, on the cover page the authors are still Bartolomeo and Pietro, but the letter written, in Latin, to the Doge is signed by Pietro only.

What does this mean? Should we infer that, even though Pietro states that the work has been carried out by himself together with his brother, Bartolomeo was dead at the time of the publication? And that Pietro had his brother's name put on the cover just as a sign of gratitude?

The fact that Pietro outlived Bartolomeo is a hypothesis that might have some grounds, because there is evidence of three other works published by Pietro, in the following two years, without his brother. In 1556 he published, always in Venice, but with another printer (Lodovico Avanzi), a medical work (in Italian): a treatise on the syphilis, the *Trattato di mal francese*.[27] In 1557 he published, in Venice, with Valgrisi and Costantini, the Italian translation of the

---

24 The full title of the book is *Le vite degli illustri filosofi di Diogene Laertio*, da'l Greco Idiomate ridutte ne la lingua commune d'Italia. On some peculiarities of this version, and mostly on the theoretical principles followed by the Rositini in translating into Italian Diogenes' biographies, see Tesi 1997 and Beta 2013, 60.

25 On the life and the works of the most active Italian printers in the 16th century, see Richardson 1994.

26 The full title of the book is *Sententiae omnes ac verba, quae in divini Hippocratis aphorismis continentur, iam recens et accurate in novum ordinem alphabeticumque digesta, ut quaevis in ipsis commemorata nunc facilius et celerius quam antea inveniri queant, ut ita medicinae studiosis maiori nimirum, quam prius, usui futura sint*.

27 The full title is *Trattato di mal francese, nel quale si discorre di ducento et trentaquattro sorti di esso male; et a quanti modi si puo prendere, et causare, et guarire. Et evidentemente si mostra chi ha il gallico male, et chi no, con segni certissimi et pronostici*, per Pietro Rostinio dottor fisico raccolto, et tradotto da quanti han scritto di mal Francese, et massime dal Brassavola (Antonio Musa Brassavola); et di più molte cose vi sono di nuovo aggiunte.

Latin handbook of surgery written by Giovanni da Vigo.[28] Finally, in the same year, he wrote, together with another brother, Lodovico, a compendium of surgery (in Italian), published by Lodovico Avanzi and his brothers.[29]

But, as I said, this is just a conjecture. In fact, in 1559 the heirs of the editor Baldassarre Costantini published in Venice *I libri di Giovanni Mesue dei semplici purgativi, et delle medicine composte*, 'nuovamente tradotti in lingua italiana': the cover page does not mention the name of the translator, but the dedicatory letter to Giovanni Manolesso, Count of Pula, is signed by the three brothers (Bartolomeo, Lodovico, Pietro Rostini, over Rossi, fratelli, medici), 'humili servitori', with the date 1558.[30]

Among the works edited by Pietro without his brother Bartolomeo, there is another book that has nothing to do with medicine. In 1546, that is, one year after the publication of the brothers' Aristophanes and Diogenes, he published (alone) the edition of a Greek text, printed by Paolo Manuzio, Aldo's son: the commentary of Ammonius Hermiae (also known as Ammonius of Alexandria) to the 'five voices' of Porphyry of Tyre, the celebrated *Isagoge* (a sort of 'introduction' to Aristotle's *Categories*).[31] It was not a first edition: as he states in the dedicatory letter written to the Abbot Francesco Loredan, the work was a corrected collation of 'other editions' — namely, the *editio princeps* printed in Venice in 1500 by Zacharias Calliergi and Nicolao Vlastos, followed, in 1545, by an edition published in Venice by Melchiorre Sessa, under the supervision of Giovan Bernardo Regazzola.[32]

---

28 The full title is *Prattica utilissima et necessaria di cirugia dello eccellentissimo m. Giovanni Di Vico, con nuove figure adornata, con il compendio dell'eccellente m. Marian Santo da Barletta suo discepolo. Tradotta nuovamente di latino in lingua volgare per lo eccellente fisico m. Pietro Rostino, a beneficio & utilità universale.* The original Latin handbook (*Practica in arte chirurgica copiosa*) had been published in Rome in 1514 and then reprinted, for at least eight times, in Lyon, between 1516 and 1561.

29 The full title is *Compendio di tutta la cirugia, utilissimo ad ogni studioso di quella, & sopra modo necessario, per Pietro et Lodovico Rosetini medici, estratto da quanti han scritto de l'antidetta cirugia, con il dissegno de gli instromenti, a tal'arte più che necessari.* The book was reprinted in 1561 by the same Venetian editor under the supervision of the celebrated surgeon Leonardo Fioravanti.

30 John Mesue is the anglicized name of Yūhannā ibn Māsawaih, a ninth-century Nestorian Christian physician born in Baghdad, whose real identity is still under dispute.

31 The full bilingual title is Ἀμμωνίου Ἑρμείου εἰς τὰς πέντε φωνὰς τοῦ Πορφυρίου ὑπόμνημα / *Ammonii Hermiae in quinque voces Porphyrii commentaria, correctionibus quamplurimis, & locorum imaginibus illustratus.*

32 *Nos ea commentaria cui nunc integritati restituerimus, quibusque erroribus repurgaverimus, ex aliarum editionum collatione lector iudicet.* The editor of the 1545 book (whose complete title

Since ancient philosophy is not my field of expertise, I cannot make a scholarly assessment of the value of Rositini's undertaking; however, the sheer fact that he considered himself worthy of taking responsibility for a similar task, and was considered as such by an editor whose competence in the publication of Greek texts was widely renowned, show sufficient evidence that, of the two brothers, he was the more proficient in Greek and was, therefore, responsible for the valuable solutions we have pinpointed in the overall poor translation of Aristophanes' *Knights*.[33]

Why the most part of this version is not up to this good quality is difficult to say: perhaps Pietro, occupied with other jobs (Ammonius, but also Diogenes), did not have time to devote to Aristophanes full time; consequently, pressed by the urge to publish both the playwright's and the biographer's works as soon as possible, to receive some benefits from the lords of Pralboino (as it might be inferred by the undertone of both the dedicatory letters) he preferred to leave most of the translation to his less expert brother.

But this is food for thought for historians, rather than philologists — and maybe for the specialists in local history, because the reputation of the Rositini brothers did not cross the borders of Northern Italy. What can be said for sure is that such an innovative approach to the translation of Greek texts, different from the *uerbum de uerbo* technique favoured by early modern scholars like Divus, would have played a significant role in promoting the knowledge of po-

---

is Ἀμμωνίου τοῦ Ἑρμείου εἰς τὰς πέντε φωνὰς τοῦ Πορφυρίου ὑπόμνημα / *Ammonii Hermiae in quinque voces Porphyrii commentaria*, Venetiis, per Ioan. Ant. & Petrum fratres de Nicolinis de Sabio, sumptu Melchioris Sessae), born in 1490 either in Venice or, more probably, in Cremona, was above all an expert in Greek medicine, but dedicated himself to philosophy as well (in 1541 he translated into Latin Aristotle's *Nicomachean Ethics* for the Giunta editors, in Venice). The dedicatory letter, signed by his surname 'Feliciano', is written to 'Aloisio Cornelio Magno, Cypri Commendatario': under this name there was probably the future cardinal Alvise Corner, also known as Luigi Cornaro, who was the grand-nephew of Caterina Cornaro, Queen of Cyprus; after having entered, still young, the Order of the Knights of St. John of Jerusalem, Alvise was then named Grand Prior of Cyprus; after a few years, he then resigned in favor of his younger brother, Federico.

33 It would be interesting to know some more about Pietro's teachers, but the role played by Pralboino in the history of Italy's early modern scholarship is yet to be studied. We know that, before becoming professor of Greek and Latin at the University of Parma, the philosopher Mario Nizzoli spent some time with the Gambara family, both in Brescia and in Pralboino; he was probably the teacher of Camillo (the dedicatee of Aristophanes' comedies) and his sister Veronica, one of the most famous Italian female poets (see Beta 2013, 57–59). It would be also interesting to know why Bartolomeo and Pietro decided to translate Aristophanes among all the Greek playwrights — but, apart from the easy guess that they did it because they had been moved by Divus's translation, there are no clues that can help us.

ets such as Aristophanes, if the outcome had been more consistent, equilibrated and elevated, qualitatively speaking.

Moreover, if the Council of Trent, which began in that very 1545, had not strongly hindered the study of the Greek language in Italy to the advantage of Latin,[34] other translators would have probably followed the trail drawn by Bartolomeo and Pietro Rositini. This would have anticipated by at least three hundred years the effort made by Coriolano Malingri of Bagnolo, senator of the Kingdom of Sardinia, who was the first man to translate and publish the eleven comedies of Aristophanes into Italian, in Turin in 1850.[35]

One thing stands out, for sure. We owe to the Rositini brothers the first rendering of the voice of the Sausage-seller, one of the most impressive characters created by Aristophanes, in a modern language. 'Che cosa gli è? Perché mi chiamate?' (l. 150: τί ἐστι; τί με καλεῖτε;): these are the first words uttered by this Rabelaisian figure in the first Italian translation of Aristophanes' *Knights* — the amazed reply of the Sausage-seller to the greetings of Demosthenes, who has just called him 'rescuer of Athens'.

Thanks to this in several respects quite imperfect work, Aristophanes, the greatest Greek comic playwright, makes his real grand entrance in the Western world, speaking the language of one of its many peoples.

---

34 On the negative consequences of the Council on the teaching of Greek, see Sonnino 2017, 13–18. This excellent and groundbreaking book is dedicated to the Italian version of four comedies of Aristophanes (*Lisistrata*, *Arringatrici*, *Festeggianti Cerere*, *Ranocchie*) translated by Michel'Angelo Giacomelli around 1750 and never published.

35 On this translation, see Quaglia 2006, 353–357, Chirico 2014, 731–733, and Sonnino 2017, 152–153. The Count of Bagnolo is, by the way, one of the most severe critics of the Rositini's translation: at p. xxxiv of his introduction, he writes 'Nè posso mettere in conto di traduzione quella fatta in prosa da Bartolomio et Pietro Rositini de Prat'Alboino, e stampata in Vinegia da Vincenzo Vaugris nel 1545 in caratteri corsivi, la quale quantunque rechi sul frontispizio, tradotte di greco, pure è fatta per comune consenso sulla pessima traduzione latina di Andrea Divo Giustinopolitano, e per certo poi ripiena zeppa di contrassensi e di passi inintelligibili'. Non too different is the judgement of another translator, Domenico Capellina, whose Italian version was published in Turin two years after Bagnolo's. At pp. liv–lv of his introduction, we read the following statement: 'L'Italia fin dal secolo decimosesto vide apparire nella sua lingua una traduzione delle commedie di Aristofane, quella di Bartolomeo e Pietro Rositini di Prato Alboino stampata in Venezia il 1545. Essa è in prosa più lombarda che italiana, fatta manifestamente sopra una cattiva versione latina con poca intelligenza di quella medesima lingua, e così priva di senso, che reca meraviglia il pensare che abbia potuto venir in capo ad alcuno di stampare un così sciocco lavoro'.

Part II: **Translating Tragedy**

II.1: Scholarly Networks: Translation Models and Functions

Alexia Dedieu
An 'Origin' of Translation: Erasmus's Influence on Early Modern Translations of Greek Tragedy into Latin

Abstract: When Erasmus has his Latin translations of *Hecuba* and *Iphigenia at Aulis* printed in 1506, he is the first to have two complete Greek tragedies translated into and printed in Latin. In the dedicatory letter addressed to William Warham, he mentions what he calls the *obscuritas* of the choral parts of tragedy. He comments on his method as a translator of ancient Greek as well as his mode of dealing with the lyric parts of Euripides' tragedies. Erasmus then becomes an example and a model for the editors and Latin translators of Euripides who come after him. In other words, Erasmus comes to be an 'origin' in the way Antoine Berman coined the term. The aim of this paper is to study how Erasmus' attempt at theorizing and translating Greek tragedy is commented upon and used by his successors in their own theories on translating Greek drama.

1 Introduction: Erasmus's Ethos as a Translator

'Many translators, according to Erasmus, excuse their ignorance and, like the cuttlefish, spread an inky obscurity round themselves to escape detection'.[1] With this unexpected metaphor, Erasmus ridicules some of his predecessors, severely discrediting their translating methods, and revealing the competitive aspects of his translation practice.[2] Indeed, Erasmus reflected upon the act of translating and his own translations of *Hecuba* and *Iphigenia at Aulis*, first printed in 1506 by Josse Bade in Paris, are supplemented by several liminary texts revealing his *ethos* as a translator.

One such liminary text is the dedicatory letter by Erasmus addressed to William Warham, the archbishop of Canterbury, which serves as a preface to the edition.[3] Here, the Dutch scholar underlines that his project is an innovation:

---

[1] Erasmus 1975, 109–110.
[2] On the competitive attitude of Erasmus as he translates, see Botley 2004 and Vedelago in this volume.
[3] Erasmus 1975, 107–110.

> I am not really surprised if even in the present fortunate age no Italian has ventured to embark on the task of translating any tragedy or any comedy, whereas several have attempted Homer.[4]

Addressing the topical difficulties of translating ancient Greek texts into Latin, Erasmus underscores the audacity of his project. He emphasises — like the translators after him — the many difficulties surrounding the Latin translation of a Greek tragedy. The scholar does more than point out the obstacles of such a venture: he shapes his *ethos* as a *nouus interpres*. Playing on the polysemy of the word *nouus*, he underlines that he is both an *innovator* and a *beginner*. The implicit rhetoric employed in this liminary text depicts a translation project deserving both admiration and leniency. Erasmus's technique as a translator of Euripides has been much studied.[5] The several liminary texts he composed present his work as propaedeutic to his upcoming translation of the New Testament, rendering his translation methods explicit. Drawing a middle ground between literal and literary translations, Erasmus offers a precise definition of his work as a translator:

> I thought it better that scholars should perhaps find me wanting in grace, let us say, and elegance of poetic style than in accuracy. Lastly, I did not wish to announce that I was but paraphrasing [...] I have chosen to reproduce the concise clarity and neatness of my original rather than a pomposity that does not belong to it and in which I take little pleasure in any case.[6]

His translation from the Greek cannot be reduced to a mere *ad uerbum* (i.e., a 'literal' translation), but it does not depart much from the original Greek either.

The first edition of Erasmus's Latin translations of Euripides was released three years after the Aldine edition, which contained the Greek text of eighteen of the nineteen plays of Euripides.[7] No complete Latin translation of a Greek

---

4 *Quo minus admiror, si ne hoc quidem felicissimo seculo quisquam Italorum ausus fuit hoc muneris aggredi, aut tragoediam aliquam aut comoediam verteret, cum plures Homero sint admoliti.* The Latin is from Erasmus 1906, 418–419, whereas the English translation from Erasmus 1975, 108.
5 Baier 2015; Rummel 1985 Waszink 1971; Wilson 1973; McCallum-Barry 2004.
6 *Maluique committere ut eruditi candorem et concinnitatem carminis in me forsitan desyderarent quam fidem. Denique nolui paraphrasten* [...] *eius quem verti, pressam sanitatem, elegantiamque referre malui quam alienum tumorem qui me nec alias magnopere delectat.* Ep. 188; the Latin is from Erasmus 1906, 419, whereas the translation from Erasmus 1975, 109–110.
7 Manuzio 1503. The Aldine edition of Euripides' tragedies announces 17 plays: *The Madness of Heracles* and *Electra* are not mentioned on the cover. Although it does not appear in the

tragedy had yet circulated throughout Europe.[8] However, even though he could not be aware of it at the time, the usual depiction of Erasmus as a pioneer in the field of Latin translations of Greek drama must be nuanced. In 1506, another similar translation was published. Giorgio Anselmi's translation of Euripides' *Hecuba* into Latin was released in Padova.[9] Diverging in many respects, both translations met sharply contrasting fates: the discreet circulation of Anselmi's translation was outshone by the outstanding fortune of Erasmus's work on Euripides' *Hecuba* and *Iphigenia*. Erasmus's Euripidean translations partly owed their fame to their second edition: in 1507, Erasmus, dissatisfied with the editorial work of the Parisian printer Josse Bade,[10] reached out to Aldo Manuzio, founder of the Aldine Press. Their ensuing collaboration made Erasmus a renowned scholar throughout Europe.[11] Thereafter, his translations went into press more than twenty times between 1506 and 1567[12] and spread throughout Europe. The scholar's name became a canonical, almost inescapable, reference among the translators of Greek tragedy in the 16th century.

Here, I will seek to demonstrate how Erasmus's shadow affects and shapes the theories of translation that emerge from the scholars who thereafter translate Euripides into Latin. First, I will focus on how those scholars refer to Erasmus as a model, and in what regard they quote and copy him. In her chapter in this volume, Angelica Vedelago studies Erasmus's eristic practice of translation and illustrates the 'imitative relationships between translators' of Euripides and Sophocles. A detailed analysis of Erasmus's influence on later translators of Euripides and Sophocles[13] will reveal how his work meets Antoine Berman's definition of an 'origin of translation.[14] Indeed, Antoine Berman studied the influence of the French scholars Nicole Oresme and Jacques Amyot on the evolution of French language and translation, as well as their political entangle-

---

initial list of plays, *The Madness of Heracles* was added at the end of the edition. Therefore, *Electra* is the only play missing from the Aldine edition.
8 Euripides' *Hecuba* had been partially translated into Latin several times in the 15th century. Some of these partial translations are recorded in Borza 2003.
9 Pertusi 1966.
10 Erasmus expresses how disappointed he is with Bade's work in Letter 207 of his correspondence, in which he also urges Aldo Manuzio to print his work: Erasmus 1975, 129–133.
11 On the role played by Aldo Manuzio in Erasmus's fame at the time, see Vanautgaerden 2012.
12 According to Howard Norland, Erasmus's translations of Euripides were then printed 22 times. H. Norland, 'The role of drama in Erasmus's literary thought'; Schoeck 1985, 551.
13 The fame of Erasmus as a translator of Greek tragedy certainly went beyond the corpus analysed in this paper, which only focuses on a limited number of cases.
14 Berman 2012.

ments. Berman shaped the idea of an 'archaeology of translation', theorizing how certain translators become translational references that later translators imitate or reject, either consciously or unconsciously.

The insistence on defining Erasmus as a 'first translator' of Greek drama into Latin naturally follows Erasmus's own self-directed *ethos*. However, this trend also conveys how influential his work must have been and contributes to turning Erasmus's translations of Euripides into a kind of 'origin'. Indeed, what Antoine Berman defines as 'origins' of translation are not the first translations into a language; they are rather the translations that '[drew], in the factual history of translation, a *before*, and an *after*'.[15] Thus defined, the concept of 'origin' perfectly situates Erasmus's translations within the theoretical discourse on translation, which was composed throughout the century.

Berman's notion is of great help when appreciating the evolution of Erasmus's influence within the theoretical discourse on the act of translating. Indeed, the 'origins', as Berman explains, do not constitute models themselves: they rather establish translational methods that are taken up either as models or as counter-models by later translators, thereby shaping the entire 'translational activity'[16] of a given language. This key concept will inform the theoretical framework for the following discussion of the Dutch scholar's authority when it comes to translating Greek drama into Latin in the 16th century.

The second part of this chapter will focus on the evolution of Erasmus's influence on the theory and practice of later translators. Four decades after Erasmus's translations were published, there appeared two Latin translations which mention him as a model: George Buchanan's translation of *Medea* in 1544,[17] and Sigismond Gelous' translation of *Orestes* in 1551.[18] Both works can be construed as answers to Erasmus's famous translation of *Hecuba* and *Iphigenia*, which were the first to circulate widely throughout Europe. A diachronic study of their discourses on the act of translating illustrates how scholars and writers who translated Greek drama departed from Erasmus's conception and methods of translation throughout the 16th century.

Misleading though it may be to call Erasmus's *Hecuba et Iphigenia* the first translations of Greek drama into Latin in the 16th century, in the first four decades of the 16th century, they outshone all other Greek dramatic translations.

---

15 'Elle dessine, dans l'histoire événementielle de la traduction, un *avant* et un *après*'; Berman, 19.
16 I translated it from the French expression 'activité traductive' Berman 2012, 19.
17 Buchanan 1544.
18 Gelous 1551.

From the time of their first publication in 1506, until Rudolf Collin's translation of the complete plays of Euripides[19] in 1541, Erasmus's translations of these two tragedies were read widely throughout Europe. In this gap of nearly 40 years, no other Latin translation of Euripides seems to have been printed.[20] Therefore, Erasmus's translations were some of the only references available in this developing field. Owing to his renown as a scholar and translator,[21] his work emerged as a reference for later translators.

A shift in translation practice occurred in the 1540s. From this decade onwards, Greek tragedies began being translated and printed on a wider scale, both into Latin and into vernacular languages. Many translations of Greek plays printed at the time made reference to Erasmus's work, whether or not they were composed in Latin. In addition to Erasmus's influence on Jane Lumley's translating method and practice, as evidenced by Vedelago in this volume, the French corpus of Euripidean translations illustrates how Erasmus's work influenced French translators. Angelica Vedelago notably demonstrates the influence of Erasmus on Jane Lumley's English translation of *Iphigenia at Aulis* entitled *The Tragedie of Euripides called Iphigeneia*. Virginie Leroux has shown how Sébillet's French translation of *Iphigenia* echoes Erasmus's translation of the same play[22] and Erasmus's influence on later French translations of *Hecuba* was brought to light by Bruno Garnier in his study of French translations of *Hecuba* in the 16th century.[23] However, the scholar did not only influence vernacular translations: his translations also had a powerful impact on the scholars who translated tragedies into Latin after him.

In the 16th century, the Latin translations considered to be the most influential after those by Erasmus were arguably those by the Scottish scholar George Buchanan. He translated two tragedies by Euripides, *Medea* and *Alcestis*, which were not printed at the same time. His Latin translation of Euripides' *Medea* was printed in Paris in 1544[24] in an edition that brought together Erasmus's *Hecuba*

---

19 In 1541, *Electra* had not yet appeared in the extant Euripidean corpus. The tragedy was brought to light and printed for the first time by Pietro Vettori in 1545 (cf. Vettori 1545).
20 This remark is based on my knowledge of the Euripidean corpus. I do not deny the possibility that some works unknown to me may be known to other scholars who studied the 16th century reception of Euripides. However, manuscript translations are deliberately excluded here because they are unique and were not printed, so any part they may have played in spreading literary ideas cannot be compared to that of printed translations.
21 Erasmus's translation of the New Testament was printed by Froben in Basel in 1516.
22 Leroux 2017.
23 Garnier 1999.
24 Buchanan 1544.

and *Iphigenia* and Buchanan's *Medea*. Thus, the very shape of this publication betrayed the clear Erasmian filiation of his enterprise. Like Erasmus before him, Buchanan composed liminary texts in which he expressed his aim as a translator of Euripides. These documents acknowledge Buchanan's intellectual debt to the Dutch scholar. Indeed, his preface to *Medea*[25] names Erasmus as an exemplar. According to Buchanan, 'only Erasmus succeeded' at an enterprise that was taken up by many.[26]

One might wonder to whom Buchanan refers in the same prefatory letter, in which he mentions the *plerique*, the 'many' who have tried to translate Greek tragedies.[27] Apart from Erasmus's translations that circulated throughout Europe, which, from 1506 to 1540 almost constituted a monopoly, the only printed Latin translation[28] was an *ad uerbum* translation of Collin printed in Basel in 1541.[29] Still, Buchanan seems to consider Erasmus's attempt as the only one worth mentioning, and his praise of Erasmus may reflect his peculiar conception of translation. If Buchanan knew of Collin's translations,[30] then acknowledging the quality of Erasmus's work as the only attempt worthy of consideration would amount to a rejection of literal translations,[31] thereby highlighting the value of so-called 'literary translations'.[32]

---

25 *Ad illustrissimum principem Ioannem a Lucemburgo Iueriaci Abbatem Georgi Buchanani Praefatio*; Buchanan 1544.
26 The Latin sentence is '*hanc a plerisque rem prius tentatam, uni Erasmo successisse*'; 'at this project attempted by many before, only Erasmus succeeded'.
27 Buchanan may well refer to the attempts of Poliziano and other Italian scholars of the 15th century, mentioned by Erasmus as his predecessors who did not go through with their translations.
28 Except for the previously-mentioned translation by Giorgio Anselmi.
29 Collin 1541.
30 Collin's translations of Euripides were printed by Winter in Basel, in 1541. The translator was close to Zwingli who had him appointed Professor of Greek in Zurich. See Hartmann 1957, as well Saladin 1996, 162–163. Collin's translation is a literal translation of the entire corpus of Euripides' plays (with the exception of *Electra*, which was only printed for the first time by Piero Vettori in 1545).
31 Erasmus, building on previously defined oppositions between *ad uerbum* and *ad sensum* translations, claimed the necessity of a moderate 'in-between' method of translation that would not be content with copying the Greek but would neither stray too far from the original. On Erasmus's methods as a translator and on his definition of the delicate balance between the literary and literal in his theory of translation of Greek drama into Latin, see Baier 2015.
32 Relying on the analysis of Jean-Frédéric Chevalier's chapter 'George Buchanan and the poetics of borrowing in the Latin translation of Euripides' *Medea*', Schweitzer analysed the poetic dimension of Buchanan's translations; cf. Schweitzer 2013.

In Buchanan's prefatory letter, Erasmus's *auctoritas* is alluded to along with that of the Roman poet Ennius. By naming Ennius too, Buchanan acknowledges two literary figures closely linked to both Euripides and Latin. Erasmus's name follows Ennius', the Roman poet who was famous (among other things) for his Latin imitations of Euripides.[33] Buchanan thus undertakes his project within a tradition initiated by a Roman poet who is commonly referred to as a poetic exemplar.[34] Mentioning those two names, Buchanan explains that he would not be upset if 'darkness should spread upon him because of their authority'[35] (*auctoritas*). Ennius and Erasmus, those two 'illustrious names' (*praeclara nomina*), are introduced by Buchanan as *auctoritates*, 'examples', 'references', or 'authorities' when it comes to translating Greek drama into Latin. Both those literary figures are essential poetic references: Ennius wrote poetry and drama, and Erasmus, as he translated Euripides, took the poetic style of Euripides into consideration. Naming them as his predecessors, Buchanan delineates a poetic filiation for his work and builds this filiation on references from famous literary figures.

Critics have already suggested that Erasmus's translations are key to understanding why Buchanan chose *Medea* for his first translation.[36] The figure of Medea could thus be seen as echoing the figure of Hecuba, selected by Erasmus nearly 40 years earlier. However, it could well mirror Ennius' work. Indeed, Ennius is not only designated by Cicero as a translator of Euripides: he is also named as a translator of *Medea*.[37] The explicit mention of Erasmus and Ennius in this dedicatory letter could be read as a manner, for the scholar, of insisting on the literary lineage of his translation: his work is thus presented as a successor both to Ennius' poetry and Erasmus.[38]

---

33 Tuilier 1962; Herzog-Hauser 1938.
34 Ennius' work is often mentioned by Cicero; cf. Cic. *Fin* I, 2. Cic. Off, I, 16, 51.
35 *Numquam aeque moleste feram, Ennii atque Erasmi auctoritate mihi tenebras offundi.*
36 Schweitzer analyses the two translations of *Medea* and *Alcestis* as an echo of the Erasmian diptych *Hecuba* and *Iphigenia*. The referential game between the two scholars is convincing, but seems to have further implications on which I will expand in relation to my study of Buchanan's translation of Euripides' *Alcestis*.
37 Cic. *Fin*. I, II, 4.
38 Buchanan's choice of *Medea* could be interpreted in many ways. Schweitzer calls Euripides' *Medea* a 'revenge tragedy before the time'. Schweitzer 2013. It could also simply be construed as an appropriation of a tragic figure that circulated through Greek and Latin cultures. Before becoming the epitome of revenge prefigured by Buchanan's translation, the Scottish translator may have chosen *Medea* for her ties with epic (since Medea was one of the main characters of Apollonios' *Argonautica*. (I offer this hypothesis here because critics have made

Seven years after Buchanan's translation, in 1551, another translation of Euripides' tragedies was published in Basel by Hans Herbst (Johannes Oporinus). Sigismond Gelous Torda was born in the city of Turda, in the Kingdom of Hungary,[39] and spent several years studying at Wittenberg in 1539, where he remained for five years.[40] Gelous quickly earned his professors' esteem and formed an enduring relationship with the two main figures of the Wittenberg circle, Joachim Camerarius and Philip Melanchthon, who were his teachers at the time.[41] His translation of Euripides' *Orestes* is less famous than Buchanan's work, although it follows similar patterns. In the dedicatory letter to the pastor Marton Kálmáncsehi,[42] Gelous justifies his choice through his appreciation for both the play and Euripides, and by his will to provide a useful tool to those who wish to learn Greek.[43] In addition, just as Buchanan did seven years earlier, Gelous mentions Erasmus as a reference, and the tragedy he chooses to translate, the *Orestes*, could also be interpreted as mirroring Erasmus's choice.

As mentioned, Erasmus's decision to translate *Hecuba* has been subject to various interpretations, and the many accounts offered by critics overlap. The foundational place held by *Hecuba* within the Byzantine triad, and within the textual tradition of Euripides, is frequently offered as one of those explanations. In the middle of the 16th century, scholars frequently interpreted *Hecuba*'s notoriety in relation to its crucial place within the printed editions. Malcolm Heath, for instance, has analysed how *Hecuba*'s traditional place within the

---

the same claim about *Hecuba*, defending the idea that the play's fame had to be explained through its ties with epic.) See Garnier, 1999.

39 Okàl 1974, 105–155.
40 Sigismond Gelous' life is mainly known from the biography written by Miloslav Okàl; Okàl 1974.
41 The correspondence of both those scholars testifies to their long-lasting friendship; Okàl 1974.
42 Marton Kálmáncsehi Santa was one of the first Calvinist pastors in Hungary, close to the ideas of Philipp Melanchthon and the Reformation. He then became a pastor in Naples. By addressing to him the dedicatory letter in his translation of Euripides' *Orestes*, Sigismond Gelous gives his project an intellectual and religious filiation. His dedicatory letter later mentions Melanchthon's translations of Euripides which were not yet released at the time. Gelous: '*Sigismondus Gelous clarissimo et doctissimo uiro Martino Calmantzehi pastori ecclesiae Neapolitanae apud pannonios ad Carpathum S. D.*'; Gelous 1551.
43 *Deinde cum mirifico autoris amore inuitatus, tum ut eis qui solidam linguae graecae cognitionem nondum essent consecuti, qualecunque praesidium ad Euripidem intelligendum adderem, statui aliquot eius fabulas in latinum sermonem numeris conuertere. Ac uersi Orestem, quae mihi tragoedia et propter argumentum ipsum, et propter multos insignes locos imprimis placet. Quantum uero in ea re operae et laboris sumpserim, docti facile iudicabunt.*

Euripidean editions was tied by scholars to an aesthetic judgement.⁴⁴ In his preface to the play,⁴⁵ the German scholar Gaspar Stiblin declares that 'this story, both on account of the diversity of plot and on account of the more than tragic atrocity, rightly holds the first place'.⁴⁶ This assessment of the tragedy parallels Gulielmus Xylander's appraisal of the play. Like Sigismond Gelous, Xylander, who was a professor of Greek at Heidelberg, gives the play preferential treatment. His printed edition of Euripides' tragedies was published twice, first in 1558⁴⁷ and again four years later.⁴⁸ The second edition presents several improvements, among which the scholar's replacing his own translation of *Hecuba* with a translation that owed much to a more illustrious scholar, Philipp Melanchthon. This anecdote could be understood as simply an episode celebrating the scholarly work of another Wittenberg professor; however, it also reflects Xylander's consideration of *Hecuba*:

> If I previously placed my own translation of Hecuba first, so that the edition would not be 'headless', I now display the Philippean one,⁴⁹ after having removed my own, so that the language and style would everywhere be identical.⁵⁰

The words chosen to name *Hecuba* outline the ascendancy of the play above the rest of the Euripidean corpus. The Latin verb *praeposueram*, 'I placed it first' could simply mean 'I preferred', but it nevertheless underscores that the play comes ahead of the extant Euripidean corpus. Xylander's fear that, without the *Hecuba*, the opus would be ἀκέφαλον, 'headless', should be tied to his appraisal of the tragedy: the Greek adjective stands out and underlines the distinct place occupied by *Hecuba* within the Euripidean corpus. Those terms reflect how scholars close to the Wittenberg Circle interpret the significance of *Hecuba*.⁵¹

---

44 Heath 2010, 42.
45 The preface was published with Stiblin's complete edition and translation of the 19 plays by Euripides in 1562 (cf. Stiblin 1562).
46 *Haec fabula propter argumenti tum uarietatem, tum plus quam tragicam atrocitatem, iure principem locum tenet*. Translated by Erin Lam, https://ucbclassics.dreamhosters.com/djm/stiblinus/stiblinusHecuba.html (last accessed 06/09/2022).
47 Xylander 1558.
48 Xylander 1562.
49 The Latin word is *Philippeam*, and refers to Philipp Melanchthon's translation of the play.
50 *Qui ante opus ne esset ἀκέφαλον, Hecubam de meo praeposueram, nunc Philippeam uobis mea sublata exhibeo ut, (quantum eius fieri potuit) una oratio ubique, unus sit stylus*; Xylander 1562.
51 The theme of the play, and the reverse of fortune it epitomises, also explains why scholars turned their interest to this play in particular, such an attitude towards certain tragedies echoes

Naturally, none of these interpretations sheds a clear light on why Erasmus first singled out *Hecuba*. Nevertheless, their discourses on the tragedy reveal their interpretation of the play's influence. The assimilation between the quality of the play and its position within the tragic Euripidean corpus is unmistakable.

Singling out *Orestes*, a tragedy that traditionally came second to *Hecuba* in the Euripidean corpus,[52] could have been a way for Gelous to establish his work in Erasmus's intellectual lineage. Since, according to Gaspar Stiblin, *Hecuba* 'rightly held the first place', Gelous naturally turned his attention towards *Orestes*, the second play of the Euripidean triad. In addition, the characters, the story and the themes of the *Orestes* are also closely tied to those of *Iphigenia at Aulis*, the second play Erasmus translated in 1506. His choice may have been reinforced by numerous manuscripts of the *Orestes* then available. Indeed, *Orestes* was one of the most copied plays during the Byzantine period,[53] as shown by the numerous manuscripts of the play and a considerable number of scholia that Sigismond Gelous later evokes in his liminary presentation of his work.

Furthermore, the reference to Erasmus as a translator of Euripides is later evidenced by an explicit reference to the Dutch scholar's work. Gelous' tribute to Erasmus evokes the tribute paid by Buchanan a few years before: 'Erasmus translated *Hecuba* and *Iphigenia at Aulis* and, in this endeavor, scholars have appreciated his diligence. Had he been willing to translate the rest of the tragedies with the same application, it would have been of much help to the young people who are keen on studying the Greek language'.[54]

To Gelous, Erasmus's translations stand out owing to the 'diligence' (*studium*) and the 'application' (*diligentia*) reflected in his work. He then adopts Erasmus's rhetoric, underscoring how scarcely Euripides' tragedies have been translated: 'I realised', remarks Gelous, 'that there had never been anyone to translate this author into Latin'.[55] Thus, Sigismond Gelous revives Erasmus's rhetoric as a translator to situate himself in his intellectual lineage, and, by doing so, defines

---

the way they read and conceived tragedy at the time. This reading of tragedy is analysed by Micha Lazarus for Sophocles in his article 'Sophocles at Wittenberg'; see Lazarus 2020.

52 Both in the Byzantine manuscript tradition and in the 16th century printed editions.
53 Diggle 1991; Turyn 1957.
54 *Conuersit Erasmus Hecubam et Iphigeniam in Aulide, et in ea re studium doctis uehementer probatur. Atque utinam ceteras quoque Trageodias pari diligentia uertere uoluisset, multum profecto adolescentes linguae Graecae studiosos iusisset.*
55 *[...] inter docendum uenit in mentem mirari, quod nondum quisquam emerserit, qui hunc autorem latinum faceret. Sigismondus Gelous clarissimo et doctissimo uiro Martino Calmantzehi pastori ecclesiae Neapolitanae apud pannonios ad Carpathum S. D.*; Gelous 1551.

his work as a translator. Gelous' choice to translate *Orestes* could be construed as an attempt to continue the work of the Dutch scholar, who is acknowledged as a model.

Buchanan and Gelous both delineate a model of Erasmus as a first translator of Euripides. Until the 1550s Erasmus is quoted as a model for translation, which is owing to the wide circulation of his translations in Western Europe. His thoroughly defined technique as a translator, as previously shown, could further explain his influence. Transcending the traditional antinomy between *ad uerbum* and *ad sensum*, Erasmus's work shaped a translational 'middle ground' in which translators could situate their own practice and theories. In that respect, Erasmus's translational attempt constitutes an 'origin of translation', as Antoine Berman defined it.[56]

Erasmus's influence, as we shall see, extends beyond the Euripidean corpus. His discourse on the choruses pervades the discourses on both Euripides and Sophocles. Nevertheless, as an 'origin', Erasmus's influence evolves. As philological methods improve, his legacy does not remain a mere undiscussed model: his work becomes the basis for theoretical and practical considerations on the act of translating.

2 Beyond Euripides: Erasmus and the Obscurity of the Tragic Chorus

The translation of the choruses is one of the aspects on which Erasmus's conception may have been most influential in the 16th century. In the letter to William Warham, which serves as a preface to his translation of *Hecuba* and *Iphigenia* in 1506, Erasmus points out that, among other difficulties, to him the *choruses* are particularly complex. Erasmus's readings and his treatment of the tragic songs evolve slightly between the translation of *Hecuba* and the translation of *Iphigenia*.

In the preface added to the Aldine edition of *Iphigenia* that was printed in Venice in 1507,[57] Erasmus quotes Horace[58] and calls the tragic songs 'harmoni-

---

[56] See Berman 2012, 19.
[57] Erasmus 1507.
[58] Hor. *Ars P.* 322. In reality, Erasmus misquotes him: in the passage he mentions, Horace does not refer to Euripides.

ous trifles' (*canoris nugis*). In his opinion, 'nowhere did the Ancients write more foolishly than in choruses of this sort'.[59]

Erasmus was primarily repelled by the excesses conveyed by the lyric songs,[60] the variety of metrical forms there employed, and their complex vocabulary. These formal excesses obscured the meaning of the songs; on his account, 'in choruses of this sort, [the ancients] destroyed clarity of expression, and in the hunt for marvellous verbal effect, their sense of reality suffered'.[61] This severe judgment on tragic choruses could already be found in the dedicatory letter to *Hecuba* dated from 1506: there Erasmus had expressed the same reluctance, though in a milder form, and mentioned the 'obscurity' of the choruses:

> The choruses [...] are so obscure, because of some sort of deliberate artifice, that they need an Oedipus, or Delian prophet, rather than a translator.[62]

Erasmus, as a mere *interpres*, is unable to decipher such obscure messages. He thus tried, in translating the choruses, to 'render verse metrically'.[63] However, he did not attempt to render them in the style of the Euripidean chorus. On the contrary, his view on tragic choruses, reinforced in the preface to the 1507 edition of his tragedies, served as justification to openly reject any attempt at rendering their style in the actual translations.[64]

---

59 *Nusquam enim mihi magis ineptisse uidetur antiquitas, quam in huiusmodi Choris.* Ep. 208; Erasmus 1906, 135.
60 Erasmus 1975, 135. *In Choris immodicam illam carminum uarietatem, ac licentiam, aliquantulum temperauimus.* Ep. 208; the Latin is from Erasmus 1906, 440, whereas the translation from Erasmus 1975, 135.
61 *[...] antiquitas [...] in huiusmodi Choris [...] uitiauit eloquentiam, dumque uerborum miracula uenatur, in rerum iudicio cessauit.* Ep. 208; the Latin is from Erasmus 1906, 440, whereas the translation from Erasmus 1975, 135.
62 *Adde nunc choros nescio quanam affectatione adeo obscuros, ut Œdipo quopiam aut Delio sit opus magis quam interprete*; the Latin is from Erasmus 1906, 218, whereas the translation from Erasmus 1975, 108. I have translated the word *interprete* differently from the translation that I am using, which has 'commentator' instead. Considering that *interpres* is also the word that Erasmus uses to define himself a few lines later, when he called himself a *nouus interpres*, I think that it refers to the act of translating and to the translator himself.
63 Erasmus 1975, 108.
64 Erasmus 1975, 133–135.

Despite several passages within Erasmus's paratexts to Euripides that clarify his position towards the tragic choruses,[65] his definition of their *obscuritas* is the only piece of Erasmus's discourse on the topic that circulates among translators. Buchanan, in his dedicatory letter to *Medea*, reflects on the lyric parts in exactly the same manner. He appears to follow Erasmus's judgment when pointing out the 'considerable obscurity in the choruses' (*summam in choris obscuritatem*). The Scottish scholar then adds that this *obscuritas* is 'in Euripides so frequent that he seems to be purposefully trying to reach it'.[66] As Erasmus did decades before when dealing with the style of Euripides, Buchanan does not offer any way to render the style of the choruses and also limits himself to mentioning their 'obscurity'.

This *topos* of the obscurity of the lyric parts, as highlighted by Erasmus at the beginning of the 16th century, spread beyond the scholarship on Euripides. The translators of Sophocles, who also regularly turned to Erasmus as a model of 'first' translator of Greek tragedy into Latin, later exploited the same *topos* to define the choruses of Greek tragedy.

The German philologist Thomas Naogeorgos used a dedicatory letter to the antiquarian Johann Jacob Fugger as a preface to his 1558 translation of Sophocles,[67] evoking 'the obscurity deployed in the choruses' (*in Choris affectatam obscuritatem*). He sets aside the choruses as the only obscure parts in Sophocles' tragedies. He mentions 'especially the obscurity deployed in the choruses': his view on Sophocles' style is that 'this only applies [...] to those parts, in which even the Greek scholia that I used cannot determine nor indicate the exact meaning but rather, by offering various interpretations, obfuscate which meaning should be chosen'.[68] As he translated Sophocles, the German dramatist singled out the tragic songs because of their 'obscurity'. The adjective he resorts to — '*affectatam*' — seems to follow Erasmus in presenting the obscurity as an intentional process of the Greek playwrights.

---

65 Erasmus clarifies his view of the Greek choruses in the second letter to William Warham (ep. 208), which serves as a preface to his translation of *Iphigenia* in 1507; Erasmus 1975, 133–135.
66 [*Obscuritatem*] *quae huic scriptori adeo familiaris est ut eam de industria sectatus esse uideatur*; Buchanan 1544.
67 'Generoso ac amplissimo viro d. Ioanni Iacobo Fuggero, Domino Vissenhorni ac Kirchpergae, consiliario Caesareo ac Regio, et patrono suo colendissimo, Tho. Naogeorgus, S. D. P.'; Naogeorgus 1558.
68 [...] *praesertim in Choris, affectatam obscuritatem: id tamen in iis factum solis puto, in quibus ne scholia quidem Graeca, quibus usi sumus, suffragantur, certumque indicant sensum, sed variis interpretationibus ambiguum faciunt quid sit sequendum.*

A year earlier, the French scholar Jean Lalemant also translated the seven tragedies of Sophocles.[69] The liminary texts to his Latin translations reflect Erasmus's influence as well. Similar to Erasmus half a century earlier,[70] Lalemant composed a *carminis ratio* explaining his metrical choices. In this text, after mentioning the influence of the Latin Comic playwrights and Cicero regarding the use of metrics, he names Erasmus, 'who wished to enjoy the same freedom in his translations of the tragedies *Hecuba* and *Iphigenia* of Euripides'.[71] The implicit imprint of the translator can also be sensed in his 'small preface' (*praefatiuncula*), where Lalemant states that 'his work would be useless and vain if [he] did not uncover the enigmatic words of Sophocles to the eyes of those who do not have an Oedipus or a Delian diver at home'.[72]

The mention of an 'Oedipus' or the 'Delian diver' whose help should be required to understand Sophocles is a direct quote from Erasmus's 1506 dedicatory letter to William Warham.[73] However, Jean Lalemant slightly shifts from Erasmus's translation method since he wishes to 'uncover the enigmatic words of Sophocles to the eyes of those who do not have an Oedipus or a Delian diver at home'. In his translation, then, Jean Lalemant intends to resolve a difficulty only mentioned by Erasmus, and Buchanan after him: he does not limit himself to mentioning the difficulties of the choral parts; on the contrary, his translations aim at 'uncovering' them.[74]

The *topos* of the *obscurity* of the choruses ends up qualifying the tragic choruses and, in Jean Lalemant's case, the entire tragic style, of Sophocles. The ubiquitous presence of Erasmus within the liminary texts, which characterises scholarship on the tragic poets[75] in the 16th century, further supports the hypothesis that the Dutch scholar, who proclaims himself the 'first' translator of

---

69 Lalemant 1557.
70 Erasmus's 1507 edition of his translations of Euripides contains a *conspectus metrorum* entitled '*Ad Lectorem*', whose aim it is to provide the readers with an explanation of the metrical forms employed in the text; cf. Erasmus 1507.
71 *Eadem libertate gaudere voluit Erasmus in illis Hecuba et Iphigenia Euripidis trageodiis.* 'In Sophoclis tragoedias praefatiuncula per Ioannem Lalamantium'; Buchanan 1557.
72 *Sic enim existimaui, fore uti noster hic labor inanis, et frustra susceptus permultis uideretur, nisi quae sub aenigmate dicta sunt a Sophocles, ob oculos eorum ponerem, qui uel Oedipum domi non habent, uel Delio egent natatore.* 'In Sophoclis tragoedias praefatiuncula per Ioannem Lalamantium'; Buchanan 1557.
73 See footnote 56.
74 Indeed, even though it is not the purpose of this paper to study Jean Lalemant's attempts at adapting Sophoclean metrical patterns, it should nevertheless be mentioned that his translations do present interesting insights.
75 Of which this chapter can only provide a mere sample. See footnote 15.

Greek drama into Latin, can be construed as an 'origin' of translation as Berman intended.

3 Setting Erasmus Aside

While Erasmus's influence pervades the scholarship on both Sophocles and Euripides, his work cannot be defined as a mere 'model'. Despite the wide circulation of Erasmus's ideas on translation through the corpus of Greek tragedies translated into Latin at the turn of the century, his method is not merely copied by translators. This makes the assimilation of his translation technique with the notion of 'origin' all the more relevant. A diachronic approach to Erasmus's discourse on the act of translating reveals that translators construe his work as a method that can be copied, improved, or rejected. Thus, they do not restrict themselves to Erasmus's discourse on translation: Erasmus's 'first attempt' becomes a starting point to their reflections on translation which they either uphold or implicitly drift away from.

In the preface to his *Orestes* composed in 1551, Sigismond Gelous had already illustrated how translators can stray from Erasmus or expand on his theories on translation. As he rejected the literal line-to-line rendering (*uerbi ex uerbo redditio*) in favor of the 'meaning' (*sententia*) of the Greek text, Gelous evoked Erasmus. Gelous also dwelt on the style of Euripides, and on the best way to render Greek in Latin. His theory on translation partly relies on Erasmus's conception of translation:

> For, to keep quiet about other difficulties, Greek speech has its own turns of phrase, and if you translate them inconveniently, you might harm very ancient phrases, mosaics almost, and the main ornaments of the work.[76]

Gelous remains silent on the exact nature of these 'other difficulties', which he elects 'not to mention'. However, they could be understood as referring to the difficulties encountered by Erasmus in 1506 when, without exemplifying his thought, he alludes to the 'difficulties of the task'.[77]

One could then infer that Gelous, because he implicitly based his discourse on Erasmus's previous theoretical attempt, considered it unnecessary to de-

---

[76] *Nam ut alias difficultates taceam, habet graecus sermo proprias dicendi formulas, quas si parum apte transtulisti, uenustissima quasi emblemata, et praecipua operis ornamenta sustilisti.*
[77] *Negocii difficultas*, Ep. 188; Erasmus 1906, 408, my translation.

scribe further the obstacles encountered by Erasmus, choosing instead to focus on an aspect of the Greek style that, until then, had remained unexplored. Gelous provides several examples of 'Greek turns of phrases', where he attempts to render the style of the Greek into Latin, and thus tries to resolve the difficulties he previously mentioned. One of those examples is Gelous' translation of *Orestes*, 129, that he introduces in this manner:

> To demonstrate this with an example, this occurs in what I translated as 'scilicet Helene est uetus':[78] to the Greeks, this is proverbial.[79]

A comparison of Gelous' translation to the Greek original is shown below:

Ἔστι δ' ἡ πάλαι γυνή.

She remains the woman of before[80]

Scilicet Helene est uetus

That is to say, she is the old Helen[81]

The 'difficulty' in this specific example resides in the insertion of the adverb πάλαι ('in olden days') between the article and the noun, a Greek turn of phrase not directly translatable into Latin. Gelous turns the adverb πάλαι ('in olden days'; 'long ago') into an adjective, *uetus* ('old'; 'ancient'). To this end, Gelous continues from Erasmus's remarks on the difficulty of turning Greek into Latin and makes those difficulties explicit. Gelous develops his view on the style of the Greek in a precise way, and in doing so, justifies his translation. His theory on Greek style is tied to an explanation of the difficulties encountered, thus allowing his audience a clear understanding of the text. His discourse on translation is close to that of Erasmus but clarifies and develops a consideration that was only alluded to by Erasmus in the preface of *Hecuba* and *Iphigenia*. Erasmus becomes a model whom translators try to outshine in different ways, or to contest.

---

78 The Latin translates the Greek Ἔστι δ' ἡ πάλαι γυνή (*Orestes* 129): 'she remains the woman she used to be'.
79 *Quale est, ut exemplo rem demonstrem, illud quod nos uertimus, 'Scilicet Helene est uetus': Graecis est παροιμιῶδες*.
80 Gelous' translation.
81 Literal translation.

Owing to Erasmus's ubiquitous presence throughout the liminary texts surrounding the translation of Greek drama in the middle of the 16th century, his absence can hardly go unnoticed. One could argue that not naming Erasmus is a way to contest his legacy and assert one's individuality as a translator. Two later Latin translations of Euripides that develop interesting thoughts on translation show no mention of the renowned scholar, and, for this reason, deserve to be closely analysed.

In Xylander's aforementioned preface to his 1562 edition of Euripides,[82] comments on his translation choice concerning *Hecuba* make no reference to Erasmus, whose name could be expected in such a context. On the contrary, Xylander praises Melanchthon's translation of the *Hecuba*, and his silence on Erasmus's previous attempt on the same play could easily be construed as taking a philological stance, setting aside a rival whose influence may have outshone Melanchthon's at the time.

During the same period, as he comes to translate *Alcestis*, Buchanan drifts away from Erasmus's *auctoritas*, whom he no longer mentions. Critics have underlined that Buchanan's translations of Euripides echo Erasmus because they form a diptych. Indeed, Buchanan's debt to Erasmus in his translation of *Medea* is explicitly acknowledged. However, a diachronic study of both Buchanan's discourse on his translations demands to reassess its Erasmian filiation. Even though the Erasmian diptych should certainly be considered as a source for Buchanan's choice to translate *Alcestis*,[83] Buchanan's translation was first printed in 1556, twelve years after his translation of *Medea*.[84] While Buchanan acknowledges the influence of Erasmus in the dedicatory letter to *Medea*, in contrast, his dedicatory letter to *Alcestis*[85] never names the Dutch scholar. Buchanan's second translation reflects how he improved as a translator of ancient Greek.[86] This improvement as a translator is accompanied by a remoteness from Erasmus, whom he presented as a model in his preface to *Medea*. Erasmus's influence thus fades in the second part of the century, as translation methods and philology improve. From his role as a model, Erasmus becomes a

---

82 Xylander 1562.
83 The link between Buchanan's translation of *Medea*, printed in 1544, and *Alcestis*, printed in 1556, has been studied by Schweitzer. Schweitzer 2015.
84 However, his translation of Euripides' *Alcestis* and Euripides' *Medea* belong to the same period, since they were written while Buchanan was at the College de Guyenne. See Schweitzer 2013.
85 'Ad illustriss. Principem D. Margaritam Henrici Secundi Francorum Regis sororem, in Alcestin Praefatio', Buchanan 1557.
86 Buchanan 1983, 313.

reference that translators use to shape their practice, and from which they drift, in order to assert their own literary independence.

4 Conclusion

Erasmus's methods and theories on the translation of Greek drama constitute a starting point for translators as they attempted to build theories illustrating their practice of translation in the first half of the 16th century. In that sense, Erasmus's work constitutes an 'origin' of translation, as Berman intended it. Erasmus's practice and theories about Greek tragedies, on the style of Euripides, and on translation from Greek into Latin were so famous that they became a reference for scholars to situate their work.

Buchanan and Xylander's striking silence on Erasmus's influence in the works they published later in the 16th century can be read as a way to set their work on an independent path. Erasmus's prestige is gradually set aside as the Wittenberg school of Melanchthon emerges and as translators of Euripides shift their attention to the political interpretations of the Greek playwright; the French writer Florent Chrestien, in the last decades of the century, barely mentions Erasmus, and claims another literary filiation: that of Scaliger.

Although Erasmus did not remain an uncontested model, the political, religious, and literary themes at the heart of the tragic diptych he assembled certainly played a major part in the translation's wider success. The repercussions of his *Hecuba* and *Iphigenia* on the translations and reception of Greek drama at the time inevitably leads to questions of how his tragic diptych may have oriented or affected tragedy's aesthetics throughout the 16th century.

Angelica Vedelago
Imitation, Collaboration, Competition Between English and Continental Translators of Greek Tragedy

Abstract: Imitation in early modern translation is traditionally seen as the phenomenon by which translators imitated their source author. However, translation entailed another kind of imitation: the one of previous translators of the same work. This chapter first examines how imitation in translation was conceived by two 16th-century theorists such as Erasmus and Laurence Humphrey, and then considers the imitation of other translators of the same text in Latin translations of Greek tragedy. Erasmus and Humphrey present imitation of previous translators as a competitive process. Their conception of imitation chime with the practice of two English 16th-century translators of Greek tragedy, Jane Lumley and Thomas Watson. Watson competes with previous translators in challenging aspects like metre; Lumley, who relies on Erasmus both as translator of Euripides and as translation theorist, engages less in a competition than in a collaboration with the humanist's version, which serves as a hermeneutical support for her own translation.

Nihil est difficilius quam cum est e Graecis tragicis uertendum.
(Hervet 1541, sig. A2v)

It is not easy to define how the relationship between translation and imitation was conceived in the early modern period. '[T]he precise point at which translation stops and imitation begins is often very hard indeed to discern': thus Glenn Most admits the difficulty of drawing a boundary between translation and imitation, with reference to classical literature.[1] This seems to hold true also for 16th-century poetry, at least in the eyes of English theorists of the same period, who wavered between the two poles of imitation and translation when critiquing the relationship of near-contemporary poets with their sources. Thomas Wyatt and

---

This chapter stems from the research for my PhD dissertation on the reception of Sophocles' *Antigone* in early modern English drama (University of Padua, 2019) and has been subsequently revised during my participation in the PRIN project 'Classical Receptions in Early Modern English Drama' at the University of Verona. I thank Dr Micha Lazarus and all the editors of this volume for their suggestions on the drafts of this chapter.

1 Most 2003, 388.

Henry Howard's debts to Petrarch were described in terms of both imitation and translation: George Puttenham regarded their poetry as 'in all imitating very naturally and studiously' Petrarch;[2] John Harington defined the two poets as 'translators out of Italian'.[3] While scholars such as Étienne Dolet, Thomas Sébillet, Pierre de La Ramée, and Andreas Schott subsumed translation under imitation,[4] most theorists, since the influential Leonardo Bruni, rather reflected on the relationship between the two practices from the perspective of translation: they considered which authors and how translators had to imitate.[5] The instability of the hierarchy between translation and imitation in the 16th century testifies to their interplay; translators were often perceived as imitators of the source author.

However, translation could entail another process of imitation, especially when the target language was Latin. In the 16th century, Latin was by far the most frequent target language for translations of Greek tragedy.[6] A translator's choice of Latin, on the one hand, guaranteed him/her a wider readership but, on the other, exposed him/her to comparison with translators who had previously attempted the same task, notably scholars of the calibre of Erasmus. This did not dissuade translators from venturing into competition; in so doing, they often ended up imitating previous versions of the same text. Even the choice of the vernacular did not make translators immune to the influence of existing Latin translations. Competition in translation could therefore trigger another process of imitation, with translators imitating previous translators of the same text. Translation theories of the time reflected on this peculiar form of imitation, i.e., competition, sometimes explicitly encouraging it.[7] This is the case with

---

2 Puttenham 1589, 50.
3 Harington 1591, sig. viii*r*.
4 On Dolet, see Worth-Stylianou 1999, 129; Norton 1974, 6; Sébillet 1548, f. 74*r*: 'la version n'est rien qu'une imitation' ('translation is nothing but an imitation'); on de La Ramée and Schott, see Hosington 2014. All translations are my own unless otherwise indicated.
5 In *De interpretatione recta* (1420 ca.), Bruni argues that translation is a creative art *per se*, entailing the imitation of the source author (Folena 1991, 63 and Bertolio 2020, xlvi–lix). On later Italian theorists discussing the relationship between translation and imitation, see Di Martino in this volume.
6 Tanya Pollard records 104 printed editions of tragedies translated into Latin and 57 in vernacular translation published or circulating in manuscript in 16th-century Europe (Pollard 2017, 243–269). The number of Latin editions excludes those preserved only in manuscript.
7 Among the wide bibliography on early modern translation theory, see Norton 1984, Hermans 2014 [1985], Rener 1989, Folena 1991, and Burke and Po-Chia Hsia 2007. With reference to Latin, see Botley 2004 and Hosington 2014; with reference to England, see Rhodes, Kendal, Wilson 2013, and Morini 2017.

Laurence Humphrey's *Interpretatio linguarum* (1559): capturing the main ideas on translation circulating in Europe at the time, this treatise challenges analyses that are nationally confined and showcases the interconnectedness of a pan-European *respublica litteraria*. Also, this treatise sheds light on the relationship between translation and imitation, presenting the latter as an essential feature of the former.

This chapter first examines how 16th-century theorists conceived of imitation in translation and then considers to what extent translations of Greek tragedy of the same period featured imitation not in its more traditional understanding as imitation of the source author but as imitation of translators of the same text. This imitative process rests on a mechanism of competition between translators. Accordingly, I first take into account two examples of translation theory, one of unquestioned prominence, i.e., Erasmus's prefaces to his Euripides translations, and the other less influential but representative of the main trends in the field, i.e., Humphrey's treatise: both theorists present imitation as a form of competition with previous translators of the same text. I then look at how the competitive dimension of imitation informs the practice of 16th-century translators of Greek tragedy, focussing on two English translators — Lady Jane Lumley and Thomas Watson. Lumley, an educated noblewoman on the outskirts of the European *respublica litteraria*, and Watson, an Englishman who refined his education on the Continent, are perfect litmus tests for measuring English translators' reliance on their continental predecessors and, more generally, the outreach of contemporary translation theories in England.

1 Theory: Erasmus and Humphrey

16th-century translators, including translators of Greek tragedy, were usually silent in relation to imitation, especially as a form of competition with other translators. Paratexts are not lavish in information in this regard as they tend to focus on the source author instead. However, there is at least one exception: Erasmus does refer to another translator in the dedicatory epistles of his translations from Euripides' *Hecuba* and *Iphigenia at Aulis* (1506). In so doing, he implicitly suggests that competition was one of the factors that led him to translate Euripides.

However, Erasmus outwardly justifies his choice to engage with Greek literature for other reasons than competition: in order to contribute to the project of 'restor[ing] or promot[ing] … the science of theology' and to prepare for his own theological studies.[8] Erasmus regards his literary translations from Euripides as ancillary to theology, as tests of his knowledge of Greek and Latin on a tough but safe ground. In so doing, Erasmus primarily hoped to avoid incurring any translation 'mistake', explicitly assimilated to a religious 'sin' (*peccatum*).[9] By working 'on a subject which, though very taxing, was secular in nature', Erasmus aimed to acquire linguistic dexterity in both the source and target languages. As he wrote in another paratext, 'nothing is harder than to turn good Greek into good Latin' (*nihil es[t] difficilius quam ex bene Graecis bene Latina reddere*).[10]

Other, more prosaic factors equally contributed to Erasmus's choice of Euripides. Carmel McCallum-Barry has suggested that, by translating Euripides, Erasmus intended to present 'his credentials as a man of letters on a wider European scene'.[11] From 1499 to 1506 Erasmus was badly in need of a patron and he may well have hoped that translating such a difficult author as Euripides would be a strong calling card. Also, *Hecuba* was a rather 'predictable' choice considering its position as the first play in the Byzantine triad.[12] Erasmus's choice of *Iphigenia at Aulis* is less obvious: it may have been due to the play's thematic consonance with *Hecuba* itself and with a work Erasmus was completing in those years, i.e., *Panegyricus* (1504), which, like the Euripidean plays, is centred on themes such as good government, selfless sacrifice for one's country, and the nature of nobility.[13]

When one considers the preface to his version of *Hecuba* and *Iphigenia at Aulis* in its entirety, yet another motive, alongside linguistic and biographical circumstances, seems to have prompted Erasmus to translate two Euripidean tragedies. After stressing the subservience of these translations to his theological studies, Erasmus underlines the difficulty of Euripides' 'various and so unfamiliar' metres (*carmen … uarium et inusitatum*), 'remarkably succinct, delicate, exquisite' style (*uerum etiam mirum in modo presso subtili excusso*) and

---

[8] Letter 188 in Erasmus 1975, 108 (trans. R.A.B. Mynors and D.F.S. Thomson); for the Latin original, see Erasmus 1969a, 216: *rem theologicam … vel restituere vel adiuvare*. All quotations in translation from Erasmus's correspondence are taken from Erasmus 1975 and the original from Erasmus 1969a unless otherwise indicated.
[9] Letter 188 (trans. R.A.B. Mynors and D.F.S. Thomson) in Erasmus 1975, 108.
[10] Erasmus's dedicatory letter to his translation from Libanius (translated in 1503; published in 1519); Letter 177 (trans. R.A.B. Mynors and D.F.S. Thomson) in Erasmus 1975, 75.
[11] McCallum-Barry 2004, 59.
[12] McCallum-Barry 2004, 60. See also Cuzzotti in this volume.
[13] McCallum-Barry 2004, 61, 66.

'obscure choruses' (*choros ... obscuros*).[14] It should then come as no surprise, he adds, that 'even in the present fortunate age no Italian has ventured to embark on the task of translating any tragedy or any comedy'.[15] However, a few lines below, Erasmus qualifies his statement by mentioning one who did translate a tragedy, albeit partially, namely Francesco Filelfo, who Latinized only the prologue of *Hecuba*:[16]

> *Franciscus Philelphus (id quod post institutam interpretationem cognouimus) primam Hecubae scenam in oratione quadam funebri traduxerit, sed ita ut nobis alioqui putidulis uir tantus animi non parum addiderit.*
>
> (Letter 188)

> Francesco Filelfo in one of his funeral orations translated (I discovered after I had begun my own version) the first scene of the *Hecuba*, but did so in such a fashion that I, usually bashful to a fault, was considerably encouraged by this great scholar's performance.
>
> (trans. R.A.B. Mynors and D.F.S. Thomson)[17]

Albeit couched in terms of conventional self-effacement, Erasmus's reference to Filelfo suggests that competition also played a role in his decision to translate *Hecuba*. As McCallum-Barry observes, '[w]hile he refers modestly to himself, Erasmus at the same time implies that he is worthy to compete with the famous scholar'.[18]

---

14 Letter 188 (trans. R.A.B. Mynors and D.F.S. Thomson) in Erasmus 1975, 108.
15 Letter 188 (trans. R.A.B. Mynors and D.F.S. Thomson) in Erasmus 1975, 108: *ne hoc quidem felicissimo seculo quisquam Italorum ausus fuit hoc muneris aggredi, ut tragoediam aliquam aut comoediam uerteret*. Erasmus's emphasis is probably here less on *hoc ... felicissimo seculo* than on *quisquam Italorum*, thereby suggesting that the fact that not even the Italians have embarked on this enterprise is surprising; I thank Micha Lazarus for drawing my attention to this point.
16 McCallum-Barry 2004, 56; Rummel 1985, 29. Alongside Filelfo, other Italians had measured themselves against Greek drama and specifically against Euripides' *Hecuba*: the play was partially translated also by Leontius Pilatus and Pietro da Montagnana (Pollard 2012, 1064 n. 14). J.H. Waszink records another translation by the Italian Giorgio Anselmi Nepote, which was published in the same year of the Erasmian version (1506), and therefore was probably unknown to Erasmus (Waszink 1969, 205–206).
17 The term *putidulis* means either 'disgusting' or 'offensive'. By translating 'bashful to a fault', Mynors and Thomson opted for the first semantic area, but they considerably lessened the strength of the term. It seems odd that Erasmus would adopt such a pejorative term as 'disgusting' but it could make sense as a gesture of excessive self-modesty with reference to his knowledge of Greek.
18 McCallum-Barry 2004, 56.

The competitive dimension is further enhanced by two inconsistencies. First, in the statement quoted above, Erasmus both acknowledges and downsizes his debt to Filelfo. While he admits knowing that Filelfo's translation existed and that he was prompted by it to pursue his own, Erasmus underlines that this was only after he had already started his translation (*id quod post institutam interpretationem cognovimus*). This contradiction is further reinforced if we compare this statement to a passage in another letter dating back to 1523:

> [A]*nnis aliquot ante quam adirem Italiam, exercendae Graecitatis causa ... uerteram Hecubam Euripidis ... Ad id audendum prouocarat F. Philelphus, qui primam eius fabulae scenam uertit in oratione quodam funebri, parum ut tum mihi uisum est feliciter.*[19]

> [S]ome years before my visit to Italy, in order to practise my Greek ... I had made a version of the *Hecuba* of Euripides ... This rash attempt was provoked by Francesco Filelfo, who translated the first scene of the play in a funeral oration, without (as I then thought) much success.[20]

As Agostino Pertusi suggests, Erasmus 'seems to remember wrongly'[21] since almost twenty years before he had claimed discovering Filelfo's version only after embarking on the translation. Or possibly Erasmus was more anxious to underline his autonomy from Filelfo in 1506 than in 1523, precisely on account of a greater need to establish his scholarly credentials back then. Be it as it may, Erasmus imitates the Italian scholar's version in several points of the prologue, although he claims he thought Filelfo had performed *parum ... feliciter*.[22] The second inconsistency lies in Erasmus's definition of his task as 'unattempted hitherto' (*rem hactenus intentatam*), while a few lines earlier he himself refers to Filelfo's version.[23] This latter contradiction is solved by understanding the word *rem* to refer to translating *Hecuba*, or indeed any Greek play, in full. Both were tasks that no one had ever achieved until then, at least, according to Erasmus's knowledge at the time.[24]

---

19 Letter 1341A in Erasmus 1906, 4.
20 Letter 1341A in Erasmus 1989, 297 (trans. R.A.B. Mynors and J.M. Estes).
21 Pertusi 1963, 404: 'sembra ricordare male'.
22 On Filelfo's influence on Erasmus, see Waszink 1969, 205. By saying that he thought that Filelfo translated 'without much ... success' (*parum feliciter*), Erasmus partly contradicts his definition of Filelfo as 'such a great man' (*uir tantus*) in the prologue to *Hecuba*. Erasmus also praised Filelfo for his rendering of a passage of Theocritus (François 2015, 400 n. 38).
23 Letter 188 (trans. R.A.B. Mynors and D.F.S. Thomson) in Erasmus 1975, 109.
24 Erasmus was probably not aware that the Paduan scholar Pietro da Montagnana had produced a prose manuscript Latin version of *Hecuba* in the mid-fifteenth century; for this version

What the preface suggests is that Erasmus was prompted to translate Euripides' *Hecuba* also by the desire to compete with Filelfo and, if not specifically with him, with all those 'who have stepped into the same wrestling-ring' (*quicunque in eandem palaestram descenderit*).[25] As becomes clear in the following lines, the *palaestra* to which Erasmus refers is not just the one of translation from Greek into Latin but that of 'turning *good* Greek into *good* Latin' (*ex bonis Graecis bona Latina facere*; emphasis mine).[26] What Erasmus means by 'good' Greek and Latin becomes clear in the rest of the epistle. For Erasmus, in order to become a translator 'from good Greek to good Latin', one has to have 'the richest and the readiest vocabulary in both languages' and 'an extremely sharp and alert intelligence', and 'an extreme erudition and precision'.[27] Erasmus further insists on the difficulty of this task, which not only requires 'someone with exceptional skill' but also — like the capture of Troy, so central to the plays he translated — 'some god accompany[ing] with a favourable wind such bold enterprise'.[28] He then goes on to stress the metrical difficulty, the obscurity and the delicacy of Euripidean verse, particularly in the choruses, which are so sibylline that 'they need an Oedipus, or Delian prophet, rather than a translator'.[29]

Moreover, although not presenting it explicitly as a motive, Erasmus relishes the positive reviews on the first steps of his translation coming from prominent scholars in England.[30] The reference to England is no coincidence, since it was there that Erasmus produced his translations of Euripides and engaged in what Erika Rummel defines as his 'friendly competition' with Thomas More.[31] The two scholars undertook the project of translating Lucian's dialogues in the same years in which Erasmus was translating Euripides and their joint effort was published in Paris in 1506. For one dialogue, *Tyrannicida*, they each con-

---

of *Hecuba*, see Waszink 1969, 204–205 and Porro 1992. Porro argues that Montagnana's version is in fact a reworking of Leontius Pilatus' version (cf. n. 8 above).
25 Letter 188 (trans. R.A.B. Mynors and D.F.S. Thomson) in Erasmus 1975, 108.
26 Letter 188 (trans. R.A.B. Mynors and D.F.S. Thomson) in Erasmus 1975, 108.
27 Letter 188 (trans. R.A.B. Mynors and D.F.S. Thomson) in Erasmus 1975, 108: *sermonis utriusque copiosa parataque supellectile ditissimum, oculantissimum uigilantissimumque*.
28 Letter 188 (my translation): *singularem aliquem artificem, quis ... deus coeptis tam audacibus dexter aspiraret*.
29 Letter 188 (trans. R.A.B. Mynors and D.F.S. Thomson) in Erasmus 1975, 108: *Oedipo quopiam aut Delio sit opus magis quam interprete*; I here translate *interpres* as 'translator' and not 'commentator' as in Mynors and Thomson's version. Erasmus refers to the choruses also in the additional preface to *Iphigenia* (Letter 208; in Erasmus 1975, 133).
30 Letter 188 (trans. R.A.B. Mynors and D.F.S. Thomson) in Erasmus 1975, 108.
31 Rummel 1985, 49.

tributed a translation, thereby 'inviting the reader to act as an arbiter'.[32] Another 'friendly rivalry' was the one between More and William Lily, who both translated epigrams from the Planudean Anthology.[33] Competition within scholarly circles, however, was not always friendly. As Erasmus tells in 1535,

> de tragoediis sparserunt rumorem uanissimum, eas esse Rodolphi Agricolae (quem mecum fatentur uirum fuisse doctissimum), meque suffuratum exemplar pro meis aedidisse. Quid malitiosius?[34]

> some spread out the absolutely false rumour that the tragedies were by Rudolph Agricola — and it is a common view, which I also share, that he was an excellent scholar — and that I had stolen a copy and published it as mine. What could be more malicious? (My translation)

The rumours surrounding Erasmus's translations from Euripides suggest that translation endeavours in scholarly circles could easily lead to an 'eristic' dimension.

In his study on imitation, G.W. Pigman has identified some imitation metaphors that reveal 'an open struggle with the model for pre-eminence, a struggle in which the model must be recognized to assure the text's victory' and which 'reveal a persistent ambivalence in emulation (which may also be called eristic imitation: admiration for a model joined with envy and contentiousness'.[35] If we apply the category of 'eristic imitation' or 'emulation' to translation, it can be argued that translation itself, especially translation from the classics, equally displays an 'eristic' quality. Translation involves a competition on two levels: 'vertically', i.e., with the source author, and 'horizontally', i.e., with other translators of the same text.[36] However, since the beginning of the 15th century, translation also served as a supplement to the source text and other translations alike.[37] Translating to integrate existing translations was a learning method for students of Greek. As Paul Botley explains, there was the notion that even 'a reader with no knowledge of Greek might deepen his understanding of a Greek

---

32 Rummel 1985, 64.
33 Botley 2004, 171–172.
34 Erasmus 1947, 184.
35 Pigman 1980, 4.
36 Gianfranco Folena has proposed the idea of two levels of translation, vertical and horizontal, according to the prestige of the languages involved (Folena 1991, 13); however, I here refer to these two levels to define the relationship not between the languages but between the people involved, i.e., authors and translators.
37 Botley 2004, 170–177; Hosington 2014.

author by collating a number of translations of the original text'.[38] New translations of the same text were seen 'not as a replacement for the earlier versions, but as a commentary or a key to open up the meaning of the original text to the reader'.[39] Therefore, translation was *heuristic* as well as *eristic*. While the didactic function of supplementary translations was heuristic and hence oriented to the understanding of the source author, the comparison with other versions of the same text created the conditions for the translator to nourish eristic ambitions.

Competition had been a major motive to translate since the previous century but it is only around the middle of the 16th century that it is given a considerable attention within a theoretical treatise, i.e. *Interpretatio linguarum* by the Oxonian theologian Laurence Humphrey. A staunch Protestant, Humphrey left England for Switzerland during Mary I's reign and became Regius Professor of theology upon his return to Oxford in 1560. *Interpretatio*, one of the works he penned during his Swiss exile, is the first treatise on translation produced in England as well as 'the longest and most comprehensive' in 16th-century Europe.[40] Printed in 1559 in Basel, this treatise, which probably enjoyed greater success than has often been admitted, captures the major ideas on translation circulating on the Continent in the mid-16th century and is conceived as a manual not only on translation but also on the 'teaching and learning of languages'.[41] The second of its three 'books' or parts is devoted to imitation and its relationship to translation; this is in itself revealing of Humphrey's attention to the interplay between the two practices.

In *Interpretatio*, Humphrey devotes one book to imitation on the grounds that translation necessarily entails some kind of imitative process:

> *Tantum enim hic de imitatione dicam, quantum erit cum hoc argumento nostro, et cum Interpretis imitatione coniunctum ... interpreti aliquem ad imitandum proponi censeo oportere ... Est igitur necessaria Interpreti futuro imitatio.*[42]

> Here I will deal with imitation insofar as it relates to our subject [i.e., translation] and to the imitation done by the translator ... I think it is necessary to provide the translator with someone to imitate ... Therefore, imitation is necessary to the would-be translator. (My translation)

---

38 Botley 2004, 173. On translation as a tool to learn Greek, see also Hosington 2014.
39 Botley 2004, 173.
40 Brammall 2017, 56.
41 Merchant 2013, 92–93; Brammall 2015, 9–10 and 2017, 72–75.
42 Humphrey 1559, 212–213.

However, this passage does not specify which author a translator should imitate. Is Humphrey referring to the source author or to other translators? And if other translators, does he mean translators of the same work? Or is he referring to another author altogether, not the author of the original text but an author in the target language who serves as universal model of style such as Cicero?

Humphrey's vague statement, therefore, leaves open three possible options as models for the translator to imitate: the source author; other translators, either of the same text or of other texts; and another target language author as stylistic paradigm. He addresses all three kinds of imitations in his treatise. With reference to the first, for Humphrey translators should always imitate source authors in order to 'preserve their diversity', be they 'tragic, comic, poet, historians, sacred or profane' authors;[43] as Humphrey puts it, 'the distinctiveness of the authors has the priority' (*proprietati autorum primus locus sit*).[44] Moreover, Humphrey brands as 'inept' and 'absurd' the 'imitation of Cicero' in translation because it makes 'Plato, Aristoteles, Moses, Christ, St Paul, Homer, Aristophanes' all sound Ciceronian.[45] In assessing Joachim Périon's translation of Aristotle's *Nicomachean Ethics*, Humphrey thinks that Périon 'has beautifully emulated but he did not intend to translate' Aristotle (*pulchre aemulatus est, sed non uoluit ... transferre*) and translated 'in a way that is more Ciceronian than Aristotelian' (*Ciceroniane magis quam Aristotelice*).[46] Périon had indeed translated Aristotle by filtering it through Cicero's language in the treatise *De optimo genere interpretandi*. Humphrey, a more moderate Ciceronian than Périon, labels this operation as a 'bad imitation' (*prava imitatio*).[47]

For Humphrey, the competitive or eristic dimension of imitation, which is encapsulated in the notion of *aemulatio* or emulation, should be avoided in translation if it entails a betrayal of the source author's *proprietas*.[48] However,

---

43 Humphrey 1559, 84–85: *diuersitatem tenere ... Tragicos, Comicos, Poetas, Historicos, Sacros, Prophanos*.
44 Humphrey 1559, 87.
45 Humphrey 1559, 85: *ineptam quandam et praeposteram Ciceronis imitationem; ut Plato Aristoteles, Moses, Christus, Paulus, Homerus, Aristophanes, non aliam sonent linguam quam Ciceronianam*.
46 Humphrey 1559, 28, 229, 252.
47 Humphrey 1559, 28. However moderate, Humphrey too points at Cicero as the best model for translation into Latin prose but under specific generic circumstances is open to other models such as Livy; Humphrey 1559, 83, 233–234.
48 The relevance of emulation is one of the novelties that, according to Sheldon Brammall bely the notion that Humphrey's *Interpretatio* is only a 'cumulative and recapitulatory' work, 'an encyclopaedia of doctrine on translation', or 'one of the summarizing statements in the history

this does not mean that Humphrey excludes emulation in translation altogether. He does envisage it but, as Sheldon Brammall has noted,[49] only on one condition, i.e., only insofar as it involves previous translators:

> Aemulatio magnum calcar est et incitamentum ut recte uertamus, contendamusque cum aliis qui ante nos quippiam uerterunt, ut cum illis de palma certemus.[50]
>
> Emulation is a great spur and incitement for us to translate correctly and to compete with others who translated something before us, so that we contend for the victory with them.

This passage in isolation, however, does not clarify which translators one should emulate. The reference to 'others who translated something before us' without context could refer to any good translator, not necessarily those translating the same work one has decided to translate. This is the view held by Thomas Sébillet in *Art poétique françois* (1548), wherein he recommends some works by contemporary French translators:

> Mais puis que la version n'est rien qu'une imitation, t'y puy je mieus introduire qu'avec imitation? Imite donc Marot en sa Metamorphose, en son Musée, en sés Psalmes: Salel, en son Iliad: Héröet, en son Androgyne: Désmasures, en son Eneide: Peletier, en son Odyssée, et Géorgique.[51]
>
> Since translation is nothing but a form of imitation, how can I better introduce you to it than with imitation? Imitate then [Clément] Marot in his *Metamorphoses*, in his *Musaeus*, in his *Psalms*; [Hughes] Salel in his *Iliad*; [Antoine] Héröet in his *Androgyne*; [Louis] Des Masures in his *Aeneid*; [Jacques] Pelletier in his *Odyssey* and *Georgics*. (My translation)

However, if one considers Humphrey's suggestion in its context, it becomes clear that he envisages two kinds of emulation, one in imitation and another in translation, as illustrated by his examples. The former is the competition with the source author and is exemplified with two ancient imitators of Homer. The latter kind of emulation involves competition between translators of the same work, with three possible outcomes: defeat, draw, and victory:

---

of translation' (Brammall 2015, 11–14 and 2017, 63–69); definitions respectively by Rhodes in Rhodes, Kendal and Wilson 2013, 263; Norton 1984, 11; Steiner 1998, 277.
49 Brammall 2015, 14.
50 Humphrey 1559, 536.
51 Sébillet 1548, f. 74r.

Itaque certamen suscipiatur cum alio artifice in hoc transferendi artificio, uel praestantissimo et sciente, ut uictus discas, uel cum aequali ut par sis, uel cum deteriori etiam ut uictor triumphes.[52]

Then competition may arise with another expert in this art of translating: either with a most excellent and learned one so that, albeit defeated, you will learn; or with one with similar abilities to yours so that you are equal to him; or with one even worse than you so that you will triumph in victory.

Humphrey illustrates the first — i.e., defeat inflicted by better translators — by referring to Cicero's translation of Plato's *Timaeus*: a comparison with his version will help the would-be translator become aware of his faults and improve his skills.[53]

Competition — or, in one of its equivalent early modern terms, *aemulatio* — is a phenomenon typical of imitation but can feature also in translation, thereby testifying to the osmotic relationship between imitative and translation processes. While in imitation, competition is traditionally associated with the ambition to surpass the source author, in translation, competition is established less with the source author than with other translators of the same work. According to Humphrey, *aemulatio* in translation should never lead the translator to betray the author's distinctiveness — Périon being a negative example in this regard. Rather, it is conceived only as competition between translators of the same work and as such is turned into a methodological approach.

2 Practice: Lumley's *Iphigeneia* and Watson's *Antigone*

Erasmus's translations from Euripides were one major catalyst for competition in translating Greek tragedy from the beginning of the 16th century onwards. His translations boosted competition between translators across Europe not

---

52 Humphrey 1559, 537.
53 He then mentions Cicero's lost translation of Plato's *Protagora*, of which only few lines quoted in Priscian are now extant — on this, see Hösle 2008, 148–149 n. 14 — and compares it to the version of Marsilio Ficino. Predictably, Cicero comes out the winner, but what is crucial to Humphrey is the comparison between Ficino and the would-be translator, who, measured against a worse model than Cicero, will appear 'if not superior, at least no longer inferior'; cf. Humphrey 1559, 537: *ut si non superior, saltem non longe inferior.*

only in Latin but also in the vernacular.⁵⁴ Editions of Erasmus's versions reached the shelves of the libraries of English noble households such as the Lumleys: in the 1550s, Lady Jane Lumley (née Fitzalan), the young wife of the first Baron Lumley, produced a manuscript English version of *Iphigenia at Aulis*, entitled *The Tragedie of Euripides called Iphigeneia*, based on Erasmus's version and Euripides' original; editions of both are registered in the family's book catalogue.⁵⁵ Regarded as the first piece of English closet drama,⁵⁶ Lumley's translation may have been read or even performed before a restricted private audience, which may have included no less than Queen Elizabeth.⁵⁷

Lumley's translation goes beyond the quality of school exercise as it displays a degree of imitation of, or, as I will suggest, a collaboration with, the most illustrious pioneer in the art of translating Greek tragedy, namely Erasmus. Such imitation in the form of collaboration affects not only Lumley's lexical choices and phrasing but, as Carla Suthren has argued, also her theoretical stance to translation, imbued with Erasmian ideas.⁵⁸ This is visible in four aspects of Lumley's version: the omission of the choral odes, her penchant for *sententiae*, the presence of Christological imagery, and the choice to translate in prose. All these features find a counterpart in Erasmus's methodological statements in his preface to the whole edition of *Hecuba* and *Iphigenia* and in the additional preface to *Iphigenia* alone, two paratexts that, as Alexia Dedieu shows in her chapter in this volume, were the touchstone of translation theory for 16th-century translators of Greek drama.

In this latter preface, Erasmus states that he 'dared to depart' (*ausi dissentire*) from Euripides by reducing the metrical complexity of the choruses, adding that, should he translate another Greek tragedy, he would 'not be reluctant to alter the style and contents of the choruses' (*non uererer chororum et stilum et*

---

54 Pollard registers 57 vernacular translations of Greek tragedies in the 16th century; cf. Pollard 2017, 260–269.
55 Jayne and Johnson 1956, 205 (no. 1736), 191 (1591a); cf. Pollard 2017, 77 n. 48. Jane Lumley's manuscript is now at the British Library (MS Royal 15.A.ix).
56 Burroghs 2019, 16.
57 Pollard 2017, 54–56. As Pollard underlines by quoting Findlay and Hogdson-Wright, a reading in a context of closet drama is not at odds with a performance in the early modern imagination (Pollard 2017, 78 n. 60; Hogdson-Wright 2000, 2–3). If indeed present, the Queen must have been particularly pleased by the performance of a Euripidean play since it seems that she was herself a translator from Euripides. A secretary of state under James I reports that Elizabeth translated a play from Euripides 'for her own amusement' (Pollard 2017, 40 n. 121; see also Suthren 2020, 75).
58 Suthren 2020, 86–91.

argumenta commutare) since for him choruses 'destroy clarity of expression' (*uitiauit eloquentiam*).⁵⁹ Accordingly, Lumley considerably cuts the original play, eliminating the choral odes altogether but preserving the chorus present onstage and using them to convey gnomic sentences.⁶⁰ Also, Lumley's manuscript has been defined as 'a commonplace book' because of the presence of Latin *sententiae*.⁶¹ In his *Iphigenia* dedication, Erasmus expresses the preference to 'treat of some commonplace' (*locurum quempiam tractare communem*) rather than wasting time rendering the choruses.⁶² Moreover, Erasmus displayed this interest in *sententiae* in his huge collection of *Adages*.

The play also contains Christian references and, if written around 1557 as some scholars have argued, also a possible topical allusion to the Protestant martyr Lady Jane Grey, who was executed on the charge of treason in 1554; if present, this allusion would have been embarrassing for Lumley's father, Henry Fitzalan, twelfth Earl of Arundel, who was a prominent actor in the events that led to the proclamation of Mary I and the execution of Lady Jane.⁶³ At a lexical level, scholars have interpreted Lumley's translation of ἔλαφος ('hind', Eur. *IA*. 1587) with 'a white hart' as an allusion to Christological symbolism.⁶⁴ The transition from the feminine to the masculine may be imputed to a mistake induced by the double gender of the Greek word, meaning either 'stag' or 'hind'; however, the Greek-Latin dictionary she may have used, the one recorded in the 1609 catalogue of the Lumley library, correctly reports the noun's double gender.⁶⁵ In any case, it is the addition of the adjective 'white' that decisively sub-

---

59 Letter 208 (trans. R.A.B. Mynors and D.F.S. Thomson).
60 Suthren 2020, 88.
61 Wynne-Davies 2008, 119. Suthren has suggested that the annotations of the previous owner of his Greek version, John Toker, also played a role: Toker added commonplace marks and inserted portion of Erasmus's translation; cf. Suthren 2020, 82–83.
62 Letter 208 (trans. R.A.B. Mynors and D.F.S. Thomson) in Erasmus 1975, 135.
63 Scholars do not seem to have reached a consensus on the date of composition of Lumley's translation. Pollard has proposed 'around 1557' (Pollard 2017, 49), whereas Miola dates it back to '*ca* 1553' (Miola 2020, 293). Purkiss equally believes that the play was probably written 'no later than 1553' because a possible connection with the execution of Lady Jane Grey would have been 'uncomfortable' for Lumley's father (Purkiss 1998, xxv). Lumley's father had a very duplicitous conduct between the death of Edward VI and the ascension of Mary I: he pretended to support the Duke of Northumberland's plan to make Lady Jane Grey the new queen but he actually acted in favour of Mary's claim behind the scenes; see also Suthren 2020, 83 and Hodgson-Wright 1998, 133.
64 The English translation is from Euripides 1958; Lumley 1998, 34, line 942; on Christological symbolism, see Purkiss 1999, xxxi.
65 Crastoni 1524, f. 48r; cf. Jayne and Johnson 1956, 202 (no. 1710).

stantiates the reference to Christ, establishing a connection with the more openly Christological symbol of the lamb.[66] Considering that Erasmus translates ἔλαφος as *cerua*, respecting the gender in the original,[67] Lumley surpasses him in filtering the Greek play through religious concerns, which, as we have seen, was always the priority for the Dutch scholar.

Finally, as suggested by Suthren, Lumley's decision to translate in prose could be equally read as a response to Erasmus's methodological statements.[68] In his preface to *Hecuba* and *Iphigenia*, Erasmus insists on the purity (*plusculum candor*), conciseness (*pressam sanitatem, presso*) and flowing quality (*fusior … dictio*) of Euripides' style.[69] Alongside cutting choral odes, Lumley opts for prose instead of verse, thereby going beyond Erasmus's notion of fluidity and pushing it to its extreme by renouncing any metrical constriction.[70]

These points of contact with Erasmus did not prevent Lumley from looking at the original, especially in syntactical terms.[71] While this may signal Lumley's intention to compete with Erasmus, she could not possibly challenge him in the way Erasmus could do with Filelfo, both illustrious members of the *respublica litteraria*: as a woman, Lumley could not compete with Erasmus on equal terms. However, as a noblewoman, she was raised according to the educational principles that Erasmus himself had established forty years before and which were condensed in pedagogical manuals such as Roger Ascham's *Schoolemaster* and Humphrey's treatise. In these manuals translation and imitation were conceived as steps to a good writing proficiency and as analytical and interpretive instruments to read texts. Translation and imitation were thus hermeneutical processes instrumental to both reading and writing, establishing 'a unity of the critical and creative acts'.[72] A reason for Lumley to translate *Iphigenia at Aulis*

---

66 Diane Purkiss connects this image to 'the white hart or unicorn as beast of the chase', which were 'figure for Christ'; Purkiss 1998, xxxi. However, the lamb was much clearer a symbol for Christ than the stag or hart, which was rather linked with 'piety and religious aspiration' due to Psalm 41 in the *Vulgate* (*Quemadmodum desiderat ceruus ad fontes aquarum, ita desiderat anima mea ad te, Deus*); cf. Ferguson 1961, 20–21, 25. The lamb as a symbol for Christ recurs in the New Testament, more frequently in the *Book of Revelation*.
67 Erasmus 1969b, 357 (line 2288).
68 Suthren 2020, 90.
69 Letter 209.
70 At the time, blank verse was not a dramatic form yet; the first play partly adopting blank verse, *Gorboduc*, was staged in 1561. Before that, English playwrights usually adopted rhyming schemes (see for instance, the metrical variety in interludes; Hardison 1989, 154). In this context, Lumley's choice of prose looks even more peculiar.
71 Suthren 2020, 85.
72 Greene 1982, 267.

may, therefore, have been a twofold desire to improve her proficiency in Greek and to increase her understanding of the Euripidean play, which she could read in Erasmus's Latin. In line with contemporary pedagogical approaches, her version can thus be seen as a sort of supplement to Erasmus's translation. Lumley's imitation of Erasmus was thus not so much competitive as collaborative.[73] In Lumley, the heuristic and hermeneutical dimensions of translation prevail over the eristic.

At an interlingual level, a translator's imitation of another translator was rare;[74] competition in translating Greek tragedy was more likely to originate in an intralingual (Latin) context, as illustrated by Thomas Watson's *Sophoclis Antigone*. By the time Watson published his translation in 1581, there were already eight Latin translations of the play circulating in Europe.[75] Watson makes no reference to these previous translators, except for Thomas Naogeorgus,[76] whose name is mentioned in a marginal note but only to acknowledge the debt to his annotations. The paratexts that accompany Watson's version also omit any reference to other translators but rather present Watson's translation as an extraordinary endeavour. In the dedicatory epistle, Watson defines his own work as 'a thing of great moment, greater than my powers had not Pallas industriously come to my aid' (*momenti res magna, meis quoque viribus impar, / ni daret ipsa mihi sedula Pallas opem*).[77] One laudatory poem vaguely defines Watson as 'the first expert in this art'.[78] Dana Sutton has glossed this definition as meaning 'the first Englishman to translate a Sophoclean tragedy, at least for publication'.[79] Indeed, Watson may well have been the first Englishman to publish a Latin translation of Sophocles but he was certainly not the first to write one. In around 1543 Ascham translated *Philoctetes* into Latin, a translation now lost, and authored what are probably the first extant translations from Sophocles

---

73 On reception as collaboration, see Pollard, 2017, 20.
74 Another example is the French translation of *Iphigenia at Aulis* by Sébillet, which also looks at Erasmus's translation; cf. Waszink 1969, 208–209.
75 Hervet 1541; Gabia 1543; Melanchton 1546; Rataller 1558; Rataller 1570; Lalemant 1557; Naogeorgus 1558; Estienne 1567.
76 On Naogeorgus and translation of Greek tragedy, see Baier in this volume.
77 Watson 1581, sig. A5v.
78 John Cooke in Watson 1581, sig. B1r: τέχνης πρῶτον τοίησδε διδακτήν (the noun διδάκτης does not exist; author might have invented it on the basis of first-declension masculine nouns such as πολίτης).
79 Sutton in Watson 1996, 119.

into English: in his *Toxophilus* (1545) he translates lines from *Ajax*, *Antigone*, and *Philoctetes*.[80]

Nevertheless, Sophocles still remained an unexplored territory for Englishmen and Watson may have wanted to fill this gap but he may have been equally motivated by the desire to compete with continental scholars. Although competition remains unvoiced in the paratextual material, what reveals Watson's attention to previous continental translations is a close comparative reading. In the very first lines on the play (Soph. *Ant.* 1–3, 11–14), Watson evidently borrows from Naogeorgus:

Watson

> *Praefatur autem Antigone.*
> Antigone:
> *O Stirpe eadem Ismena germanum caput,*
> *Superatne nunc ex Oedipi quicquam malis,*
> *Quod non adhuc effudit in nos Iuppiter*
> ?
> [...]
> Ismene:
> *Sermo de amicis nullus Antigone mihi*
> *Nec laetus accessit, nec ingratus, duae*
> *Ex quo sumus duobus orbae fratribus*
> *Una die manu peremptis mutua.*[81]

So Antigone speaks first
Antigone:
Oh Ismene, sisterly head from the same progeny, is there now any remaining evil from those coming from Oedipus which Jupiter has not thrown on us so far?
[...]
Ismene:
No word about our friends has come to me, Antigone, neither pleasant nor disagreeable, since we are both deprived of our two brothers who died on one day each at the other's hand.

Naogeorgus

> *Praefatur autem Antigone.*
> Antigone:
> *Chara soror Ismene, atque germanum caput,*

---

80 Smith 1988, 201; Ascham 1865, 29, 56, 58–59, 92.
81 Watson 1581, 17.

> *Num scis malorum quippiam emergentium*
> *Ab Oedipode, nobis adhuc uiuent[ibus]*
> *Quod Iuppiter non faciat?*
> Ismene:
> *Mihi Antigone quidem*
> *Nullus de amicis sermo nec iucundior*
> *Nec tristior uenit, duobus fratribus*
> *Ex quo duae nos pariter orbatae sumus,*
> *Manibus peremptis mutuis una die.*[82]

> So Antigone speaks first
> Antigone:
> Dear sister Ismene and sisterly head, do you know an evil deriving from Oedipus which Jupiter has not accomplished against us who are still living?
> [...]
> Ismene:
> No word has come to me, Antigone, truly, neither
> more joyful nor more sorrowful, since the moment
> we were both deprived of our two brothers who died each at the other's hand.

The first speaker, Antigone, is introduced with the same formula which, albeit quite conventional, does not appear in most of the other translations.[83] Many phrases are modelled on Naogeorgus: *germanum caput*;[84] *Sermo de amicis nullus*; *ex quo sumus ... orbae*; *Una die manu peremptis mutua*. Also, Watson replicates many of Naogeorgus's marginal notes and commonplace marks.[85]

However, we should not overestimate Naogeorgus's influence. There are two reasons for not doing so: because Watson's version features verbal parallels with other Latin translations or with the original, and because it displays autonomous stylistic qualities. Watson probably used multiple pre-existing Latin translations simultaneously. Alongside Naogeorgus's, he may well have consulted one of George Rataller's versions.[86] Franciscus Portus' 1567 literal version may be behind the phrase *calamitatis capax* as well as the sequence of nega-

---

[82] Naogeorgus 1558, 204.
[83] Except for Melanchthon and Winsheim, who opt for *praeloquitur Antigone* instead; Melanchton 1546, sig. O3r.
[84] The phrase appears also in two other translations: Gabia 1543, 82; Melanchton 1546, sig. O3ʳ.
[85] Naogeorgus 1558, 211, 217–219; Watson 1581, 22, 26–27.
[86] The verb *effudit* could be based on Rataller's *effuderit*, *conspexi* on *conspicata sim*; Rataller 1558, 92.

tions (Estienne 1567, 739).[87] However, the negations could be based also on the original, which Watson may have read alongside Portus' translation in Estienne's edition:

οὐδὲν γὰρ οὔτ' ἀλγεινὸν οὔτ' ἄτης ἄτερ
οὔτ' αἰσχρὸν οὔτ' ἄτιμόν ἐσθ', ὁποῖον οὐ
τῶν σῶν τε κἀμῶν οὐκ ὄπωπ' ἐγὼ κακῶν
(Soph. Ant. 4–6; Estienne 1567, 738)[88]

No, there is nothing painful or laden with destruction or shameful or dishonouring among your sorrows and mine that I have not witnessed.

Other clues indicate that Watson possibly looked at the original Greek, particularly in syntactical terms. In the second episode, Antigone attributes the silent dissent of the Thebans against Creon to fear, which 'shuts their mouths' (εἰ μὴ γλῶσσαν ἐγκλῄοι φόβος, 'if it were not that fear shuts their mouths'; Soph. Ant. 505; Estienne 1567, 781). Watson reproduces the Greek syntax more faithfully than Naogeorgus, who breaks the clause with an enjambement:

Si non tacitus astringeret linguam metus.
(Watson 1581, 30)

If the silent fear did not bind their tongues.

Ni metus
Linguam coerceat.
(Naogeorgus 1558, 223–224)

If fear did not restrain their tongue.

By means of a hypallage, Watson attributes the silence to fear rather than to the tongue, thus graphically enclosing the word *linguam* between the verb and the noun. At the beginning of the fifth stasimon (Soph. Ant. 1115–1117), Watson perfectly replicates the word order of the original, unlike Naogeorgus:

---

87 In Estienne 1567, *Antigone* is attributed to 'F.P.'; behind the initials, scholars have identified the Cretan scholar Franciscus Portus (Weinberg 1971, 198).
88 The textual variants from modern editions are here irrelevant. All the abbreviations Soph. Ant. refer to Sophocles 1994. All translations from the Greek are by Hugh Lloyd-Jones except in the passages in which the Stephanus and the Loeb editions differ.

Celeberrime, Cadmeiae
nymphae decus summum, Iouis-
que grauisoni genus
                          (Watson 1581, 47)

Nominibus inclyte plurimis
Bacche, atque Cadmae decus
puellae, et altisoni Iouis
                          (Naogeorgus 1558, 247)

Πολυώνυμε Καδμείας
νύμφας ἄγαλμα καὶ Διὸς βαρυβρεμέτα γένος
                          (Estienne 1567, 833)[89]

You who have many names, pride of the Cadmean bride and child of Zeus the loud-thunderer.

Examples of this kind could be multiplied and show that Watson's translation is overall scholarly and closer to the original than his main translation model, Naogeorgus.

Watson's evident engagement with the original could be interpreted as an attempt to challenge previous versions in this regard. This can equally be appreciated in Watson's attention to the metrical aspects of his translation, particularly in the choruses, which are preceded by the headings indicating the metrical scheme, usually a mixture of lyrical patterns (Watson 1581, 26; 19; 33; 38; 42; 47; 51). The presence of these headings shows how important it was for Watson that choruses had recognizable metrical patterns, which is already significant considering that Alessandro Pazzi de' Medici in his translations from Sophocles and Gentien Hervet in his version of Sophocles' *Antigone* renounced adopting a metrical scheme.[90] To translate Sophocles' choruses was therefore a particularly difficult task as well as a decisive proving ground. What is even more significant is Watson's explicit claim that he applied the same metres used by Sophocles in the parodos and the first stasimon: *carmen choricum ex uariis metri generibus ac eisdem, quibus utitur Sophocles*; *carmen choricum uarie mixtum, et eiusdem generis cum Graeco* (Watson 1581, 19, 26). Erasmus had claimed

---

89 Here the colometry and the order of the words in Manuzio 1502 differs from the one of modern editions.
90 Borza 2013, 65–68; Hervet explicitly declares he had renounced adopting a metrical scheme; cf. Hervet 1541, sig. A2v: *Huius tamen lectores admonitos uolo, me in choris uertendis nullam penitus carminis rationem habuisse*; 'However, I want to warn my readers that I did not adopt any metrical scheme whatsoever in rendering the choruses'.

something similar in the letter to the reader in his *Hecuba* with reference to Polymnestor's monody: *ex uariis metrorum constat generibus, ac ferme iisdem quibus usus est Euripides* (Erasmus 1969c, 220).

They were probably few those who after him claimed this direct affiliation to the model.[91] Hence, Watson's use of the heading quoted above — in which he significantly drops Erasmus's mitigating adverb *ferme* — signals his intention to reach, if not to challenge, Erasmus's translations of the choruses.[92] However, in his translation of *Iphigenia at Aulis*, Erasmus himself soon abandoned the intention to reproduce the original's metre and changed technique.[93] Except for the parodos, he started conforming to Seneca's treatment of the choruses; this latter solution is the one which would be adopted by other distinguished scholars such as George Buchanan and Hugo Grotius tackling Greek tragedies.[94] In the choral odes, Watson overall attempts to reproduce — and often successfully reproduces — the metrical variety of the original, thereby recuperating the challenging approach that Erasmus adopted in his *Hecuba* and later abandoned in *Iphigenia at Aulis*.[95] In so doing, he distances himself from Naogeorgus, who instead aligned himself with Erasmus's later approach and thus adopted regular sequences of iambic and anapaestic dimeters in the choruses.

Alongside a greater faithfulness to the original in some passages and in the metre of the choral odes, there are two other features that potentially point to Watson's competition with Naogeorgus. First, Watson inserts mythological references that are absent both in the original and in Naogeorgus's version, mostly using names from Roman rather than Greek mythology. On many occasions, gods are turned into the Roman Penates, thereby domesticating his translation according to the target language (Watson 1581, 22, 39, 42). Similarly, in the parodos, the chorus invokes 'the beam of Phoebus' (*Phoebi o radie*, Watson 1581, 19), whereas Naogeorgus retains the imagery of the original without clarifying the mythological reference, having *o radius solis* (Sophocles, 1558, 208; ἀκτὶς ἀελίου, Soph. *Ant.* 100; cf. Estienne 1567, 746). Moreover, πυρός (from πῦρ, 'fire', Soph. *Ant.* 475; Estienne 1567, 778) becomes *uolcano* in Watson (Wat-

---

[91] Another instance before Watson is in the fifth stasimon of George Rataller's *Antigone*, in which he writes *uarie mixtus, eodem pene carm[ina] genere, quo est usus Sophocles*; Rataller 1558, 140; Rataller 1570, 110.
[92] On a similar attempt to surpass Erasmus in metre, see the example of Jean Lalemant, as discussed by Alexia Dedieu in her chapter.
[93] Waszink 1969, 202–203.
[94] Waszink 1969, 202–203, and Erasmus 1969b, 272, footnote to line 9, 280, footnote to line 197.
[95] A detailed analysis of Watson's metrical choices in the choral odes is beyond the scope of this chapter; on metre in Watson's choruses, see Vedelago 2021.

son 1581, 30), remaining *igne* in Naogeorgus (Sophocles, 1558, 222). In the fourth episode, in Antigone's *kommos*, Watson glosses the mythological allusion to Niobe (Watson 1581, 39), unmentioned in the original (Soph. *Ant*. 824–825), thus incorporating the name which Naogeorgus indicates in the marginal note (Naogeorgus 1558, 216).

Second, Watson displays a tendency to *enargeia* or *euidentia* (vividness).[96] Erasmus defines it as the 'description of things, of time circumstances, of places, and of people', in which the object is 'expressed in colours, as if it were meant to be contemplated in a painting, so much so that it seems that we [the authors] are painting, not narrating, and that the reader is contemplating, not reading'.[97] Watson often adds realistic details aiming at *enargeia* in his translation, for example, in the guard's account of how he caught Antigone burying her brother. While denouncing Antigone to Creon, the guard claims to have seen her *his orbibus* ('with these eyes', Watson 1581, 28), whereas the Greek original only has ἰδόν (literally 'seeing', Soph. *Ant*. 405)[98] and Naogeorgus *uidi* (Naogeorgus 1558, 220).[99] The woods that are tormented by the storm become sonorous in Watson's translation: *sylvae sonantis* ('resounding woods', Watson 1581, 28), whereas in the original they are said to 'cover the ground' (ὕλης πεδιάδος, Soph. *Ant*. 420)[100] and in Naogeorgus are defined 'trees of the plain' (*campestrium arborum*, Naogeorgus 1558, 220). Creon refers to Haemon as 'a man whose cheeks have not been adorned by a beard yet' (*Ab homine, cui uix barba decorauit genas*, Watson 1581, 37), while the Greek text only has ἀνδρὸς τηλικοῦδε ('a man of your age', Soph. *Ant*. 727); Naogeorgus renders *a tantulae aetatis ... uiro* ('by a man of so young an age', Naogeorgus 1558, 232). Antigone's hand casting the dust on her brother's corpse becomes *tenella* ('soft', Watson 1581, 28), whereas Naogeorgus only has *manibus* (Naogeorgus 1558, 221). By means of subtle *euidentia* effects such as these, Watson enlivens what overall remains a version close to the original and thereby strikes a balance between a literary and literal translation.

By focusing on translations of Greek tragedies — texts that by virtue of their difficulty represented an alluring but challenging task for scholars — this chap-

---

96 Mack 2011, 332. For a full discussion on *enargeia*, see Plett 2012.
97 Erasmus 1988, 202: [D]*escriptione rerum, temporum, locorum, personarum*; [rem] *coloribus expressam in tabula spectandam ..., ut nos depinxisse, non narrasse, lector spectasse, non legisse, uideatur*.
98 Estienne 1567, 773.
99 The Loeb edition has the participle in the masculine rather than the neuter form, thus correctly attributing it to the speaker: ἰδών.
100 Estienne 1567, 773.

ter has explored the imitative relationships between translators of the same text in order to establish whether they resulted in a form of competition, an aspect discussed by 16th-century translation theorists such as Erasmus and Humphrey. By further limiting the scope to English translators, I have looked at Lumley's *Iphigenia* and Watson's *Antigone* as case studies for measuring the outreach of Continental translation theories and versions of Greek tragedy in England.

Both Lumley and Watson imitate previous translators of the same text: albeit in different ways, Lumley imitated Erasmus, Watson imitated Naogeorgus and others. In this regard, then, theory and practice coincide, as previous translators are involved; in the case of Lumley, the correspondence is even more marked, as she follows Erasmus both as a translator of Euripides and as a theorist on translation. However, as a woman without the stature of an established scholar, Lumley could not aspire and had probably no ambition[101] to enter the public *palaestra* of the *respublica litteraria*. By applying Erasmus's ideas on translation, Lumley engages less in a competition than in a collaboration with the scholar. Also, as a manuscript by a young noblewoman, her effort rather aligns with the contemporary notion of '[t]ranslation as a learning tool',[102] which enabled the translator to improve his/her linguistic proficiency and his/her hermeneutical skills. By contrast, Watson, an erudite budding poet, silently challenges previous translators such as Naogeorgus by translating more closely to the original, by imitating multiple previous translations simultaneously, and by adopting other stylistic strategies such as *euidentia* effects; in reproducing the original metres, he dares challenge even Erasmus.

This analysis has addressed the issue of imitation in 16th-century translation of Greek tragedy and has shed light on two of its features: the dialogue between theory and practice, even far from the Continent, and the different forms that imitation of previous translators can take. The case studies of Lumley and Watson respectively exemplify two forms: imitation as collaboration with a hermeneutical function; imitation as competition with an eristic dimension.

---

101 Diane Purkiss has argued that Lumley's translation was a display of her excellent classical education, which confirmed her suitability as a member of the nobility and brought prestige to their household as a whole (Purkiss 1998, xv).
102 Hosington 2014.

Thomas Baier
Why Translate Greek Tragedy? Melanchthon, Winsheim, Camerarius, and Naogeorgus

Abstract: In 1534, Philipp Melanchthon was ill-tempered: he was professor in Wittenberg, but badly wanted to leave 'barbarian' Saxony for England. Unfortunately, he had to wait for permission from his sovereign, Kurfürst Johann Friedrich von Sachsen. In this situation, he found solace in reading Sophocles with Camerarius's newly published commentary. In a letter to Camerarius, he combined Sophocles' *Antigone* with dangerous remarks on the political situation of his times. Here, the Greek language and Greek tragedy in particular turned out to be a means to communicate 'under cover'. Why translate Greek tragedy at all? Translations were obviously designed *ad usum Delphini* and used for the purpose of education. One of the first translators of Sophocles in Germany was Veit Winsheim, a student of Melanchthon's. He prefaced his translations with interpretative essays written by his teacher. Camerarius had Winsheim's translation in mind when he wrote about how to teach Greek and when he produced his famous edition of Sophocles with a commentary in 1534. The present chapter will examine the role of translations in 16th-century Germany.

1 Melanchthon and Winsheim

In October 1534 Melanchthon wrote a morose letter to his friend Joachim Camerarius.[1] In that year, he was a professor in Wittenberg, but badly wished to leave 'barbarian' Saxonia. He had just been made an offer by Herzog Ulrich von Württemberg to become a professor at Tübingen University. Unfortunately, he had to wait for permission by his sovereign, Kurfürst Johann Friedrich von Sachsen. In this situation he found solace in reading Sophocles with Camerarius's newly edited commentary. Melanchthon, of course, read Sophocles in the original Greek. This commentary, which Melanchthon had welcomed so enthusiastically, is the first attempt of a scientific approach to Greek tragedy.

This was during a time when early modern scholars in Germany were becoming interested in Greek and when knowledge of this ancient language was

---

[1] MBW 1505 (= *Corpus Reformatorum* 2, 791–793 Nr. 1222).

https://doi.org/10.1515/9783110719185-007

slowly but steadily being increased.² The Reformation of the church had roused interest in the original wording of the New Testament and, in the same course, paved the way for the study of classical Greek texts. The beginning of the 16th century marks a turning point in the reception of Greek tragedy, even a rediscovery thereof. But strangely enough, translations were not what people desired most. On the contrary, Melanchthon saw himself as an advocate of reading the original. In 1549 he published a fervent plea for studying Greek, the *Oratio de studiis linguae Graecae a Vito Winshemio dicta*.³ It was a university lecture held at Wittenberg and read out by his pupil Veit Winsheim.

The speech was written in the wake of the Schmalkaldic War (1546–1547) and its devastating consequences. From his early youth, Melanchthon was what one would today call a pacifist. As a seven-year-old boy, he must have been deeply upset when his father was injured during the siege of his home town Bretten.⁴ In the *oratio*, he praises the study of Greek as a remedy against the hardship and toils of war. He adopts the attitude of an intellectual who retires from the world and takes refuge in his books. In the opening of the speech, he refers implicitly to the Schmalkaldic War⁵ and sees the devil at work bringing destruction to the church and to the schools. According to Melanchthon, it is a sign of the times that nothing is firm, nothing stable. In this situation of uncertainty, he finds footing and support in his studies.⁶ In this speech, he even goes as far as to presume that the Fathers of the Church and the prophets were sent by God to bring not only the gospel of peace, but also science and literature. The Greek language was chosen as the only vessel worthy of containing and transporting this precious knowledge: *Voluit Deus hanc linguam eius doctrinae potissimum nuntiam et ministram esse*.⁷ From the fact that God had the New Testament written in Greek, Melanchthon concludes that the pagan literature which

---

2 Nevertheless, Greek was still seen as an obstacle during the 16th century, cp. Daskarolis 2000, 128f.
3 Melanchthon 1570, 317–333 = Nürnberger 1961, 135–148.
4 Scheible, 1993, 222.
5 Nürnberger 1961, 135, n.
6 Nürnberger 1961, 136: *Si uero ullum umquam tempus fuit, quo apparuit, quam nihil firmi sit in rebus humanis, nihil stabile, haec, opinor, tempora nos id satis manifeste docuerunt. Ad hunc igitur portum salutis dirigamus animos atque oculos nostros, ut sanam puramque doctrinam verae pietatis nunc magis quam umquam antea ac pertinacius amplectemur et studiis nostris, quae ad gloriam Dei, ad eiusdem doctrinae sacrae propagationem pertinent, summa cura ac diligentia incumbamus atque in his temporum procellis auxilium et liberationem ab aeterno ac clementissimo Deo, patre domini nostri Iesu Christi, et petamus et exspectemus.*
7 Nürnberger 1961, 139.

was transmitted in the same language had the same dignity and was equally worth reading. While Lorenzo Valla saw the Latin language as a *sacramentum*,[8] Melanchthon does so with the Greek language. He even goes so far as to criticize parents who let their children learn vernacular languages for commercial or financial motives. This is, in his eyes, a waste of time and even dangerous.[9] What is so dangerous about 'barbarian' languages? Language forms a person's character and influences their way of thinking. Therefore, barbarian languages might harm one's moral health.

It is obvious that a man like Melanchthon would not readily support any sort of translation from Greek. He even starts a violent attack against translations:

> As far as translations are concerned, we have seen how miserable they make those who have to rely on them. Besides the fact that a faithful translation can never be done, that it is impossible to translate the content into another language with the same aptitude and clarity, there are many other shortcomings. Often the subject becomes obscure or unrecognisable (*in aliam quasi speciem*) or is being perverted and made unintelligible, so that the result of the translation is rather a metamorphosis than a version of the same text.[10]

According to Melanchthon, it was God's will that the Gospel be written in Greek, and it was also his will that all the treasures of knowledge and all the wisdom of philosophy be transmitted in that very language. So, it would be most desirable for all human beings to learn Greek. He also deems it indispensable for those who deal with literature and science.

So why translations at all? As we know, Melanchthon possessed the first complete translation of Sophocles written on German soil. The author was his own pupil Veit Winsheim. Vuinshemius, as he called himself, was born as Veit Oertel in 1501 in the Franconian town Windsheim. In 1528 he became master in philosophy, in 1550 doctor in medicine. His *peregrinatio academica* had led him from Deventer to Vienna and Ofen (Buda), and, finally, in 1523, he joined Me-

---

8 Valla 1526, 3: *Magnum [...] Latini nomen sacramentum est, magnum profecto numen.*
9 Nürnberger 1961, 140: *immo uero si turpis lucri spe saepe non una barbarica lingua cum ingenti temporis iactura nec sine vitae periculo discitur.*
10 Nürnberger 1961, 140: *Nam quod ad uersiones attinet, uidemus, quanta miseria sit, si quis illis solis niti cogatur. Nam praeterquam quod vix fieri potest, ut sententia ubique eadem felicitate ac perspicuitate in alienam linguam transfundatur, multa etiam alia incommoda interpretationes sequuntur, fitque saepe ut uel inter reddendum natiuus sensus obscuretur, vel in aliam quasi speciem transformetur, atque ita peruertatur, ut uix eundem agnoscere possis, et non raro usu uenit ut uerius metamorphosin, quam interpretationem talem uersionem dicere possis.* (Translations my own unless noted otherwise)

lanchthon in Wittenberg. The famous scholar was only four years his senior but had great influence on him. Conversely, Melanchthon thought very highly of his pupil and occasionally transferred his own teaching load upon him when necessary.

Winsheim's translation, *Interpretatio tragoediarum Sophoclis, ad utitilitatem iuuentutis, quae studiosa est Graecae linguae, edita a Vito Winsheimio* (1546),[11] declares already in the title that it was written for the 'benefit of young people', that it had merely didactic purposes. In his dedicatory letter to prince Edward, the later king Edward the VI, Winsheim presents the prince with his translation as a means to provide a moral education. He particularly emphasizes the connection between guilt and punishment that can be learned from tragedy.[12] Even the church, he says, has the habit of proposing examples of divine revenge in order to deter the faithful from malfeasance.[13] Winsheim draws analogies between the Old Testament and Greek mythology. He sees both as moral historiography, written in order to teach the youth modesty.[14] At the same time, he advertises for his own scholarly profession, i.e., he insists on the necessity of having professors for Latin and Greek and of paying for their salaries.

The second aspect Winsheim puts forward is the stylistic quality of tragedy. Reading Sophocles and Euripides is advisable *eloquentiae causa*. As proof he quotes Horace's famous lines from the *Ars poetica*: *Vos exemplaria Graeca nocturna versate manu, versate diurna* ('Read the Greek models by night and by day', AP 268f.). And he adds from the same work: *Grais dedit ore rotundo Musa loqui* ('the Muse turned the Greeks into well-rounded speakers', AP 323f.).[15] It goes without saying that Winsheim connects both quotations from the *Ars poetica* to the Greek text of Sophocles. But in his letter to the English prince, he sees his translation as a suitable tool to convey the *eloquentia* of the original as well as the *lumina uerborum et sententiarum*.[16] This is rather surprising, because Winsheim's translation hardly lets the elegance of the original shine through. Obviously, he understands *eloquentia* and *lumina* to refer to content, not to style.

---

11 On the structure and content of the volume cp. Schultheiß on Winsheim 1546.
12 Winsheim 1546, A4r.
13 Winsheim 1546, A5r: *Recitantur ergo in Ecclesia inde usque ab initio tristissimae tragoediae, furores et poena*.
14 Winsheim 1546, A5v: *Ad hunc usum cum scriptas esse tragoedias non dubium sit, [...] ut (iuuentus) consideratione humanarum miseriarum ad modestiam flectatur*.
15 Winsheim 1546, A6v.
16 Winsheim 1546, A7r.

After the dedicatory letter Winsheim prints the introduction, *De autoribus tragoediae*,[17] from Camerarius's 1534 edition of Sophocles. Here, Camerarius serves as a witness for the specific qualities of Sophoclean tragedy, namely the *vis orationum*, the rhetorical vigour.[18] Oddly enough, Winsheim does not even try to transfer the *vis oratoria* into his Latin version. On the contrary, he produces a *uerbum de uerbo* translation with no stylistic aspiration, whatsoever. A small sample of four verses might illustrate Winsheim's method. At the beginning of Sophocles' *Ajax*, Odysseus answers to Athena observing him:

Ὦ φθέγμ' Ἀθάνας, φιλτάτης ἐμοὶ θεῶν,
ὡς εὐμαθές σου, κἂν ἄποπτος ᾖς, ὅμως
φώνημ' ἀκούω καὶ ξυναρπάζω φρενί,
χαλκοστόμου κώδωνος ὡς τυρσηνικῆς.
(Soph. *Ai.* 14–17)

O uox Minervae, charissmae mihi ex Diis
Quam facile perceptibilis: tuam, etsi inconspicua eras, attamen
Vocem exaudio, et adpraehendo mente
Tanquam sonum tubae Thyrrenicae.[19]

The first and the third line keep the word order of the Greek original. In the second line εὐμαθές is rendered by *perceptibilis* which is not a classical word. It occurs in St. Augustine and the Church Fathers. The compound word χαλκόστομος is not translated at all but paraphrased by *tubae Thyrrenicae*, which in turn has to be explained in a marginal commentary.

It is obvious that a brilliant classicist like Winsheim did not pretend that his translation could in any way render the stylistic qualities of the original. He must have conceived it as a help for his pupils and as a substitute for those who did not know Greek. The reader who had worked himself through the *littera nuncupatoria* must have been disappointed — unless he had the Greek text lying next to him. No doubt, Winsheim's Latin version and his rare but useful marginal comments make it easier to understand Sophocles. We can therefore conclude that Winsheim's translation was written *ad usum Delphini*, for educational purposes. It was certainly not written for the stage — and maybe not even to be read without the Greek text.

Unfortunately, we do not know what Melanchthon thought about his pupil's translation. It is beyond question that Melanchthon knew about Wins-

---

17 Winsheim 1546 A8r-B1r = OC 0139.
18 Winsheim 1546, B1r.
19 Winsheim 1546, B3r.

heim's work and, indeed, influenced it. In 1545, one year before Winsheim's translation was published, Melanchthon had written a preface to Camerarius's edition of Terence's comedies.[20] In this *cohortatio ad legendas tragoedias et comoedias*[21] he enumerates the same educational motives which Camerarius and Winsheim had already praised:

> These events [scil. in Greek tragedies] impressed upon men *the causes of human misfortunes*, which they saw in these examples being brought about and exacerbated by *depraved passions*. And, just as Pindar [P. 2.40ff.] said that Ixion, tangled on the wheel among the dead souls below, cried out the following words repeated by Vergil, 'Be forewarned! Learn Justice and not to scorn the Gods!' [*discite iustitiam moniti, Aen.* 6.620]: Thus, *in all the tragedies, this is the main subject. This is the thought they wish to impress upon the hearts of every man: that there is some eternal mind that always inflicts severe punishments upon atrocious crimes*, while bestowing mostly a more tranquil path for the moderate and just. And although now and again accidental misfortunes can fall upon men – for there are many mysterious causes – still, *that fundamental, unmistakable principle cannot be dispelled*: clearly *the Erinyes and cruel misfortunes are always the companions of heinous misdeeds*. This thought persuaded many to temper their actions and ought to move us even more since we know that it was often delivered to the Church by the clear voice of God.[22]

Just like Melanchthon's *cohortatio*, Winsheim's *epistula nuncupatoria* to Prince Edward also contains the example of Ixion next to the Vergil quote.[23] The close similarities between Melanchthon's preface to the edition of Terence and his pupil's letter to Prince Edward arouse the suspicion that Melanchthon himself had instigated the production of the translation. Winsheim remained silent about the method and purpose of his work, nor does Melanchthon give away any theories on translation. But, implicitly, he makes it clear that it is the goal for students to read the Greek original. Even in his introduction to Terence, where the question of translating from Greek to Latin does not arise, his aversion to translations has not waned. According to Melanchthon, the *lumen orationis*, the *splendor uerborum* comes forth only when reading the original. From this perspective, he even judges Plautus and Terence as mere translators. On

---

20 Camerarius 1546, A2r-A6r. See Gindhart on OC 0487; MBW 3782 (= *Corpus Reformatorum* 5, 567–572 Nr. 3108).
21 See Lurje 2004, 49–56. See also Deloince-Louette 2017, 11–14 on Melanchthon's 'lecture rhétorique' of Terence.
22 Translation from Lurje 2012, 443 (= Melanchthon in: Camerarius 1546, A2v). Camerarius's edition of Terence is printed in 1546, Melanchthons *cohortatio* is dated on 1st of January 1545, cp. Gindhart on Terenz 1546.
23 Winsheim 1546, A3r.

this point, of course, he can call on the support of Cicero,[24] but in so doing, he does not do the Latin authors justice. Unfortunately, classicists until the 19th century have followed the *praeceptor Germaniae* all too eagerly and regarded Latin authors as epigones. In Melanchthon's eyes, Plautus and Terence are not of interest for their own sake, but because they give us an idea of how graceful and elegant the Greek originals were.[25]

When even Roman literature is a mere substitute for the lost Greek originals, this applies all the more to Latin translations. From Melanchthon's silence about the translations created in his environment we can deduce that he did not take them seriously but saw them as mere preliminary exercises for higher educational purposes. He was far from alone in this attitude.

1.1 Camerarius

Joachim Camerarius the Elder (1500–1574) was one of the most prolific scholars in early modern Germany, and one who is often compared to Erasmus in his importance.[26] In Erasmus, we can see the dawning of a new way of understanding ancient texts. Before setting his sights on the New Testament, he tried his pioneering new method on two ancient tragedies: he translated the *Hecuba* of Euripides and later the *Iphigenia Aulidensis* by the same author into Latin verse.[27] In doing so, he had practically no role models to serve as orientation. While Filelfo's translation of the prologue of the *Hecuba* did reach Erasmus's notice, this was, as a letter informs us, only after he had already finished working on the relevant part himself.[28] He is the undisputed pioneer in Northern Europe when it comes to translating tragedy. Camerarius studied and greatly

---

24 Cic. ac. 1, 10; fin. 1, 4.
25 Melanchthon in: Camerarius 1546, Aa5: Nam ex *Latinis* utcumque aestimari potest, quantum uenustatis in *Graecis* fuerit, et fragmenta sunt elegantissima. [...] Postquam uero monumenta horum interierunt, reliquiis fruamur, *Plauti* et *Terentii* fabulis ('For from the Latin plays one can immediately appreciate the grace that the Greek ones possessed, and the fragments are most elegant. [...] After their texts have perished, let us enjoy the remains, i.e., the comedies of Plautus and Terence').
26 Stählin 1936, 2; Hamm 2011.
27 See Baier 2015. *Hecuba* has always been the first Euripidean play read in class according to the Byzantine curriculum, and it maintained this position when Greek scholars came to Italy. It was therefore the most accessible one, a fact which might have influenced Erasmus's choice, see Wilson 1973, 87.
28 Ep. 188 (to William Warham), line 40–42, ed. Allen 1906. See also Vedelago and Dedieu in this volume.

admired Erasmus's translations when he embarked on the project of the edition, translation and commentary of Sophocles.

In a letter to Franz Burchart, who also went by Franciscus Vinariensis,[29] sent on the 13th of March 1534,[30] Camerarius praises Erasmus's translations as being *duae elegantissimae uersae ab Erasmo Roterodamo in Latinum tragoediae* (two most elegant tragedies, translated into Latin by Erasmus), stressing: *quod ego cum summa utilitate discentium futurum fuisse existimo* ('which I think will be of the highest value for those who learn Greek').[31] Camerarius was speaking from his experience as a pupil, as Erasmus's translation from 1506 was apparently the only contact he had with Greek tragedy while still in school. In this letter, Camerarius reveals his penchant and interest for Greek tragedy: *spirat tragicum*, to put it in the words of Horace. About Roman tragedy, however, he is not quite as enthusiastic. While all of its representatives from Republican times are lost, based on Seneca's extant tragedies, Camerarius feels justified to regard them as inept imitations. Though he does not pass judgement explicitly, his silence speaks for itself: *De quo quidem in uniuersum quid sentiam non habeo dicere necesse* ('I feel no need to express myself on the whole topic').[32]

Camerarius begins by defining tragedy, following Aristotle's *Poetics*.[33] He seems to be using select pieces from that treatise when he distinguishes between μίμησις and ἁπλὴ διήγησις δι' ἀπαγγελίας,[34] that is, between dramatic imitation and non-scenic report. No direct quotations from the *Poetics* are to be found, however. He says μίμησις exists in prose as well as poetic speech, that the former are dialogues, the latter dramas. Regarding dramas he makes a distinction between plays with οἰκονομία of the plot, like comedies and tragedies, and those which resemble short skits such as the *mimus*. He regards dialogical bucolic poetry as an intermediate form. The same goes for the satyr play, which

---

29 At the time, Burchart was *professor in schola Wittenbergensi*. He was in close contact with Philip Melanchthon.
30 Camerarius 1534, II, A2r-A5r = OCEp 1401. The letter has been transmitted as a paratext to OC 0139 = *Commentarii interpretationum argumenti Thebaidos fabularum Sophoclis, authore Ioachimo Camerario*, in: Camerarius 1534. On the structure and content of the volume cp. Schultheiß on Sophocles 1534; on the letter itself cp. Schultheiß on OCEp 1401.
31 Camerarius 1534, II, A3r (OCEp 1401).
32 Camerarius 1534, II, A2v-A3r (OCEp 1401).
33 The *editio princeps* of the *Poetics* was published in 1508 by Aldo Manuzio in Venice. Camerarius may therefore have known the Greek text. He mentions the *Poetics*, although he does not quote it verbatim, in his Sophocles-edition of 1534 and in the preface to Winsheim's edition (1546, reprint 1549).
34 Camerarius 1534, II, A2r (OCEp 1401).

he connects with dramatic satire.³⁵ The fundamental distinction between μίμησις and διήγησις is derived from the third book of Plato's *Republic*, which he quotes directly.³⁶ Closely following Plato, Camerarius sees a mixture of μίμησις and διήγησις in cases where the poet speaks through one of his characters. Besides the speech of Chryses in the *Iliad*, which already Plato had cited, he also gives that of Juno in the *Aeneid* as examples. While he does take Plato's criticism of mimetic poetry³⁷ seriously, he thinks it should only apply to those who do not read comedies with sufficient understanding: *Si forte recte intellecta minime contumeliosa illis inveniantur* ('As long as they are interpreted correctly there is very little to be found causing offense').³⁸ Thus, he indirectly justifies his undertaking to comment on tragedy as serving proper understanding.

In the introductory section of his commentary, he briefly sketches the origins of tragedy and speculates as to its name's origin, always closely sticking to the ancient tradition. His division of the parts (*argumentum, personae, sententia, elocutio, modi, actio*) corresponds to that of Aristotle.³⁹ Following Euripides, he deems the συμφορὰ θεήλατος ('divinely sent misfortune'), to be the essence of the tragic.⁴⁰

The commentary comprises the Sophoclean tragedies of the Theban Cycle: *Oedipus Tyrannus, Oedipus Coloneus* and *Antigone*. Camerarius says he adduced the aid of Greek *interpretatiuncula* from ancient *scholia*, which often proved to be riddled with errors, however. He also claims to have accepted *quae in codicibus uulgatis exstarent*. In places where those commentaries seemed unsatisfactory, he took recourse to his own *iudicium*. Lastly, he attaches great weight to the fact that he is open to having his commentary augmented and improved upon

---

35 It seems that Camerarius confuses the dramatic *satura*, which we know from Liv. 7.2, with the satyr play — an error that was only cleared up by Casaubonus in his treatise *De satyrica graecorum poesi et romanorum satira libri duo*, Paris 1605. Camerarius 1534, II, A2r-A2v (OCEp 1401): *Quare cum* σατυρικῶν δραματῶν *mentionem satyrorumque factam legimus, sciendum id genus quoddam fuisse fabularum in quibus agrestium numinum personae introducerentur* ('When we read that the dramatic *satura* and the satyrs are mentioned, we must know that they were a specific genre of plays in which rural deities came on stage').
36 Plat. rep. 3.393 b 7-393 c 4.
37 Moss 2000, 415, sums up Plato's reproach as follows: 'imitators are concerned with images far removed from the truth about what they represent (596a–598b); many people are too foolish to distinguish imitation from reality and thus accept ignorant imitators as experts and guides (598c–602b)'. Obviously, Camerarius considers educated readers to be immune to this danger.
38 Camerarius 1534, II, A3r (OCEp 1401).
39 Camerarius 1534, II, A6r (OC 0139); cp. Arist. poet. 6.1450a9-10: μῦθος καὶ ἤθη καὶ λέξις καὶ διάνοια καὶ ὄψις καὶ μελοποιία.
40 Camerarius 1534, II, A7r (OC 0139).

by later scholars, *si inuenietur proferetur que aliquando melius quid*. It seems that he thought of his commentary as a *work in progress*, continually to be iterated on.[41] In explaining the Greek text, as Camerarius himself tells us, he confined himself to the *loca obscura*. The rest he left up to the reader, *quasi spicilegium*, that is as 'prepared ears of corn merely to be picked up'. For, if a commentary were to be too detailed, that only served *ostentatio* ('boasting'), but not *utilitas* ('usefulness').[42] Accordingly, in this commentary, Camerarius confines himself to brief explanations of individual verses.

This edition[43] with commentary,[44] first printed in 1534, forms the beginning of Camerarius's studies on tragedy. Twenty years later he published the translation of the *Hecuba* by Heusler, prefaced with a dedicatory letter dated to 13 April 1554,[45] in which he set out the objectives (*rationes*) for the study of Greek Tragedy. In praising Heusler, he makes it clear what commenting is all about: 'This is made apparent by the diligence spent on explaining the basic forms (*primas voces*) from which, by declension and conjugation (*flexu ac declinatione*) other forms are derived as well as the derivation of words from their verbal roots (*etymorum indicatio*). Much is said about this for the sake of teaching, which is required in textbooks (*institutiones*) of this kind. In etymological derivations, too, the investigation goes only so far as to reach something that possesses a high degree of plausibility (*probabilis coniectura*)'.[46] Here, again, Camerarius's pedagogical focus finds emphasis. Above all else, he sees the commentary as an aid for pupils. Heusler was originally a trained physician, and Camerarius intimates that his efforts relating to his students' education were just as valuable as those regarding their physical wellbeing.

In 1556, at last, Camerarius expanded his commentary about the Theban plays into one that treated the entirety of Sophocles. He included two translations, of *Ajax* and *Electra*, but without an accompanying Greek text. In 1568 finally, this commentary and the two Latin translations were included in Stephanus' edition.[47]

---

[41] Camerarius 1534, II, A3v (OC 0139).
[42] Camerarius 1534, II, A4r (OC 0139).
[43] OC 0140.
[44] OC 0139.
[45] Camerarius 1554, A2r-A3r = OCEp 1457.
[46] Camerarius 1554, A2r-A2v, cp. Schultheiß on OCEp 1457.
[47] Camerarius 1556 and 1568. See Schultheiß on OC 0631.

2 Camerarius as a Translator

For Camerarius, translations are part of the philological work on the classic text. Further details about the development and publication of the translations are revealed by the dedicatory letter to the printer Hans Herbst (Johannes Oporinus), written on the 15th of March 1556.[48] There, Camerarius gives explanations about the genesis of the work and the pursued methodology. It is therefore one of the very rare documents with explicit remarks on the theoretical basis of translating.[49] We learn that Camerarius saw the translation as a prerequisite of the commentary. He first began to compile the translation according to two different premises: the translation should, on the one hand, be literal and keep the word order of the original as closely as possible; on the other hand, it should meet the requirements of the target language: *Coeperam interpretari bifariam, ut et uerbis conversio inhaereret, et sensum liberius exprimeret* (4). He denotes two different concepts of translation. Accordingly, his own translations represent both types — one is literal, the other literary. When Camerarius talks of *bifaria interpretatio* he therefore has two separate translations in mind, namely the two he had produced himself: in the translation of the *Ajax,* he did not attribute any importance to elegance and, in so doing, had no regard for Classical Latin style; he qualifies it as an *interpretatio ad uerbum*.[50] The translation of the *Electra,* however, being a prose translation largely adhering to the Greek text, is qualified as an *interpretatio libera*.[51] It is different in that it gives more weight to the target language. But most importantly, it respects the rules of Latin syntax. It is a convenience translation which only preserves its origin language in so far as Latin will allow. In the letter to Herbst, Camerarius comments on both translations saying that they, to some extent, represented examples not so much of his industriousness as of his method (*quasi specimen, non tam industriae meae quam consilii,* 4). The *consilium* in this case is to help the better understanding of the original. As a side effect, Camerarius promises his readers that they will profit

---

[48] Camerarius 1556, 3–7 = OCEp 1406. The following summary is based on Schultheiß on OCEp 1406.
[49] Before Camerarius had got to know Winsheim's work, he had completed the translation of two pieces, *Ajax* and *Electra*. As soon as he had learned about his colleague's version, he stopped his own efforts. As for the rest of the tragedies he points to Winsheim's already existing translation, cp. Schultheiß on OCEp 1406.
[50] Camerarius 1556, 107 (OC 0630).
[51] Camerarius 1556, 257 (OC 0632).

from his achievement for a better understanding of their own vernacular language (*ad proprii et puri sermonis cognitionem*, 4).

As we can see, neither Melanchthon, nor Camerarius, nor Winsheim deemed translating worthy of detailed theoretical considerations. Nor did they translate tragedies in order to provide a text which could be used on the stage. In their view, translations of tragedies were purely functional and, it seems, educational. It was Camerarius's objective to facilitate access to the plays, not to win renown by his own translations. In addition, he understood translation as being a composition exercise, meant to improve the pupils' Latin language skills.[52] It appears that Camerarius sees himself as part of a scholarly network whose job it is to make as many ancient texts as possible accessible to a broader readership.

2.1 Method of Translation – *Ajax*

The translation of the *Ajax*,[53] being titled *Interpretatio ad uerbum*,[54] proceeds line by line trying to replicate the original's syntax, even its word order as faithfully as possible. In essence, Camerarius has created an interlinear translation which is exceedingly useful for understanding the original. In doing so, he had to forego keeping the metre, which is what Camerarius means by *interpretatio*

---

52 Schultheiß on OCEp 1406 notes that Camerarius was working under pressure and that other duties (*uaria, et saepe de improuiso oblata negotia*, 3) prevented him from completing the work as he would have liked to (*neque elaboratione nostra perfecta, neque descriptione explanata*, 3). It is also noteworthy that Camerarius gives Herbst free reign in the printing. He was to correct what seemed wrong to him and is warned by Camerarius not to be misled by his unintelligible handwriting (*scriptura indistincta*): He asks Herbst to be careful not to read anything nonsensical from it (4f.). In a post scriptum to this letter, he mentions that detailed interpretations about the Sophoclean plays had been published in France at some point in the past (*in Gallia editas esse nescio quando explicationes copiosas fabularum Sophoclis libro grandi*, 6). In light of this, he was wondering if he should hold back on publishing his edition until he could take the French work into account. He goes on to write that, at last, he made the decision to publish the work in its current form, as, even though the work ended up somewhat short, an attentive reader could certainly profit from it. And if others had achieved more, they were not to be envied but rather congratulated. Lastly, Camerarius restates his permission granted to Herbst to either publish or withhold the book (*potestatem edendi vel supprimendi*, 6), even to save it or to destroy it (σαωσέμεν ἢ ἀπόλεσθαι, 6f.). The French *explicationes* about Sophocles are those of Adrien Turnèbe, published in 1553, as a letter of Camerarius to Turnèbe shows, cp. Hubert/Huth on OCEp 0376.
53 Camerarius 1556, 107–174 = OC 0630.
54 Camerarius 1556, 107 (OC 0630).

ad uerbum. In his imitation of Greek syntax, he even goes so far as to apply Greek's facility in forming composite nouns to Latin. He turns χέρας ξιφοκτόνους (10) into *manus ensicidas*. The idiom, consistent with tragic style,[55] Εὖ δέ σ' ἐκφέρει / κυνὸς Λακαίνης ὥς τις εὔρινος βάσις· (7f.), 'moving like a Spartan hound with keen scent, you travel quickly to your goal',[56] is translated literally: *te deducit / Canis Lacaenae instar sagax ingressio*.[57] In his commentary, Camerarius gives the following explanation: *Canum laus: odore enim feras vestigant. et huius organum nares sunt. Notum autem, Laconicas canes fuisse appellatas, sagaces istas, et indagatrices* [...] ('Praise for the dogs, because they use their sense of smell to track down wild animals. The organ for this is the nose. It is well known that these sharp-sniffing dogs were called Spartan dogs').[58] This explanation, while accurate, does not go far beyond lexical matters. It is to be doubted if the Latin translation could be understood without the Greek original and Camerarius's own commentary. That Camerarius's first postulate *ut et verbis conversio inhaereret* asserts itself in a quite dominant fashion will have become obvious from these two examples from the prologue.

In several places, Camerarius has marked lines of his translations with a *diple*. About these Cressida Ryan has made deliberations, reaching the conclusion that it is mainly passages related to the topics ὕβρις, ἄτη, σωφροσύνη and κακία which are marked in such a manner.[59] In my view, Camerarius has probably marked those passages which possess a sentential quality and contain a statement about the *condicio humana*. In the 1534 edition of *Ajax* the lines 125f. and 131–133 are marked (125–133):[60]

> Ὁρῶ γὰρ ἡμᾶς οὐδὲν ὄντας ἄλλο πλὴν
> εἴδωλ', ὅσοιπερ ζῶμεν, ἢ κούφην σκιάν.
> ΑΘ. Τοιαῦτα τοίνυν εἰσορῶν ὑπέρκοπον
> μηδέν ποτ' εἴπῃς αὐτὸς ἐς θεοὺς ἔπος,
> μηδ' ὄγκον ἄρῃ μηδέν', εἴ τινος πλέον
> ἢ χειρὶ βρίθεις ἢ μακροῦ πλούτου βάρει·
> ὡς ἡμέρα κλίνει τε κἀνάγει πάλιν
> ἅπαντα τἀνθρώπεια· τοὺς δὲ σώφρονας
> θεοὶ φιλοῦσι καὶ στυγοῦσι τοὺς κακούς.

---

55 See Jebb 1896, 12, *ad. loc.*
56 Translation: Lloyd-Jones 1994.
57 Camerarius 1556, 107f. (OC 0630).
58 Camerarius 1556, 23 (OC 0631).
59 She recognises in this a moralistic tendency which she sees even more prominent in the 1556 translation than in the edition of 1534, Ryan 2017, 164.
60 Camerarius 1534, A5r-E1v = OC 0140, esp. A7v.

[...] because I see that all of us who live are nothing but ghosts, or a fleeting shadow. (Ath) Look, then, at such things, and never yourself utter an arrogant word against the gods, nor assume conceit because you outweigh another in strength or in profusion of great wealth. Know that a single day brings down or rises up again all mortal things, and the gods love those who think sensibly and detest offenders![61]

The marked verses are about the power of the gods and the comparative weakness of humans. Verses 127 and 130, which call for *moderatio* when dealing with others, have not been marked with a *diple*.

Camerarius translated verses 125–133 in his 1556 edition like this:[62]

Video enim nos nihi aliud esse, nisi
Simulacra, quotquot vivimus, aut levem umbram,
Nullum unquam dixeris in deos dictum.
Neque elationem suscipias ulla, si quo plus
Aut manu vales, aut grandis opulentiae pondere
Nam dies flectit atque reducit retro
Cuncta humana. Bonos autem
Di diligunt, et odêre malos.

It is immediately obvious that Camerarius did not attribute any importance to elegance and that he, in so doing, far exceeded the boundaries of classical style. Translating *elatio* for ὄγκος may have been suggested to him by association with the following form of αἴρειν, as both *ecferre* and αἴρειν mean 'to uplift'. On the other hand, *elatio* meaning 'arrogance' can also be found in Ambrosius' commentary on the *psalms* (psalm 4.8) and the *sermons* (serm. 17.36). Arnobius (2.63) uses the word in conjunction with *arrogantia*. Besides that, *elatio* can be found with the same meaning in the Vulgata (2 Macc. 5.21), which may affirm Ryan's hypothesis that Camerarius brought a Christian perspective to ancient tragedy.[63]

Camerarius also wrote a relatively long comment on this same passage. While he usually limits himself to explaining words as needed for translation, in this passage he draws parallels to sections from the *Philoctetes*, the *Antigone*, the *Odyssey*, the *Iliad* and the Euripidean *Helena*.[64] Thus it would appear that the notion contained here is important to him. About the word εἴδωλα (126) he notes:

---

61 Translation: Lloyd-Jones 1994.
62 Camerarius 1556, 107–174 = OC 0630, esp. 113–114. In the translation verses 125–126, 128 and 131–133 are marked with a *diple*.
63 Ryan 2017, 161–165.
64 Camerarius 1556, 38f. (OC 0631).

Haec de misera conditione, et incerta fortuna uitae hominum, γνωμικῶς intulit. εἰδώλου autem et σκιᾶς similitudine, de inanitate, et euanescentia, et contemtu, et nullo momento usus est. [...].[65]

This much about the miserable human condition and man's unstable luck. He has used the metaphors *phantasm* and *shade* in order to explain inanity, vanity, condescension and futility.

At the end of the marked passage, regarding ὡς ἡμέρα (131), he explains once more using nearly the same words:

Subiecta ratio instabilitatis fortunae, et iudicii, ac sententiae diuinae. Nam et fluxae res sunt, atque caducae hominum, et Deus improbitatem odit: contra autem, propitius est probis, quos nunc vocat σώφρονας, temperantes, modestos, frugi, sobrios, pudicos.[66]

It is about the impermanence of fate, of judgement, of divine will. For human things are in a state of flux and decline, and God hates iniquity. Instead, he is merciful to the pious, whom he calls here prudent, moderate, modest, restrained, devout and chaste.

In this example, too, the author's Christian way of thinking can be demonstrated, for example by the way he replaces the pagan gods with the one God. Through his commentary, then, he transfers this pagan text into the conceptual world of his contemporaries. Simultaneously, Camerarius, always the schoolmaster, connects a vocabulary exercise on the semantic field 'moderate' with this moral lesson.[67]

2.2 *Electra*

The translation of the *Electra*[68] passes itself off as an *interpretatio libera*.[69] It is not an interlinear but a prose translation. It sticks closely to the Greek text, and it puts more of an emphasis on the target language. Most importantly, it pays heed to the rules of Latin syntax. As such, it is a convenience translation which only respects its origin language in so far as Latin will allow. The end of the prologue, spoken by the *paedagogos*, even closes with a Ciceronian clausula:

---

65 Camerarius 1556, 38 (OC 0631).
66 Camerarius 1556, 39 (OC 0631).
67 For the moral implications of tragedy and especially of the Aiax figure in the 16th century, see Wagniart 2015.
68 Camerarius 1556, 257[68]312 = OC 0632.
69 Camerarius 1556, 257 (OC 0632).

ὡς ἐνταῦθ' ἵμεν ἵν' οὐκέτ' ὀκνεῖν καιρός, ἀλλ' ἔργων ἀκμή.

since in this place this is no occasion to hesitate, but it is time to act.[70]

Quippe eo loci versamini, ut non cessandum magis, sed ad opus accingendum esse videatur.[71]

The translation by *ésse videátur* is not suggested by the Greek text. It seems obvious that Camerarius went out of his way to create a typically Latin jingle[72] and thereby remind his intended audience of pupils of the importance of ending sense units with a rhetorical clausula. There can be no doubt that Camerarius could compose Latin verse and would easily have been able to produce a verse translation.[73] His abstaining from verse translation on this occasion can therefore only be intentional and for pedagogical reasons.

3 Naogeorgus

The first German translator of tragedies who produced a Latin verse translation of Sophocles was Thomas Naogeorgus (1508–1563). He is known as a writer of theological treatises and especially as a dramatist. In 1558, having already earned a reputation as a successful writer, he published a translation of all Sophoclean plays in iambic trimeters.[74] Naogeorgus claims to be the first translator of all Sophoclean tragedies,[75] which proves that he had no knowledge of Winsheim, although his book appeared only two years after Winsheim's with the same printer, Hans Herbst, in Basel. Naogeorgus's translation is much more elegant than everything else in the field that had appeared before it. Therefore, he addresses two sorts of readers, those who are scholars of Greek and find pleasure in reading a Latin version of Sophocles and those who do not know

---

70 Translation: Lloyd-Jones 1994.
71 Camerarius 1556, 257 (OC 0632).
72 Catalectic dicretic.
73 One only needs to take a glance at his *Eclogae* (1568, newly edited by Mundt 2004). On genesis, structure and content of this poetry collection (partly in Greek) cp. Schultheiß on Eclogae 1568. Camerarius even wrote Greek poetry in iambic senarii, e.g. Περὶ μεσοτήτων ἢ μέσων ἀνάλογον τριῶν καὶ ἀριθμητικῆς καὶ γεωμετρικῆς καὶ ἁρμονικῆς, σύνοψις ἔμμετρος διαλαμβάνουσα τὰ κατὰ φύσιν, εὕρεσιν, γένεσιν καὶ χρῆσιν ἐκείνων (1554) = OC 0600.
74 See Daskarolis 2000, 177–181, on the moral evaluations in Naogeorgus' translation.
75 Naogeorgus 1558, 4: *opus magnum et difficile, a nulloque antea tentatum.*

any Greek.[76] He also is the only one who gave any explicit remarks in the dedicatory letter about his method. He focuses on two points: the metre and adequate reproduction of the content. His discussion of the problems of translation shows that he is far beyond the naïve idea that a translation could convey all of the original's nuances and shades of meaning or reproduce its tone perfectly. He even gives the impression that, in a sort of disclaimer, he defends himself preventively from attacks he is expecting, and he does so in a rather impassioned way as if he already knew his prospective adversaries:

> *Quamquam hercle fieri potest, ut non ubique sensum Poetae sim assecutus, propter locorum quorundam, praesertim in Choris, affectatam obscuritatem: id tamen in iis factum locis puto, in quibus ne scholia quidem Graeca, quibus usi sumus, suffragantur, certumque indicant sensum, sed variis interpretationibus ambiguum faciunt quid sit sequendum.*[77]
>
> Even though, by Jove, I might not always have found a proper translation because of the affectation and obscurity, especially in the choruses, I think these shortcomings are rare and to be found only in those parts, where not even the scholia were of any help but gave themselves ambiguous interpretations.

His maxim could be paraphrased as follows: as literally as possible, as freely as necessary.[78] Concerning the metres, he declares to have used iambic trimeters and is rather detailed in guiding his readers, if they should wish to analyse his verses.[79] In rendering the chorus-parts he seems to be aware of the impossibility to reproduce the variety of rhythm of the original.[80] But he is very specific about his choices and gives a meticulous list of the metres used and he also points out in which cases he differed from the usual habits: *praeter aliorum consuetudinem*. He finishes his chapter with another disclaimer taking the wind out of the sails of his prospective critics:

> *Haec ideo commemorare uisum est, ut si quis uersus examinare ac metiri velit, habeat quid sequatur. Atque haec de mea opera ac studio dicta sufficiunt.*[81]

---

76 Naogeorgus 1558, 3: *gratum id non tantum Graecarum literarum studiosis fore, verum iis etiam, quibus Graeca non admodum sunt cognita et expedita, magnam allaturum utilitatem.*
77 Naogeorgus 1558, 5, see Borza 2007, 131.
78 Naogeorgus 1558, 4f.: *me summa qua potui fide versatum, ut si non verba omnino omnia [...] sensum saltem Latinis verbis dilucide redderem.*
79 Naogeorgus 1558, 5, see Borza 2007, 131.
80 Naogeorgus 1558, 5: *In Choris dimetris usus sum partim Iambicis, partim Trochaicis, partim etiam Anapaesticis.*
81 Naogeorgus 1558, 5f.

> I thought it necessary to explain these things. If anybody wants to check and examine the metres, he shall know the method I followed. Enough said about my work and my efforts.

Naogeorgus's defensive remarks show that at his time there was a discussion about how to translate. Unfortunately, we do not have many testimonies of the debate. We can conclude that the early translations of Winsheim and Camerarius were composed to explain the Greek text, but not to replace it. One gets the impression that Naogeorgus at least tried to produce a work of art which could be put on the stage.

4 Conclusion

Melanchthon and his pupil Winsheim saw no intrinsic value in translations but regarded them as aids to an audience ignorant of Greek. They contributed little to translation theory.[82] This changed with Camerarius, who was strongly influenced by Erasmus, but took a more philological perspective than the latter. Both scholars were advocates of a true-to-text-translation.[83] Furthermore, Camerarius seems to justify the requirement of translational accuracy from the adherence to Aristotelian rules. In the introduction to his Sophocles edition (1534), titled *De tragico carmine et illius praecipuis authoribus apud Graecos*, he faithfully renders the Aristotelian definition of tragedy according to his own understanding,[84] foregoing any Christian moralising.[85] This treatise, striving for appropriate representation of its subject matter, is addressed to an audience of experts. As we have seen, his later translation from 1556 is tinged with Christian expressions, but this is mainly to ensure greater clarity for his Christian audience and to make it easier for him to impart general wisdom. The Christian terms are a concession to pupils. By no means should this be thought of as a Christian reimagining. Camerarius interpreted Sophocles according to the guidelines set out by Aristotle, and it is these guidelines to which he laboured to stay true.

Naogeorgus shared the same views on translation independently of Camerarius, considering his work primarily as a help to understanding the Greek

---

[82] Botley 2004, 164–177 has distilled some categories of translation with regard to Italian scholars.
[83] For Erasmus see Baier 2007, 103.
[84] Camerarius 1534, II, A5r-A8v (=OC 0139).
[85] See Lurje 2004, 96, who uses the example of *Oedipus Tyrannus* to show that Camerarius (unlike Winsheim) does not advocate a moralising interpretation of tragic catharsis.

text. Nevertheless, like Erasmus at the beginning of the century, he strove for a pleasing form of translation. He reflected on the metre and considered the right balance of literal and free translation. One could have staged his works.

For all authors treated here the following applies: in dealing with Greek tragedy there was no space for poetic licence. If that was what someone desired, they were free to compose their own verse and enter into the wide field of Latin Drama, but that is another story.

II.2: Proto-National Dynamics and Vernacular Translating

Giovanna Di Martino
Translating Ancient Greek Tragedy in 16th-Century Italy

Abstract: The present chapter provides an analysis of the interplay and overlap between translations of ancient Greek tragedy and the creation of new tragedies aimed at establishing the tragic genre in 16th-century Italy. It makes the case that the theoretical roots of imitation in this period lay in Aristotle's *Poetics*, which was used to justify and ground the generally free and emulative approach to ancient Greek tragedy in its translation as well as recreation. The chapter demonstrates how the playwrights and translators were fully aware of their imitative approach which resulted in the hybrid nature of their works, in between translations and adaptations. The hybridity of these tragedies/translations also emerges from the very labels attached to them by later scholarship. The latter part of the chapter thus focuses on 'volgarizzamento' in particular, its history as a term and its validity for 16th-century translations of ancient Greek tragedy.

The present chapter focuses on the interplay and overlap between translations of ancient Greek tragedy and the creation of new tragedies aimed at establishing the tragic genre in 16th-century Italy. It inserts these works back into the intellectual, literary, and theatrical history of the period, as well as into the history of the theory and practice of translation more generally.

It addresses the topic first by exploring the very aesthetic principle guiding the production of new literary creations in 16th-century Italy, i.e., imitation, a concept mainly grounded in the 'rediscovery' of Aristotle and his *Poetics*. The substantial (and purposeful) assimilation of the composition of tragedy into the translation of ancient tragedy and vice versa results in the hybrid nature of these texts, which are somewhere in between translations and new tragedies; hence the use of a slash between the words 'tragedies' and 'translations' throughout this chapter. Such hybridity is especially visible in the use of various defining labels in the many paratexts that accompany the publication or donation of some of these works, which will be at the heart of the second section.

I would like to thank Francesca Bortoletti, Giulia Fiore, Miriam Leonard, Fiona Macintosh, Angelica Vedelago, Maria Wyke, and the other editors of this volume, for reading earlier drafts of this chapter and for their invaluable comments.

https://doi.org/10.1515/9783110719185-008

Yet, most importantly, the hybrid nature of 16th-century tragedies/translations has led to a general disregard of some of these texts as either too derivative of, or too distant from, their source texts, deploying a normative and fidelity-based conception of translation that simply does not account for the wide variety of translation approaches in the period, especially those of and for the theatre.[1] The third and last section of this chapter puts these works in dialogue with the history of the theory and practice of translation in this period. It does so by discussing the ubiquitous but late presence of the word 'volgarizzamento' as a functionalised and broad category into which these works might fall, so as to eschew the terminological impasse arising from their hybridity. It thus makes a step into the study 'of the theory of vulgarization from classical languages to the vernacular' on which, as Marco Sgarbi has recently argued, 'almost nothing has been written',[2] by combining the scholarship on 'volgarizzamento', 'volgarizzare', and translation theory and practice in this period with the rich scholarship on so-called 'Italian Renaissance tragedy'. Finally, it brings to the surface how the general disregard of 16th-century volgarizzamenti is connected to important questions of literary style, class, and national agenda.

1 Imitation as Literary Creation

Such are the words of the author-character Antonio Sebastiano Minturno in the section on the tragic genre contained in the dialogue-treatise *Arte Poetica*, published in Venice in 1564:

> Because we do not have one tragic poet whom we can be sure to take example from, I will resort to the Greeks, and amongst them to Sophocles, as someone who was awarded first prize in this type of poetry, and to one of his tragedies, entitled *Antigone*, as this is one of the best he wrote, and one that has already been made ours by Mr Luigi Alemanni, whose style and intelligence deserve high praise; this has been made ours so much so that one could hardly distinguish it from the Greek if it wasn't for the different language.[3]

---

[1] For further discussion on early modern as well as contemporary conceptions of translation, see the Introduction.
[2] Sgarbi 2019, 390.
[3] 'Poiché noi tragico poeta non abbiamo da cui certi esser possiamo di vero essempio prendere, avrò ricorso a' Greci, e tra quelli a Sofocle, come a colui al quale in questa poesia la palma si diede, et in una delle tragedie di lui *Antigone* chiamata, sì per esser quella una delle più eccellenti ch'egli scrivesse, e sì per esser fatta nostra da messer Luigi Alemanni, il cui stile et inge-

Indeed, Minturno's *Arte Poetica* is only one of the many treatises on poetics published in the 16th century which stand alongside, underpin, and are generally influenced by, the coeval, prolific and experimental production of new tragedies/translations.[4] Unsurprisingly, these treatises on poetics heavily draw on Aristotle's own *Poetics* — whose editions, translations, and commentaries (again) stand alongside, underpin, and are generally influenced by, the production of new treatises on poetics, including a number of discussions around the composition of tragedy more specifically.[5]

Minturno's reference to Sophocles in the above quotation provides a good example of this intricate web of mutual influence between 16th-century commentaries on and translations of Aristotle's *Poetics*, new treatises on poetics, and the composition of tragedy. Unlike other genres for which there exist scholar-poets within the Italian literary tradition,[6] Minturno concedes that the tragic genre lacks native 'examples' to imitate (or any that he would recommend, at least). It thus becomes necessary to resort to the ancient Greek models themselves when discussing the composition of tragedy, he argues, and not just to any of the Greek tragedians, but to Sophocles in particular, in line with 16th-century readings of Aristotle's *Poetics*.[7] Indeed, even if Aristotle draws many of his examples from Sophoclean tragedies, and the *Oedipus Tyrannus* in particular, it is rather the 16th-century's obsession with finding tragedy's perfect model and rules that leads to the over-privileging of Sophocles' importance in translations of and commentary on Aristotle's *Poetics*, as well as treatises derived therefrom.[8]

---

gno merita somma laude, e talmente fatta nostra che dalla greca non si conoscerebbe se la favella non fosse diversa' (Minturno 1564, 65, 75). Henceforward, all translations are my own.
4 See Weinberg 1970, 566–581 for a list of the most important publications on poetics in the 16th century. For a discussion of treatises on tragedy, see Mastrocola 1998 in particular.
5 See Weinberg 1970, 566–581 for a list of the editions and translations of and commentaries on Aristotle's *Poetics* in the 16th century (to which one should add Alessandro Piccolomini's *Annotationi* (1575), on which see especially Cotugno 2006).
6 Cf. when Minturno identifies Petrarch's *Trionfi* as a primary example for imitation for the epic genre alongside Virgil and Homer (Minturno 1564, 22–23).
7 See Fiore in this volume.
8 In his introduction to Aristotle's *Poetics*, Stephen Halliwell asserts that the 'the *Poetics* does *not*, either explicitly or implicitly, put forward a view of tragedy derived directly from the plays of Sophocles, still less from the *Oedipus Tyrannus* alone' (1987, 9). On the importance of Oedipus as a model in 16th-century Italy, see Fiore in this volume and Mastrocola 1996 (convincingly arguing that both *Antigone* and *Oedipus Tyrannus* are primary models for 16th-century tragedy) and 1998 (arguing for the predominance of the model of Oedipus in treatises on tragedy and, ultimately, in tragic compositions).

Sophocles held 'first prize' amongst 16th-century Italian scholars, as Minturno suggests: not only was he credited with adding the third actor, according to Niccolò Rossi, a member of the Olympian Academy at Vicenza, in his *Discorsi intorno alla tragedia* (1590); he is also responsible for bestowing 'gravitas' onto tragedy by means of eliminating 'satyrs' from the stage, inserted to entertain the audience and lengthen the performance.[9] His *Antigone* and *Oedipus Tyrannus* in particular were undisputed models for Italian tragedians/translators:[10] Oedipus had even been upheld as tragedy's 'idea(l)', as the 16th-century scholar, poet, tragedian, and member of the Accademia degli Oziosi in Naples, Gabriele Zinano, suggested.[11]

The successful tragedian Giovan Battista Giraldi Cinzio's *Didone* (1543), for example, was accused of not being sufficiently like *Oedipus Tyrannus*. However, as Giraldi Cinzio argued in his own defence, whilst *Didone* was not *Oedipus* in terms of its subject matter, it was like *Oedipus* in terms of its 'artificio' ('artifice') – namely, in following the structure of tragedy that Sophocles' *Oedipus* was said to embody.[12] Another example comes from Rossi's already mentioned *Discorsi*, where, though praising Gian Giorgio Trissino's tragedy *Sofonisba* (1515; the first 'regular' tragedy) and considering it as exemplary as Sophocles' *Oedipus Tyrannus*, he confesses that:

> If all those beautiful parts which Aristotle identifies in *Oedipus Tyrannus* with regards to reversal [*peripeteia*] and that admirable recognition [*anagnorisis*] cannot be found in this tragedy [Trissino's *Sofonisba*], this should not be imputed to the divine intellect of Mr Gi-

---

9 Rossi 1970, 67. Rossi asserted to have grounded such statement in Alessandro Piccolomini's *Annotationi* (1575), where in fact Piccolomini confutes the interpretation by which Sophocles should be credited with ridding tragedy of satyrs (which Piccolomini ascribes to Maggi-Lombardi 1550) and bestowing 'gravitas' onto the genre (which he ascribes to Robortello 1548). The interpretation seems to derive from a misreading of τὸ μέγεθος (1449a), which, Piccolomini argues, must refer to the 'length' of performances only, and should be detached from Sophocles, from whom Aristotle seems to have moved away (cf. Piccolomini 1575, 85–86).
10 Mastrocola 1998, 185 contains a table with the main tragedies/translations derived from these two models. For *Antigone*, these include Gian Giorgio Trissino's *Sofonisba*, Giovanni Rucellai's *Rosmunda* and Luigi Alamanni's *Antigone* (incidentally, but rather tellingly, all part of the same academic circle); for *Oedipus Tyrannus*, these include Giovanni Andrea dell'Anguillara's *Edippo*, Orstatto Giustiniani's *Edipo*, Pomponio Torelli's *Tancredi* and Torquato Tasso's *Torrismondo*.
11 Zinano 1970, 132.
12 Giraldi Cinzio 1970, 484; see Fiore in this volume.

oan Giorgio, but to the subject matter to which he adapted his tragedy, which did not lead to such perfection.[13]

Again, Rossi seems to impute to the modern tragedy that it is not like *Oedipus* in all respects and that this is why it falls short of perfection.

But Aristotle's influence was especially visible in 16th-century tragedies and discussions on poetics precisely because his *Poetics*, in particular, provided the conceptual ground upon which the very literary system was built. Minturno's words might be useful again here:

> But this one [the dramatic poet], whom we are about to discuss now, is clothed in otherness from the beginning, as it so happens in the Tragedies by Sophocles and Euripides, a number of which have already been made ours thanks to the work and effort of [Lodovico] Dolce, and [Luigi] Alemanni, two most brilliant jewels of our language, [...].[14]

In this passage, Minturno reveals *en passant* the sort of engagement that seems to be required in the (re)creation of such models in order that tragedy can be founded as a genre in the Italian vernacular. Lodovico Dolce and Luigi Alamanni are commendable for having already begun this process of imitation and emulation of the ancients: Alamanni's *Antigone* is even representative in this respect, he argues, as it can hardly be 'distinguished' from its 'original', so much so that it has become 'ours'.

The theoretical implications of these statements are of paramount importance when grappling with translation theory and practice in this period, and the translation of Greek tragedy, in particular. Once it has been established that the models are the ancients, it is only by appropriating and imitating such models — by clothing oneself 'in otherness from the beginning', as Minturno suggests — that it will be possible to create anew, to make these models 'ours'. Such an assumption is more than just a nod to Aristotle's *mimetic* theory of poetry, upon which rested the entire aesthetic and literary system that was be-

---

13 'E se tutte le belle parti che considera Aristotile intorno alla trasmutazione dell'*Edipo tiranno* di Sofocle con quella mirabile recognizione non si scorge in questa tragedia, non si dee incolpare il divino ingegno del signor Gioan Giorgio, ma il soggetto a cui adattò la sua tragedia, che non comportò tanta perfezione' (Rossi 1970, 84).
14 'Ma questi [il poeta scenico], del quale ora parliamo, dal principio infin all'estremo è vestito dell'altrui; sì come nelle Tragedie di Sofocle e d'Euripide, delle quali già nostre alquante, per l'opera e fatica del Dolce e dell'Alemanni, duo chiarissimi ornamenti della nostra lingua, si sono fatte, [...]' (Minturno 1564, 65, 75).

ing developed at this time.¹⁵ Indeed, on the same (Aristotelian) principle by which poetry (and tragedy) imitates nature (an action) and the mimesis of such nature (action) results from a selection, arrangement, and improvement of nature (actions),¹⁶ 16th-century tragedians need to select, imitate, and emulate the most successful tragic models. Representative of this mimetic paradigm is the ancient painter Zeuxis, who features above all in treatises on poetics and figurative art as the model for the imitation (of models).¹⁷ Lodovico Castelvetro's gloss on Aristotle's mention of Zeuxis as connected with the 'impossible' of poetry (τὸ ἀδύνατον; *Poet.* 1461b.9ff) in his commentary on the *Poetics* (1570) is also very interesting. Here, Castelvetro strenuously defends Zeuxis' choice of 'assemblage' in the portrayal of Helen as an 'impossible' that is not only allowed, but even required in poetic compositions.¹⁸ Indeed, to the potential criticism that Zeuxis' Helen could not be found in nature, Castelvetro argues that Aristotle would respond with:

> ἀλλὰ καὶ πρὸς τὸ βελτίον. It is true that they [people] can't be such by nature, but Zeuxis pictured them as such because it would be better if they looked like that; similarly, the poet would do [their job] well if they made things [that is, the object of their poetry] resemble how they should be, even when it were impossible to find them in such a state [naturally].¹⁹

---

15 On the pivotal importance of 16th-century literary production in the 'founding of Italian literature', see Dionisotti 1967, 39; on imitation as the founding principle of 16th-century poetics, see Weinberg 1970, 541–562 and Quondam 1999, 399ff; on tragedy and imitation more specifically, see Mastrocola 1998, 55ff.
16 Cf. especially Ar. *Poet.* 1447a.14–17, 1454.b10, and 1460b.20. Cf. also the difference between the poet and the historian at 1451b.1–19. In his treatise *Della Poetica* (1536), Bernardino Daniello, also a successful translator of Virgil's *Georgics* and *Aeneid* 11, clarifies that though art has its origin in nature, it doesn't limit itself to mere imitation, but it 'betters' the object of its 'imitation' and 'makes it perfect' (Daniello 1970, 230).
17 Zeuxis is particularly present in treatises on the figurative arts (cf. the occurrences of 'Zeuxis' in treatises on art assembled in Barocchi 1960).
18 Castelvetro also quotes Cic. *De Inv.* II.I.3, where Cicero retrieves Zeuxis and his artistic technique to justify his own choice of 'excerpting' the best from many authors in writing his book of rhetoric (cf. *De Inv.* II.I.4). Indeed, this discussion around model(s) tapped into a longstanding debate which had received an important push with Erasmus's publication of the *Ciceronianus* (1528) at the beginning of the century (see, for example, Giulio Delminio Camillo's response to the debate in his treatise *Della Imitazione*, composed a few years later, ca. 1530, but published posthumously in 1544). See also Dedieu and Vedelago on the topic.
19 Cf. *Poet.* 1461b.13; 'ἀλλὰ καὶ πρὸς τὸ βελτίον, egli è vero che per natura non è possibile che sieno tali, ma Zeussi le dee dipingere tali perché meglio sarebbe se fossero tali, sì come il poeta

The example of Zeuxis is thus read as a paradigm for literary imitations, for which one need elect the models to imitate as well as select and assemble the best elements of such models in their newly created (imitative) works. Indeed, it is only within this imitative and emulative relationship with the ancients (modelled on the Aristotelian 'inevitable' and 'natural' mimesis of nature)[20] that one can create anew; as the scholar Amedeo Quondam states, for 16th-century writers 'the imitation of nature and its models [...] is the productive principle' of their whole literary system.[21]

2 Prefacing Hybridity: Routing Ancient Tragedy onto New Tracks

Tragedies/translations of this period perfectly inscribe themselves into this productive understanding of imitation as literary creation, the result of a carefully selective and creative process involving adaptation of the ancient models into a new context. Whilst Alamanni's *Antigone* bears the same title as Sophocles' famous tragedy, it also reproduces its model rather freely, particularly in the case of the choral odes where the last two supplant the original stasima with new ones.[22] But it is equally the case that there are other tragedies which seem to bear little resemblance to the ancient models yet which adapt the (known) plot to other stories or pepper their tragedies with references to the ancients.[23]

Particularly important for this imitative-creative interrelationship with the ancients is the information that one can garner from the paratexts of these trag-

---

farà bene se rassomiglierà le cose come steano meglio, ancora che sia impossibile che si truovino tali' (Castelvetro 1570, 328–329). Cf. also Piccolomini (1575, 412ff.) on the same passage.
20 Cf. Ar. *Poet.* 1448b.5–10.
21 For Quondam, the literature of the 'Ancient Regime', a historical period identified with the 'Europe of the Courts' and abruptly ending with the French Revolution, rests on a 'system wholly rooted in the principles of authority and tradition and thus on the positive function of the reuse of its [models]' (1999, 80).
22 Cf. Alamanni 1997, 53–55 and 62–63. It was indeed common practice to tweak and adapt the original's stasima when composing/translating tragedies; see, for example, Marcantonio Cinuzzi's translation of Aesch. *PV* in Cinuzzi 2006, 33; cf. also Di Martino 2021. See also Coriolano Martirano's Latin translation of the choral odes of the same play (cf. Di Martino 2019, 138). Cf. Porro 1981, 491–492 in particular for a general survey of the usual treatment of choral odes in 16th-century translations of Greek tragedy.
23 See the rich apparatus of references to ancient tragedies in Cremante 1988 and also Mastrocola's table mentioned in fn. 8.

edies/translations, which disclose the authors' general concern with presenting their work as a (conceptual and concrete) hybrid space between the 'old' and the 'new'. The prolific translator Alessandro Pazzi de' Medici, the author of an *Oedipus Tyrannus*, an *Electra*, a *Cyclops*, an *Iphigenia in Tauris* and a *Dido in Carthagine*, introduces his *Iphigenia* in this way:

> And so I put myself to writing the Tragedy *Iphigenia in Tauris*, which Euripides composed, following not just the disposition of its author, but also the meaning constantly, though not limiting myself to the laws of translating, but striving to bring the substance of his lines across to our own language as much as I was allowed to.[24]

Pazzi eloquently describes the imitation game in which he is competing with both his contemporaries and the ancients: with his *Iphigenia*, he follows the disposition of the original Euripidean tragedy and its meaning, but also adapts it to meet the needs and potential of the new language as he makes the ancient Greek tragedy part of his own literary repertoire, just as Alamanni does with Sophocles' *Antigone*. And if the dichotomy between 'substance' and the 'laws of translation' might echo the long-standing debate between a *uerbum uerbo* translation versus one *ad sensum*, between *uerba* and *sententiae*,[25] Pazzi seems only

---

[24] 'Et così mi missi a scrivere la tragedia di *Iphigenia in Tauris*, composta da Euripide, osservando in quella non solo la dispositione in tutto del proprio authore, ma anchora il senso continuatamente, non mi ristringendo però alle leggi del tradurre, ma ben quanto mi fusse lecito nello idioma nostro sforzandomi di trarre la sustantia di tutti li versi suoi' (Sorella 2013, 149–150). Interestingly, Pazzi here employs a whole series of expressions and verbs to try and define his work ('writing', 'following the disposition', 'striving to bring the substance'), whilst carefully avoiding to use 'translating', which features here as the less creative approach to the ancient text.

[25] See, for example, Leonardi Bruni's *De interpretatione recta* almost a century earlier (1424–1426), where he explicitly plugs into the debate by suggesting a re-unification of *verba* and *sensum*: *Hec est enim optima interpretandi ratio: si figura prime orationis quam optime conservetur, ut neque sensibus verba neque verbis ipsis nitor ornatusque deficiat* (Bertolio 2020, 8–9). It was from a corrected interpretation of the famous Ciceronian passage *nec converti ut interpres, sed ut orator* (*De opt.* 14) that translation received its defining push out of the realm of 'imitation' and into that of 'philology' in the second half of the century (cf. Di Martino 2019). Relevant in this respect would be Fausto da Longiano's treatise in 1556 (cf. 1556, 77ff.), but also the works of other prominent intellectuals of the period, who were mainly interested in and translators of philosophical and/or rhetorical works; see especially Castelvetro 1543 in Cardillo 2010, 10ff., Piccolomini 1575 in Cotugno 2006, 213, Toscanella 1575, 35, and Catena 1581 in Baldassarri 2006, 140, for a discussion of the long-standing issue relating to reproducing the author's 'concepts' (*sententiae*) and/or 'words' (*verba*). The majority of these discussions rely on a rather strict recontextualization of some of the most popular passages related to translation from antiquity (Cic. *De opt.* 14 is indeed a pivotal one, but Hor. *Ars Poet.* 133ff. also plays an im-

vaguely interested in the debate and instead is much keener on presenting his *Iphigenia* as a literary 'imitation' — a new tragedy yet anchored to the ancients.

Even when referred to as 'translations' by the translators themselves, these 16th-century works reserve surprises. A good example is the translation of Aeschylus' *Prometheus Bound* by Marcantonio Cinuzzi, a prolific *letterato* from Siena and a member of the Accademia degli Intronati. In the dedication letter to the Duke of Urbino Francesco Maria II Della Rovere (1578), the translator carefully construes his *Prometeo* as an accurate reproduction of the original ('fonte'):

> If, by any chance, your excellency might find any Greek or Latin text where there might be different characters from the ones I have put here, he should not be surprised as these are indeed overt mistakes, because in the source text of the tragedy there appear no other characters than those I put in here.[26]

But it is not long before Inachus rather than Io appears amongst the main characters: the dialogue between Prometheus and Io (*PV* 562–886) is replaced by one with Inachus; and this, together with Io's *rhesis* (*PV* 640–686, here replaced with a long speech by Prometheus to Io's father), is a reworking of Io's story as told by Ovid in his *Metamorphoses* (*Met.* 1.568–746), which in turn is now adapted to meet the dramaturgical needs of the (translated) Aeschylean episode.[27] The two ancient models are merged and adjusted to fit the new, modern retelling of Io's story.

In his dedication letter to Filippo del Migliore, Giovan Battista Gelli, a member of the Accademia Fiorentina, speaks of his *Hecuba* (1519–1524) as a 'traduttione', though not from the Greek itself, but from Erasmus's Latin:

> And don't be surprised if you find our translation somewhat discordant with Erasmus's Latin in some parts (not in meaning, but in the words and the way of saying), as it seemed to me more convenient to follow the meaning of the author in some parts and accommodate it to our language, rather than translating his [Erasmus's] words *ad literam*, which it would not have been possible to do, not without some harshness and difficulty.[28]

---

portant role, for which see, amongst others, Fausto da Longiano 1990, 87ff., Toscanella 1575, 28–29, and Piccolomini in Refini 2009, 166–167).

26 '… se per aventura venisse alle mani di vostra Eccellenza reverendissima alcun testo greco o latino nel qual fussino altri interlocutori di quelli che son qui posti non si maravigli perciò che sono errori manifesti atteso che dentro nel fonte de la tragedia non si trova che parlino altri che i preposti qui' (Cinuzzi 2006, 33).

27 Cf. lines 769–1014 in Cinuzzi 2006; see also Di Martino 2021.

28 'E non pigliare admiratione se questa nostra traduttione da quella latina di Erasmo in qualche parte (non in senso ma nelle parole e nel modo del dire) troverrai discorde, perché mi è

Along the same lines as Pazzi's preface, Gelli's words briefly touch upon the *ad uerbum/litteram* versus *ad sensum* debate, which subsumes even more interesting traits here because Gelli himself explicitly presents his work as a translation of a translation, one that had become iconic for the translation of Greek drama more generally.[29] As with Pazzi, Gelli's interest is not so much in adding to the debate using his work as an example; rather, the *ad sensum* option, far from being discussed in detail, is used to justify his adaptive techniques as being necessary: an in-depth linguistic (*largo sensu*) relocation seems to be required of these imitative literary creations. Along these same lines is the dedicatory letter to another *Hecuba* by the learned Dominican Matteo Bandello, this time translated from Euripides — or so it is claimed — and made wholly 'Italian', as he argues.[30]

Yet, it is probably the prolific Venetian translator/tragedian Lodovico Dolce who offered some of the most interesting paratextual insights into translating/composing (ancient Greek) tragedy in 16th-century Italy. In the dedication letter to the 1560 edition of all of his tragedies addressed to the senator of the Republic of Venice Marcantonio da Mula, Dolce explains that he 'composed the present Tragedies' by means of 'extract[ing]' — à la Zeuxis — 'the inventions, sentences, and texture from the ancients'.[31] *Medea* (1557) is presented as a 'new Tragedy' ('nova Tragedia') in the prologue; 'new', Dolce explains, 'because it has been newly clothed with new garments'.[32]

Even more eloquent is the prologue to Dolce's *Ifigenia* (1551). Following the example of the finale of Giraldi Cinzio's *Orbecche* (produced in 1541 and published in 1543), 'La tragedia a chi legge' ('Tragedy to the readers', lines 3141–

---

parso più conveniente in qualche luogo pigliare il senso dello autore et al nostro idioma vulgare accomodarlo, che tradur le parole di quello *ad literam*, il che senza qualche durezza e difficultà sarie quasi stato impossibile a fare' (Gelli 2016, 4).

29 See Dedieu and Vedelago in this volume.

30 Cf. 'Per tanto havendo io già di molti dì per mio trastullo l'Hecuba di Euripide Poeta Tragico fatta Italiana, e messa a modo mio in rima, sempre con altre cose mie l'ho tenuta nascosa, affine, che l'occasione si levasse a questi maledici questa mia picciola fatica biasimarmi' (Bandello 1813, 12–13). The translation seems to carry political relevance, not least because at the time of Bandello's dedication letter (1539) to Marguerite de Navarre (née Marguerite d'Angoulême), queen of Navarra, Bandello's patron, Cesare Fregoso, was in the service of François I, Marguerite's brother.

31 'Havendo io ... composte le presenti Tragedie, togliendo le inventioni, le sentenze, e la testura da gli antichi'; Dolce 1560, 2.

32 'Nova dico, per esser novamente / con nuovi panni da colui vestita'; Dolce 1557, 2.

332),³³ Dolce has Tragedy introduce herself (and the *fabula* of Iphigenia) to the audience onstage:

> I am she, whom the Greeks called
> Tragedy; and I was born then, when on earth
> unfair Tyranny was conceived
> [...] From thereon at length
> Was I under muddy wrecks
> [...]
> But then more than anybody else
> Sophocles held me up, magnificent
> and the illustrious Euripides; they both
> made me play with a clear trumpet
> for the whole of Greece. And as I stayed on the Ilisus
> for many years; so I didn't like it when I
> lived on the Tiber.³⁴

Thus, whilst tragedy enjoyed herself in Greece with Euripides and Sophocles, she rather spurned her time in Rome. Here, Dolce's words reflect the 'imitative-emulative' relationship that 16th-century tragedians/translators established with their models: discussions revolved around which sources to use (Greek, Roman, or historical)³⁵ as well as which structure — the division into acts (Horace-derived: Hor. *Ars* 189–190) or the 'Greek' episodes. Whilst debates around which sources to use were inextricably tied up with the Aristotle-derived issue of whether the *fabula* should be of a historical or fictitious nature (*Poet.* 1451b–52a), those around structure also involved considerations about the performative function of the chorus. In defence of his *Didone*, for example, Giraldi Cinzio explains that the Roman structure allowed for a better treatment of the chorus, who, in marked contrast to the Greek model, was not onstage the whole time, eavesdropping on members of the royal family, but, according to the needs of 'verisimilitude', left the stage in every act so that there could be an 'empty stage', which signalled the end of an act.³⁶

Yet, here Dolce successfully nods at both the Greek and Roman traditions: he follows the five-act structure which imposed itself as the most popular choice

---

33 Cf. Giraldi Cinzio 1988, 433–448 and Cremante's introductory note (1988, 261–282).
34 Cf. the original Italian in fn. 40. Cf. also Giraldi Cinzio's different take on tragedy in Roman times (1970, 446ff.).
35 See, amongst others, Trissino 1970, 15ff.; Giraldi 1970, 479ff.; Giraldi 2002, 214ff.; Minturno 1564, 74ff.; Rossi 1970, 68ff. and 90ff.; Strozzi 1970, 30ff.
36 Giraldi 1970, 477–480.

after the success of Giraldi Cinzio's *Orbecche*,[37] and he also explicitly has 'tragedy' express her preference for the Greek models.[38] The Graeco-Roman tradition is unsurprisingly combined here with the nascent Italian vernacular tradition, onto which Dolce carefully grafts his own tragedies:

> [...] Now, to the Arno
> I was made to turn much pompously:
> it was he who cried over Sofonisba's end;
> he who of Antigone and Haemon
> renewed the compassion, faith, and love;
> and then this other one, who pushed Orbecche;
> and he who sang Rosmunda's disdain;
> and he who [sang] this new and not-to-be-seen-after example
> of Macareus' wicked love;
> and no less this brilliance who dignified
> Horatia with her great father's ears.[39]

Along with making sure that his *Ifigenia* is seen as following in the footsteps of the ancients (Roman and Greek), i.e., the 'old', Dolce also ably positions his new work within the newly established genre of tragedy in the Italian vernacular, i.e., the 'new'. His tragedy appears to have its origin in the ancient models, but as part of the 'imitation' aesthetics of the literary creations in early modern Italy, it is as much new as it is old:

> Thus, I resorted to Euripides; and extracting
> the beauty, which made me noble and honourable,
> I gave it to one of your fellow citizens and servants;
> so that in another language, and in another form,
> as he does, he might introduce me to you.[40]

---

37 Trissino 1970, 22 attempted to reconcile both traditions by identifying the Greek prologue and exodus with the first and fifth Horatian acts and the (series of) episode(s) in between these two as the third act, itself divisible into three acts (choral odes seem irrelevant to the division of tragedy into acts). Discussions around tragedy's ideal structure and sources were never really resolved and still visibly embroiled later tragedians such as Vittorio Alfieri (18th century) and Alessandro Manzoni (19th century) (cf. Mattioda 1994 and Di Martino 2019a).
38 Euripides was indeed Dolce's source for his *Ifigenia*, though mediated via Erasmus's famous translation; on Dolce's tragedies, see Giazzon 2014 and 2016.
39 Cf. Giraldi Cinzio's own list of tragedians who came before him in Giraldi 1988, 445ff.
40 'Io son colei, ch'addimandaro i Greci / Tragedia; e nacqui alhor, ch'in terra nacque / La Tirannide iniqua, [...] / Indi gran tempo / Condotta fui sotto fangose larve [...] / Ma più ch'altro giamai m'alzò superba / Sofocle, e'l chiaro Euripide, ambedoi / Facendomi sonar con chiara tromba / Per Grecia tutta. E come sù l'Ilisso / Stetti molt'anni; cosi a me non piacque /

Dolce's *Ifigenia* should thus be aligned with other similar works — notably, Trissino's *Sofonisba* (whose main models are *Alcestis* and *Antigone*), Alamanni's *Antigone*, Giraldi's *Orbecche* (whose main models are Seneca's *Thyestes* and Boccaccio's story of Ghismunda and Guiscardo, *Decameron* 4.1), Rucellai's *Rosmunda* (whose main model is *Antigone*), Sperone Speroni's *Canace* (whose main models are Ovid *Her.* 9; Virgil *Aen.* 1.50–80),[41] and Pietro Aretino's *Orazia* (mainly adapted from Livy *Ab urb. cond.* 1.25ff.).[42]

As Dolce explains, Tragedy has resorted to Euripides once more, and yet, it is distilled Euripides that has been delivered to Dolce: the Euripidean text extracted from its former context and adapted to the new one in language and form. Far from applying any defining label to the nature of his work, Dolce envisages it as hybrid: if mapping it onto the classical tradition gives prominence and prestige to his literary endeavour, openly situating it in a new context as a distilled extraction of the ancient 'beauty' validates it as part of the new literary tradition. As a new tragedy with a new owner, it contributes to the founding of the tragic genre in the Italian vernacular.

But there is more. The adaptive freedom with which the tragedians treat their tragedies is itself conceived of as a licence afforded by the ancients and inscribed into the 16th-century (mimetic) literary system. In the prologue to his *Altile*, which he presents as a 'tragicomedia' in a way that meaningfully retraces Mercurius' words in the prologue to Plautus' own *tragicomoedia*, the *Amphitruo* (Plaut. *Amph.* 50–63), Giraldi Cinzio argues:

> And thus our Poet now believes
> that the laws imposed on Tragedy
> might in fact not be so strict as to forbid
> stepping out of that which has been prescribed, in some way.
> [...]

D'habitar sopra il Tebro. Hor sopra l'Arno / Volger mi fece il piede assai pomposa / Quei, che già pianse il fin di Sofonisba, / E quello, che d'Antigone e di Hemone / Rinovò la pietà, la fe, e l'amore, / E quell'altro dapoi, che spinse Orbecche / E chi cantò lo sdegno di Rosmunda; / E chi con nuovo e non più visto esempio / Lo scelerato amor di Macareo, / Ne men quell'alto ingegno, che fe degna / L'Horatia de l'orecchie del gran padre, [...] / Ond'io ricorsi a Euripide; e togliendo / Il bel, che mi fe nobile e honorata, / Lo diedi a un vostro cittadino servo; / Perche con altra lingua, et altra forma, / Com'egli suol, l'appresentasse a voi'.

41 Maslanka Soro 2010 identifies Seneca's *Phaedra* and *Thyestes* as well as Sophocles' *Antigone* as additional models for Speroni; I would also add *Oedipus Tyrannus* (cf. Mastrocola 1998, 205ff.).

42 Aretino's *Orazia* is in fact inspired by Jacopo Nardi's translation of Livy's retelling of the conflict between Horatii and Curiatii (cf. Spera 1995, 787).

> And the poet knows with much certainty
> That if the ancient poet were here now,
> he would seek to accommodate these times,
> This audience, and the new subject matter;
> And the poet holds true that these laws change,
> As we have seen the Greeks themselves often
> Departing from the first instructions,
> And the Romans, though inheriting
> Their way of composing tragedy from the Greeks,
> leaving the Greek footsteps behind,
> And composing tragedy as time and custom
> of their own required them to.[43]

Dealing freely with the material and with the instructions laid down before the modern poet is seen as only a superficial departure from the ancients. In fact, departing from the ancients is seen as just another way of imitating the ancients — or, better, it is imitating the way the ancients went about creating literature in the first place: by free imitation. The Greeks inherited yet departed from the 'first instructions' just as the Romans inherited yet departed from the Greeks: because the ancients' literary system is itself mimetic and emulative, so too is the modern, which is modelled upon and in direct dialogue with the ancient. Thus, any disobedience perpetrated with a view to accommodating content and structure to the tastes of the poet's contemporaries is not only permitted but required: it is a choice inherently written into the ethics of imitation of the period as the productive principle at the foundation of new literary creations.

---

43 'E perciò crede hora il Poeta nostro, / che sì ferme non sian le leggi poste / a le tragedie, che non gli sia dato / uscir fuor del prescritto in qualche parte, / [...] Et egli tien per cosa più che certa / che s'hora fusser qui i poeti antichi / cercherian sodisfare a questi tempi, / a' Spettatori, a la materia nova. / E che sia ver che varin queste leggi, / vedesi che più volte i Greci istessi / si sono da i primi ordini partiti, / et i Romani, anchor ch'avesser presi / il modo di componerle da' Greci / lasciare a dietro le vestigia Greche, / E si diero à comporle, come l'uso / dei fatti lor, dei lor tempi chiedeva': Giraldi 1970a, 489; see also Giraldi 1970, 484–485: 'E se forse in qualche parte mi son partito dalle regole che dà Aristotile per conformarmi co' costumi de' tempi nostri, l'ho io fatto coll'essempio degli antichi. [...] Et oltre a ciò lo mi ha concesso il medesimo Aristotile, il quale non vieta punto, quando ciò richiede o luogo o tempo o la qualità delle cose che sono in maneggio, il partirci alquanto da quell'arte ch'egli ha ridotta sotto i precetti che dati ci ha'.

3 'Volgarizzamento' and Italy's Intellectual and Literary History

As we have seen, the cross-pollinating nature of imitation as the productive motor of new literary creation characterises the composition, translation and production of old and new tragedies in 16th-century Italy. Their inherent hybridity has rendered these works hard to define, and they have only recently become the object of serious scrutiny.

That these works are of a puzzling nature is testified by recent editions of some of these texts, which are located in a kind of terminological (translation or tragedy?) and disciplinary (Classics or Modern Languages?) limbo. Indeed, if some tragedies are categorised and published as theatrical texts belonging to so-called 'Italian Renaissance tragedy',[44] others feature more specifically as 'translations' of classical texts.[45] In modern scholarship, these works are often referred to as 'volgarizzamenti'.[46] In his 2002 *Italian Tragedy in the Renaissance*,

---

[44] Cf. for example, Renzo Cremante's edition of some of the most famous 16th-century tragedies, including, amongst others, Trissino's *Sophonisba* (1524), Rucellai's *Rosmunda* (1525), and Giraldi's *Orbecche* (1543), which are (re)published under 'Theatre' in the book series *La Letteratura Italiana. Storia e Testi* (Cremante 1988). Some of Alessandro Pazzi de' Medici's translations/tragedies (*Dido in Carthagine, Iphigenia in Tauris, Cyclope, Edipo Principe*) have recently been re-assembled and edited as texts belonging to Italian literature and theatre under the title *Alessandro de' Pazzi e il Rinascimento fiorentino. Dalle posizioni machiavelliane ai Medici e a Bembo* (Sorella 2013; 'Alessandro de' Pazzi and Florentine Renaissance. From Machiavelli's positions to the Medici and Bembo'). The most recent editions of Michelangelo Buonarrotti il Giovane's *Ecuba* (Buonarroti 2017) and Giovanni Andrea dell'Anguillara's *Edippo* (Anguillara 2020) feature in a book series devoted to theatrical texts (*Voci Di Repertorio* and *Il Parlaggio*, respectively).

[45] Cf. for example, the edition of Giovanni da Falgano's *Ippolito* and *Ecuba* (Da Falgano 1995) for Olschki, which bears the subtitle 'volgarizzamenti inediti dal greco' ('unpublished vernacularisations from the Greek'), or that of Marcantonio Cinuzzi's *Prometeo*, published as a 'traduzione' ('translation') in a series that is otherwise mainly devoted to Greek and Latin texts, Adolf M. Hakkert (Cinuzzi 2006). Dolce's *Tieste* (1543; Dolce 2010) and *Medea* (1557; Dolce 2005), as well as Alamanni's *Antigone* (1532–1533; Alamanni 1997), are (re)published as part of the book series Echo – 'Collezione di traduttori' ('Collection of translators'), whose aim is to gather the most important and influential Italian translations written between the 16th and 18th centuries. This editorial project as a whole publishes texts mainly belonging or relevant to the study of Italian literature.

[46] Cf. amongst others, Neri (1904) 95ff., Bertana (1905) 35ff., Dionisotti (1967) *passim*, Pertusi (1966) *passim*, Porro (1981) *passim*, Folena (1990) *passim*, Guthmüller (1990, 1993), Di Maria (2002), Montorfani (2006).

Salvatore Di Maria explains early on that 'the eagerness to divulge to a wider audience the content of newly found ancient texts led to translations into the vernacular and reworkings *appropriately called* "volgarizzamenti"'.[47]

However, even if we concede that some 16th-century 'translations' are more evidently anchored to their models than others, it remains terminologically problematic to state which might fall into the category of 'translation' and which might be 'appropriately called' volgarizzamenti, especially when the term 'volgarizzamento' is by and large absent from discussions about the tragedies/translations of the period.[48] Indeed, it seems as though volgarizzamento has functioned as a *passepartout* in order to evade the terminological impasse that arises when defining all translated products of the period, starting with the copious catalogues of volgarizzamenti drawn up between the 17th and 18th centuries by avid bibliophiles and manuscript collectors. This is the case, for example, with Scipione Maffei's *Italian Translators, i.e. a list of the volgarizzamenti of ancient Greek and Latin writers* (1720),[49] Jacopo Maria Paitoni's *Library of the ancient Greek and Latin authors put into the vernacular* (1766),[50] and Filippo Argelati's *Library of Volgarizzatori*,[51] first published in 1766–1767 after his death, with additions by Angelo Teodoro. In these massive collections, 16th-century volgarizzamenti are variously gathered together with much later (18th-century), as well as much earlier (as early as the 13th-century), translated prod-

---

47 Di Maria (2002) 19, *my italics*.
48 Whilst the forms 'volganamente' adv. > 'volgarmente' adv., 'volgare' adj./s.m., 'volgarizzare' v., 'volgarizzato' adj., 'volgarizzatore' s.m., 'volgarmente' adv., are indeed present, there are no instances of 'volgarizzamento' in the database *Tesoro della Lingua Italiana delle Origini* (TLIO), the online historical dictionary of ancient Italian, which contains all available textual attestations beginning with the first 'Italian' text in the 13th century to the end of the 14th century. A search for the term 'volgarizzamento' amongst the 67,811 pieces of bibliographical information from 1501 to 1600 collected in the database Edit 16 also yields no result. To my knowledge, the term is also altogether absent from prefaces and works listed in 18th-century catalogues that collect volgarizzamenti beginning with the origins of Italian literature up to the 18th century, except for Castelvetro 1576, in which he uses the term 'vulgarizzamento' as a way to distinguish his translation of Aristotle's *Poetics* from its commentary (1576, 12, 14, 16). The *Biblioteca Italiana* (*BI*) database records four occurrences of the term prior to the 18th century, though these appear only in the titles of later (post-18th-century) publications.
49 'Traduttori Italiani o sia notizia de volgarizzamenti d'antichi scrittori Latini e Greci, che sono in luce'.
50 'Biblioteca degli autori antichi greci, e latini volgarizzati'.
51 'Biblioteca degli Volgarizzatori'.

ucts,⁵² all categorised as volgarizzamenti but conceptually belonging to completely different translation-related activities.

A rather interesting occurrence of 'volgarizzamento' appears in the first edition of the *Vocabolario degli Accademici della Crusca*, published for the first time in 1612. Although the term is only equipped with a proper dictionary entry in the third edition of 1691, it features extensively in the 1612 preface. Juxtaposed with 'translations' ('traslatamenti') as if they were a hendiadys, the volgarizzamenti seem to refer to the many renditions 'of other authors' works, some from Latin, some from provençal',⁵³ which were 'transposed into this language by those authors of ours belonging to the good century';⁵⁴ and such works are mentioned as important sources for the compilation of the dictionary.⁵⁵ In other words, volgarizzamento designates a very specific type of translation in this instance, one that occurred between the 13th and 14th centuries in Italy and which, as Alison Cornish argues, pinpointed the move 'between an already well-established literary language' (Latin, but also other vernaculars) 'into one that [was] not yet'.⁵⁶ It was a practice of domestication devoted to 'popularising' (*vulgus*) and simplifying texts to make them available to illiterate people.

However, according to the *Crusca*'s compilers, these volgarizzamenti are rather important texts and thus appear as sources *despite* their being translations. Indeed, there are many 'mistakes' in these texts, the dictionary's compilers confess, mistakes that derive from 'the little knowledge of Latin at the time' and the translator's 'steering away from the true nature/sentiment of the Latin au-

---

52 See under Cicero, for example, where there are listed, amongst others, a volgarizzamento of the *Rhetorica ad Herennium* by Guidotto da Bologna (13th century) (now attributed to Bono Giamboni), and one of the *Pro Quinto Ligario* by Brunetto Latini (1220 ca. – 1294 ca.) (Argelati 1767, IV, 230, 225).
53 Artale-Guadagnini 2018, 385 explain that here 'provençal' is to be identified with any vernacular 'beyond the Alps'.
54 'Traslatamenti d'opere altrui, tratti parte dal Latino, e parte dal Provenzale, e recati da' nostrali autori, di quel secol buono, in questo linguaggio'; the text is published online in *Lessicografia della Crusca in Rete* (henceforth: LCR). See also Folena's definition in 1990, 32: 'la traduzione da altri 'volgari' romanzi e da lingue diverse come anche dal latino'.
55 Artale-Guadagnini 2018 republish the table of all the writers quoted in the 1612 edition of the dictionary, which is divided between 'antichi' and 'moderni': if the first section counts 55 volgarizzamenti among the 180 sources quoted from the 'good century', the second has only one volgarizzamento, from the 16th century, out of the 51 sources employed from 1400 to 1600. 'This huge difference' in numbers, Artale-Guadagnini argue, 'is to be connected with the fact ... that' for the compilers of the *Crusca* dictionary 'translations offer a [linguistic] testimony of paramount importance in the early period', but 'don't in later ones' (2018, 387).
56 Cornish 2013, 11.

thor'.[57] These works are, in fact, most valuable as precious linguistic testimonies of a certain use of the vernacular. The compilers explain that the language employed therein coincides with the vernacular of the 'good century' ('buon secolo'); that is, from the 'time of Dante', 'or a little before then …, to the death of Boccaccio'.[58]

It was precisely this period that had been held up, not long before 1612, as a model for 16th-century writers, including translators:[59] Dante, Petrarch, and Boccaccio had been selected as literary exempla to follow and play a part in the wider programme of 'aristocratisation' of the vernacular so as to raise it to literary status, i.e., remove it from the *vulgus* — a move that was the opposite of the project which the vernacular (and vernacular translation) had been engaged in two centuries earlier and one that had much to do with class, as suggested at the beginning of this chapter.

But there is more: this programme of 'aristocratisation' of the vernacular finds its justification, once again, in the ancients. As the pivotal literary figure in this shift of status of the vernacular, Pietro Bembo, explained in his influential *Prose della volgar lingua* (1525), putting literary endeavours off limits from the likes of the 'moltitudine' ('multitude') and reserving them for the appreciation of the few 'dotti' ('learned') was grounded in examples that came from the Graeco-Roman tradition. Demosthenes, Aristophanes, and Terence, for example, 'have indeed reasoned with the people in a way that they could understand', but not 'in the way the people may have reasoned with them'.[60]

---

57 'Ne' libri volgarizzati, per la poca intelligenza, in que' tempi, del latino idioma, sono molti e diversi errori, non tanto per essersi lasciato il volgarizzatore tirare a molte voci, e locuzioni di quella lingua, quanto per essersi discostato non poche volte dal sentimento più vero del latino scrittore'; in Artale-Guadagnini 2018, 384.
58 '[…] Abbiamo stimato necessario di ricorrere all'autorità di quegli scrittori, che vissero, quando questo idioma principalmente fiorì, che fu da' tempi di Dante, o ver poco prima sino ad alcuni anni, dopo la morte del Boccaccio'; in LCR.
59 Cf., for example, Dolce's following the linguistic rules and literary models (Dante, Petrarch, and Boccaccio) set by Bembo in his translation of Ovid's *Metamorphoses* (cf. Guthmüller 1993, 511–512).
60 'Simigliantemente averne di Demostene tra' Greci; e poco meno in quell'altra maniera di scrivere, d'Aristofane e di Terenzio tra loro e tra noi. Per la qual cosa dire di loro si può, che essi bene hanno ragionato col popolo in modo che sono stati dal popolo intesi, ma non in quella guisa nella quale il popolo ha ragionato con loro'; Bembo 1966, 37. For a general overview of and bibliography related to Pietro Bembo's influential *Prose della volgar lingua*, see Dionisotti 1966 and 1967, 136–137; in his *Rinascimento e Classicismo*, Quondam asserts that the 'structuring of the vernacular into a linguistic system can be safely dated back to the 1530s, between the

It is in following 16th-century linguistic *auctoritates*, such as the 'illustrious cardinal Bembo' (and his *Prose della volgar lingua*, 1525), 'those charged with amending Boccaccio in 1573' (a committee of learned men carefully chosen to cleanse Boccaccio's *Decameron*, which had made the *Index Librorum prohibitorum* in 1559),[61] and Lionardo Salviati (a pivotal figure in the Accademia della Crusca and its *Vocabolario*),[62] that the dictionary's compilers decided to limit themselves to works belonging to the 'good century'. Writers before that date were 'much antiquated', they report, quoting Salviati, whereas those after 'corrupted the purity of speaking of the good century'.[63]

So, in this normative linguistic endeavour, 'volgarizzamento' is a technical term that encompasses a translating activity which may be criticised for its inaccuracies as translation but is commendable for its good use of the vernacular. The volgarizzamenti are thus employed by 16th-century linguists to move the vernacular beyond the 'vulgus' and into the hands of an elite that is more numerous than before, but is still very much an elite.

It is precisely this type of volgarizzamento that has received most attention in scholarship. For scholars, it provides important linguistic testimonies to a vernacular that was to become *the* vernacular a few centuries later and as rather early products of a translating activity that had few or no equivalents in Europe at the time.[64] The historical dictionary specifically devoted to the origins of the Italian language (TLIO: *Tesoro della Lingua Italiana delle Origini*) includes a substantial number and a complete bibliography of all the volgarizzamenti up

---

first edition of *Prose della volgar lingua* (1525) and the translation of Aristotle's *Poetics* into Italian (1538), via the first edition of Baldassarre Castiglione's *Libro Cortegiano* (1528) (1999, 372).
61 On the philological and linguistic cleansing of Boccaccio's *Decameron* in 1572, and then again in 1582 at the hands of Lionardo Salviati, see Gargiulo 2009 and Maino 2012.
62 On Salviati's role in the *Vocabolario*, see Artale-Guadagnini 2018, 384 for a bibliography.
63 'Nel compilare il presente Vocabolario (col parere dell'Illustrissimo Cardinal Bembo, de' Deputati alla correzion del Boccaccio dell'anno 1573, e ultimamente del Cavalier Lionardo Salviati) abbiamo stimato necessario di ricorrere all'autorità di quegli scrittori, che vissero, quando questo idioma principalmente fiorì, che fu da' tempi di Dante, o ver poco prima sino ad alcuni anni, dopo la morte del Boccaccio. Il qual tempo, raccolto in una somma di tutto un secolo, potremo dir, che sia dall'anno del Signore 1300 al 1400, poco più, o poco meno: perché, secondo che ottimamente discorre il Salviati, gli scrittori, dal 1300 indietro, si possono stimare, in molte parti della lor lingua, soverchio antichi, e quei dal 1400 avanti, curuppero non piccola parte della purità del favellare di quel buon secolo'; in LCR.
64 Cf. Cornish 2011, 1–7.

to 1400, compiled by Elena Artale and available online.[65] This is indeed only one of the most important results of an interest that has attracted much attention in Italian scholarship at least since the 1960s.[66]

An important project concerned with cataloguing and scrutinising volgarizzamenti was instituted by the Ministry for Assets and Cultural Activities (Ministero per i beni e le attività culturali) in 2003. Though it extends beyond the early volgarizzamenti and includes (as well as publishing) a number of 16th-century translations from ancient Greek (none of which is ancient Greek tragedy, however),[67] its survey, census and editorial endeavours stop at 1527 and have privileged translations from Greek into Latin.[68] Indeed, translation from Greek into Latin is invested with linguistic importance for scholars in Classics because it is part of the life and development of Latin in the early modern period. The case of 16th-century translation of ancient Greek drama is further complicated by its hybrid nature, as has been amply documented throughout this chapter: unless the texts under scrutiny have been deemed to fall within the category of new, original tragedies, and have thus been published by scholars in the Modern Languages departments as early modern tragic plays, neither the Latin nor the vernacular engagements with Greek tragedy in this period have

---

65 The project is part of the Italian Dictionary (OVI: *Opera del Vocabolario Italiano*), which has been financed and promoted by the Italian National Council of Research (CNR: *Consiglio Nazionale delle Ricerche*) since 1965.

66 Cf. bibliography in Romanini 2007, 382; Dionisotti 1967 certainly represents a pivotal starting point.

67 Funding was suspended in 2011. A quick look at the digital census of the translations of Greek texts in early modern Italy (ENTG: *Edizione Nazionale delle Traduzioni dei testi greci*) reveals a vast number of mostly anonymous, unpublished manuscripts containing translations of Greek drama into Latin especially, which have been catalogued but have seldom received the attention they deserve. Furthermore, the manuscripts therein recorded represent just over half of those actually available in libraries, as can be seen if one scouts through (hardcopy and digital) library catalogues in Italy. A (tentatively) complete list of all volgarizzamenti of ancient Greek tragedy between 1400 and 1600 is in preparation, see Di Martino-Fiore forthcoming 2023.

68 The project is eloquently titled *The Return of the Classics during Humanism* (*Il Ritorno dei Classici nell'Umanesimo*) and comprises four publishing series: 'I. The national edition of comments to Latin texts during humanism and renaissance; II. The national edition of the early volgarizzamenti from Latin texts to the Italian vernacular; III. The national edition of translations of Greek texts during humanism and the renaissance [ENTG, cf. footnote above]; IV. The national edition of texts relating to humanistic historiography' (Cortesi 2007, 2). Interestingly, it distinguishes volgarizzamenti (belonging to the earlier period of the Italian vernacular(s)) from translations (belonging to the later period, identified with so-called humanism and renaissance). One need only look at the publication page of the ENTG to see that translation from Greek into Latin has been privileged to translation into the vernacular.

interested many scholars in Classics or in Translation Studies; indeed, rarely have these texts been considered to be of particular importance for the history of Italian literature or translation in the early modern period.[69]

Beyond those mentioned above, there is also another more interesting, yet hidden, reason for the neglect of 16th-century volgarizzamenti and the privileging of the early ones, one which has long haunted Italian scholarship and which, as Quondam argues, goes back to the Risorgimento's creation of a literary history that was subsidiary to the creation of the Italian nation; it is indeed a reason that has much to do with Italy's national agenda, as suggested at the beginning of this chapter.[70]

As the influence of the Romantic genius and the invention of originality inevitably divorced from the category of imitation as the inherent productive principle of literary creation, recently unified Italy (1861) was scouting out its (literary) heroes to parade in the construction of its national past, for its '*Ossian*' and 'Shakespeare'.[71] The identification of Dante, Petrarch and Boccaccio as the par-

---

69 Projects that are subsidiary to the scrutiny of late-15th and 16th-century volgarizzamenti are, amongst others, the online census database of all printed books in the 16th century (Edit16), a government-funded project run by the Central Institute for the Union Catalogue of Italian Libraries and for Bibliographic Information (*Istituto centrale per il catalogo unico delle biblioteche italiane e per le informazioni bibliografiche*); the AHRC *Vernacular Aristotelianism in Renaissance Italy, c. 1400–c. 1650* (2010–2013), followed by the ERC project *Rethinking Renaissance and Early-Modern Intellectual History* (c. 1400–c. 1650) (2014–2019), both based at the University of Warwick; the AHRC-funded project with the British Library and Royal Holloway entitled *The Italian Academies, 1525–1700: The First Intellectual Networks of Early Modern Europe* (2010–2014), with an online database; and FRIDA (Festivals in Renaissance Italy: A Digital Atlas), which 'recreates early-modern festivals as multimedia digital events through a dynamic, web-based platform – a digital Atlas – that restores the mosaic-like fragments of festivals to the form in which humanists, artists, and poets first conceived them' (FRIDA 2021). On the APGRD's *Translating Ancient Drama* research project run at the APGRD see Macintosh-Di Martino 2021 and Gillespie in this volume.
70 Quondam identifies Francesco De Sanctis's *History of Italian Literature* (Storia della letteratura italiana; 1817–1883) as the 'founding text' of this narrative, a narrative which continued to thrive for at least another full century, if not more, and which contributes to explain why serious studies on early modern Italy were first conducted outside of Italy, particularly in the United States (see, for example, Fantoni's edited volume *Gli Anglo-americani a Firenze. Idea e costruzione del Rinascimento*, 2000).
71 Quondam 2002, 42. Italy was unable to reconcile itself with its 'classical' past, its inevitably 'Christian-centric' and 'classics-centric' culture, unless it rid itself of those centuries which had built their aesthetic and literary systems around the classics. Other European countries had found a way to deal with, and even celebrate, their own 'Ancient Regime and its culture', such as France, which, Quondam argues, had made peace with its past to such an extent that the

adigmatic pillars of Italy's literary history went hand in hand with another historical narrative which presented itself as particularly useful to those charged with finding (and founding) a national identity after Italy's political unification. In Quondam's words, 'in origin there was the freedom of the comuni [during the 'good century'], that is the creation of the idea and institutions of the republic; there [followed] a most long transition from the crisis and decadence of republican freedom to the reconquering of the desire at least to return to being a free and republican nation'.[72] The emperor Charles V's siege and conquest of Florence in 1530 was identified as a watershed between a republican, free Italy and one enslaved to foreign powers.[73]

The re-integration of 16th-century volgarizzamenti into Italy's intellectual, literary and dramatic history, as well as, most importantly, the reception history of the 'original' ancient texts these volgarizzamenti are adapted from, inscribes itself into a general re-appreciation of this period's literary and dramatic production that does away with the imitative-derogative equation and historicises its outputs as stemming from, and belonging to, a different value system. If it is indeed true that 'almost nothing has been written on the theory of vulgarization from classical languages to the vernacular in the Italian Renaissance',[74] we hope that this chapter has contributed not only to interrogating the validity of 'volgarizzamento' as a defining label, but also to highlighting the historical, linguistic, cultural and political importance that these 16th-century texts and paratexts have for a history of the theory and practice of translation of and for the theatre in this period.

19th-century historiographer Jules Michelet consecrated it forever with the invention of the 'âge Classique' (cf. ibid.).
72 Quondam 2002, 44.
73 Cf. Quondam 2002, 39.
74 See fn. 1.

Claudia Cuzzotti
The Italian Translation of Euripides' *Hecuba* by Michelangelo Buonarroti the Younger (1568–1647)

Abstract: The present chapter focuses on the Italian translation of Euripides' tragedy Hecuba by Michelangelo the Younger, the great nephew of Michelangelo Buonarroti. Michelangelo the Younger was a leading figure in the artistic and political scene of 16th- and 17th-century Florence, and he had strong relations with the ruling Medici family. His long activity at the court led him to write for the theatre. He is the author of several comedies; the translation of Hecuba is his only extant tragic work and it has only recently been published (Cuzzotti 2017). His translation stands out for his attempt to remain close to the Greek text; unlike many 16th- and 17th-century translators, Michelangelo translated directly from the original; he also made use of a Latin translation and of a couple of Italian versions. This chapter compares Michelangelo's version with other versions of Hecuba and with translations of other Euripidean tragedies in 16th-century Italy.

1 The *Ecuba* by Michelangelo Buonarroti the Younger: An Introduction

Translations were one of the several interests of Buonarroti the Younger (1568–1647), the great nephew of Michelangelo Buonarroti. He was a leading poet on the cultural scene of 16th- and 17th-century Florence: he worked for the Medici court and was a close friend of Pope Urban VIII and Galileo; he was a friend and collaborator of the well-known singer Francesca Caccini, and became a member of various academies, both in Florence, where he joined the Accademia Fiorentina and the Crusca Academy, and in other Italian cities, such as Pavia. Besides poetry and theatre, Buonarroti was also interested in art, music, painting and heraldry. His literary production, partly still unpublished, ranges from theatrical plays to be staged in courts (the most important are *La Tancia* and *La Fiera*, the latter known above all for its lexical experimentalism) to lyric, religious and music poetry, to satire and other genres related to the activity of academies.[1]

It is against this multifaceted background that one should consider his translation of *Hecuba*, kept in the Buonarroti Archive in Florence (manuscript 92).[2] As the manuscript shows, the text was extensively revised by Buonarroti and a total of six different translations exist. Only one can be precisely dated, as recorded in Buonarroti's correspondence: it is the version sent to Maffeo Barberini (the future Pope Urban VIII) in 1599 and kept in the Vatican Library (Barb. Lat. 3949).[3] Subsequent translations, on the other hand, are not precisely datable, but Buonarroti is likely to have worked on them for several years. The final version cannot be considered a finished work, as it contains some textual alternatives and partial directions on acts, scenes and characters.[4] Among the various versions, two have great importance: the *Ecuba Barberini* and the last version of this translation, which I will refer to as Ecuba throughout this chapter. Being very different from each other, they were published side by side in my 2017 edition of Ecuba, with two distinct critical apparatuses. In between these two versions is a very literal translation, which is of great importance for understanding the evolution from the *Ecuba Barberini* to the last version.

---

[1] For a short biography of Buonarroti the Younger, see Buonarroti 2017, 43–54. Comprehensive information can be found in two publications by Janie Cole dedicated to Buonarroti's poetic compositions for music (Cole 2007) and his role as mediator in the field of music and entertainment between the 16th and 17th centuries (Cole 2011).

[2] Manuscript 92 is entirely devoted to translations. *Ecuba* is the only work taken from a Greek play, while the others are from works in Latin prose; see Buonarroti 2017, 56–58. *Ecuba* is also the most challenging text, while the other translations are incomplete (with the exception of two), and sometimes are not very long. Some translations from Greek into Latin can be found in manuscript 96: they are interlinear versions probably carried out as an exercise (among them there is also a large part of *Hecuba*: see Cuzzotti 2011, 20 and 20 n. 24).

[3] I refer to this version as *Ecuba Barberini*. In manuscript 92 this version is included as a correction on the text of a previous version. See Buonarroti 2017, 9–11; 59–60.

[4] The long working process and the incompleteness of the play was typical of Buonarroti, who repeatedly revised what he had already written, also because he was frequently asked to write for the court (in particular dramas to be performed during the numerous celebrations held) and he often had to interrupt the other works he was doing. *La Fiera* is the best example of his *modus operandi*: started as early as 1604 and staged in 1619, during the Carnival, it was extensively reviewed and the author was unable to publish it in his lifetime. There are therefore two versions: the 'performance script', as it were, and the revised version, which exceeds 30,000 verses. The first version was edited by U. Limentani (see Buonarroti 1984); the second one, published in 1726 by A.M. Salvini, was edited more recently by O. Pelosi (see Buonarroti 2003).

2 *Hecuba* and the Other Euripidean Translations in 16th-Century Italy

Buonarroti began composing his *Ecuba* in the late 16th century. At that time, a long tradition of reading and translation of this tragedy had already been established.[5] As a matter of fact, amongst all the Euripidean plays rendered into Italian, *Hecuba* was the one that enjoyed the greatest success. Compared to other Euripidean plays, it also had the largest number of renderings. This was due to the fact that, from the Byzantine period onwards, *Hecuba* had become the major focus of scholarly interest. It was the lead play of the 'Byzantine triad' (along with *Orestes* and *Phoenissae*) as well as of 16th-century Euripidean editions.[6] It was the first of Euripides' tragedies to be translated into Latin, in 1362 by Leonzio Pilato, who translated the first 466 lines for Boccaccio, and in the 15th century by an anonymous translator, who produced a full version of the tragedy. Later on, it was translated by the Dutch scholar Erasmus, and subsequently enjoyed a great number of Latin and Italian versions.[7]

Stiblin, a 16th-century translator of the Euripidean corpus into Latin, argued that the tragedy *iure principem locum tenet* ('justly holds a prominent position'),

---

[5] See Pollard 2012, 1063–1070.
[6] Two editions of Euripides' plays are worth mentioning: the Aldine edition (1503), which was considered the *editio princeps* (see Manuzio & Grigoropoulos 1503) and contained all plays except the *Electra,* first edited by Pietro Vettori in 1545 (see Vettori 1545) and the complete edition by Willem Canter in 1571 (see Canter 1571).
[7] The 15th-century version is included in the Code Marc. lat. XIV 54 (4328), ff. 90r–100r. Several hypotheses on the identity of the anonymous translator have been formulated (see, for example, Pertusi 1963, 402 and Porro 1992, 343–362). Among the Latin translations, the most famous were the *Hecuba* and *Iphigenia in Aulide* by Erasmus, first printed in Paris in 1506 and the following year in Venice by Aldo Manuzio (see Erasmus 1506; Erasmus 1507). These translations became a model for several subsequent versions (for example Giovan Battista Gelli's and Lodovico Dolce's *Ecuba*. It is Gelli himself who, in the dedication letter of his translation, tells us that he used Erasmus's text. For information on Dolce's models, see Giazzon 2011, 36, 180, and Di Martino in this volume). Latin translations of the entire corpus were made by Rudolf Collin in 1541 (see Collin 1541; this translation did not contain the *Electra,* for obvious chronological reasons), by Caspar Stiblin in 1562 (see Stiblin 1562) and by Emilio Porto in 1597 (see Porto/Canter 1597). Collin's translation (as well as the aforementioned translation by Erasmus) provided a model for Dolce, while Buonarroti used Porto's version for his own translation from the Greek. For further information on translations from Euripides in the 15th and 16th centuries, see Pertusi 1963, 401 ff.; Petrina 1999, 213–217; Cortesi-Fiaschi 2008, 470–476. See Vedelago and Dedieu in this volume for more on Erasmus's influence on translating practices and discourses about translation.

due to its extremely varied content and the atrocities presented in it. The play was seen as morally useful, visible in the deterrent power of the punishment inflicted on the wicked and in the numerous gnomic sentences present in the tragedy.[8]

Limited to the texts edited until today, the importance of the *Hecuba* among the Euripidean titles during the 16th century is attested by six plays composed by the following scholars: Giovan Battista Gelli, Matteo Bandello, Lodovico Dolce, Giovanni da Falgano, Giovanni Balcianelli, Buonarroti the Younger; *Troades*, having four renderings, is at the second place; in the same period, eleven further translations were inspired by ten Euripidean titles, i.e., *Alcestis, Andromache, Bacchae, Cyclops, Hippolytos, Iphigenia Aulidensis, Iphigenia Taurica, Medea, Phoenissae,* and *Supplices*.[9]

Fewer than half of these texts were published in the 16th century, while the majority appeared later, from the 18th century onwards (this is the case of Buonarroti's *Ecuba*). Finally, among the unpublished translations, Michelangelo Serafini's *Le Fenisse* is worth mentioning: this is actually the first known attempt of a direct translation of the tragedy in the Tuscan language, i.e., without the mediation of a Latin translation of the original Greek.[10]

This corpus broadly illustrates two translative practices. Some of these works include the presence of new characters and/or new scenes, or a combination of different models (e.g., the use of characters and scenes from another play, or even from a non-tragic source), and the choice of a new title or of a different setting.[11] So that although translating of ancient and other material

---

8 See Heath 1987, 40–68.
9 See the table at the end of the book.
10 For further information on *Le Fenisse*, see Porro 1981, 481–508.
11 There are also examples of Euripidean fragments inserted in plays that are not otherwise inspired from Euripides, as in Giovan Giorgio Trissino's *Sofonisba*, or Giovanni Rucellai's *Rosmunda*. In *Sofonisba*, the story of the Carthaginian queen, inspired by Livy's prose narrative, contains a scene taken from *Alcestis* (where Alcestis bids farewell to her children and leaves her material possessions); however, the character of Alcestis' husband is replaced with that of Erminia, a dear friend to whom Sofonisba entrusts her children. At the beginning of the play, then, the dialogue between Sofonisba and Erminia recalls the dialogue between Agamemnon and the servant in *Iphigenia Aulidensis* (compare lines 134–155 of *Sofonisba* with lines 16–33 of *IA*). The relationship between *Alcestis* and *Sofonisba* had already been discussed in the 17th century by Giovan Battista Parisotti in the notes to his own translation of *Alcestis* (see Parisotti 1735). *Rosmunda* reproduces the story of *Antigone* setting it in Lombardy. Rosmunda is the daughter of the king of the Gepids, defeated and killed by the Lombard king Alboin. Like Antigone, the girl attempts to bury a relative, despite the prohibition of the king. Although the main model is Sophocles, there is a clear influence of the Euripidean *Hecuba*. The dialogue

does indeed occur, the final products are not full-length *translations* of one of Euripides' plays.¹² The most significant examples are transpositions of ancient Greek Euripidean tragedies by Lodovico Dolce's works (*Giocasta, La Medea, Le Troiane, Ifigenia*); other examples include Rucellai's *Oreste* and the two works by Bongianni Gratarolo, taken from Troades.

Others, instead, follow one source text and maintain the structure as well as general wording of the original, such as Giovan Battista Gelli's, Matteo Bandello's, Giovanni da Falgano's and Buonarroti the Younger's versions of Euripides' *Hecuba*, together with Cristoforo Guidiccioni's works (*Andromache, Bacchae, Supplices, Troades*) and Pazzi de' Medici's *Cyclope* and *Iphigenia in Tauris*.¹³ Lodovico Dolce's *La Hecuba* features among this group of works, even if it deals freely with the original here and there, since the author did not combine sources, or add new material, as he did in most of his other tragedies.¹⁴

The plays following the first translative practice often combine Euripidean and Senecan sources. In Dolce's *Giocasta*, for instance, a scene from Seneca's *Oedipus* is inserted into a plot inspired by Euripides' *Phoenissae*.¹⁵ Dolce also included in his plays non-tragic ancient sources. An interesting example is *Medea*, where he inserted part of Cicero's speech *Pro Sexto Roscio Amerino* into a dialogue on patricide between the Nurse and Bailo.¹⁶ Sometimes the sources are both ancient and modern: this is the case of Bongianni Gratarolo's *Polissena*, mainly inspired by Seneca's and Euripides' *Troades*, and Euripides' *Hecuba*, but also by Dolce's *Le Troiane*.¹⁷

The introduction of new characters and/or new scenes mainly occurs when different sources coexist, but can also be found when the early modern text is

---

between Faliscus (an official of Alboin) and Rosmunda is modeled on the dialogue between Hecuba and Odysseus. Similarly, in predicting Rosmunda's future as a slave, Faliscus uses the words spoken by Polyxena in the scene in which she claims to prefer death to slavery. See also the Introduction for further discussion on 'translating' in the early modern period.
12 See Introduction.
13 *Iphigenia in Tauris* was published by Sorella in 2013 together with other unpublished works by Pazzi (see Sorella 2013), while the *Cyclope* was published by Angelo Solerti in 1887 (see Solerti 1887); this edition contained also some lines of the *Iphigenia in Tauris* as an example of the metres used by Pazzi in his translations.
14 For an in-depth study of Dolce's tragedies, see Giazzon 2011.
15 It is the scene in which Tiresias and Manto observe the entrails during a sacrifice (Dolce adds a priest, while Manto has a more marginal role). For *Giocasta*, see Giazzon 2011, 178–221.
16 See Giazzon 2011, 284.
17 The peacemaker in the dispute between Agamemnon and Pyrrhus is taken from Dolce's *Le Troiane*. Dolce takes the dispute scene from Seneca's *Troades* (where, however, there is no peacemaker): in Dolce the peacemaker is Menelaus, while in Gratarolo it is Nestor.

drawn from one source only. Another alley explored in freer rewritings is to give greater importance to a specific character present in the source text, but who has a silent part or merely pronounces one or two very short lines. This is the case with children, like Orestes in *Iphigenia Aulidensis* or Medea's children. In his versions, Dolce gives voice to children, obtaining strong dramatic effects (for example when Orestes bids farewell to his sister). Another example is Maffeo Galladei's *Medea*. In this play, Medea's children praise the Spanish king Philip II, to whom the work is dedicated, thus making the text politically relevant to the period (they say the monarch will bring back the Golden Age).[18]

Conversely, new titles appear in Giovanni Rucellai's *Oreste* and Lodovico Dolce's *Giocasta*. His *Oreste* is a rewriting of *Iphigenia Taurica*, while *Giocasta* is inspired by Euripides' *Phoenissae*. In both cases, the new title attests to the key importance of the characters. Rucellai highlights Orestes and his friendship with Pylades, while Dolce focuses his tragedy on Giocasta, the unfortunate heroine modelled on Hecuba.

Finally, works set in a different context and period have in common that they were all written in the first decades of the century: Giovanni Rucellai (*Rosmunda*) and Giovan Giorgio Trissino (*Sofonisba*), linked to Florence and to the Orti Oricellari circle.

3 The *Ecuba* by Michelangelo Buonarroti the Younger as 'Translation'

Buonarroti's *Ecuba*[19] is a somewhat close rendering of the original Greek, even if he also used Emilio Porto's Latin version as an intermediary text.[20] His translation generally steers away from features which are typical of freer translations of ancient Greek drama published in the same century, such as a large use of *amplificatio* (which is only moderately used by Buonarroti), deletion of stichomythic passages and the simplification of mythological references. Of the three

---

18 Maffeo Galladei's *Medea* is an adaptation of Seneca's play, but it is important to our analysis. The political relevance of the text is particularly evident in Dolce's tragedies. See Giazzon 2011, *passim*.
19 With the title Ecuba, I refer to the last version of the translation, therefore the quoted text and the numbering of the lines are from the final version.
20 Buonarroti used the Latin translation by Emilio Porto; this translation also contains the original Greek edited by Willem Canter in 1571, but research has shown that Buonarroti used the Greek text edited by Aldine (see Buonarroti 2017, 20–26).

characteristics mentioned, *amplificatio* is certainly the most evident and widely used in the translations of Euripides' plays mentioned in the previous section. *Amplificatio* is the addition of more or less extended sections which are absent in the model, mainly in the choral song. Poets can use it for a variety of reasons: perceived obscurity of the original text; a desire to show off their skills within a section, such as a stasimon, which may be disconnected from the action and therefore can be more easily modified; and finally, a desire to explain the myths contained in the choral songs. In general, all the translations from Euripides depart from the model by amplifying it in various ways, in particular with adjectives. These are often arranged in pairs according to the Petrarchan model and their use is meant to obtain dramatic effects (this is the case, for instance, with unfortunate old and young people, such as Hecuba, Polydorus and Polyxena).[21]

Like other authors, Buonarroti too adopted a free approach in translating the choral songs compared to the other parts of the play, which shows he had some difficulties in understanding the Greek text: indeed, one of the few instances showing a misunderstanding of the original text concerns the final lines of a stasimon.[22] In general, however, Buonarroti limits himself to adding one line only or part of it, following recognisable models. In some cases, he uses *amplificatio* to obtain tragic and pathetic effects: examples are adjectives and appositions referring to unfortunate characters such as Priam, Hecuba, Polydorus, Polyxena. In the prologue, Priam is referred to as 'infelice', 'unhappy', a Virgilian quotation; when Polydorus announces that Polyxena is going to die, he calls her 'l'amata mia sorella', 'my beloved sister'; when Hecuba comes out of Agamemnon's tent, she is described as 'pavida e trista', 'fearful and sad', using two adjectives typical of the Petrarchan tradition.[23] In other cases, Buonarroti resorted to *amplificatio* to embellish the text. Some relative clauses, for example, were introduced when Hecuba invokes various divine entities after entering

---

21 For instance, Giovanni da Falgano's *Ecuba* (65–67): 'così la madre mia (the speaker is Polydoros) due *dolci* figli, / Polyxena infelice et me *tapino*, / vedrà con gl'occhi suoi *ancisi et spenti*', 'so my mother will see her two sweet children, the sad Polyxena and me miserable, with her destroyed and lifeless eyes' (cfr. 45–46); Buonarroti the Younger's *Ecuba* (54–55): 'che (*sc.* Hecuba), tolta a Troia *prigioniera e serva*, / qui fa dura dimora', 'that, led away from Troy, imprisoned and slave, will have a very hard life here'; cf. Diggle 1984, line 34. Henceforth the edition and line-numbering referred to for the Greek text is from Diggle's edition, referenced as Diggle 1984.
22 These are the last two lines of the third stasimon (*Hec.* 950–951; *Ecuba* 1342–1343). See Baier, Dedieu and Vedelago in this volume on the difficulty in translating metre.
23 See *Ecuba* 5; 66; 87–88. The adjective referring to Priam is to be compared with 'infelix Priamus' (Verg. *Aen.* III, 50 ed. Paratore).

the scene: 'folgore di Zeus', 'Zeus' lightning bolt', (ὦ στεροπὰ Διός, 68), 'tenebrosa notte', 'dark night' (ὦ σκοτία νύξ, 68), 'veneranda terra', 'venerable earth' (ὦ πότνια χθών, 70). In the original text, only the earth is followed by an apposition: Euripides calls her 'madre dei sogni dalle ali nere', 'mother of dreams with black wings' (μελανοπτερύγων μᾶτερ ὀνείρων, 71). Buonarroti extended apposition to other divine entities as well: 'folgore di Zeus', 'Zeus' lightning bolt', becomes 'folgorante Giove', 'striking Jupiter', to whom the following relative clause refers 'il cui sguardo ogni cosa apprende, e vede', 'whose look finds out and sees everything' (*Ecuba* 107), echoing Dante ('quella il cui bell'occhio tutto vede', 'of her whose beautiful eyes can see everything' *If*. X, 131); the relative clause 'che sola / dell'occulte ombre tue scorgi i sentieri', 'the only one who can see the paths in the dark shadows' (*Ecuba* 108–109) refers to the expression 'tenebrosa notte', 'dark night'. The apposition referred to the earth is amplified, albeit to a lesser extent: in *Ecuba* 113–114 it is described as 'feconda madre', 'prolific mother', and no longer just 'madre' degli 'alati bruni sogni', 'mother of winged dark dreams'. There are also emphasizing repetitions:

> Così ne sforza lei destin crudele
> in questo infausto giorno uscir di vita
> e in questo infausto giorno
> ohimè, vedrà la dolorosa madre
> le membra esangui di due figli estinti.
> (*Ecuba* 70–74)

So a cruel fate will force her to die *on this unlucky day* and *on this unlucky day* alas, the sad mother will see the dead body of her two children.

> Ma di celarmi *a lei* sia mio consiglio,
> *a lei* che move 'l piè fuor delle tende
> d'Agamennone re, *pavida e trista*,
> *pavida e trista* (se di nudo spirto
> sgombro da' sensi mai vero è 'l presagio)
> per l'empio sogno che di me, trafitto,
> ha palesato a lei sembianza fiera.
> (*Ecuba* 85–91)

But I think it is better to hide *from her, from her,* while she is coming out from Agamennon's tents. She is *afraid and anguished, afraid and anguished* (as if the omen felt by a dead man can ever be reliable) for the cruel nightmare she had where she saw the atrocious image of my dead, stabbed body.

Finally, functional *amplificationes* are found in speeches, such as the introduction of verbs of utterance, not present in the Greek text: 'Stupor non fia, *dirò*, se steril terra', 'no astonishment, *I'll say*, if the fruitless earth' (*Ecuba* 861); 'Cose nefande, detestabili, empie, / incredibil, né mai / da tollerarsi *io narro*', 'I'm *telling* terrible, dreadful, sacrilegious, incredible events / which should never be tolerated' (*Ecuba* 1018–1020).[24]

Among other translators, Lodovico Dolce and Matteo Bandello made extensive use of *amplificatio*, albeit in different ways: the former used it with greater ease, introducing new lines within an already existing dialogue, while the latter merely embellished the source text, without adding new lines and thus remaining closer to the original text.[25]

Despite this difference in use, both authors significantly expanded their source text: Dolce's *Hecuba* has 2590 lines compared to the 1376 lines of Erasmus's Latin version, and Bandello's text has more than 3000 lines, thus more than doubling the 1295 lines of Euripides' play. *Amplificatio* was also used, although to a lesser extent, by Giovanni da Falgano in his *Hippolytus*, which has 2300 lines compared to the 1466 of Euripides' play.

These are undoubtedly significant increases in the overall number of words, even allowing for the fact that Italian lines are per se slightly shorter, in the number of syllables, than Greek lines, so that all translations legitimately need to be expanded, especially if one wants to render terms that do not have perfect equivalents, or to rearrange syntactical structures that are not acceptable in the target language.

Buonarroti's intent to offer a translation close to the original text is also attested by his choice to reproduce every line of the tragedy and avoid any simplification of the mythology, something that we find extensively in other translations of Euripides' plays at the time. This technique consisted in deleting patronymics, genealogies and place names, to make the text easier to understand for modern readers; it was used in particular by Dolce and Gelli. Both deleted, for example, part of Polydorus' genealogy at the beginning of their Ecubas, omitting to say that Hecuba is the daughter of Kisseus.[26] Further, some translators reduced to one the adjectives referring to the characters' different nationalities when there was more than one alternative: for instance, Gelli used 'Greci' ('Greeks') to translate different adjectives such as Argives, Pelasgians, Danai, Achaeans.[27] On the other hand, with regards to the translation of each verse of the tragedy, common was the deletion of lines perceived as unim-

---

24 The corresponding verses of the Greek are respectively 592 and 714–715. My italics.
25 For an example of Dolce's practice, see Giazzon 2011, 43.
26 See Tramontana 2016, XXIII; Giazzon 2011, 37.
27 See Tramontana 2016, XXIII.

portant, especially in the stichomythic passages. Such a technique was aimed at obtaining a more fluent text: there are examples of this in Gelli's *Ecuba*, where he deleted many lines from the final dialogue between Hecuba and Polyxena, before the death of Polyxena.[28]

Gelli's free approach to the original text echoes Dolce's, although differently, insofar as the former subtracted from, whereas the latter added to the original. Such freedom, however, is much more evident in Dolce: his version is in between a free translation and an adaptation;[29] Gelli's *Ecuba*, on the other hand, comes across as an overall faithful translation, if one leaves aside the methodological approach (i.e., the freedom with which he treats the model in translating stichomythic passages).

Indeed, among Euripidean translations composed in the 16th century, the *Ecuba* by Buonarroti seems to be the closest to the source text, as well as that by Giovanni da Falgano and the works by Cristoforo Guidiccioni and Pazzi de' Medici. All these translations, as well as the *Ecuba* by Matteo Bandello, were from Greek, although Buonarroti used a Latin version as an intermediary text, in line with 16th-century translation practice. Actually, translators who were working from the Greek did not always have a deep knowledge of the Greek language. However, there were also skilled scholars, such as Pazzi de' Medici (translator among other things of Aristotle's *Poetics* into Latin),[30] who did not use a Latin text as none existed for him to use at the time.[31]

Hints at Buonarroti's process of translation are contained in a manuscript including annotations that he wrote to make the literal translation after the *Ecuba Barberini*.[32] For instance, regarding line 1503 of the *Ecuba Barberini*, he annotated the Latin '*rerum quid pateris?*' (AB 93, c. 46v) as a translation of the original Greek τί πάσχεις; (1127). Many annotations show Buonarroti's intention

---

28 See Tramontana 2016, XXIII; XXIII no 66; 78.
29 For instance, in the dialogue between Hecuba and the Chorus at the beginning of the first act Dolce inserts several new lines in order to make the text 'more lively' (see Giazzon 2011, 43).
30 See Pazzi de' Medici 1536 and Fiore in this volume.
31 The first Latin translation of the Euripidean corpus appeared in 1541, whereas Pazzi composed *Iphigenia in Tauris* and *Cyclops* in 1524–1525 (see Cosentino 2015).
32 For the *Ecuba Barberini* and the different *Ecuba* versions by Buonarroti, see pages 1–2 and footnote 3. The notes made by Buonarroti on his translation are available in the manuscript 93 of the Buonarroti Archive (AB 93), along with the advice given by Alessandro Sertini, a friend of Buonarroti, on the Italian form of one of the first translations of the *Ecuba*, which Buonarroti had sent him to view, as was his custom (this is also the reason why he sent his text to Maffeo Barberini).

to translate the Greek text literally, while others explain why, in some passages, he adopted a freer approach.

Most of the notes deal with lexical problems. An example is the expression 'versar dal seno', 'bleeding from the breast wound' (*Ecuba Barberini* 189): in the related annotation, Buonarroti stated that the text 'dice collo', 'reports the word "neck"', (AB 93, c. 36r) and consequently he modified subsequent versions, writing 'dal collo', 'from the neck' (*Ecuba* 210 and see related criticism), a literal translation of the Greek ἐκ [...] δειρῆς (151–152). In the annotation to 'greco terreno', 'Greek land' (*Ecuba Barberini* 609), translation of Δωρίδος ὅρμον αἴας (450), he stated that the text 'non dice il greco in generale, ma dorio o dorico', 'it does not say Greek in general, but Dorio or Doric' (AB 93, c. 40r); thus, the expression was first changed into 'dorica riva' and later into 'dorica arena', 'doric shore' (*Ecuba* 651 and see related criticism). Even his literal version, which he produced about halfway through the translation process, shows that Buonarroti did not want to lose contact with the source text. It is a condensed version (about 1530 verses), very close to the original but not very elegant, which is why Buonarroti decided not to use it for later translations, reevaluating, in several cases, the lexical choices made in the first versions.[33]

In producing his own *Ecuba*, Buonarroti may have also used previous translations, in particular Gelli's *Ecuba*. There are indeed several elements in Buonarroti's text recalling Gelli's *Ecuba*; they can be found in translations chronologically following the *Ecuba Barberini*, seemingly indicating that he had (or made use of) Gelli's text after sending the play to Barberini. For example, in the line 'ohimè, vedrà, la dolorosa madre', 'alas, the sorrowing mother will see', (*Ecuba* 73) contained in the prologue, the adjective 'dolorosa', 'sorrowing', does not appear in the Greek and in the Latin texts (46; transl. Porto; transl. Erasmus). Its use seems to have been influenced by Gelli, who also used it in the prologue (54 Gelli), a few lines after the exclamation. Buonarroti added this adjective in a version subsequent to the *Ecuba Barberini*, which still contained the expression 'la propria madre', 'your own mother' (*Ecuba Barberini* 62). Another comparison can be made between the line 'ma dov'er'ei per lo troiano eccidio?', 'but where was he in the Trojan massacre?', (*Ecuba* 1089), introduced by Buonarroti in his last version, and the corresponding line 'dov'era questo, quando fu l'excidio?', 'where was this man during the massacre?' (775 Gelli).[34]

---

33 See Buonarroti 2017, 38–39.
34 The translation of the passage is not literal, at least from a syntactic point of view. Rather, the original line (767: ποῦ δ' ὢν ἐτύγχαν', ἡνίκ ὤλλυτο πτόλις;) is closer to Buonarroti's transla-

4 The *Ecuba* by Michelangelo Buonarroti the Younger: Formal Features

Compared to other coeval translations, Buonarroti's *Ecuba* presents, overall, similar features in terms of metre and vocabulary, which are influenced by the literary tradition of Petrarch and Dante. In most 16th-century translations, the metres used are unrhymed hendecasyllables and less frequently heptasyllables, employed to render the narrative parts and dialogues, whereas choral songs are most commonly modelled on the 'canzone' structure used by Petrarch, consisting of hendecasyllabic and heptasyllabic stanzas (with the same syllabic pattern and the same rhyming scheme). This metrical choice became common practice after Trissino, whose *Sofonisba* had turned into a model for many subsequent tragedians (he first used unrhymed hendecasyllables to translate iambic trimeters and the 'canzone' for choral parts). In the realm of Euripides' translations, exceptions are Bandello's *Ecuba*, which is completely rhymed, and Pazzi de' Medici's *Cyclope*, where unrhymed twelve-syllable lines are used instead.[35] As for choral songs, unrhymed verse can also be found: for example, Gelli does not use rhyme; the parodos in Buonarroti's *Ecuba* is in unrhymed hendecasyllables and heptasyllables; the first stasimon in Guidiccioni's *Baccanti* is in unrhymed heptasyllables. Pazzi de' Medici uses a greater variety of meters in the choral songs of his *Cyclope*, also adding octosyllables.[36] Unrhymed verse, mainly heptasyllables, hendecasyllables (and less frequently five-syllable lines as in Giovanni da Falgano and Rucellai) are used to translate the lyrical parts in the *kommoi* and in the monodies.[37]

---

tion in his intermediate literal version: 'ma dov'er'ei quando cadeva Troia?', 'but where was he when Troy fell?' (see *Ecuba* 1089 and related criticism).

35 In his *Ecuba*, Bandello made wide use of the 'canzone' structure, consisting of hendecasyllables and heptasyllables, to which a 'congedo' is often added. The constraints imposed by this metric structure may explain, among other things, Bandello's peculiar use of *amplificatio*, whereby he adds short parts throughout the translation (which considerably extends the length of the text).

36 In particular, in this translation Pazzi uses stanzas of rhymed octosyllables; sequences of three unrhymed heptasyllables and one hendecasyllable; unrhymed heptasyllables. In the introduction to the edition of 'metrical tragedies', Solerti analyses Pazzi's metrics in depth (see Solerti 1887, 27 ff.).

37 For more information on the metric pattern in Rucellai's *Oreste*, see Cosentino 2003, 239–240; on Giovanni da Falgano's translations, see Caciolli 1995, 7–48.

Most plays are divided into five acts, according to the Latin model, which became common after Giraldi's theatrical reform in the 1540s (*Orbecche* was written in 1541).[38] In this regard, it should be noted that the vast majority of the texts analysed in this chapter were written after this date; the division into acts thus indicates adherence to the dominant taste of the time. Earlier plays, such as Rucellai's *Oreste* and Pazzi de' Medici's *Cyclope* and *Iphigenia in Tauris* were not divided into acts as they followed the Greek model; in contrast, *Oreste*, edited by Scipione Maffei in 1723 with no internal division, was divided later, in particular in the critical edition by Guido Mazzoni (1887). Likewise, in Bandello's *Ecuba*, the division into acts and scenes may have been a choice of the 19th-century editor. Gelli's *Ecuba*, on the other hand, was not divided into acts, which was perhaps due to a choice made by the poet or to its dating back to the early decades of the 16th century.[39] Giovanni da Falgano's works date back to the 1570s but are not divided; it is not known whether this was due to the author's choice or to the fact that his plays were not revised to be published. The several later versions of *Ecuba* by Buonarroti, except for the last one, do not present any division either.

The final version of *Ecuba* contains 1835 lines (written in hendecasyllables and heptasyllables) and presents a partial indication that the play is organized in five acts and scenes. The characters present in the scene and, sometimes, the place where the events take place are also indicated, in line with the author's interpretation. These annotations, however, are incomplete too, due to the fact that the play did not undergo a final revision, as shown by the number of textual alternatives annotated throughout the text.[40] Similarly, the list of characters and the indication of the theme of the play are missing, while they were included in the intermediate version sent to Maffeo Barberini (where, however, the division into acts and scenes was not indicated).

Buonarroti used unrhymed hendecasyllables and heptasyllables to translate narrative parts, dialogues, lyrical meters and the parodos, while stasima follow the structure of the 'canzone', according to the following metrical pattern:

---

38 With his tragedies (especially the first: *Orbecche*) and his theoretical essay, *Discorso ovvero lettera intorno al comporre delle commedie e delle tragedie* (1543), G.B. Giraldi Cinzio left the Greek model embodied in Italy by Trissino's *Sofonisba* to follow Seneca's Latin model. This also presented the division in five acts and scenes, together with detached prologues.
39 The date of Gelli's *Ecuba* is controversial: see Tramontana 2016, X–XVII.
40 See Buonarroti 2017, 72–74.

- *Ecuba* 643–698 (444–483, first stasimon): seven stanzas of *ode-canzone* consisting of hendecasyllables and heptasyllables, with the rhyme scheme aBCBacDD.[41]
- *Ecuba* 915–947 (629–656, second stasimon): three stanzas of *ode-canzone* consisting of hendecasyllables and heptasyllables, with the rhyme scheme aBcaBdCdEdE.
- *Ecuba* 1290–1343 (905–951, third stasimon): six stanzas of *ode-canzone* consisting of hendecasyllables and heptasyllables, with the rhyme scheme AbCcAbDEE.[42]
- *Ecuba* 1449–1466 (1024–1034, choral interlude): three stanzas of *ode-canzone* consisting of hendecasyllables and heptasyllables, with the rhyme scheme AbaBcC.

The language of the play echoes the Italian literary tradition, in particular Petrarch and Dante, but also Trissino.[43] The expression 'non è sì duro cor', 'no heart is so hard', (*Ecuba Barberini* 389) echoes Petrarch, and can be compared to 'non è sì duro cor che, lagrimando, / pregando, amando, talor', 'no heart is so hard that by weeping, / praying, loving sometimes' (*RVF* CCLXV, 12–13); the same expression can also be found in a reversed order in the *Canzoniere* (*RVF* CLXXI, 10: 'del bel diamante, ond'ell'à il cor sì duro', 'her heart is hard like a beautiful diamond'). Significantly, Buonarroti also used the next line of the poem to describe Polyxena's chest during her sacrifice (*Ecuba* 818: 'quasi un bel marmo che si mova e spiri', 'like a beautiful marble which moves and breathes'; see *RVF* CLXXI, 11: 'l'altro è d'un marmo che si mova et spiri', 'the other one consists of a marble that moves and breathes'). Similarly, the following phrases can be found in Petrarch: 'agre rampogne', 'bitter reproaches', (*Ecuba* 62–63 'con agre rampogne / l'esercito arrestare', 'halting the army with bitter reproaches'; see *RVF* CCCLX, 76–77: 'il mio adversario con agre rampogne / comincia', 'my enemy starts his speech with bitter reproaches'), and 'nudo spirto', 'naked soul' (*Ecuba* 50, 88; see *RVF*, XXXVII, 120: 'o spirto ignudo od uom di carne et d'ossa', 'or naked soul, or man of flesh and blood'; see also *RVF* CCCLIX, 60: 'spirito ignudo sono', 'I am a naked soul'). The latter also recalls the naked souls of the damned (*If.* III, 100; XIV, 19; XXIV, 92; XXX, 25).

---

41 For more information on the structure of the ode-canzone, see Beltrami 2011, 377.
42 In the penultimate stanza, the rhyme b is limited to the assonance 'arene': 'speme'.
43 Quotes from Dante, Petrarch and Trissino are taken from Contini, 1964 (*Canzoniere* by Petrarch); Petrocchi 1966–67 (*Commedia* by Dante); Trissino 1977 (*Sofonisba* by Trissino).

Echoes of Dante can be found in the expression 'affetto ardente', 'the passionate love' (*Ecuba* 577–578: 'a lei perdona / l'escusabil materno affetto ardente', 'the forgivable motherly affection / forgives her'; see *Pa.* XV,43: 'e quando l'arco de l'ardente affetto / fu sì sfogato', 'and when the bow of passionate love was slackened'), in the use of the verb 'attoscare', 'to poison' (*Ecuba* 642: 'ch'attoscò co' begli occhi Ilio felice', 'that poisoned the happy Ilium through eyes'; see *If*. VI, 84: 'se 'l ciel li addolcia, o lo 'nferno li attosca', 'if Heaven softens them, or Hell poisons them') and in the past participle 'oltracotato', 'insolent' (*Ecuba* 585: 'giovine braccio, oltracotato e fiero', 'young soldier, insolent and proud' and *Ecuba Barberini* 1417: 'per non mirar l'oltracotato Trace', 'not to observe the insolent Thracian'; see *Pa.* XVI, 115–116: 'l'oltracotata schiatta che s'indraca / dietro a chi fugge', 'the insolent lineage that, like a dragon, chases the fugitives').

Other examples are drawn from Trissino's *Sofonisba*, like the question forms contained in the first line (*Sofonisba* 1: 'lassa, dove poss'io voltar la lingua?', 'how unlucky, who can I talk to?') and in line 547 (*Sofonisba* 547: 'in che voce poss'io sciogler la lingua?', 'what can I say?'), which Buonarroti combined in one line: 'lassa, come debb'io sciogler la lingua?', 'how unlucky, how can I talk?' (*Ecuba Barberini* 192).

Finally, a comparison can be made between two lines mirroring each other; the first is by Trissino: 'o figlio mio, tu non avrai più madre', 'oh my dear son, you will no longer have a mother', (*Sofonisba* 1907) and the second by Buonarroti: 'o madre mia, tu non avrai più figlia', 'oh my dear mother, you will no longer have a daughter' (*Ecuba* 275).

In conclusion, we can say that the *Ecuba*, the first versions of which date back to the late 16th century, can be considered a close rendering of the original Greek. The translating process was long and complex and the last version produced cannot be considered a finished work. Buonarroti translated from the Greek, but he also used the Latin version by Porto (1597) and almost certainly Gelli's *Ecuba*. While resorting to *amplificatio*, like almost all other scholars of the period, he employed this technique with moderation and awareness. The manuscripts attest to his great care in the careful and accurate choices to translate some Greek words. The form of the play is in line with many other translations of its time: it is divided into five acts and scenes; it uses unrhymed hendecasyllables and heptasyllables in the narrative parts and in the dialogues; the choral songs follow the 'canzone' structure (but in the parodos Buonarroti uses unrhymed hendecasyllables and heptasyllables); and, finally, the language is redolent with echoes from Dante, Petrarch and Trissino.

Therefore, with his *Ecuba*, Buonarroti provides us with a text perfectly in line with the cultural scene of his own time, philologically accurate, poetically elegant and drawing on the Italian literary tradition.

Maria Luísa Resende
Sophocles in 16th-Century Portugal: Aires Vitória's *Tragédia del Rei Agaménom*

Abstract: Published in 1555, Aires Vitória's *Tragédia del Rei Agaménom* is the only translation of a Greek tragedy produced in Portugal during the 16th century. The strong resemblance to Pérez de Oliva's Spanish version *La venganza de Agamenón* reveals that Vitória did not render it from the original; his version is instead a moralised adaptation of Sophocles' *Electra*. The analysis of both Aires Vitória's and Pérez de Oliva's translations highlights the main differences between the two works and discloses the singularity of Aires Vitória's version, anchored in a deep understanding of classical texts as vehicles of Christian morality.

Aires Vitória's *Tragédia del Rei Agaménom* was the first tragedy translated into Portuguese and published among very few other translations from ancient Greek authors produced in 16th-century Portugal.[1] Due to the easy access to editions and translations imported from Italy, France, and other countries in Northern Europe, the production of translations, both in Latin and the vernacular, was extremely rare and often linked with scholarly exercises.[2] It is indisputable, however, that Sophocles' work — as well as Aeschylus' and Euripides' — was read and studied in scholarly circles, namely by advanced students of

---

I would like to thank the editors of this volume for their valuable assistance in preparing this paper for publication.

---

[1] This is the case of Jorge Coelho's Latin translation of Lucian's *De Dea Syria*, published in 1540 (see Resende, chapter 1, *forthcoming*). Diogo de Teive's translation of Xenophon's *Cyropedia* is unfortunately lost but, apart from these, there is a Portuguese translation of the first eight cantos of the *Iliad* dubiously attributed to D. Jerónimo Osório (Resende, 2020) and some free renderings of the *Anacreontea* and of Moschus' *The Runaway Love* by António Ferreira and Pero Andrade de Caminha (Pereira 2008, 38–42; 54–56). On translations of Aristotle and Galen, see Pinho, 2006, 316–317.
[2] See especially Tarrío 2015, Fouto 2015, 92–93 and Resende, chapter 2, *forthcoming*.

Greek, as several editions confirm its diffusion in Portugal and contain marginal notes that testify to its circulation.[3]

The performance of tragedies in academic contexts, such as the Colégio das Artes and other Jesuitic colleges, also contributed to the dissemination of ancient theatre.[4] Even though George Buchanan's *Jephtes* and *Baptistes* had not been published by the time he was teaching at the Colégio das Artes, between 1547 and 1550, it is quite probable that they were performed there, as they were in the College of Guyenne, where he and Diogo de Teive had previously taught.[5] In fact, despite a major preponderance of Seneca's theatre, the influence of Buchanan's plays — and even possibly his translations of Euripides — on Portuguese 16th-century tragedies, namely Diogo de Teive's *Ioannes Princeps* and António Ferreira's *Castro*, has been demonstrated by scholars.[6]

However, the *Tragédia del Rei Agaménom* does not relate to a scholarly reading and study of Sophocles. Firstly, it was not translated from the original Greek, being instead an adaptation of Pérez de Oliva's Castilian version of *Electra*;[7] and secondly, even though we know almost nothing about the author and the circumstances of his translation,[8] from the features it displays it is possible to argue that it was intended for a wider audience with no proficiency in either Latin or Greek.

---

[3] Brandão, 1933, ccxxxvii. 16th-century copies of Sophocles' works still preserved in Portuguese libraries display marks of their circulation, namely in the University of Coimbra and amongst its professors. See especially *Sophoclis Tragoediae VII. In quibus praeter multa menda sublata, carminum omnium ratio hactenus obscurior, nunc apertior proditor*. Antuerpiae: ex officina Christophori Plantini, 1579. BNP, L. 4877, which presents the manuscript mark 'he do mestre de grego' ('it belongs to the professor of Greek') and *Sophoclis Tragoediae septem cum interpretationibus uetustis & ualde utilibus*. Florentiae: apud Iunctam, 1547, BNP L. 4880 A., fl. 63v, with several marginal translations consistent with the scholarly study of Greek. Inventories of Renaissance libraries also testify to the existence of Sophocles' works in Greek, namely D. Teodósio I's, head of Casa de Bragança (Buescu 2016, 220).
[4] Martyn 1987, 121–122 and Soares 2006, 183–184.
[5] On the date of composition of Buchanan's plays, see Sharrat and Walsh 1983, 1–5. See also Martyn 1986, 89–91 and Soares 1996, 87–91.
[6] See Martyn 1986; 1987, 137–157, Soares 2006, 186–187, Earle 2012, 293–294 and Fouto 2015, 102. On the influence of Seneca, see especially Soares 1996, 31–47; 133–159 and 1999, 81–96.
[7] On Pérez de Oliva's translation, see especially Ansino Domínguez 1999, 17–20, Bañuls Oller et al. 2006, 39–121, Calderón Calderón 2011, 25–29 and Hernández López 2019, 53–82.
[8] We know that Aires Vitória was from Porto. Vitória 2011, 37: 'Começa a tragédia de Orestes tirada de grego em romance trovada por Anrique Aires Vitória, natural do Porto [...]'. ('The tragedy of Orestes begins, which was translated from Greek into a Romance language, and was versified by Anrique Aires Vitoria, who is from Porto [...]'). See Camões 2011, 7–8.

The analysis that follows will highlight the main differences between the two versions and demonstrate how these enhance the singularity of Aires Vitória's translation, especially when considering his understanding of classical texts as vehicles of Christian morality.

The title of the Portuguese translation informs us that this version, printed in 1555, is in fact a second edition, which suggests a generalised interest in Vitória's work. The first one might have been issued sometime after 1536, but there are no extant copies that confirm this supposition, which is drawn from the author's own words:[9]

> Tragédia da vingança que foi feita sobre a morte del rei Agaménom. Agora novamente tirada de grego em linguagem, trovada por Anrique Aires Vitória, cujo argumento é de Sófocles, poeta grego. Agora segunda vez impressa e ēmendada e anhadida pelo mesmo autor.[10]

A comparison between the two versions reveals that Vitória sought to adapt his work to Portuguese theatrical plays, as he not only changed Pérez de Oliva's prose into verse, but also recurred to rhyme and to the traditional metres *redondilha maior*. This choice is of the utmost significance if we consider that, in order to achieve the opposite reaction, António Ferreira made use of the Sapphic line in his tragedy *Castro*, which, as Thomas Earle points out, contributed to emphasise its strangeness and novelty.[11]

More importantly, however, Aires Vitória also removed the Chorus and replaced it with two female characters (Climenes and Etra) with very reduced

---

9 The 1536 edition is lost and, according to Camões 2011, 10–11, there is only one extant copy of the 1555 edition. Francisco Maria Esteves Pereira published Aires Vitória's *Tragédia del Rey Agaménom* in 1918, a version which Joana Tinoco Silva reedited in 2008. There is also a manuscript copy of Francisco Maria Esteves Pereira's edition in Biblioteca da Academia das Ciências (1559, Manuscritos Série Azul). In 2011, José Camões published a new edition (Vitória 2011), which is also available in Centro de Estudos de Teatro, Teatro de Autores Portugueses do Séc. XVI – Base de dados textual [online] (http://www.cet-e-quinhentos.com – last accessed 01/09/2022).
10 Vitória 2011, 37. 'Tragedy of the vengeance that recounted the death of King Agamemnon, once again translated from Greek into the vernacular, and versified by Anrique Aires Vitoria, who based his version on the plot of Sophocles, a Greek poet. This copy has since been printed for a second time, corrected and elaborated by the same author'.
11 Earle 2012, 300: 'The effect of the heavy, pounding rhythm is to suggest the dance, which was a feature of the choruses of Greek tragedy, if not necessarily of Seneca. But more important, perhaps, is the strangeness of the hypnotic pulse, without parallel in earlier Portuguese verse, which forces the audience to realize that it is witnessing, not a homely Vicentine *auto*, but something entirely new, a classical tragedy, but in Portuguese'.

dramatic roles, almost limited to being the protagonist's confidents. Pérez de Oliva had already diminished the role of the Chorus by eliminating most of the lyrical parts in his translation, and replaced the original episode-choral ode structure of the tragedy with a scene-by-scene division. However, neither the Castilian nor the Portuguese version display fundamental changes in the plot, as the prologue corresponds, in general, to the first scene; the parodos to the second, and the episodes to the third, fourth and sixth scenes, respectively. Since the exodus is consistent with the seventh scene, only the fifth, which consists of a dialogue between Orestes, Pylades and the Servant on the value of friendship, is an innovation by Pérez de Oliva, also reproduced in Vitória's translation. Furthermore, the final 'Exhortation to the Reader' is not found in the Castilian source, being original to the Portuguese version.[12]

Even though Vitória's elimination of the Chorus did not significantly alter the development of the action, it resulted in further distancing his translation from a classical conception of theatre, like the one embodied by Diogo de Teive and António Ferreira, who, following the principles of Horace and Giraldi Cinzio, preferred the five-act structure and did maintain a Chorus throughout.[13]

Overall, the formal changes undertaken by Vitória seem to be an attempt to tailor Sophocles' tragedy to Portuguese readers, strongly suggesting an intention to achieve the largest possible dissemination.[14] It is also conceivable that such amendments were intended to encourage the performance of such translation, even though there is a lack of evidence to confirm this.[15]

Vitória's modifications were not limited to the structure: the fact that he was dealing with a translation, and not the original, probably added to his freedom. Indeed, besides transforming Pérez de Oliva's prose into verse and eliminating the Chorus, he also resorted to paraphrases, adjectivisation and metaphors to elaborate on the most lyrical and pathetic parts. This is particularly evident in the description of Clytemnestra's dream, which had already been altered by Pérez de Oliva:

---

12 For an analysis of the structure of Pérez de Oliva's version, see especially Hernández López 2019, 57–63. The structure of the Portuguese version was analysed by Serra 2011, 14–15.
13 Soares 1996, 50; 113–115. On the Chorus of Diogo de Teive's *Ioannes Princeps* and António Ferreira's *Castro*, see Martyn 1987, 128–130, Soares 1996, 110–113 and Earle 2012, 297–309.
14 Pérez de Oliva's defence of the Castilian as a literary language may also reflect the same purpose. See Bañuls Oller *et al.* 2006, 48–54 and Hernández López 2019, 22–24; 34–36.
15 Camões 2011, 7, mentions the absence of stage directions to argue against the performance of the play.

Esta noche postrera soñaba que veía Agamenón, nuestro padre, beber en una fuente de sangre, así herido como lo enterraron.¹⁶

Following closely the Castilian version, Vitória amplifies his source as he emphasises the description of Clytemnestra's reaction to the dream, by insisting on her anxiety and disquiet, and depicts Agamemnon's action in greater detail, with a reference to the sound of him drinking his own blood:

> Esta noite derradeira
> espertou com mil fadigas
> que lhe davam grã canseira.
> Com grã dor de coração
> espertou alvoroçada
> dizendo com grã paixão
> que ela vira Agamenão
> nũa fonte ensanguentada.
> E daquela água bebia
> com muito grande roído,
> o qual vinha assi ferido
> como foi na terra fria
> despois de morto metido.¹⁷

As Ansino Domínguez points out,¹⁸ Pérez de Oliva's alteration must be understood in light of his attempt to Christianise the Greek plot, because what was interpreted by the Chorus as a prediction of the arrival of the moment of venge-

---

16 Pérez de Oliva 2019, 183. 'This last night she dreamt that she was seeing Agamemnon, our father, drinking from a fountain of blood, and that he was wounded as when he was buried'. Cf. Soph. *El.* 416–423: λόγος τις αὐτήν ἐστιν εἰσιδεῖν πατρὸς / τοῦ σοῦ τε κἀμοῦ δευτέραν ὁμιλίαν / ἐλθόντος ἐς φῶς· εἶτα τόνδ' ἐφέστιον / πῆξαι λαβόντα σκῆπτρον οὑφόρει ποτὲ / αὐτός, τανῦν δ' Αἴγισθος· ἔκ τε τοῦδ' ἄνω / βλαστεῖν βρύοντα θαλλόν, ᾧ κατάσκιον / πᾶσαν γενέσθαι τὴν Μυκηναίων χθόνα. Transl. Hugh Lloyd-Jones 1994, 205–207: 'They say that she was once more in company with your father and mine, who had come to the world of light; and then he took the staff which he used to carry, and which Aegisthus carries now, and planted it beside the hearth and from it grew up a fruitful bough, which overshadowed all the land of the Mycenaeans'.
17 Vitória 2011, 65. 'This last night / she woke up with a thousand fatigues, / which gave her a great deal of trouble. / And with extreme pain in her heart, / she woke up, much agitated, / declaring, with strong emotion, / that she had seen Agamemnon / in a fountain of blood. / And, as he was drinking from that water, / with great noise, / he was wounded, / like he had been when in cold earth / he was buried, after he had been killed'.
18 Ansino Domínguez 1999, 19. See also Bañuls Oller *et al.* 2006, 83–84.

ance[19] becomes a way of illustrating Clytemnestra's remorse for killing her own husband.[20] In the Portuguese translation, this idea is further exploited, as Electra stresses the torments of those suffering from remorse and guilt when trying to convince Chrysotemis to reveal their mother's dream:

> Irmã, as grandes maldades
> elas são as vingadoras
> de tais torpes torpidades,
> recrecendo a todas horas
> aquessas tais novidades,
> trazendo no pensamento
> a maldade cometida
> que lhe dê grave tormento,
> nam tendo segura vida
> nem em si contentamento.
> Quando velam tem tristeza
> quando dormem sobressaltos,
> sonhando sua crueza
> de temor nunca são faltos
> nem lhes vale sua riqueza.
> E andam acompanhados
> contino de gram temor
> o qual tem este primor:

---

19 Soph. *El.* 473–477: εἰ μὴ 'γὼ παράφρων μάντις ἔφυν καὶ / γνώμας λειπομένα σοφᾶς, / εἶσιν ἁ πρόμαντις / Δίκα, δίκαια φερομένα χεροῖν κράτη· μέτεισιν, ὦ τέκνον, οὐ μακροῦ χρόνου. Transl. Lloyd-Jones in Sophocles 1994, 211: 'If I am not a mistaken prophet, lacking in wise judgement, Justice that has predicted the outcome shall come, carrying off just triumph with her strength; she shall come after them, my child, in no short space of time'.

20 Pérez de Oliva 2019, 182–183: 'Las grandes maldades, Chrisothemis, ellas son vengadoras de sí mismas, que continuamente representándose delante el pensamiento de quien las cometió lo atormentan, sin poderse defender. Velando tienen tristeza y durmiendo los sueños se les tornan en semejanza de las penas que merecen. Porque es propiedad de la culpa traer simpre el temor por compañero. Este nunca deja los culpados descuidarse en los placeres, nunca olvidarse en las tristezas, antes metido dentro en el alma es allí su perpetuo atormentador. Así ahora nuestra madre, habiendo sido causadora de tan grave mal, las sombras temerá, y los rayos que del cielo caen creerá que son todos a ella enviados'. ('Great evils, Chrisothemis, are their own avengers, for they continually present themselves in the thoughts of those who have committed them, tormenting them in a way that they are not able to defend themselves. In their vigil they suffer, and in their sleep their dreams become the sorrows they deserve. For it is the property of guilt to always have fear as a companion. This fear never lets the guilty disregard it, even in their pleasures, never lets them forget their sorrows, but is their perpetual tormentor within their souls. So now our mother, having been the cause of so great an evil, will fear the shadows, and she will believe that the rays that fall from the sky, they are all sent to her'.

que nunca deixa os culpados
descuidar de seu error.
No pesar os acompanha,
no prazer os traz cercados
de milhares de cuidados
que nunca os desacompanha,
assi os traz atormentados.
Assi nossa mãe agora,
com o medo que terá
de ser ela a causadora
de tanto mal, cuidará
do que é merecedora.[21]

Despite maintaining the same ideas already conveyed by the Castilian version – namely the total subjugation of the culprit to the torment of her remorse, while awake or asleep, in sorrow and in joy — the Portuguese version seems to be able to express Clytemnestra's anguish more firmly. Through the fast rhythm of the verse and the repetitive structures — notice, for instance, the verses 'quando velam [...] quando dormem' and 'no pesar os acompanha / no prazer os traz cercados' — Electra's discourse almost attains the force of a litany, thus amplifying the consequences of Clytemnestra's guilt and the pious nature of the coming revenge.

In addition to the transformation of the prophetic dream into a depiction of Clytemnestra's remorse, and the reduction of a scene of dramatic tension to a mere expression of guilt, other amendments reveal Pérez de Oliva's intention of Christianising the Greek plot,[22] also evident in his translation of Euripides' *Hecuba*.[23] Thus, the libations ordered by Clytemnestra are replaced with incense and perfume,[24] and the urn with the supposed ashes of Orestes becomes a coffin

---

21 Vitória 2011, 64. 'Sister, great evils / are the avengers / of such dreadful infamies. / Growing every hour, / these novelties / bring to mind / the committed evil, / to give them grave torment, / preventing them from having a secure life / and contentment in themselves. / In their vigil they have sorrow, / in their sleep, they are troubled, / while they dream, their cruelty / does not let them be free from fear, / nor can their wealth save them. / And they are continually / accompanied by great fear, / which has this perfection: / that never leaves the guilty / free from their error. / It accompanies them in their sorrow, / surrounds them in their pleasure, / never releases them / from a thousand concerns / and thus torments them. / So our mother, / fearing that / she is the cause / of such an evil, / will heed what she deserves'.
22 See Bañuls Oller *et al.* 2006, 84, Ansino 1999, 19–20 and Hernández López 2019, 81.
23 Hernández López 2019, 80–82.
24 Soph. *El.* 406. Cf. Pérez Oliva 2019, 182 and Vitória 2011, 63, 65.

with his embalmed corpse.²⁵ More importantly, however, he rejects most of the allusions to Greek religion, as the characters of the tragedy turn to the Christian God instead for help and guidance:

> Y pluguiese a Dios, mi ayo, que lo que vas a decir fuera verdad, si por algún estorbo de fortuna, que suele ser enemiga de los buenos, yo no he de cumplir mi deseo. Pero yo confío en Dios todo poderoso [...].²⁶

Although Vitória retains some of these amendments — namely, the references to incense and perfume instead of libations, and the coffin rather than the urn –, he also introduces references to pagan deities ('deoses'), in order to restore the Greek context that Oliva sought to erase:

> Aio, pera haver entrada,
> e *aos deoses* aprouvesse
> que verdade se fizesse
> essa morte desastrada.
> Se me houvesse d'estrovar
> a Fortuna mui cruel,
> pois que sói de contrastar
> aos bons té os matar
> e aos maus é fiel...
> Porém eu em *Deos* confio
> pois que é tam poderoso
> que nam me dará desvio
> pera me sair baldio
> meu desejo desejoso.²⁷

Vitória's lack of access to the original Greek text may explain the few pagan references he adds to his translation, mainly in the form of mythonyms, such as referring to the sun as Phoebus,²⁸ or commentaries to clarify mythological allu-

---

25 Soph. *El.* 53–58. Cf. Pérez de Oliva 2019, 179 and Vitória 2011, 47.
26 Pérez de Oliva 2019, 174: 'And may it please God, my servant, that what you are about to say be true, and prevent that by some hindrance of fortune, which is usually the enemy of the good, I do not fulfil my wish. But I trust in almighty God [...]'. See Ansino 1999, 19.
27 Vitória 2011, 46: 'For starters, that sounds / good to me, my servant, / and may *the gods* wish / that such a disastrous death / actually occurs. / Even if cruel Fortune hinders me, / for it is usually adverse to the good / until it kills them, / being faithful to the evil ones, / nevertheless, I trust *God*, / since He is so powerful, / that He will not let me deviate / that I might fail / in my longing desire'.
28 Vitória 2011, 45: 'Também o tempo nos falta / pera conselho tomar / nesta empresa tam alta, / e pois que Febo se esmalta / será bom determinar'. ('Time is also lacking, / for us to take advice / on such a high enterprise, / and given that Phoebus is tinged, / it would be good to

sions, such as explaining that Diana was a goddess or that Paris was the son of Priamus, king of Troy.[29] Yet, this mixture of pagan and Christian references — which is not at all uncommon in Portuguese theatre, even in the Vicentine *autos*[30] — not only contributes to distance the Portuguese version from its Castilian source, but also appears to stem from Vitória's aim of affording the translation with a 'classical' aura. Contrary to Pérez de Oliva, Vitória is not seeking to Christianize the original, on the contrary, as we will see later, in the prologue, he even argues that classical myths and authors are in fact able to transmit Christian values.[31]

The moralization of the plot and the attempt to present it according to Christian principles is nevertheless present in both translations. In fact, by displaying Clytemnestra and Aegisthus as terrible and unjust characters and, most importantly, by downplaying Clytemnestra's reasons to kill Agamemnon,[32] the

---

decide'). Cf. Pérez de Oliva 2019, 173: 'Ya la noche es pasada y el sol muestra las puntas de sus rayos, así que nos queda poco tiempo de tomar consejo [...].' ('The night is already gone and the sun shows the tips of its rays, so we have little time left to take advice').

29 Vitória 2011, 40. Cf. Pérez de Oliva 2019, 170.

30 On the use of mythology by Gil Vicente, see Pociña López, 2016. Earle 2008 analyses the use of mythology in 16th-century Portuguese Literature in general.

31 See, e.g., Vitória 2011, 39: 'nam podia deixar de me parecer que traria doutrina aos que a lessem com aquela entenção' ('I could not help thinking that this translation would bring doctrine to those who read it with the utmost attention').

32 Pérez de Oliva 2019, 196: '[...] Ifigenia, mi hermana, cuando iba a morir decía – según he oído – que bienaventurada era su sangre, pues por ella Grecia había de ser honrada. [...]. Si te parece que porque Agamenón mató mereció muerte, haces ley muy mala para ti, y no respondes a toda la culpa que te ponen; porque, después de la muerte de Agamenón, es otra culpa principal haber casado con Egisto, donde bien muestras que te movió más el encendimiento de tu sucio amor que la piedad que hubiste de tu hija'. ('When my sister Iphigenia was about to die, she said, as I have heard, that blessed was her blood, for by it, Greece was to be honoured. [...] And even if it seems to you that, for killing her, Agamemnon deserved to die, you are making a very bad law for yourself, and you are not giving an answer for all the blame you are accused of; because, after Agamemnon's death, it was your main fault to have married Aegisthus, and hence you showed that you were more moved by your dirty love than by the pity you had for your daughter'). Cf. Vitória 2011, 87–88: 'Porque eu ouvi dizer / que, levando-a, dezia / nam ter em nada morrer / pois que por ela podia / toda Grécia honrada ser. [...] / Fazes má lei pera ti, / todos grã culpa te dão, / que despois de morto assi / o triste de Agamenão / maior culpa houve aí / a qual foi tu te casar / com Egisto, matador, / e dás bem a demostrar / encender-te o sujo amor / pera isto se ordenar'. ('For I've heard / that, when she was taken, / she was saying that she did not mind dying, / since, with her death, / all of Greece would be honoured. [...] / You make a bad law for yourself, / and everyone finds you guilty, / for, after you killed / sad Agamemnon, / you were even more to blame / for getting married / to his killer,

tragedy is discharged of its complexity, being thus transformed into a simple case of crime, and its resultant punishment.[33]

Such a simplification of Sophocles' play leads to the fact that, even when dealing with the intricate question of matricide, divine support is never questioned, and the righteousness of Orestes' action is legitimised by a strong sense of justice, as is clear from the following excerpt of Pérez de Oliva's version:

> Ya pues no falta sino buena ocasión para nuestro hecho; del cielo la espero, en cuyo desacato se cometió tan gran maldad. Ayudadme, los que allá estáis, a limpiar de tan sucia fama la tierra por donde se ha divulgado la grave querella de la muerte de mi padre Agamenón. Y tú piedad, que sueles atar las manos en la venganza, suelta ahora las mías, que si te parecieren crueles cuando las vires bañadas en la sangre de mi madre, mirando cuánto más debo a mi padre, te parecerán piadosas. Principalmente que mi madre, en el arrepentimiento de me haber engendrado, pierde el derecho de ser de mí acatada; y en ser tan mal ejemplo en la vida, merece la muerte de mano de quien sea más cruel, porque teman, los que supieren, que todas las maldades tienen iguales castigos.[34]

The same idea is present in the Portuguese translation, as Clytemnestra's death is characterised as a fair and pious punishment, despite its cruelty:

> Do céu ajuda espero
> pois que em seu vitupério
> se fez um caso tam fero
> e do celeste império
> virá o castigo mero.
> E tu pois sóis, piedade,
> atar as mãos à vingança
> soltar-mas-á crueldade,
> como eu tenho esperança,
> pera vingar tal maldade.
> Se cruéis, vendo-as banhadas

Aegisthus. / Thus, you clearly revealed / that you were burning with dirty love, / for this to have happened').

33 Serra 2015, 98–99.

34 Pérez de Oliva 2019, 188. 'Now there is but one good occasion for our deed; from heaven I wait for it, in whose contempt so great an evil was committed. Help me, you who are there, to cleanse from such a foul fame the land where the grievous complaint of the death of my father Agamemnon has been spread. And you, pity, who usually bind your hands in vengeance, now let go mine, for if they seem cruel to you, when you see them bathed in my mother's blood, seeing how much more I owe my father, they will seem pious to you. Mainly because my mother, in her repentance of having begotten me, loses the right to be respected by me; and for being such a bad example in life, she deserves death by the hand of whoever is more cruel, so that they fear, those who know that, for every evil, there is an equal punishment'.

no sangue de minha mãe,
te parecerem, untadas,
vendo o que devo a meu pai
piedosas serão chamadas,
principalmente que ela
perde o dereito devido,
pois se maldiz com querela
por me haver concebido
polo qual desejo vê-la.³⁵

As Serra points out,³⁶ the elimination of the oracle of Apollo in Pérez de Oliva's translation not only conforms to his principle of minimising pagan allusions, but also reduces the ambiguity linked to the act of matricide and the consequences of such a crime. It is the Servant who formulates the need to resort to the death of Clytemnestra without indicating any uncertainty as to its legitimacy, understood, on the contrary, as a necessity given the cruel destiny of Agamemnon and the pending threat that falls upon Electra.³⁷

However, there is a tendency, in the Portuguese version, to avoid direct allusions to Clytemnestra's hatred, and it appears that only Aegisthus would be responsible for trying to kill the infant Orestes,³⁸ and only he intends to impris-

---

35 Vitória 2011, 74–75. 'From heaven I expect help / for, in its vituperation, / a case has been made so great, / that from the heavenly empire / clear punishment will come. / And even if you, pity, as usual, / bind the hands of revenge, / cruelty will unleash them, / for I have hope / that I will avenge such an evil. / If, seeing them bathed / in my mother's blood, / they seem cruel to you, greased, / seeing what I owe to my father, / pious they will be called, / mainly because she / loses the right that was due to her, / when she curses herself with quarrel / for having conceived me, / and this is why I wish to see her'.
36 Serra 2011, 17–19.
37 Vitória 2011, 43–47. See Calderón Calderón 2011, 28–29.
38 Vitória 2011, 43: 'E aqui foste livrado / por Eleca, irmã tua, / daquele tredor malvado / de Egisto, reprovado, que te dera morte crua'. ('And here you were released / by Electra, your sister, / from that evil traitor / wicked Aegisthus, / who would have given you a cruel death'). Cf. Pérez de Oliva 2019, 172: 'Aquí tu hermana Elecha te livró de los cuchillos de tu madre [...]'. ('Here your sister Electra freed you from your mother's knives'). The same idea is repeated by Electra. Vitória 2011, 56: 'Muito me é obrigado, / a mim, Orestes, de sorte / que ele por mi foi livrado / querendo-lhe dar a morte / aquele Egisto malvado'. ('Much does he owe / to me, Orestes, for / it was I who freed him / when that wicked one, Aegisthus, / wanted to kill him'). Cf. Pérez de Oliva 2019, 178: 'Dél, al menos, yo tengo mucho merecido; porque mi madre y Egisto, queriendo dél hacer como de mi padre, yo lo libré y lo di a un viejo honrado que lo criase escondido en buenas costumbres'. ('At least I deserve a lot from him, because when my mother and Aegisthus wanted to do to him what they did to my father, I freed him and gave him to an honest old man, who raised him with good habits').

on Electra.[39] Clytemnestra's sin is thus closely associated with the death of Agamemnon and her marriage to her husband's murderer.[40] Yet, Vitória's constraint when describing the cruelty of Clytemnestra as a mother, when compared with his Castilian source, gives rise to a problem as to the legitimacy of the matricide. Indeed, the need to justify Orestes' action is clear from the final exhortation to the reader, a part which is original to Vitória, and which stems from the need to ensure that the moral of the tragedy is understood. Thus, possibly due to the influence of Seneca's character, which, according to Edith Hall, had a predominant impact until the 19th century,[41] Vitória reduces Clytemnestra's complexity to her adulterous conduct and advises women to love their husbands if they wish to avoid a similar fate:

> Atente também toda sábia molher
> a Clitmnestra, que foi tam malvada,
> a morte que houve tam desastrada
> sem seu estado lhe a isso valer.
> Procurem todas de gram amor ter
> a seus maridos e tê-los amados,
> nam lhe acontençam tam desastrados
> casos que aqui se podem bem ver.[42]

By presenting Sophocles' *Electra* as a portrayal of divine justice, in which unjust tyrants are condemned while the virtuous prevail, Vitória reveals a moralistic conception of tragedy, in line of Chaucer, Isidore of Seville, and Lazare de Baïf,

---

39 Vitória 2011, 60: 'Egisto está inclinado / a te dar prisão mui forte / por Orestes ser livrado / por tua mão de crua morte'. ('Egisto is inclined / to give you a harsh imprisonment / since Orestes was freed / from a cruel death by your hand'). Cf. Pérez de Oliva 2019, 180: 'Egisto y Clitemnestra, nuestra madre, viendo que tú diste la vida a Orestes, que temen no sea él cuchillo de la venganza, y que agora lo provocas con quejas tan ahincadas, han determinado ponerte en prisión [...]'. ('Seeing that you gave life to Orestes, Aegisthus and Clytemnestra, our mother, fear that he might be the knife of your vengeance, and since you are now provoking him with such intense complaints, they have determined to put you in prison [...]').
40 Serra 2015, 98.
41 Hall 2005, 63–70.
42 Vitória 2011, 108. 'Pay attention, every wise woman, / to Clytemnestra, who was so wicked, / and whose death was so disastrous, / with no salvation from her condition. / Look out all of you, have great esteem / for your husbands and love them, / for may not such disastrous cases occur, / as the one you can see here'.

who, according to Alonge, reduces Electra to 'the image of a pure and heroic princess fighting against the evil Clytemnestra'.[43]

This interpretation of the myth, which is crucial for adapting Greek tragedy to a contemporary audience and ensuring its favourable reception, is in fact expressed by Vitória in the Prologue, where he advocates the reading of pagan texts as vehicles of Christian virtues. Insisting on the idea that the fate of Clytemnestra and Aegisthus was a consequence of their adulterous and wicked conduct, Vitória is of the opinion that one can 'draw great moral doctrine' from 'those ancient poets':

> [...] acho nam haver aí nenhũa fábula escrita por qualquer daqueles antigos poetas, que eram grandes filósofos, da qual nam possamos tirar grande dotrina moral [...]. E assi nesta presente obra Egisto, que era adúltero, vivendo e permanecendo em vício sem se querer dele apartar, foi a punhaladas por Orestes morto, que outra cousa é senam os maus ensistindo em sua maldade nam poderem acabar em bem? E por Clitemnestra, molher del rei Agaménom, conhecemos de quanta culpa são dinas e quanto mal pera si buscam e causam a outrem as que de tais excessos e dilitos são cometedoras, e assi pelo contrario dinas de eterna memória e grande louvor as que sempre hão vevido bem e honestamente [...].[44]

Let us not forget that the prologue has no parallel in the Castilian version and appears to stem not only from Vitória's need to justify the translation of a Greek tragedy, but also to legitimize the reading of Sophocles in a way that ensured its continuous relevance in the 16th century. Therefore, the insertion of motifs and references to pagan gods, which had been eliminated by Pérez de Oliva, is intended to present the tragedy as a Greek, rather than a Christian work, and indicates his edifying conception of the classics, as he confirms in his own words.

Thus, the changes undertaken by Vitória throughout his translation — whether the use of verse and *redondilha maior*, the elimination of the Chorus or

---

[43] Alonge 2019, 149. On moralistic interpretations of Greek tragedy, see especially Reiss 1999, 229–231, Serra 2015, 96–97, and Finglass 2017, 489–491. The interpretation of the prince's death in Diogo de Teive's *Ioannes Princeps* as a vehicle for criticizing the king and his politics of expansion would also fall under this moral conception of tragedy (see Fouto 2015, 102–107).
[44] Vitória 2011, 38–39. 'I think that there is no fable written by any of those ancient poets, who were great philosophers, from which we cannot draw great moral doctrine [...]. And so, in this present work, Aegisthus, who was an adulterer, who lived and remained in vice without wanting to depart from it, was killed by Orestes with a dagger. What else does it mean, if not that the wicked who insist on their wickedness cannot end well? And from the example of Clytemnestra, wife of King Agamemnon, we know how much guilt they deserve and how much evil they seek and cause to others, those who commit such excesses and crimes. And, on the contrary, how worthy of eternal memory and great praise are those who have always lived well and honestly [...]'.

even the development of the scenes describing Clytemnestra's guilt, aiming to bring the tragedy closer to traditional Portuguese plays — should be understood as a means to facilitate a wider understanding of the original play by a less literate audience.

In conclusion, Vitória's translation differs from Pérez de Oliva's because it does not present the Greek characters as Christians but rather preserves the original pagan traits and exhorts a reading of the classics as vehicles of Christian virtues, thus promoting their diffusion beyond the scholarly and academic contexts.

Cécile Dudouyt
Translating Ancient Greek Drama into French, 1537–1580

Abstract: Through a detailed analysis of two important treatises on French poetry, one by Thomas Sebillet (1549, *Art Poétique françoys*), and the other one by Joachim du Bellay (1549, *Deffense et illustration de la langue françoyse*), this chapter argues that translation shifts from being thought of as a highly creative enterprise, much like writing a poem, to becoming the polar opposite of new literary creation. This shift correlates with a change in translation practices: from the 1550s onwards, translating ancient Greek drama becomes a much more covert and fragmentary endeavour, aimed at recasting the (hidden) sources into new 'original' texts so as to contribute to the creation of France's national literature.

Almost all 16th-century French translations of ancient Greek drama were produced over roughly two decades. Between 1537 and 1549, seven ancient Greek plays were translated into French — five of which were translations from Euripides (*Supplices*, *Troiades*, *Hecuba* and *Iphigenia Aulidensis*, translated twice), and three from Sophocles (*Electra* and *Antigone*, translated twice as well).[1] It was also around the mid 1540s that Ronsard translated a fragment of Aristophanes' *Plutus*, and Jean-Antoine de Baïf the prologue of Euripides' *Helena*. Both were published much later — respectively in de Baïf's *Euvres en rimes* (1573) and Ronsard's *Recueil* (1617)[2] — but were likely school exercises dating from the time the two future poets of the 'Pléiade' were studying Greek with the Greek scholar Jean Dorat.[3] If Ronsard's 16th-century biographer, Claude Binet, is to be believed, the same Jean Dorat had translated a lost *Prometheus Vinctus* into French for his pupils, which inspired Ronsard to translate Aristophanes' *Plutus* and have it performed at the collège de Coqueret. By way of comparison, there

---

[1] Binet 1586, 11. There are no extant full-length translations from Aeschylus in French before Lefranc de Pompignan's and La Porte du Theil's translations in the 18th century. On the 18th-century reception of Aeschylus in France, see Lechevalier 2007 and Macintosh 2009.
[2] Laumonier 1967, 364–389 and Marty Laveaux 1966, 270–274.
[3] In 1556, the poet Pierre de Ronsard gave the name 'Pleiade' to the poetic group he formed with poets, translators, playwrights and literary theoreticians Joachim du Bellay, Antoine de Baïf, Jacques Pelletier du Mans, Etienne Jodelle, Pontus de Tyard and Remy Belleau. For a history of this 16th-century poetic movement, see Chamard 1939–40 and Fauconnier 2001.

were by 1550 only two translations of Roman tragedies — both anonymous, unpublished and undated (*Hercule Furieux* and the pseudo-Senecan *Octavie*).

In the second half of the 16th century, however, only one ancient Greek play appeared in print (du Baïf's *Antigone* in 1573), whereas more Roman tragedies went on to be published, namely three *Agamemnon* by Charles Toutain (1557), Louis-François Le Duchat (1561), and Roland Brisset, the latter presenting in the same volume four Senecan tragedies (*Octavie, Hercule Furieux* and *Thyeste*) (1589), all attesting to the growing influence of Seneca on French tragedy in the second half of the 16th century. It would, however, be a mistake to conclude that Greek drama had no impact on the French stage. Even if the production of full-length *translations* of ancient Greek tragedies stopped short for over a century, *translating* had become one of the tools of early modern playwrights, so that translated fragments of Sophocles, Euripides and Aristophanes contributed to the fashioning of early modern French drama.

To present this multi-faceted reception of ancient Greek drama in translation, I propose, after a short presentation of the different plays and their translators, to replace them in the wider context of early modern discourses on translation in early modern poetics. This includes the well-documented rise of the word 'traduction' in French, which had gradually replaced the older term 'translation' by the mid-16th century, and the simultaneous erosion of the prestige accorded to both translators and translations. One of the main theoretical counterparts of this lexical and symbolic evolution was the opposition drawn by Joachim du Bellay between 'imitation' and 'traduction' and the respective roles he assigned to the two practises in the constitution of a national French literature in *La Deffence et illustration de la langue françoyse* (1549). In spite of this denial of the creative powers of translation, the technique of translating fragments of multiple sources and combining them with new material became quite common among 16th-century playwrights who contributed to fashion the new national canon of French dramatic literature. Pierre Le Loyer's *La Néphélococugie* (1578), and Robert Garnier's *Antigone ou la piété* (1580) or *La Troade* (published in 1579 and probably performed in 1581) illustrate this practice, which goes beyond oppositions between imitation and translation, and testifies to the dramaturgical and poetic impact of Greek plays on early modern French drama.

Tab. 1: Table of French plays drawn from an ancient Greek argument. (Publication dates are in bold, dates of first performances in italics, and comedies are underlined. In the translation columns, I have placed texts that follow one main ancient source in full, irrespective of any comment on the 'closeness' or 'looseness' of the relationship between target and source.)

Translations from Greek Drama	Proto-classical Tragedies and Comedies in French (non-exhaustive)	Translations from Roman Drama
1537 Lazare de Baïf *Electra* **1542** Calvy de la Fontaine *Antigone* [Soissons, Bibliothèque Municipale, 201 (189 A)] **1542–47** (?) Amyot (?) three undated anonymous manuscript translations: *Troade* [Musée de Condé n°1688] *Iphigénie à Aulis* [BnF ms. fr. 22505] *Les Suppliantes* **1544** (second edition in **1550**) Guillaume Bochetel *Hécube* **1544-47**? Ronsard <u>*Plutus*</u> (264 lines) **(1617)** du Baïf *Hélène* (prologue) **(1573)** **1549** Thomas Sébillet *Iphigénie à Aulis*		**1504** Anonymous *Amphitryon* **1530–1550** (?) Two anonymous manuscripts: *Octavie* [BnF ms. fr. 1720], *Hercule Furieux* [BnF ms. fr. 1640] **1537** pseudo des Périers *L'Andrienne* **1539** *Le grant Thérence* (sic)
	1553 Jodelle *Cléopâtre Captive*, <u>*L'Eugène*</u> *1555* (?) Jean de la Péruse *Médée* *1556* (?) Mellin de Saint-Gelais *Sophonisbe* *1560* Jean de la Taille *Didon* *1565* Jean-Antoine de Baïf <u>*L'Eunuque*</u> **(1573)** *1567* Jean-Antoine de Baïf <u>*Le Brave*</u> **1572** Jean de la Taille *Saül le furieux* (composition date 1562) **1573-78** Robert Garnier *Hippolyte, Cornélie, Marc-Antoine* **1578** Pierre Le Loyer <u>*La Néphélococugie*</u> **1579** Robert Garnier *La Troade* (**1581?**) **1580** Robert Garnier *Antigone ou la piété*	**1557** Charles Toutain *Agamemnon* **1561** François Le Duchat *Agamemnon*
1573 Jean-Antoine de Baïf *Antigone*		**1589** Roland Brisset, *Hercule furieux, Thyeste, Agamemnon, Octavie*. Pierre Mathieu *Clytemnestre*

As can be seen in this table, there is a clear preference for translating ancient Greek tragedy between 1530 and 1550, in the last 20 years of the reign of François I, and the first few years of Henri II's. I am tempted to plot three main translating hubs: one around François I (Amyot and Bochetel), another in the extended marotic circle (Calvy and Sébillet), and a third, initiated by Lazare de Baïf, continued by his son Jean-Antoine, and fostered by the poetic ideals formulated by the Pléiade.

The upper half of the middle column is empty, but this should not be interpreted to mean that there were no dramatic productions in France before Jodelle's *Cléopâtre Captive* and *L'Eugène*. Up to the 1550s, the popular dramatic genres in French were the comedic 'farces' and 'sotties', the serious 'moralités', and religious theatre, the 'mystères'. These performances were produced by a variety of 'confréries' ('brotherhoods'), the better known of which are 'Les Enfants sans souci' ('the careless Children', specialising in farces, sotties, and moralités), 'les Basochiens' (law students performing sotties and moralités) and the 'Confréries de la Passion' ('mystères'). In 1548, the Parliament of Paris gave to one such 'Brotherhood of the passion' ownership of the main indoor theatrical venue in Paris, the Hotel de Bourgogne, at the express condition, however, that no religious 'mystère' should ever be performed on its stage — one of the many examples of the push against religious drama in anti-reformation France. Simultaneously, a new generation of poets created new plays following the example of ancient comedy and tragedy. As can be seen in the table, this renewal of dramatic genres under the tutelage of Henri II first took the form of full-length translations of ancient drama in the mid-16th century, and then of new plays built on ancient models.

1 Overview of 16th-Century Translators and Translations of Ancient Greek Drama

Of the eight full-length translations of ancient Greek drama, all of which are tragedies, four (*Hécuba*, and the three manuscript translations: *Les Suppliantes*, *La Troade* and the first *Iphigénie à Aulis*) do not bear the name of the translator. In the early 20th century, René Sturel attributed both *La Troade* and *Iphigénie à Aulis* to Jacques Amyot,[4] who presumably made them when he was a tutor in Bourges, in the early 1540s. As for *Les Suppliantes*, the long-lost manuscript was

---

4 Sturel 1913, 269–296, 637–52.

found only recently by Tristan Alonge, who traces it back to Amyot as well.[5] If all these attributions are correct, the figure of Jacques Amyot looms very large on the first reception of Euripides into French. Indeed, Sturel designated Guillaume de Bochetel as the author of the fourth anonymous translation (published in 1544 and reprinted in 1550), *Hécuba*, which was previously thought to be by Lazare de Baïf. He drew this conclusion on the strength of the preface, in which the unnamed translator addressed the king and explained that he retranslated the Latin version that his children had produced under the supervision of their tutor, who, in the early 1540s, happened to be no other than Jacques Amyot himself.

The social trajectory of Jacques Amyot, celebrated by both his contemporaries and posterity as the translator of Plutarch's *Lives*, illustrates the prestige accorded to the translator and translation in the early 16th century.[6] His accomplishments as a Greek scholar and translator from ancient Greek allowed this impecunious son of a modest merchant family based in Melun to reach the pinnacle a man of his condition could aspire to by becoming the tutor of the future kings, Charles IX and Henri III, in 1557; the almoner to their father, Henri II, in 1561; and the bishop of Auxerre, in 1570. The translator of Plutarch and presumed translator of Euripides was not an isolated example; translations of ancient Greek drama were attempted by poets, legal scholars and prelates, men of note on the royal payroll or occupying positions as administrators in urban centres. The first translator of a Greek tragedy in French, Lazare de Baïf, was François I's ambassador to Venice from 1529–1534, before becoming one of his masters of request ('maître des requêtes de l'hotel du roi') in 1537, on the same year his *Electre* was published. Guillaume Bochetel, mentioned above, was a diplomat too, and a royal secretary sent by François I to negotiate with Charles Quint (in 1538) and Henry VIII (in 1546). All these early translators worked directly for the king, for François I until 1547 and Henri II after, attesting to the royal favour accorded to translation and translators.

Calvy de la Fontaine, the first translator of *Antigone*, and Thomas Sébillet, one of the translators of *Iphigenia at Aulis*, did not belong to the same sphere as Jacques Amyot, Guillaume de Bochetel or Lazare de Baïf.[7] Less is known about their lives, but both were minor poets as well as translators, and belonged to the poetic circle around Clément Marot, the most prominent French poet of the first half of the 16th century, and the translator of the first five books of Ovid's *Met-*

---

5 Alonge 2016, 109–126.
6 Gresy 1848.
7 On Sébillet's translation of *Iphigenia at Aulis*, see Di Martino and Baudou in this volume.

amorphoses. De la Fontaine was active in the quarrel opposing Marot, who leaned towards protestantism, to the catholic François de Sagon from the Sorbonne.[8] Thomas Sébillet, on the other hand, who studied law and became a lawyer at the Parliament of Paris was also the author of an *Art poétique* (1548), in which he praised not only Marotic poetry itself but Marot's method of poetic creation through translation.[9]

In the next generation, the playwright Robert Garnier and the polygraph Pierre Le Loyer both studied law in Toulouse in their early twenties, then spent time in Paris where they met with Ronsard and the poets of the Pléiade, before settling as *conseillers du Présidial*, Garnier in Le Mans and Le Loyer in Angers.[10] Their fellow playwright Jean-Antoine de Baïf, son of Lazare, produced a few plays drawn from ancient material: *Antigone*, and two comedies, *Le Brave, ou le Taille-Bras* (presented to the king in 1567) drawn from Plautus' *Miles Gloriosus*; and *L'Eunuque* from Terence's *Andria*. Whereas the earlier translations of ancient Greek plays were clearly meant for reading, the ones produced by that younger generation — de Baïf's son, Garnier, and Le Loyer — are clearly scripts intended for performance.[11] Interestingly, de Baïf's reworking of the Sophoclean tragedy followed the source text more closely than his comedies, but with only one tragedy and two comedies, it is difficult to draw conclusions about a differential treatment of the two genres. Antoine Du Verdier, in his *Bibliothèque* (1585), a bibliographical list of notable books and authors, claims that he saw manuscripts of translations by de Baïf of Euripides' *Medea*, Sophocles' *Trachiniae*, Aristophanes' *Plutus* and Terence's *Heautontimorumenos*: 'all of the above, ready for the press as I have seen them complete and written in his own hand'.[12] Unfortunately, all these translations are now lost; they were presumably never published and, after 1572, the practice of translating ancient Greek drama into French drew to a stop for over a century. The next translations of ancient Greek drama on the record are Anne Le Fèvre's *Le Plutus et les Nuées d'Aristophane* (1684) and her husband André Dacier's *L'Œdipe et l'*Electre *de Sophocle* (1692).[13]

---

8 Berthon 2020, 163–182.
9 Sébillet 1910, 190; de Noo 1927, 1–2, 22–23.
10 Le Loyer 2004; Chardon 1970.
11 Dudouyt 2016, 181; Lebègue 1977, 141.
12 'Tout cela prest à imprimer comme ie l'ay veu paracheué & escrit de sa main'; Du Verdier 1585, 641. For more information about Ronsard's and Baïf's *Plutus*, see Bastin-Hammou 2015.
13 Le Févre 1684; Dacier 1693. On Anne Dacier's translations of Aristophanes, see Bastin Hammou 2010.

2 Thomas Sébillet's *Art Poétique Françoys* (1548): Translation as Poetry

The high social regard for translators until the mid-16th century is reflected in the prominent position Thomas Sébillet gives translation in the first ever treatise on French poetry, *L'Art poétique français* (1548).[14] He writes: 'A Version or Translation is today the most common Poem as well as the best received among renowned Poets and cultivated readers'.[15] In the mind of this 16th-century jurist, translator, and man of letters, there was no contradiction between the terms 'traduction' or 'version' and 'poème': here, a text is not considered as secondary simply because it 'turns' a foreign text into French. The very use of the verb 'tourner', etymologically close to the meaning of 'version', is reminiscent of the artisanal vocabulary used for poetry itself. Sébillet recognised that the translinguistic reception of ancient and Italian material in particular had been influential in shaping and driving early modern French poetic creativity, through the introduction of novel poetical forms into the target language.

This acknowledgement is anything but surprising, in view of the influential verse translations of the first half of the century. Ancient poetry was almost never translated into prose; every translation of ancient Greek drama was in verse, and when a poem was translated both into prose and verse, the poetic version won acclaim and recognition. This was the case, for example, of Jehan Samxon's prose retranslation of Lorenzo Valla's Latin version of the *Iliad*, first published in 1523, and soon replaced by Hughes Salel's celebrated verse translation of the first ten books in rhyming decasyllables (with a rhyming pattern AA BB).[16] The *Iliade* went on to be retranslated twice in the 16th century, each time in verse; in the paratexts, none of the translators mentioned the possibility of translating the epic in prose for greater accuracy, as would become the norm from Anne Dacier's 1699 translation onward.[17]

The short poetic paratexts to Salel's *Iliad* by Barthélémy Aneau play both on the spatial meaning of the word *translatio* in Latin (journey), and on the warlike

---

14 Jacques Pelletier du Mans published an *Art poétique* in 1545 but it is a translation of Horace's Poetics, not a treatise on French Poetics (Pelletier 1545). He published one ten years later (Pelletier 1555).
15 'La Version ou Traduction est aujourd'hui le Poème plus fréquent et mieux reçu des estimés Poètes et des doctes lecteurs'; Sébillet [1549] 1910, 187.
16 Homer, *Il.* transl. Samxon 1530.
17 Homer, *Il.* transl. Certon 1615. Homer, *Il.* transl. Jamyn 1605. Homer, *Il.* transl. Dacier [1699] 1712.

subject of the *Iliad*, and present poetic translation as a 'literary deportation': 'Reduced in France from the Hellad [...] more than itself the *Iliad* is made'.[18] The boast, also translated in Greek and in Latin verse, equates 'réduire' and 'traduire' to 'reduce to slavery' — it is verse translation, and not prose translation, which truly incorporates the ancient material to form the new early modern French canon, establishing the creative powers of French poets and of the French language. Salel is compared to Lucan's Gallic Hercules, the rhetorical hero, who with the golden chains of his eloquence, both imports (or deports) the source text and magnifies it — even if there is a trace of the tension between ancient prestige and modern ambitions in the oxymoron: although the poet vanquishes or 'reduces' a text he still has to make it 'greater'.[19]

Discussing translation in a treatise on French poetics thus made perfect sense, and Sébillet developed the poetic merits of translations in chapter 14 of his *Art Poétique françoys*: even if time is 'powerful enough' ('assez puissant') to produce new poetic forms, translating ancient genres to embellish the French language is the best way of preparing the poet both for imitating them and for inventing new poetic forms. Sébillet gives the example of the 'long poem' ('grand oeuvre') which was rare in French; imitating either the *Roman de la rose* or, which he presents as even better models, Homer, Virgil, or Ovid, would be a way of introducing longer poetic forms in the language.[20] It is clear throughout that there is no opposition in Sébillet's mind between imitation, version and translation. All 'yield the pure and silvery invention of Poets gilded and made richer by our own language'.[21] Here translation is presented as a process in which something is gained, going from silver to gold, reversing the ancient trope of golden times devolving to baser metals in the course of history, and expressing an optimistic view of artistic and linguistic progress. But in the same sentence, that new hierarchy is questioned: 'and both man and work are truly worthy of praise who were able to formulate properly and idiomatically in one's language, what another had written *even better* in his own'. The two criteria mentioned here are 'propriety' and 'nativeness', that is to say acceptability in the target language.[22] In this context, the hallmark of a good translator-poet is that they may be able to produce a translation that sounds idiomatic to native

---

18 'Réduire en la France d'Hellade [...] plus grande que soit or se fait l'*Iliade*'.
19 Bompaire 1993, 59–62.
20 Sébillet 1548, 186.
21 'Rendre la pure et argentine invention des Poètes dorée et enrichie de notre langue'; Sébillet 1548, 188.
22 'Et vraiment celui et son œuvre méritent grandes louanges qui a pu proprement et naïvement exprimer en son langage, ce qu'un autre avait mieux écrit au sien'; Sébillet 1548, 188.

readers, without any residual awkwardness to indicate that it was not first produced in that language. This ideal is one of appropriation and domestication, but this domestication is not in any way presented as antagonistic to maintaining the resemblance between source and target texts: 'Yet the dignity of the author, and the energy of his discourse expressed in such a curious way, that it is impossible to present his face itself, let your work show as much as the mirror would'.[23]

Paradoxical as it may seem, this conception of translation as 'faithful domestication' is concerned with adapting cultural references, avoiding neologisms, and general target text acceptability, as well as with paying attention to stylistic features in the source text. This can also be found in prose. Amyot did not preface the anonymous verse translations of ancient Greek drama he is said to have authored, but in the paratexts of the *Vies Parallèles* (1559), he shows no signs of considering that domesticating the text, through the use of well-known cultural references and the use of 'native' language that readers can relate to, was in any way contradictory with providing an accurate portrait of the author's style:

> the task of the translator is not just to give the meaning of the author, but also represent and outline the form and way of speaking peculiar to him, so as not to blunder like the painter who, tasked with making a likeness of a living model, would make him long when he is short, and fat when he is thin, even if he takes care to make the face a good likeness.[24]

In this comparison, the meaning of the text is compared to the features of the model's face, but producing a good likeness is not the only duty of the translator/painter, the author's writing is also to be considered. This passage refers to the practice of *amplificatio*, doubling adjectives or expanding on the source text to make it more explicit.[25]

---

23 'La dignité toutefois de l'auteur, et l'énergie de son oraison tant curieusement exprimée, que puis qu'il n'est possible de représenter son même visage, autant en montre ton œuvre, qu'en représenterait le miroir'; Sébillet 1548, 190.
24 L'office d'un propre traducteur ne gît pas seulement à rendre fidèlement la sentence de son auteur, mais aussi à se représenter aucunement et à adombrer la forme du style et manière de parler d'icelui, qu'il ne veut commettre l'erreur que ferait le peintre, qui ayant pris à portraire un homme au vif, le peindrait long, là où il serait court: et gros, là où il serait grêle, encore qu'il le fît naïvement bien ressembler du visage. Amyot 1559, NP XI.
25 Cf. Piccolomini's similar view on this in Beta, footnote 16, in this volume.

Going back to Sébillet's conception of poetic translation, as long as the readers' ears are not scratched, ('n'égratigne et ride les oreilles rondes')[26] translators are to be praised for their arduous but fruitful task: 'To him is due the same praise as he receives the man who by dint of long and strenuous efforts draws out of the womb of the earth the hidden treasure, in order to share it with everyone'.[27] The methodology Sébillet outlines here is inspired from Etienne Dolet's *Manière de bien traduire d'une langue en autre*: linguistic proficiency and preference for the 'sentence' ('idea') rather than to the 'mots' ('words').[28] But Sébillet introduces the metaphor of the dancer; once the source text is understood, the translation is the nimble and graceful expression of a linguistic body — who only needs, in order to caper and turn, to have full mastery of the source and target languages.

This presentation of translation as a way of enriching both one's language and the art of writing itself bears testimony to a way of conceptualisation translation that did not see writing translations and writing poetry as antithetical, but potentially identical occupations, as long as the translator poet was able to 'dance' on their two linguistic legs. Indeed, translation was seen as both propaedeutic to writing poetry and a valid poetic strategy in its own right: domesticating a foreign text and providing a mirror image of that text were not conceptualised as sets of irreconcilable translation strategies. A poet, translator, and theorist of translation and poetry like Sébillet encompassed in one sentence both the losses and gains of translation, and ended on an encomium of translation as the sharing of the treasures of the past with future generations.

Sébillet drew this logic to its conclusion in his *Art Poétique*. Since writers are imitators, and translators are imitators, then the best poetic advice Sébillet gives to future poets is to imitate the first generation of French poet translators:

> so imitate Marot in his *Metamorphoses*, in his *Musée*, in his *Psalmes*; Salel, in his *Iliade*, Héroet, in his *Androgyne*, Démasures, in his *Enéide*, Peletier in his *Odyssée* and his *Georgiques*. Imitate all these divine minds, who, as they followed in the footsteps of others, made the path smoother to follow, and are themselves followed; [...] follow them step

---

26 Sébillet 1548, 31.
27 'Et lui est due la même gloire qu'emporte celui qui par son labeur et longue peine tire des entrailles de la terre le trésor caché, pour le faire commun à l'usage de tous les hommes'.
28 Dolet 1540, 15. Dolet's distinction between 'sentence' and 'mots' harkens back to the longstanding debate between *verba* and *sententiae*, for which see Di Martino, footnote 22, in this volume.

by step like a child follows his nurse, wherever he will happen to venture in the meadow of Poetry.²⁹

In the first flush of translating ancient sources into French, poetic freedom and translative fidelity are presented here walking hand in hand. But Sébillet's view of translation as an opportunity for poetry rather than as its opposite, reflecting the enthusiastic poetic translation of the first half of the 16th century, was about to be rejected and replaced with a radically opposite one.

3 The Translator and the Poet: Textual Ownership and Cultural Prestige

Sébillet had compared the process of translating poetry into verse, that he also called imitation, to that of following a well-trodden path: just as it is easier and safer to walk where others have walked before, imitating is the best way of learning poetry, both at an individual and national level. A few years later, Barthélémy Aneau used the same image to make the exact opposite point: 'it is harder and more bothersome to follow others in unknown and narrow paths, placing one's feet in their footprints, than, with free and bold steps, walk at will on a smooth and wide uncovered path'.³⁰ In the first comparison, translation is the royal road to poetic excellence, in the second, it has become an inglorious and inconvenient byway.

This shift in perception is well documented. Guillerm was the first to retrace it in the prefaces of early-modern translators, and to give 1540 as a watershed. More recently, in the third volume of the *Histoire de la Traduction en Langue Français*, Véronique Duché confirmed her analysis: 'starting from a precise point in the period under study, around 1550, identified by L. Guillerm as a watershed and confirmed by additional investigations now made possible by

---

29 'Imite donc Marot en sa *Métamorphose*, en son *Musée*, en ses *Psalmes*; Salel, en son *Iliade*, Héroet, en son *Androgyne*, Démasures, en son *Enéide*, Peletier en son *Odyssée* et *Géorgique*. Imite tant de divins esprits, qui suivant la trace d'autrui, font le chemin plus doux à suivre, et sont eux-mêmes suivis. [...] les suivre pas à pas comme l'enfant la nourrice, partout où il voudra cheminer par dedans le pré de Poésie'; Sébillet 1548, 26.
30 'Il est plus difficile et fâcheux suyvre autry par chemin incogneu et estroict, arrrestant ses peids sur ses traces, que par livre et franche marche s'en aller esbatant à son plaisir par lain et large chemin descouvert'; quoted in Guillerm 1988, 382.

the large number of translations available online, the neutral, and at times positive, discourse on that practice becomes derogatory'.[31]

This reversal calls for interpretation. Did something change around that date in the social reality of translators? Guillerm argues that this negative perception of translation was not justified by real changes in the socio-economic circumstances of translators. On the contrary, the number of translations continued to peak until 1560; they increasingly bore the name of the translator, whose copyright was recognised by the Parliament; and the prestige surrounding ancient material provided translators with some negotiating powers with publishers: 'the claim that the translated work is inferior in status to the original work does not even amount to a representation, which could trigger real-life consequences, it is a mere trope found in theoretical discourses'.[32] This trope opposes two cultural figures who used to be one and the same agent: the free-ranging author and the chained translator.

The inequality between them is expressed in terms of ownership of the text. Jacques Pelletier du Mans, in a dizain published with his translation of Horace's *Art Poetique* (1545) muses, 'little booklet that is only half mine, should I publish you?'.[33] Ten years later, in his own *Art Poetique*, he explores the ramifications of textual ownership and the ways in which the Poet can appropriate a subject (*inventio*) that belongs to everyone. He takes Ovid's *Metamorphosis* as an example. Ovid did not invent the stories, but made them his own:

> This is the way of choosing one's stories and one's topic, and this is how, even if we appropriate them in front of all the world, we will not be accused of theft. This, as Horace said, is how public material becomes private. Here is how we make it our own [...] as long as we do not adhere to the curious notion that we should follow the whole thread of the Author we take it from.[34]

---

31 'À partir d'un moment précis de notre période, autour de 1540, date charnière identifiée par L Guillerm et confirmée par les sondages complémentaires que permet aujourd'hui la mise en ligne d'un nombre important de traductions, le discours neutre, voire valorisant, de présentation de l'exercice se convertit en dévalorisation'; Duché 2015, 133.
32 'L'affirmation du statut inférieur de l'ouvrage traduit par rapport à l'œuvre originale apparaît donc, non pas même comme une représentation partiellement active, qui pourrait produire des effets en retour sur le réel concret, mais comme *un fait de discours*'; Guillerm 1988, 422.
33 'Petit livret qui n'est mien qu'à demi / dois-je te mettre en vue?'; Pelletier 1545, 6.
34 'Voilà le moyen de choisir ses arguments et son sujet: et comme, encore que nous le prenons devant tout le monde, nous ne serons point pourtant accusés de larcin. Voilà comme disait Horace, qu'une matière publique devient privée. [...] pourvu que nous ne nous arrêtons à ne sais quelle curiosité de suivre tout le fil de l'Auteur dont il est pris'; Pelletier 1555, 21.

Here, the same image, of walking after a previous author is presented as larceny. The best imitation will always be translation, but if an author wants the text to be their own, to belong to them as Author, they should take their distances. Merely following, as translators are bound to do, means losing symbolic ownership of the text, and all the cultural prestige the text will be able to garner is afforded to the poet while all the disrepute goes to the translator, either as a bad translator or as the translator of a bad author.

In the middle of the 16th century, concomitantly with this reversal in the cultural prestige accorded to following ancient sources, there was the progressive rise of a new term to refer to the producer of a target text, the act of producing it and the product itself. The words 'traduire', 'traduction' and 'traducteur' gradually came to replace 'translater', 'translation' and 'translateur' — the older terms came from the 14th-century royal programme of the *translatio studii* initiated by Charles V: 'the agenda of the *translatio studii* was intrinsically linked to the transfer of powers (the *translatio imperii*), so that cultivating the language was a way of furthering on the cultural level, the influence that France was looking for politically. Translating ancient texts in the vernacular remains, as in Oresme's time, one of the ways of providing symbolical legitimacy to the monarchy, at a time when the Church benefitted from the prestige of Latin'.[35] The royal support of translation given by François I and Henri II was the continuation of the efforts of previous monarchs who strove to ground the monarchy in artistic and scientific achievements.

The term 'translation' primarily referred to the transfer of knowledge rather than the reproduction of textual forms. Its most prominent figure, the translating scholar Nicole Oresme, who followed a trajectory reminiscent of Amyot's almost two centuries before him, was born in a modest family, but noticed for his intelligence and ability to translate Aristotle's treatises, he became a close advisor of the king and finished his life as a bishop. In his preface to the *Ethique* (1370), the synonym he uses to 'translater' is 'bailler' (to give), highlighting translation as a semantic transmission as opposed to Sébillet's use of the verb 'tourner' (turn), presenting translation as a craft.

---

35 'La *translatio studii* étant intimement liée au transfert du pouvoir (la *translatio imperii*), enrichir la langue est en effet une manière de prolonger, sur le plan culturel, le rayonnement que la France cherche sur le plan politique. La traduction des textes de l'antiquité en langue vernaculaire demeure, comme au temps d'Oresme, un des moyens de donner une assise symbolique au pouvoir royal, alors que l'église jouit du prestige du latin'; Duché 2015, 145.

4 Du Bellay's Deffense et Illustration de la Langue Françoyse (1549): Traduction and Imitation

The author who was most influential in redefining *traduction* as an ancillary and constrained exercise and who most strongly opposed the translator to the poet was Joachim du Bellay, himself both a poet and a translator of poetry. Sébillet had advised future poets to imitate the imitative ways of the poet translators of Marot's generation; du Bellay's treatise advocates for the opposite in what can be seen as a prototype of 17th-century quarrels opposing admirers of ancient Greeks and Romans, the *anciens*, to the advocates of the *modernes*, who extolled the merits of their contemporaries. According to du Bellay, the French language was sufficiently rich and powerful to accommodate any foreign text:

> our language, previously so rough and unpolished, [has been] made elegant and if not as copious as it could hope to become, at least, a faithful interpreter of all the others. And so it happens that philosophers, historians, doctors, poets, Greek and Latin orators, have learned to speak French.[36]

He carefully avoids crediting translation explicitly for the 'fertility' of the French language, but the implication is clear, if the French language is now more polished than it was before the reign of François I, and if it can now translate all kinds of foreign texts, it is thanks to the work of generations of translators. The true 'cultivateurs' (cultivators or gardeners) of the language who 'grafted' ancient branches onto the national fruit tree were the old 'translateurs', thanks to whom: 'all the sciences can be faithfully and eloquently treated in it, as can be seen in so many Greek and Latin books, and even Italian, Spanish or other, translated into French by many excellent writers of our time'.[37] But the title of the next chapter firmly contradicts Sébillet's advice: 'translations are not enough to perfect the French language'.[38]

---

36 'Notre langage, auparavant scabreux et mal poli, rendu élégant, et sinon tant copieux qu'il pourra bien être, pour le moins, fidèle interprète de tous les autres. Et qu'ainsi soit, philosophes, historiens, médecins, poètes, orateurs grecs et latins, ont appris à parler français'; du Bellay 1549, 49.
37 'Toutes sciences se peuvent fidèlement et copieusement traiter en icelle, comme on peut voir en si grand nombre de livres grecs et latins, voire bien italiens, espagnols et autres, traduits en français par maintes excellentes plumes de notre temps'; du Bellay 1549, 49.
38 'Les traductions ne sont suffisantes pour donner perfection à la langue française'.

Du Bellay sets out to demonstrate this claim with the help of Quintilian's five rhetorical canons: *Inventio* (finding the subject matter), *dispositio* (arranging it in a cogent way), *elocutio* (formulation of the ideas), *memoria* (memorisation of the speech for public display) and *actio* (delivery of the speech). He discards three of them: memory and delivery because they depend on natural qualities and hard work, and cannot be learned from theory. He also leaves composition (*dispositio*) aside on the grounds that there are no rules or precepts for it either: 'in as much as historical events, geographical location, living conditions and the diversity of situations are innumerable' — perhaps an acknowledgment of the evolution of cultural taste, although this is not stated explicitly.[39] Instead, he chooses to base his opposition between translation and poetry on invention and eloquence. His rationale is that although it is possible and praiseworthy to follow the invention of foreign authors, it is impossible to follow another poet's *elocutio*: 'I will never believe that it is possible to learn all that from translators, because no one can formulate it as gracefully as the author did: all the more so as every language has a je-ne-sais-quoi belonging only to itself'.[40] In his view, a poet's *elocutio* is untranslatable because with a language comes an indescribable originality, a 'naïveté', a 'je ne sais quoi' that cannot be derived from anything foreign and cannot be reproduced in another language. Later, he argues implicitly that in poetry *inventio* cannot be separated from *elocutio*: 'poets, a kind of author whom if I knew or wanted to translate I would the least consider, because of the divinity of their invention, [...] the loftiness of their style, magnificence of their words, gravity of their maxims, the daring and variety of their tropes, and a thousand other lights of poetry'.[41] He goes on to equate the poetry contained in the text with the 'immortal soul' residing in the body.

To attempt to duplicate this spiritual essence born of quasi divine inspiration and the genius of a language is not only doomed, but sacrilegious; 'O Apollo, O Muses! To defile in this way the sacred relics of antiquity'.[42] This awe is one

---

39 'Vu que les événements du temps, la circonstance des lieux, la condition des personnes et la diversité des occasions sont innumérables'; du Bellay 1549, 51.
40 'Je ne croirai jamais qu'on puisse bien apprendre tout cela des traducteurs, pource qu'il est impossible de le rendre avec la même grâce dont l'auteur en a usé: d'autant que chacune langue a je ne sais quoi propre seulement à elle'; du Bellay 1549, 52.
41 'Poètes, genre d'auteurs certes auquel si je savais, ou voulais traduire, je m'adresserais aussi peu, à cause de cette divinité d'invention, [...] grandeur de style, magnificence de mots, gravité de sentences, audace et variété de figures, et mille autre lumières de poésie'; du Bellay 1549, 54.
42 'O Apollon! O Muses! Profaner ainsi les sacrées reliques de l'antiquité'; du Bellay 1549, 54.

of the earliest expressions of the near metaphysical cultural prestige attributed to writing, and particularly poetry in the constitution of a French identity. Yet it is built on a statement of untranslatability which was far from obvious at the time.

Barthélémy Anneau, the author of the anonymous *Quintil Horacien* — an almost line for line critique of *La Deffence* — starts with a translation of a few lines from Horcace's *Poetics*, in order to prove du Bellay wrong in deed, before demonstrating it with words: 'These are Horace's lines. That which I have not *traduit* (as you say) for I am no *traducteur* and do not want to be: but I have turned or *translatés*, [...] to show that it is not so difficult to turn Poets into French as you repute it to be impossible in chapter 6 of book I'[43] The 'as you say' is revealing, showing that Anneau sensed du Bellay was redefining the practice and using the more recent term 'traduire' to formulate a new ideal of translation. He picks up on the fact that in the *Deffence*, du Bellay widens the semantic gap between, on the one hand, old ways of translating and the old term used to name them, and, on the other hand, a new conception of 'traduire' under its new name.

So if, according to du Bellay, 'traduction' is not the way of making the French language the greatest in Europe, what is? The answer comes in chapter 8: 'to amplify the French language by imitation of ancient Greek and Roman authors'.[44] Imitation is the method true poets should use to make their language illustrious. This creates an opposition between imitation and translation which did not exist in Sébillet, who used 'translater', 'imiter', 'traduire' and 'tourner' as synonyms. And yet, even if du Bellay reviles 'traduction' and extolls 'imitation', it is difficult to spot actual differences in the way he describes the two. In chapter 5, he used the intranslatibility of *elocutio* as his strongest argument against translation, but in chapter 8 it is made clear that imitation only makes sense if the imitated source is foreign and that, when imitating, it is important to take *elocutio* into account: 'in the same way that it is not harmful but greatly to be praised to borrow from a foreign tongue maxims and words, and appropriate them; it is greatly reprehensible and detestable for any reader with a liberal nature, to see this imitation happening within one same language'.[45] If *imitation*

---

43 'Tels sont les vers d'Horace. Lesquels je n'ai pas traduit (comme tu parles) car traducteur ne suis, et ne veux être: mais les ai tournés ou translatés [...] pour montrer qu'il n'est si difficile à tourner les Poètes en Français comme tu le fais impossible au 6 chap. Du I. livre'; Anneau 1555, 2.
44 'D'amplifier la langue française par l'imitation des anciens auteurs grecs et romains'; du Bellay 1549, 58.
45 'Comme ce n'est point chose vicieuse mais grandement louable, emprunter d'une langue étrangères les sentences et les mots, et les approprier à la sienne; aussi est-ce chose grande-

should only be translinguistic, and if it is concerned, in the end, with *elocutio* as well as *inventio*, the difference between the two is not one of nature, but simply of degree. Du Bellay uses the word 'traduire' to express a heavier sense of duty towards the source, and an almost religious translative ideal, that of transfering the source into the target language, so to say, without touching it, without introducing any change. If translation is defined in these terms it is indeed impossible.

When du Bellay implicitly redefined what translation should be (i.e., perfect adequation to the source), the translated text became unfit to perform its task, that of both enriching the French language and ensuring the cultural prestige of France in 16th-century Europe. This is a shift in the relationship to the ancient source which can be analysed in the light of Descriptive Translation Studies as a change in the translative norm, linked to a reappraisal of the source text in the cultural landscape, called by Even Zohar the cultural system of systems, the polysystem. The poetic source becomes sacred, untouchable, and the ideal translation is redefined as its most faithful copy, which necessitates a degree of foreignisation, of importation of foreign stylistic and cultural alienations into the target culture, which heighten the equivalency but lowers the acceptability of the translation. Du Bellay's *Deffence* formulates this tension between, on the one hand, shifting translative norms and, on the other hand, the translative task of providing the French language with the 'thousand lights of poetry'.[46]

As a consequence of the clash between new translation norms and the main cultural purpose of translation, translation becomes impossible. This provides some context to the fact that only one full-length translation of ancient drama was published after Sébillet's *Iphigénie à Aulis* in 1549. When du Bellay opposed the poet and the translator, he redefined poetry in terms of genius and originality. This foundational ideological opposition between creation and translation has pervaded the construction of national identities around a canon of poetic and literary texts from the 16th century onward, laying the groundwork for the enduring denial of foreign intertextuality which has pervaded conceptions of French national literature well into the 20th century.

---

ment à reprendre voir odieuse à tout lecteur de libérale nature, voir en une même langue une telle imitation'; du Bellay 1549, 59.
46 'Mille lumières de poésie'; du Bellay 1549, 54.

Part III: **Beyond Translation**

Lucy Jackson
Translation *Ad Spiritum*: Euripides' *Orestes* and Nicholas Grimald's *Archipropheta* (1548)

Abstract: One of two surviving plays by the English sixteenth-century scholar and poet Nicholas Grimald tells the story of John the Baptist's last days. In many ways this play, the Archipropheta (published in Cologne in 1548), adheres to the trends of Latin drama of the time, drawing on the plays of Plautus and Terence for structure, metre, and tone and taking a well-known biblical story as its focus. What has escaped the notice of scholars so far, however, is the way Grimald's drama takes inspiration from, and translates *ad spiritum*, certain aspects of ancient Greek tragedy and one play in particular — Euripides' Orestes. In this paper I explore the Hellenic attributes of Grimald's tragedy and show how the Archipropheta would provide a vehicle for Greek tragedy, in subtle and subterranean ways, to haunt the Latin drama of the sixteenth century.

The focus of this chapter is the way that Greek tragedy could be and was translated in original Latin plays produced in 16th-century Europe. These original Latin dramas were written and performed in astonishing numbers across the continent and constituted a significant part of theatrical culture more generally, interacting with vernacular drama of various kinds. Many, if not most, of the authors who wrote these original dramas, in Latin and in the vernacular, were scholars well-versed in ancient Roman drama. But many also will have known the language and literature of ancient Greece as study and scholarship of the language proliferated across western Europe from the mid-15th century onwards. A central premise in what follows is that this education in Greek literature, including its drama, led to an infusion of elements from Greek plays appearing in those original Latin works.

Greek tragedy was translated in the 15th and 16th century for a variety of reasons, as many of the chapters in this volume make manifest. The kind of translation considered in this chapter is one that this volume has been explicit about including in its capacious definition(s) of the concept i.e. it concerns translating rather than a translation.[1] It is not one bounded by lexical equivalence, verbal echoes, paraphrase, or even explicit allusion. It is, rather, a kind of translation *ad spiritum*. Theatre historian Marvin Carlson uses a metaphor for

---
1 See Introduction, p. 4.

https://doi.org/10.1515/9783110719185-012

theatrical allusion that is central for the approach taken in this chapter to translation more generally — that of 'haunting'.[2] This metaphor and its related imagery of ghosts and uncanny (sometimes inexplicable) presences, memories, and fuzzy outlines lies at the root of my discussion of translation *ad spiritum*. In doing so I wish to provoke further thought about the possibilities of recasting the traditional translational dyad of either *ad uerbum* or *ad sensum* translation that tends to dominate in early modern European translation theory.[3] I take as a case study the way that the 'ghosts', the translations *ad spiritum*, of Greek drama, haunted one Latin play in particular; Nicholas Grimald's *Archipropheta* (1548). Not only will this explorative study further expand the limits of this volume's discussion of translation more generally, but it will also demonstrate how a broader range of 16th-century playwrights, and not just recognised scholars of Greek and Latin, incorporated and deployed elements from Greek drama in original (although often biblical) contexts, i.e., that Greek drama had a crucial role to play in 16th-century drama more widely and much earlier than is often supposed.[4]

Recognising the place of Greek drama in original Latin dramas has several advantages.[5] First, bringing together pagan Greek and Christian biblical characters and ethical questions gives rise to particularly interesting, complicated, often ambiguous and polyvalent texts. The 'Christianization' of Greek drama was not a straightforward endeavour. As the various Reformations and Counter-Reformations across Europe rumbled on, pagan Greek texts were defended or contested in all confessional quarters. Attention to the different ends to which the ghosts of Greek drama might be used in the context of contemporary religious discourse is a rich but still largely unstudied aspect of Latin drama studies of the 16th century. In looking at the translation *ad spiritum* of Greek drama, we find further ways to appreciate the rich textures of these Latin plays.

But we also gain a key piece in the puzzle of the cross-pollination, or cross-contamination,[6] of different kinds of dramatic texts being read and created. The presence of elements and motifs in Latin plays that resonate strongly with those of Greek tragedy will have, in turn, shaped the reading and reception of those same Greek plays as the 16th century continued. Audiences of these haunted Latin plays would have taken on and become primed with a certain set of asso-

---

2 Carlson 2001.
3 See Di Martino, n. 22, in this volume.
4 See Di Martino and Fiore, this volume.
5 See also Bastin Hammou, this volume, for another important example.
6 See Martino-Baudou this volume.

ciations with the translated elements even *before* they came into contact with the Greek plays themselves. The students who may have seen a performance of Grimald's play at Christ Church College in Oxford in the mid-1550s would, I argue, go on to read and understand Euripides' *Orestes* with a particular set of biblical characters and, in turn, biblical ghosts in mind. First audiences of Latin plays need not recognise the allusions to Greek drama for those allusions still to have a powerful influence on the general understanding of Greek drama throughout their lifetimes. The frame put around certain characters or moral dilemmas by translating them into a biblical context would act powerfully on the 16th-century reception of those same Greek tragedy characters or dilemmas in their original contexts. This anti-chronological mode of reception and translation is something I shall return to in the conclusion.

A final note before we turn to our case study. The haunting of Latin drama by Greek drama's ghosts is something that was potential and in action all over Europe, wherever ancient Greek was being studied and original Latin plays being produced. This may, however, have been a mode of translation and reception that was particularly prevalent in England. Tanya Pollard notes, '[i]n the arena of print, England's engagement with Greek drama lags behind that of the continent, but England's recorded performances of Greek or Greek-inspired plays during the 16th century were considerable, suggesting both that performance was an important medium for English encounters with Greek plays, and that education institutions that typically produced them had an especially important shaping role'.[7] This case study will therefore keep prominently in mind potential aspects of performance as integral to the dramatic text as a whole.[8]

1 Nicholas Grimald's *Archipropheta* (1548)

The *Archipropheta* is one of two plays by Nicholas Grimald (1519–1562) that are extant. Like a number of other Latin dramas written in Europe in the 1530s and 1540s, it takes the figure of John the Baptist as its central figure and dramatises his last days and eventual demise at the hands of King Herod and his wife Hero-

---

[7] Pollard 2017, 59.
[8] On the importance of thinking about these texts in and as performance, David Greenwood says, '[s]o much of the meaning of several of the Latin plays is conveyed by the significant use of action, costume, *domus*, and stage apparatus, that unless this fact is constantly borne in mind, they cannot be appreciated or even properly understood.' (1964, 311).

dias.⁹ Grimald probably wrote the play in the 1540s while engaged in teaching and other literary work in Oxford.¹⁰ He dedicated the play to the newly chosen dean of Christ Church, Dr Richard Cox, in 1546. There is no record of a performance in Oxford but it seems highly likely, especially since Grimald writes in that dedicatory letter of the 'greatest consequence' in presenting characters 'as though living and breathing; when time, place, words, and deeds are vividly depicted; when the whole action is brought before your eyes and ears, so that it seems not so much to be told, to be narrated, as to be done, to be enacted'.¹¹ The play was published in Cologne in 1548 by Martin Gymnicus.

Grimald had, however, been surrounded by dramatic experiments in both Cambridge and Oxford for some years, and this was not his first experience of writing drama. The theatrical experiments in various Oxbridge colleges were profoundly shaped by an intensive focus in the first half of the 16th century on placing classical, and specifically Greek, texts at the heart of education. Cambridge had been a centre of ancient Greek learning since the founding, on the instructions of Lady Margaret Beaufort (1443–1509), of St John's College in 1511. This college was to be the home to such influential teachers and scholars of ancient Greek as Richard Croke, John Cheke,¹² and Roger Ascham. With the foundation in 1517 of Corpus Christi College in Oxford, the centres of Greek learning in England multiplied. By 1518 there was already a backlash *against* Greek learning in Oxford – a sure sign of the vitality and impact of the subject.¹³ 1524 saw new statutes introduced at St John's College Cambridge, based on those already in place at Corpus in Oxford, which required daily lectures on Greek grammar and literature. By 1535 several wealthy colleges at Oxford and Cambridge were required to provide lectures in Greek and attendance by all students, including those from less well-resourced colleges, was mandatory.¹⁴

---

9 John the Baptist seems to have been something of a key figure for the Protestant movement (see Edwards 2004, 9). However, playwrights usually steered clear of direct comment and comparison with contemporary figures or disputes, see Blackburn 1971, 100. For a very positive appraisal of this play in the context of the 'other' Baptist plays being written and performed at the time, see e.g., Edwards 2004, 12 and Norland 1995, 334.
10 For further details of this phase in Grimald's career, see Merrill 1925, 14–34.
11 [...] *cum personae tamquam rediuiuae ac spirantes introducuntur, cum locus, tempus, dicta, facta illustrantur: cum omne negotium ita sub aspectum auditumque subiicitur, ut non tantum dici aut commemorari, sed fieri iam de geri uideatur*; Merrill 1925, 233–235.
12 'Nobody did more to develop Greek studies as a humane discipline in the 16th century'; Rhodes 2018, 40. Cheke was appointed a Fellow of St John's in 1529 and was the first Regius Professor of Greek in 1540.
13 Pollard 2017, 47 and Lazarus 2015, 442.
14 Lazarus 2015, 443.

This intensive focus has not always been fully recognised by modern scholars of 16th-century classical learning in England, and goes some way to explaining how Greek drama's imprint has gone undetected in much drama written in England in the earlier part of the century. As has been pointed out by Micha Lazarus, there has been an unhelpful conflation between scholarship on ancient Greek texts with *literacy* in ancient Greek; and it would have been the ability to read and engage with Greek texts, and drama particularly, which would have created the conditions for a greater range of nascent and future playwrights to translate aspects of Greek drama into their new and original works.[15] Greek drama had a central place in all this vibrant culture of Greek teaching and learning early in the century. As noted by Pollard, the first editions of Greek tragedy may have been produced in Florence and Venice at the turn of the 16th century, but the broader dissemination of Greek tragedy 'began with Erasmums's Latin *Hecuba*', a work the great scholar translated in London 'with support from English patrons'.[16]

Aside from patrons, Erasmus interacted with a number of scholars of ancient Greek who had been active in England's educational establishments from the end of the 15th century onwards — Thomas Linacre, William Grocyn, William Latimer, and Cuthbert Tunstall.[17] It was from these figures (and the provisions they put in place at Oxford and Cambridge) that many of England's leading literary lights of the 16th century, Nicholas Grimald among them, would have learnt their Greek and been exposed to Greek drama.[18] An often-quoted, and immensely valuable, testimonium to the place of Greek drama amongst the more general Greek learning is found in a letter from Roger Ascham, writing in 1542. He says:

> Aristotle and Plato are read by the young men in the original, but that has been done among us at St John's [Cambridge] for the last five years. Sophocles and Euripides are here better known than Plautus used to be when you were up [...] Our Cheke's effort and example has lit and fed this flame of literary zeal, for without pay he has publicly lectured on all of Homer, all of Sophocles, and that twice, as well as all of Euripides, and nearly all of Herodotus.[19]

---

15 Lazarus 2015, 433–437.
16 Pollard 2017, 43. On Erasmums's influence on 16th-century translations and translators, see also Dedieu, Di Martino-Baudou, and Vedelago in this volume.
17 On these early titans of ancient Greek learning and pedagogy in England, see Lazarus 2015, 438–439 and Pollard 2017, 72 n. 5 for further bibliography.
18 See Lazarus 2015, 456–458 for a formidable survey of just how many English literary figures would have come into contact with Greek learning in this way.
19 Giles vol. 1, 1864, 32; English translation in Williams 1967, 1070–1071.

When Nicholas Grimald arrived in Cambridge in 1535, the stage was set for his immediate attention to and absorption of Greek language, literature, and drama. Hailing from Lincolnshire, his early experiences of drama were likely of mystery plays.[20] When he came to Cambridge, however, he would have found many contemporaries and lecturers not only reading and talking about Greek drama, but also experimenting with new forms of theatre. It seems that in Oxford and Cambridge biblical tragedy especially was becoming fashionable.[21] Thomas Watson's Latin play *Absolom* was written sometime between 1535 and 1544, and John Christopherson's *Jephthah,* written in ancient Greek and performed ca. 1544 would have been known to Grimald. George Buchanan's popular *Baptistes* may also have been circulating in manuscript and would have been available when Grimald was writing his own Baptist tragedy in the mid-1540s.[22]

So, it is no surprise that, having graduated from Christ's College, Cambridge with a B.A. in 1539–1540, and having travelled to Oxford to begin the next phase of his scholarly career, he turned to writing a play himself. He spent his first few months in Oxford at Brasenose College while he was waiting for his books to arrive and in this time was encouraged by his peers to set down a dramatic work that he had already been planning.[23] This was his first drama, his *Christus Redivivus*, a mixture of tragedy and comedy. In the dedicatory epistle appended to the published play he notes that Roman dramatists, particularly Plautus, are a key touchstone for this work; and indeed the motifs of Roman comedy are evident throughout.[24] We know regrettably little about Grimald's many other plays.[25] What is discernible in the *Archipropheta*, however, is a significant shift in tone from his earlier work, a shift that is in part attributable to a deeper engagement with Greek tragedy. Alongside certain recognisable Roman motifs and language, there are

---

20 Blackburn 1971, 15.
21 Blackburn 1971, 77–81.
22 The *Baptistes*, according to the preface of the published version (1576) Buchanan's first play ([...] *primus est foetus*..), see Sharratt and Walsh 1983, 97. On the ghosts of Sophocles' *Antigone* in this play, see Jackson 2020.
23 See the *Epistola Nuncupatoria* (Merrill 1925, 98–101).
24 Cf. a reference to Plautus *Captivi* in the *Epistola Nuncupatoria* (Merrill 1925, 110–111). See also the allusion to the opening of Plautus' *Amphitryo*, a thoroughly Greek tragedy-inspired comedy, in the Syrian *ancilla*'s use of 'tragoedia' (see Plaut. *Amp.* 50–54). The *Archipropheta*, and the figure of the Syrian *ancilla* especially, moves from comedy to tragedy, while the *Amphitryo* begins as a tragedy and ends as a comedy.
25 For discussion, see Merrill 1925, 24–27.

also elements that we do not find in the Roman comedians or in Seneca. It is to these elements that have been translated *ad spiritum* that we now turn.

2 Herod as Orestes *Furens*

One of the remarkable features of Grimald's dramatic telling of the last days of John the Baptist is a lengthy scene of banqueting in Herod's palace, filled with songs, dancing, celebration (pp. 328–347) culminating in Herodias' daughter requesting, and getting, the severed head of John the Baptist on a platter (*in patella postulo / Iohannis à cervice divulsum caput*; 344).[26] After such a lengthy build up to the crucial moment of the Baptist's death, the turn from jubilation to horror at the end of Act four is sudden and jarring. Act five begins with several characters' reactions to the events: Jehovah himself, Herodias, the disciples of John the Baptist, one of the servants of Herodias' house, and the Syrian *ancilla* (on whom, more below). After this, Herod himself appears on stage, in some distress and wracked with guilt.

> *Hui qua irrequietu animu gero? furiis quibus*
> *Incensus agitor? Inire somnos dum uolo,*
> *Qui me tremores? quae auferunt insomnia?*
> *[...]*
> *Videor mihi interdum partriis e finibus*
> *Exul, inops, cuique contemptus mortalium [...]*

> Alas, what a troubled mind I bear with me! What furies madden and drive me! When I would sleep, what trembling seizes upon me, and what restlessness! [...] Sometimes I seem to see myself exiled from my fatherland, needy and despised of all men [...]
> (Merill 1925, 354–355)

The mention of a troubled mind, of the Furies, a thwarted desire for sleep, seizures and trembling, and an imminent, lonely exile are striking in themselves, but will put many in mind of the Furies' most famous quarry, the matricide Orestes.[27] We should note that by the 16th century, the image of 'Orestes *furens*' was not confined to Greek tragedy. Robert Miola traces the spread of this motif

---

26 All references to text and translation are from Merrill 1925.
27 Other subjects of the Furies' relentless pursuit were Alcmaeon (see e.g. Ap. *B*. 3.7.5), and the sons of Oedipus (Pind. *Ol*. 2.38–42). Virgil is the first to name the Furies as three figures, Alecto, Tisiphone, and Megaera — *Aen*. 6.570–572; 7.324–326; 12.845–848). Grimald invokes Alecto the Fury in *Christus Redivivus* Act 4 scenes 4 and 5.

from Virgil's comparison of Dido to Orestes *furens* (*Aen.* 4.471–473), to Plutarch and Longinus,[28] as well as a host of references to the moral complexity of Orestes' dilemma in Cicero, Horace, Quintilian, and others — all authors that were read with frequency by early 16th-century students and scholars. It is worth noting as an aside that Orestes is not a figure featured in any Senecan drama.[29] And yet, the details given in Grimald's play resonate with Euripides' presentation of Orestes in his play of that name and suggests a closer relationship. The lines quoted above distil a detailed picture of Orestes' mental torment and the siblings' desperate plight, discussed at some length by Electra and the chorus (Eur. *Or.* 34–51, 88–90, 153–210) and depicted by the character of Orestes himself (Eur. *Or.* 211–236, 253–315). Equivalence of vocabulary is not in evidence and nor need we seek it out. What we see in the figure of Herod as presented by Grimald at this point in the play is a haunted character — a translation of Euripides' Orestes *ad spiritum*.

We can feel confident in positing a close relationship between the two texts in light of the particularly easy access to Euripides' play which 16th-century students and scholars enjoyed. It was, along with the *Hecuba* and *Phoenician Women*, one of the three plays chosen by Byzantine scholars as exemplars for their students and, as such, these three plays are usually found at the beginning of printed editions of Euripides' works. These same students and scholars would have been encouraged towards the Euripidean play, too, by the fact it was quoted by other popular and often-read works at the time, as noted above. Longinus, as well as discussing the Oresteian dilemma in general terms, quotes two passages from the Euripidean play, both from the scene where Orestes is overtaken with a Fury-inspired frenzy.[30] While scholars have noted these contextual factors in explaining how Orestes was to be a significant figure throughout the theatrical creations of the 16th and 17th centuries, the appearance of an Orestes *furens*, and a thoroughly Euripidean Orestes at that, this early in the 16th century, has not been adequately recognised by modern scholars.[31] The ghost of Euripides' Orestes very clearly haunts Herod's character at this late stage in the *Archipropheta*, an act of translation not *ad uerbum*, or *ad sensum*, but *ad spiritum*.

---

28 Plut. *Mor.* 465 D (*Tranquility of Mind*) and 501 C (*Affections*), [Longinus], *Subl.* I:8.
29 See Seneca's *Agamemnon* 1012 for a very light allusion from Cassandra.
30 [Longinus] *Subl.* 15.2 and 15.8 cf. Eur. *Or.* 255–257, 264–265.
31 Miola 2017.

3 Unexpected Messengers

Herod's Orestes-like outburst in Act five, however, is by no means the most significant ghost or moment of translation *ad spiritum* in Grimald's play. In the style of Greek tragedy, the actual act of murder occurs offstage, and the fullest account of the death of John the Baptist is given by a messenger figure.[32] Rather than this report being given by a new character whose express purpose is to communicate the information (as is commonly the case in Greek tragedy) or by an enslaved character in a hurry (a *servus currens*, as is commonly the case in New Comedy), here the report is given by a female attendant of Herodias', a Syrian *ancilla*. This is someone we have seen in many scenes throughout the play, praising Herodias' beauty (pp. 261–263), acting as a Senecan-style confidant and moderator of her mistress' fiery passions (pp. 290–291), and delivering a quasi-prophetic soliloquy of foreboding (pp. 290–291). Just prior to Herod's own entry, discussed above, the Syrian *ancilla* bursts onto the stage to speak to the Chorus of People and to the Baptist's disciples, two groups still unaware of the decapitation that has just occurred at the end of the previous act. She says:

> Atrocem ô regem: flebile ô spectculum:
> O dirum, ô horrendum, ô tyrannicum scelus.
> Ferro ablatum insontis est nefario caput.
>
> O cruel king! O doleful spectacle! O dire, terrible, and tyrannical crime! The head of the innocent man has been cut off by a wicked sword. (pp. 350–351)

In light of her connection as attendant to the queen, it is surprising that she displays such distress at the fate of John the Baptist, a fate desired and all but ordered by her mistress Herodias.[33] Made all the more prominent by the abundance of elision in these lines when spoken aloud,[34] the vocative exclamations not only make for a striking entry speech but also give clear performative cues for the actor to imitate the heaving sobs of fresh distress. Signs of how personally invested the Syrian *ancilla* is in the fate of John the Baptist are clear as her

---

[32] We can compare this Greek tragic style of announcement with that found in Buchanan's *Baptistes*, delivered by a 'Nuntius' (1316 ff.).
[33] She has by this point already expressed her immediate horror at the presentation of the head (pp. 344–345 *Deum immortalem. Quod peractum nun scelus est?/ Non ista poscit hoc tempus spectacula* – 'Immortal God! What crime has been committed now? the time demands no such sight as this'. Merrill notes that the last line is a close echo of Vir. *Aen.* 6.37).
[34] Atroc' o regem: flebil' o spectculum:/ O dir' o 'rrend' o tyrannicum scelus.

conversation with the disciples continues. She is scarce able to look upon the feasting inside following the presentation of the Baptist's head and, as well as clearly physically leaving the palace, flees 'from body and soul' in horror (*mente quas* [*sc. epulae*, 'feasts'], *et corpore fugio*). The impact of the murder is, in her eyes, not only an injury (*damnum*) to her alone, but to the people at large (*Haud meu./ Sed publicum est*). She restates for the disbelieving disciples what has just occurred in lines with heavy poetic repetition:

> *Est, est humeris abscissum Baptistae caput,*
> *Caput humeris abscissum, heu, quam crudeliter?*
>
> The head of the Baptist has been cut from his shoulders! How cruelly, alas, has his head been cut from his shoulders!

After her dialogue with the Baptist's disciples in iambic trimeters, she moves into a longer more formally recognisable 'messenger' speech, but shifting from the expected spoken iambics into a lyric metre; phalaecian hendecasyllables.[35] The use of a variety of lyric metres earlier in the play means that in one sense this is not too surprising. However, within the context of the formal features of both Greek and Roman drama, the use of lyric to report events that have happened offstage *is* unusual, and conspicuous. It does, however, have one famous parallel in Greek tragedy; the sung messenger speech in Euripides' *Orestes*, delivered by an enslaved Phrygian attendant (πρόσπολος) of Helen's. It is here that we find, I argue, Grimald's clearest and boldest moment of translation *ad spiritum* in the *Archipropheta*.

The moment when the enslaved Phrygian appears on stage in Euripides' *Orestes* is entirely unexpected and incongruous, a fact that caused much comment amongst ancient scholars and continues to be a landmark in Euripidean and Greek tragic dramatic technique.[36] In that scene we also have a lyrical mode deployed to report information and, like the Syrian *ancilla*, by a speaker in some

---

[35] This metre has already been used once, briefly, earlier in the play (pp. 310–313) by the enslaved Syrian man, perhaps suggesting the metre was reserved for the Syrian figures of the play. It is a common enough metre in 16th and 17th century epigrams, popularised by its familiarity in the works of Catullus, Statius, and Martial.

[36] '[...] nothing could have prepared us for the bizarre scene that follows. We have been led to expect that the doors will swing open to reveal Helen's corpse on the *ekkyklêma*, but this turns out to have been yet another skilful piece of misdirection. Instead the 'wrong' character appears, from the 'wrong' part of the stage, and behaves in a most unexpected way: it is a Phrygian slave who appears on the roof, descends to the *orchêstra*, and bursts into song.' Wright 2008, 45.

considerable distress. 'Oh the murderous sufferings, the lawless woes I have seen, have seen in the royal palace!'[37] — cries that echo the Syrian ancilla's: 'O cruel king! O doleful spectacle! O dire, terrible, and tyrannical crime!' (pp. 350–351). Like the *ancilla,* the Phrygian is attempting to flee the scene.[38] The identity of this singing figure is markedly 'foreign' or 'other', just as the Syrian (and perhaps the whole Herodian court) would have read as 'foreign' to Grimald's Oxford audience and a broader western European audience too.[39] It is suggestive too that the events being reported — a murder or attempted murder — resonate with intriguing clarity.[40] Aware of the impact of having such an unusual and virtuosic cameo as the Phrygian reporting traumatic and climactic events within the house, Grimald seems to have taken and translated the moment into his original play, and into a character that would be just as surprising a messenger figure and into just as lyrical a mode of performance — the hendecasyllable. Once again Euripides' *Orestes* can be seen as haunting this 16th-century original Latin play.

However, the plot thickens. A second ghost might possibly be haunting this climactic moment in Grimald's tale; that of Cassandra in Aeschylus' *Agamemnon*. In the Aeschylean play, Cassandra acts as a prophetic messenger, alluding to the acts that are, at that very moment, happening in the house and those that are about to happen.[41] Like the Syrian *ancilla*, she is enslaved, and has an identity marked as 'foreign', and for a great deal of her appearance sings in highly emotional lyric. The images summoned by both the Syrian *ancilla* and Cassandra resonate uncannily. The text in Aeschylus that describes the slaughter of

---

37 φονίων παθέων ἀνόμων τε κακῶν/ ἅπερ ἔδρακον ἔδρακον ἐν δόμοις τυράννων (Eur. *Or.* 1455–1456).
38 Cf. Syrian: *fugio* with the Phrygian's πέφευγα [...] φροῦδα φροῦδα [...] φύγω, Eur. *Or.* 1368–1379.
39 On the connotations of the term 'Syrian' in a 16th-century context, we should consider that 'Syrian' is not a term found in the Hebrew bible and is not a name that was used by the Arab population from the seventh century CE onwards: 'Syria' is used as a term in the Septuagint as a translation for Aram and Aramaeans. (Shehadeh 1994). For Herod being frequently 'identified by contemporary marks of foreignness' in early modern drama, see Bushnell 1990, 86. However, the connotation of Syrian identity may be more complex. In the early 16th century, Lucian, a Syrian writer of the 2nd c. CE was recommended as a good place to start learning Greek, see Rhodes 2018, 36–38.
40 Eur. *Or.* 1107 they are planning to slit Helen's throat. Eur. *Or.* 1199 Hermione is threatened with throat-slitting.
41 'You wash your husband, who shares your bed, in the bath [...] Is it, is it, a net of death? [...] She traps him in the robe, the black-horned contrivance and strikes — and he falls into the tub full of water.' (Aesch. *Ag.* 1107–1128, trans. Sommerstein 2008.)

Thyestes children by his brother Atreus is uncertain,[42] but the allusion to the impious feast of those murdered (beheaded?) children in the Greek play coheres with the Syrian *ancilla*'s disgust at 'these feasts' (*istae epulae*, p. 350).[43] The waiting chorus of disciples and their initial consternation at what the Syrian *ancilla* is telling them echoes the Aeschylean chorus' initial confusion ('Why are you wailing like that about Loxias? He is not the sort to come in contact with one who laments' 1074–1075): *Quid est, que sic gemitus das post conuiuium* [...] *Itane uero? Dic, dic, Syra, facta praedicas?* (p. 350). And, specifically, their perception of improper lamentation on the part of the Syrian — *Alacrem epulae debeant reddere* — coheres with the Old Men's confusion at Cassandra's inappropriate invocation of Apollo ('Here she is again, making an ill-omened invocation of a god for whom it is in no way appropriate to be present amid cries of grief' Aesch. *Ag.* 1078–1079).

What makes this ghost all the more intriguing is the peculiar nature of the textual transmission of Aeschylus *Oresteia* in the 16th century. The Aldine *editio princeps* of the trilogy, produced in 1518, omits lines 311–1066 and 1160–1673, i.e. the majority of the *Agamemnon*, combining that play and *Libation Bearers* and resulting in a drama that promotes Orestes as central and has Agamemnon entirely absent. The first part of Cassandra's scene with the chorus was, therefore, more prominent for readers of this edition.[44] If this was a source of inspiration, and was translated *ad spiritum* by Grimald, this would be a remarkable instance of mid-16th-century reception, and one that was entirely possible in light of Grimald's exposure to the texts of Greek tragedy during his time at Oxford and Cambridge, and his command of the language. Aeschylus was not often looked to or, if Ascham's letter quoted above is to be believed, lectured on. The ghost of Euripides' *Orestes* may be more likely if we take into account what we know of the easier access to and discussion of Sophoclean and Euripidean texts. However, the presence of Cassandra, too, at this point in Grimald's play should give us pause. There is no way that Grimald would not have access to an

---

[42] There seems to be no satisfactory emendation to Triclinius' text in line 1091.
[43] The comparison of the opulent feast in the palace of Herod and the feast of Atreus raises a further resonance between Herodias and Aerope, the wife of Thyestes, then his brother Atreus — both women are, in this sense, incestuous by marrying their brothers. See *Archipropheta* pp. 292–293 — 'You, violating honour and your brother's marriage vows, have seized upon his wife, and taken her away while he is still living [...]'.
[44] And the subsequent 1552 edition edited by Robortello and published by Turnèbe in Paris, and the Latin translation of the truncated text by Jean Saint-Ravy in 1555. On the early editions of Aeschylus see Mund-Dopchie 1984. The full text was not published until 1557 in Vettori's Latin translation, published in Geneva.

Aldine edition of the tragedies while at Cambridge or Oxford, and we should not rule out the possibility of independent discovery and absorption of Aeschylean text, along with his Euripides.

4 Herodias and the Dilemma of Orestes

The fuzzy outlines of ghosts from Euripides' *Orestes* allow for multiple characters in Grimald's play to 'host' these spectral, translated, figures. The tormented Orestes appears again when we see the Queen Herodias reacting in private to the murder that she herself so vehemently desired.

> *Heu quam ingens aestuat in corde intimo pudor?*
> *Furens ut amor? Mens ut facinoris conscia?*
> *Me turbat ut misto dolore insania? ut*
> *Insultat accusatrix cogitatio?*
> *Scio, acerba me multorum circumstant odia.*
> *Quid deinde? Oderint me hercle, dum metuant modo,*
> *Regina si maneo, mea quid interest?*

> Alas! what great shame wells up from the depths of my heart! How love rages! How conscious the soul is of guilt! How madness mingled with grief confounds me! How accusing thought reviles me! I know that the fierce hatred of many surrounds me! What then? By Hercules, let them hate me so long as they fear me! If I remain queen, what care I? (pp. 348–349)

L.R. Merrill has highlighted the surface allusion to Virgil here, and the description of an ashamed Turnus in book 12 (*aestuat ingens/ uno in corde pudor mixtoque insania luctu/ et furiis agitatus amor et conscia virtus*, 'within that single heart surges mighty shame, and madness mingled with grief, and love stung by fury, and the consciousness of worth', *Aen.* 12.666–668).[45] The proximity to the two ghosts of Euripides' *Orestes* discussed above, however, supports a comparison of Herodias with the figure of Orestes and one of his most famous (certainly to the scholars of 16th-century Europe) and much-discussed lines. In his dialogue with Menelaus, a potential saviour for Orestes and his sister in the hostile environment of Argos, he describes the suffering he currently endures as ἡ σύνεσις, ὅτι σύνοιδα δείν' εἰργασμένος — 'Understanding: the awareness that I have done dreadful things' (Eur. *Or.* 396). The ghost of Orestes haunting the

---

[45] Trans. Fairclough and Goold 1999. Cf. also *Aen.* 10.905–906 — *Scio acerba meorum/ Circumstare odis*.

figure of Herodias here puts a distinctive spin on the Virgilian elements of shame, madness, and love. What torments Herodias at this point in the play is not just these strong emotions but the *awareness* of them (*Mens ut facinoris conscia*).[46] As Jed Atkins has noted, this line of Euripides *Orestes* 'was the *locus classicus* for medieval treatments of conscience'.[47] The Queen Herodias does move quickly on from this questioning of herself and her deeds, inhabiting the garb now of the stereotypical tyrant (*Oderint* [...] *dum metuant modo*). And yet this brief translation *ad spiritum* of Orestes' dilemma and his consciousness of the crime committed places an extra layer of complexity onto Grimald's guilty queen.

5 Herodias and the 'Bad Women' of Greek Tragedy

The figure of Herodias in Grimald's play is unusually porous, a ready host for a number of different spirits from Greek tragedy. Her own gender lends itself to comparison with the remarkable women of tragedy — often royal and filled with passion and purpose. In the preface to his Latin translation of Euripides' *Alcestis* (published in 1556), addressed to Marguerite de France (1523–1574) daughter of François I, George Buchanan wrote: 'there will be no mention beyond this point of parricide and poisoning and of all the other wickedness with which other tragedies are filled' (*parricidii vero et veneficii et reliquorum quibus aliae tragoediae plenae sunt scelerum nulla prorsus hic mentio*, ll. 10–12),[48] an attempt no doubt to anticipate the common suspicion of Greek tragedy, and in particular those agents of 'poisoning', the women, especially, and contrasting that reputation with the praiseworthy figure of Alcestis — 'the good wife'.[49] The ghosts of these bad women are often indistinguishable from their articulations in Latin (particularly Senecan) and post-classical texts.[50] Herodias, the luxurious inspirer of uxorial devotion acts as a lightning rod for these ghosts and, in turn, will

---

46 For other comparable uses of *conscius* in the Vulgate, see 1 *Kings* 2.44, *Leviticus* 5.1, and an explicit denial of the ability to be *conscius* in 1 *Corinthians* 4.4.
47 Atkins 2014, 2.
48 Sharratt and Walsh 1983, 211.
49 On the suspicion of Greek tragic women, see e.g., Heavey 2015 and Pollard 2017.
50 For example, I do not discuss the clear echoes between Herodias and Seneca's Medea at, e.g., p. 297 where Herodias rails against the prospect of Herod abandoning her — *Haeccine/ Sacra illa est confirmata coniugio fides?* [...] *Certe ego famae, pudori, patriae, uiro,/ Ac omnibus te rebus unum praetuli* [...] cf. Sen. *Med.* 488 *tibi patria cessit, tibi pater frater pudor*.

have shaped later readings of Clytemnestra, Medea, Aerope, and Phaedra. None of these is so clearly translated, however, into Herodias' character as the figure of Helen, someone who, like Orestes, holds nothing like as prominent a place in the Senecan dramatic corpus as she does either in the Greek tragedies available to 16th-century readers, or in the Euripides' *Orestes* itself.[51]

The emphasis on beauty, wealth, and opulence at the court of Herod, and around Herodias especially, is conspicuous in Grimald's play. The enslaved Syrian man and the Syrian *ancilla* early on emphasise Herodias' sumptuous physical beauty — eyes, teeth, nose, hair, snowy neck and trim bosom.

> Ebori' instar candidi dentes. Labellula/
> Suffusa nativo quodam velut minio.
> Nasus elegans venusto libratur spatio,
> Eöae pulchra par est aurorae coma.

> Her teeth are white as ivory, and her dainty lips, delicately coloured, are parted a little. Her fine nose is well poised amid lovely surroundings. Her hair is as beautiful as the dawn [...] (pp. 261–263).

Her daughter is named Tryphera,[52] the meaning of the name (drawn from the Greek word τρυφή, luxuriousness) borne out in Act 4.2 when she is dressed by Herodias in an impossibly rich array of jewels and fine clothes:

> *Margaritas idcirco sumes: coloribus*
> *Corpusculum fucabis: torques, et aureos*
> *Geres annuluos, et armullas* [...]
> *Profer (puella) chirothecas, anulos,*
> *Gemmas, crepidulas, et mundum omenmen relliquum.*

> Therefore put on your pearls. Paint your little body with colours, wear your necklaces, your rings of gold, and your bracelets [...] Quick, girl, my ring-cases, my rings, jewels, sandals, and all the rest of my ornaments. (pp. 312–313).

Herodias then adorns herself in even greater riches (pp. 312–313). The same scene takes the opportunity to highlight that Herodias, like Helen, is a woman

---

[51] She appears in one scene of his *Trojan Women*. Her opening lines, and association of marriages that are 'funeral and joyless' (*funestus, inlaetabilis,* v. 861) indicate that this version of her character diverges greatly from Herodias, whose passion for her husband is one of the most remarkable features of this play.

[52] Grimald would have known Josephus' account of this story and also the name of Salome given there, *Antiquities of the Jews* 18.109. See Blackburn 1971, 95 on Grimald's use of multiple sources.

with two husbands, as the fool (another appropriately Greek-named character) Gelasimus jokes with the Queen:

> Herodias. Now tell whose [wife] I am.
> Gel. The wife of Herod.
> Her. But of which? (pp. 314–315)

The translation of a particularly indulged and luxury-oriented Helen, as is depicted in the Euripides play, into this biblical setting and the figure of Herodias serves Grimald's drama in two ways. First, the crime of incest which the Baptist accuses Herod and Herodias of is given further cultural weight through the comparison with Helen's adultery with Paris. But second, the famed wealth of Troy and Phrygia, noted at several points in Euripides' play and presented as corrupting and negative by a range of characters, is here transmuted in a biblical context into a critique frequently levelled at the Catholic church throughout this stage of the Reformation — a corrupting and negative association with idols, luxury, and wealth.[53] In this brief example, then, we see how translation *ad spiritum*, allows for subtle but utterly contemporary comment on the confessional disputes that were rife still in the 1540s.

6 Conclusions

Grimald's *Archiuropheta* did not leave a hefty footprint in the literary records of English or European drama. His *Christus Redivivus*, published earlier in 1543, went on to be performed in Germany, and it was also produced at Augsburg in 1556, and is one of the plays on which the original Passion Play of Oberammergau was based.[54] Grimald was also a major contributor to Tottel's Miscellany — the first printed anthology of English poetry (1557) and one of the most influential of these kinds of publications during the reign of Elizabeth I in England.[55] And yet, despite his literary reputation at the time and many biblical and classical works (most of which are no longer extant), he is a relatively obscure figure in terms of English literary history. This may well be due to his shadowy dealings as a double agent during the religious conflicts of the mid-16th century, a

---

53 Dutton notes that the jewels worn by Tryphera and Herodias are 'a certain signal to Grimald's audience of [their] doctrinal error', Dutton 2020, 169.
54 On the huge influence of this play in Germany, see Merrill 1925, 61–89.
55 On this publication, see, recently, Warner 2013.

fact that makes the not-so-veiled critique of Catholic idolatry in the figure of Herodias all the more intriguing.[56] The better play, perhaps, than other Baptist-focused works, it has suffered from relatively little attention. This should be taken into account when looking to the *Archipropheta* as a key text for the shaping of later attitudes towards Greek tragedy. And yet what I hope to have shown here is that the process of translation *ad spiritum* was one that *did* occur, especially once we factor in the certain backdrop of Greek drama being translated and read with renewed intensity, certainly in Oxford and Cambridge, right from the earliest decades of the 16th century. By appreciating this translation *ad spiritum*, we gain a great deal in how we understand Greek drama to have been an active ingredient in all kinds of dramatic production at a much earlier point than is usually posited.

Plays like *Archipropheta*, however and whenever they were read or seen in performance, would have bolstered motifs, such as Orestes *furens*, in the general literary imagination of the time. In circling back to an ancient Greek articulation of that motif, the image has a new specificity, just as we see in the complication of Herodias' guilt and rejection of the awareness that, in the light of some Christian doctrine, could have been her salvation. The kind of translation of Greek tragedy we see Grimald performing also shows us how playwrights of original Latin plays might take on dramaturgical techniques found in the ancient Greek plays, such as a climactic messenger speech being delivered by a 'foreign', singing, enslaved and othered voice, perhaps prompting rather unsettling feelings of sympathy in the audience. A pagan Greek ghost could also add complexity to traditional representations of certain biblical figures. The casting of Herod, through his association with Orestes overcome with Fury-driven madness, in a more ambivalent, if not exactly sympathetic light, is an interesting counterbalance to the usual presentation of Herod as an outright tyrant, something that would only become more standard as the century continued.[57] If we are to follow my suggestion that, unusually, we might also find a play of Aeschylus' being translated into this biblical drama, we can find new avenues for identifying the presence of less-vaunted, but still available, dramatic texts in the development and proliferation of dramatic experiments in the first half of the 16th century.

The advantages of, with caution, broadening our view of what translation might mean when it comes to Greek drama in this period, are considerable. This

---

56 Merrill 1925, 36–50.
57 See Bushnell 1990, 84 on Hamlet's comment, to 'out-Herod's Herod'. See also, e.g., Leo 2019 on later entanglements between tragedy, Herod, and the Furies.

chapter has begun to point at these advantages, but much more work and discussion remain, especially regarding the understudied early Latin dramas of the 16th century.

Giulia Fiore
Interpreting Oedipus' *Hamartia* in the Italian Cinquecento: Theory and Practice (1526–1570)

Abstract: Building on Hartmut Böhme and Johannes Helmrath's concept of reception as 'mutual transformation', which emphasises the interdependency between antiquity and early modern cultures, the present chapter contributes to exploring the mutual influence between ancient Greek tragedy, Aristotle's *Poetics* and 16th-century tragedies and theoretical treatises. More specifically, it investigates the multiple facets of the notion of *hamartia* in the mid-16th-century translations of Aristotle's treatise — from Pazzi de' Medici's Latin translation of the *Poetics* (1536), to Robortello's commentary (1548), and Castelvetro's first Italian commentary of the *Poetics* (1570) —; debates about vernacular tragedies, such as the literary quarrel around Speroni's *Canace*; and early modern Oedipus plays, such as Pazzi de' Medici's *Edipo Principe* (1525–26) and Anguillara's *Edippo* (1565). Shedding new light on the precarious balance between conservation, rejection, and recombination of the ancient sources, this approach thus highlights the active role of the receiving culture in appropriating and reconstructing the classical past.

Giovan Battista Giraldi Cinzio, an intellectual at the Court of Ercole II at Ferrara and author of the first tragedy in the vernacular ever performed in Italy, *Orbecche*,[1] wrote in his apologetic *Lettera sulla tragedia* in 1543 in defence of the criticism addressed to his play, *Didone*:

> Mi volgerò a rispondere alla sesta accusa ch'egli mi ha data, cioè che la *Didone* non è simile all'*Edipo tiranno*. E ciò gli concedo io senza questionare quanto alla materia, imperò che il soggetto dell'*Edipo tiranno* è tale che un simile non fu mai prima, né ora è, né sarà forse mai. E se Aristotele si scelse questa favola come per Idea del compor tragico, fece egli ciò con quel giudizio ch'egli ha usato in tutte le altre sue composizioni: perché questa materia è veramente tra le altre singolare [...]. Confesserò io adunque, senza esser ponto celato, che la *Didone* in quanto alla materia è diversa dall'*Edipo tiranno*. Ma non voglio già concedere che nelle parti che alla tragedia convengono e nell'artificio ella non sia tale quale è l'*Edipo*, quanto ha potuto portarne il soggetto tratto da Vergilio che io ho avuto per le ma-

---
1 See Guastella 2006, 177–183; Schironi 2016, 135f.

> ni. E se forse in qualche parte mi son partito dalle regole che dà Aristotele per confrontarmi co' costumi de' tempi nostri, l'ho io fatto coll'esempio degli antichi.

> I will answer the sixth accusation addressed to me, according to which the *Didone* is not similar to the *Edipo Tiranno*. And I admit this without question as for the subject matter, though the subject of the *Edipo Tiranno* is such that a similar plot was never created before, nor is it now, nor will it ever be. Aristotle posited this plot as the idea for composing tragedies because this subject is really unique among the others [...]. I will confess that the subject matter of the *Didone* is indeed different from the *Edipo Tiranno*. But I will not concede that in those parts specifically concerning tragedy it is not like the *Edipo*, as much as the subject taken from Virgil that I worked on allowed it to be. And even if, somehow, I moved away from Aristotle's rules to meet the customs of our times, I did it on the example of the ancients.[2]

Giraldi makes an admission of guilt: he declares that his *Didone* is not similar to Sophocles' *Oedipus Tyrannus*, but he defends his play by arguing that, even if he occasionally departed from Aristotelian rules, he did it following the example of the ancient authors.[3] Undoubtedly, composing a tragedy in mid-16th-century Italy without strictly following the plot structure of the *Oedipus Tyrannus* meant violating Aristotle's rules. This passage testifies to the beginning of the theoretical debate developed in Italy around the 1540s and aimed at defining the tragic genre, a debate that was indeed centered around the 'rediscovery' of Aristotle's *Poetics* and its appraisal of Sophocles' *Oedipus Tyrannus* as the best example of a well-structured play.[4] What makes *Oedipus* the perfect tragedy? What must early modern tragedians keep in mind in order to make a play 'similar' to the ancient model? Bernardo Segni, a member of the Florentine Academy and author of the first vernacular translation of the *Poetics* (1549), explains the reasons behind his translation choices in the preface to his vernacular *Oedipus Tyrannus* (1551) by referring to the Aristotelian treatise, and in the process sheds light on the dramatic elements that make the *Oedipus Tyrannus* a paradigmatic plot:

---

2 Giraldi, *Lettera sulla tragedia*, in Weinberg 1970, 1. 484f. Unless otherwise specified, all of the English translations are mine.

3 See also Giraldi's prologue to his *Altile* (1583). By using the expression 'coll'esempio degli antichi', Giraldi is probably referring not only to Aristotle's *Poetics*, but also to the rules attributed to Aristotle – sometimes arbitrarily – and often filtered through Horace's *Ars Poetica*. See Herrick 1946; Cronk 1999; Conte 2002.

4 On the reception of ancient drama in early modern Italy, see Di Martino and Cuzzotti in this volume and Di Martino 2019; see also Di Maria 2002 and 2005; Guastella 2006, 167–206; Schironi 2016.

> È in questa tragedia tutta l'arte, che ha espressa Aristotile nella sua *Poetica*; dalla quale come da perfetta regola ha ei cavato tutti i documenti, che s'appartengono alla poesia tragica [...]. Il fine che debbe aver la Tragedia; le persone da esservi introdotte, che non debbon esser cattivi Principi; la durazione del tempo; la ricognizione con la peripezia appariscono in questa eccellentemente: ed insomma, ci si esprime dentro, come in uno specchio, l'esempio bellissimo ed ottimo della perfetta Tragedia.

> All the art that Aristotle expressed in his *Poetics* is in this tragedy; from this [tragedy] he has extracted all the elements belonging to tragic poetry as a perfect rule [...]. The aim of tragedy; the characters to be introduced, that they may not be wicked princes; the duration of time; the recognition and the reversal appear in this tragedy marvellously: in short, the beautiful and excellent example of the perfect tragedy are expressed herein as in a mirror.[5]

Aristotle states that the *Oedipus Tyrannus* is the only play showing a perfect overlap between the *anagnorisis* ('recognition') and the *peripeteia* ('reversal'). Oedipus who, unaware, began investigating his real identity, was led by this investigation to the eventual discovery of parricide and incest and to his downfall: 'la ricognizione con la peripezia appariscono in questa eccellentemente', Segni claims, thus referring to chapter 11 of the *Poetics*.[6] Above all, Aristotle considers Oedipus the ideal 'middling character', specifically because of his *hamartia*. In chapter 13, Aristotle identifies the core of tragedy with the failure of human action: the concept of *hamartia* is the causal element that leads the tragic hero/heroine to his/her downfall. Aristotle declares that the ideal protagonist of the best kind of tragedy is a middling character who is neither pre-eminently good nor bad and must elicit pity and fear by falling into adversity not because of his or her evil and wickedness,[7] but 'because of a certain fallibility' (δι' ἁμαρτίαν τινά):

> ὁ μεταξὺ ἄρα τούτων λοιπός. ἔστι δὲ τοιοῦτος ὁ μήτε ἀρετῇ διαφέρων καὶ δικαιοσύνῃ μήτε διὰ κακίαν καὶ μοχθηρίαν μεταβάλλων εἰς τὴν δυστυχίαν ἀλλὰ δι' ἁμαρτίαν τινά, τῶν ἐν μεγάλῃ δόξῃ ὄντων καὶ εὐτυχίᾳ, οἷον Οἰδίπους καὶ Θυέστης καὶ οἱ ἐκ τῶν τοιούτων γενῶν ἐπιφανεῖς ἄνδρες.[8]

> We are left, then, with the figure who falls between these types. Such a man is one who is not preeminent in virtue and justice, and one who falls into affliction not because of evil and wickedness, but *because of a certain fallibility*. He will belong to the class of those

---

5 Segni 1811 [1551], 20–21.
6 Arist. *Poet.* 11, 1452a32–34.
7 Cf. Segni 1811 [1551], 20: 'le persone da esservi introdotte, che non debbon esser cattivi Principi' (the characters to be introduced, that they may not be wicked princes).
8 Arist. *Poet.* 13, 1453a7–12.

who enjoy great esteem and prosperity, *such as Oedipus*, Thyestes, and outstanding men from such families.[9]

Thus, the notion of *hamartia* within the Aristotelian framework is the hinge of a good plot and renders Oedipus the ideal middling character. However, the meaning of *hamartia* is ambiguous, and is the subject of a still-unresolved scholarly debate, since its semantic field covers a wide range of nuances, including an 'error resulting from ignorance', an 'error of judgement', a 'character flaw' or a 'moral fault', thus making it difficult to determine to what degree the tragic character is responsible for his or her own downfall.[10]

This chapter aims to offer a comprehensive view of the most recent scholarship on the new methodological perspectives outlined by early modern reception studies and to explore new challenges posed by the heterogeneity, interdependency, and syncretism of 16th-century texts; it will also discuss the specific case study of the interpretation of Oedipus' *hamartia* in the Italian Cinquecento through an analysis of selected key passages in theoretical treatises, commentaries on and translations of Aristotle's *Poetics*, as well as vernacular adaptations of Sophocles' *Oedipus Tyrannus*.

1 Reception as 'Transformation' in 16th-Century Italy

The interpretation of Oedipus' *hamartia* already played a pivotal role in the 16th-century debate on the tragic genre. Since Aristotle's theory — or what was supposed to be 'Aristotelian' — was considered to be the only authoritative key to understanding ancient drama, interpretations of Greek tragedy were inextricably intertwined with the *Poetics*. One of the main exegetical problems was caused by attempts to reconcile the concept of *hamartia* with Christianity: the indeterminacy of the notion, admitting the presence of contingency, thereby implying that human agency could never be entirely autonomous, was not compatible with the Christian conceptualisation of free will. Indeed, the influence of Christianity deeply impacted the reception of Aristotle's *Poetics*: translators, commentators, theoreticians, and tragedians increasingly interpreted the

---

9 Translation by Halliwell 1987.
10 The number of scholarly contributions to the history of the interpretation of *hamartia* is remarkable; see especially Adkins 1966; Bremer 1968; Stinton 1975; Saïd 1978; Schütrumpf 1989; Sherman 1992; Donini 2004; Witt 2005; Kim 2010.

term *hamartia* — in both Latin and the vernacular — with reference to a notion of personal responsibility and various alternating lexical variants, such as *error/errore* and *peccatum/peccato*.

Scholarship on the early modern interpretation of *hamartia* has developed significantly starting from the early 2000s. Michael Lurie, in his book *Die Suche nach der Schuld* (2004), stresses the moralising re-interpretation of the *Poetics* in early modernity, leading to 'the Aristotelization of both tragedy and tragic theory [...], to the Christianization of Greek tragedy' and, consequently, to 'a hermeneutical disaster'.[11] Early modern (mis)interpretations of the *Poetics*, however, had already been analysed in fundamental works, such as Bernard Weinberg's *A History of Literary Criticism* (1961), along with his *Trattati di poetica e retorica del Cinquecento* (1970–1974), as well as in Baxter Hathaway's *Age of Criticism* (1962), which surveyed the landscape of Cinquecento poetics. Both Weinberg and Hathaway emphasised the moral and rhetorical influences exerted by Horace's *Ars Poetica*, Cicero, Quintilian, as well as Aristotle's *Rhetoric* on the reception of the *Poetics*, whose moral function, they argued, served as justification and response to Plato's condemnation of poetry.[12] This moralising line of criticism has recently been called into question in a number of studies by Brigitte Kappl, Daniel Javitch, Terence Cave, Cristina Savettieri, and Bryan Brazeau.[13] If indeed early modern interpretations of Aristotle's *Poetics* are misinterpretations, this is not due *exclusively* to their authors' desire to moralise and justify the tragic genre from an ethical — or even religious — perspective. Rather, such (mis)interpretations should be read as part of a wider programme of cultural translation and vulgarisation directed at domesticating the *Poetics* for a 16th-century Christian audience[14] and at establishing modern theatrical practice and theory for the tragic genre.[15] Even if it is indeed true that the late antique and

---

11 Lurie 2012, 442. On the interpretation of Aristotelian *hamartia* in relation to Sophocles' *Oedipus Tyrannus*, see Lurie 2004.
12 *Pl. R.* X 595a–608b.
13 On the most recent approaches to the study of the reception of Aristotle's *Poetics*, see Javitch 2001; Cave 2001; Kappl 2006 and 2016; Brazeau 2020b. On the notion of *hamartia* in 16th-century Italy, see Savettieri 2018; Brazeau 2018 and 2020a: the following analysis is particularly indebted to the reflections contained in their recent contributions. Concerning the early modern reception of Aristotle's *Poetics*, see Lowry 1994; Javitch 1999; Reiss 1999; Conte 2002; Schmitt 2002; Zanin 2012a.
14 See Brazeau 2018 and 2020a.
15 See Javitch 2001; Kappl 2006; Savettieri 2018.

medieval traditions[16] played a crucial role in the formation of the early modern framework that 'received' the *Poetics*, this does not imply that this moralising interpretative lens, which involved answering to moral or religious concerns, was a fixed scheme applied to every reading of the Aristotelian text.

Since the reception of the *Poetics* was deeply influenced by the rise of new theatrical practices and by contemporary cultures, it should be considered in its own right, independently from thorough assessments of Aristotle's text.[17] This is the essential premise of the innovative approach proposed by Brazeau in his 2020 edited volume containing new perspectives on the study of early modern poetics, *The Reception of Aristotle's Poetics in the Italian Renaissance and Beyond*. Through an interdisciplinary, transnational, and diachronic approach, Brazeau's book aims at providing insight into a number of interpretative and cultural frameworks that shaped the reception of Aristotle's *Poetics* and that have only recently begun to garner proper attention. The impact of the Catholic Counter-Reformation on poetic treatises has recently been highlighted, as well as the need to avoid reading early modern poetics exclusively through a religious lens.[18] In fact, many 16th-century translators and commentators often interpreted Aristotle's text, and especially problematic passages like chapter 13, by referring to other works in the Aristotelian canon – including the *Nicomachean Ethics*, the *Politics*, the *Rhetoric* and *On the Soul* – or to the Aristotelian traditions of commentary. Others, instead, used Aristotle's text to justify their literary experimentalism in response to the emergence of a renewed tragic genre, both in theory and practice.

Moreover, some fundamental studies – including Enrica Zanin's *Fins Tragique* (2014) – have begun to consider the impact (specifically concerning the ethical issues) that the 16th-century Aristotelian debate had on a European scale in relation to the foundation of a new model of tragedy.[19] Dramatic theory and theatrical practice mutually influenced each other: this interpretative reality should inform new perspectives in the study of early modern drama and liter-

---

16 For a reconstruction of the tragic genre between Antiquity and the Middle Ages, see Kelly 1993. On late antique and medieval influences on modern tragedy, see Zanin 2014a, 2017a and 2017b; Savettieri 2014 and 2017.
17 See Javitch 2001, 128; Cave 2001, 200.
18 See Brazeau 2018 and 2020a.
19 On the mutual relationship between theoretical debate and theatrical practice, see Mastrocola 1998 (on 16th-century Italian tragedy); Zanin 2011, 2014a (on 16th- and 17th-century Italian, French and Spanish tragedy).

ary criticism to a much greater degree.[20] Furthermore, as Brazeau argues, the Aristotelian text should be explored in both its Latin and vernacular traditions.[21] The same approach should be applied to early modern adaptations of ancient drama by exploring their production in both Latin and the vernacular contexts and investigating the interdependency of their renderings.[22]

The last decade has witnessed an increasing theoretical interest in exploring what Julia Kristeva first called 'intertextuality', a term coined in the 1960s to highlight the relationship between different texts communicating and interacting with each other.[23] The recent resurgence of interest in early modern reception studies has led to interesting new methodological frameworks, amongst which is that proposed by the Berlin-based research group *Transformationen der Antike*.[24] Hartmut Böhme and Johannes Helmrath purport to change the terminology of, and the critical viewpoint on, what has been called 'classical tradition' or 'classical reception'. The term they use, 'transformation', along with the model of *allelopoiesis* (from the Greek ἄλληλον, 'mutual', 'reciprocal', and ποίησις, 'creation'), describes the relationship of interdependency and reciprocity between antique and early modern cultures. Most of all, what this approach stresses is not the classical past (the 'reference sphere') but the receiving culture (the 'reception sphere'), thus highlighting the active role of the receiving culture in appropriating and reconstructing the past.

In light of the most recent methodological approaches discussed above, the aim of the following sections is to apply the new interpretative framework to the 16th-century reception of Aristotle's *Poetics* and Sophocles' *Oedipus Tyrannus* through a series of readings around Oedipus' *hamartia*, and to underline the

---

20 In this regard, at least three research projects are worth mentioning: *Les Idées du Théâtre*, directed by Marc Vuillermoz (Université de Savoie), aims at highlighting the theoretical, moral and philosophical reflections emerging from the dramatic texts and an analysis of the liminal texts of 16th- and 17th-century Italian, French and Spanish tragedies; *IThAC – L'invention du théâtre antique*, led by Malika Bastin-Hammou (Université Grenoble-Alpes) and Pascale Paré-Rey (Université Lyon III), aims at investigating the reception of ancient drama in 16th-century Europe, through the analysis, the translation and the digital edition of the liminal texts; *Translating Ancient Greek Drama in the Early Modern Period* (see the Introduction to this volume).
21 Two research projects have recently refocused on the vernacular Aristotle: the *AHRC Vernacular Aristotelianism in Renaissance Italy* project (2010–13) carried out at the University of Warwick and the Warburg Institute (led by David Lines, Simon Gilson and Jill Kraye) and the *ERC Aristotle in the Italian Vernacular* (2014–2019), led by Marco Sgarbi (Ca' Foscari, Venice) and David Lines (University of Warwick). On the vernacular Aristotle, see Refini 2020.
22 See Villari 2016.
23 See Kristeva 1969.
24 On 'transformation theory', see Baker/Helmrath/Kallendorf 2019.

interpretations of early modern scholars, not merely as part of the transmission of the ancient texts into a set of pre-existing moralising and rhetorical ideas, but in their active 'transformation' of such texts in their contemporary context.

2 Theorising Oedipus' *Hamartia*

After the publication of the *editio princeps* of the *Poetics* in 1508, for almost thirty years Aristotle's theory had little relevance for learned Italian readers. The first reliable Latin translation was composed in 1524 and published in 1536 by Alessandro Pazzi de' Medici, who was also the author of the first Latin and vernacular translations of Sophocles' *Oedipus Tyrannus*. His text, far more reliable and complete, followed the first printed Latin translation of the *Poetics*, Giorgio Valla's 1498 Latin translation, much more indebted to Horace and Diomedes than Aristotle,[25] which did not gain any traction among his contemporaries and fell into oblivion.

The publication of Pazzi's translation in 1536 was a real turning point. Far superior from a philological point of view, it immediately became the most used translation of the *Poetics*.[26] Pazzi's interpretation of *Poetics* 13 is crucial for our purposes here. His choice to translate δι' ἁμαρτίαν τινά as *humano quodam errore*[27] is worthy of attention: he seems to follow Valla's translation – *errore aliquo eorum*[28] – but he adds the adjective *humanus* to modify the error, thus stressing 'the protagonist's agency and human responsibility'.[29] From the mid-16th-century onwards, *hamartia* was increasingly translated as *peccatum*/*peccato*. However, a few translators and commentators preferred to use Valla's and Pazzi's translation of it as *error* and/or interchanged it with the terms *peccatum*/*peccato*.[30]

---

[25] On Valla's translation of the *Poetics*, see Weinberg 1961, 361–366; Tigerstedt 1968, 14–20; Zanin 2014a, 93.
[26] On Pazzi's translation, see Weinberg 1961, 371–373.
[27] Pazzi 1536, 32.
[28] Valla 1498, 4.
[29] Brazeau 2018, 24.
[30] In his *Rettorica et poetica d'Aristotile* (1549), the first vernacular translation of the *Poetics*, Bernardo Segni renders δι' ἁμαρτίαν τινά as 'per qualche errore'. Antonio Minturno, in his Latin treatise *De poeta* (1559), renders ἁμαρτία as *error quidam humano*, and in his Italian treatise *L'Arte poetica* (1563) as *humano errore*. Gian Giorgio Trissino, in his *Divisione quinta sulla Poetica* – written around 1549–50 and published in 1562 – renders ἁμαρτία with the term 'inadvertenza' ('oversight') combined with the expression 'grave peccato' ('serious sin').

The first extensive and influential commentary on Aristotle's *Poetics* was written by Francesco Robortello and published in Florence in 1548. It followed Pazzi's translation of *hamartia* as *humanus quidam error*, but he chose the verb *peccare* in his commentary. With regard to the tragic character, he says:

> Plane inter bonum ac malum is est collocandus, qui peccat quidem, sed imprudens peccat; huiusmodi enim neque bonus appellandus, quia iam peccavit; neque rursus malus, quia non consulto peccavit, sed per imprudentiam.

> He is clearly to be placed between good and bad; he who *sins* indeed, but *sins imprudently*; in fact, such a man should not be called good, because he *sinned*, nor, on the other hand, should he be called evil, because he did not sin on purpose, but *through imprudence*.[31]

In his commentary, Robortello refers to book III of Aristotle's *Nicomachean Ethics* to explain the tragic error through the distinction between voluntary and involuntary action, taking the case of Oedipus as an example:

> Qui vero per ignorationem agit, scit quidem quid aequum, quid oportet; imprudenter tamen, & invitus agit. Hic quidem particulare ignorat, quod agit, ut Oedipus, qui peremit Laium patrem, sciebat enim nefas esse perimere patrem; sed ignorabat illum esse patrem. Hi quidem igitur, qui per imprudentiam peccant, excusatione, & commiseratione digni, ut idem ait Aristoteles libro tertio Ethicorum sub initium, his verbis. ἐν δὲ τοῖς ἀκουσίοις συγγνώμης, ἐνίοτε δὲ καὶ ἐλέου γινομένου. Si igitur huiusmodi commiseratione digna patet referri posse ad tragoediam, quae eam perturbationem in primis studet excitare in animis auditorum.

> He who acts *on account of ignorance* knows what is just and what is necessary; he acts imprudently, however, and against his will. Indeed, this man ignores the one detail which he performs, just as *Oedipus, who killed his father Laius, knew it was an impious act to kill his father; but he did not know that that man was his father. Therefore, these men who sin because of imprudence are worthy of exemption and pity*, as Aristotle says in the third book of the *Ethics* after the beginning with these words: those [scil. actions] that are involuntary are condoned and sometimes even pitied. Therefore, if such actions are worthy of pity, it appears that it might be possible that this [scil. pity] may be referred to as tragedy, which chiefly seeks to elicit that emotion in the souls of spectators.[32]

Although Robortello's translation follows Pazzi's text in choosing to render *hamartia* as *humanus error*, he clarifies his choice in the *explicationes*: by referring back to the *Nicomachean Ethics*, he describes *hamartia* as an involuntary deed committed *per imprudentiam et ignorationem*. According to Aristotle's *Ethics*,

---

31 Robortello 1548, 131.
32 Robortello 1548, 131.

this is an involuntary action committed δι' ἄγνοιαν ('because of ignorance'); that is, the only kind of ignorance (the so-called 'ignorance of particulars') that deserves pity (ἔλεος) and pardon (συγγνώμη) because involuntary actions are *not* caused by wickedness, but by ignorance itself.[33] *Hamartia* is thus caused by ignorance and imprudence: it seems that Robortello did not choose these terms accidentally as synonyms; rather, he wants to explain Aristotle's *Poetics* via Aristotle's *Ethics*. Thus, his use of the verb *peccare* clearly does not imply culpability of the agent, nor necessarily 'sin' in its Christian meaning.[34]

Moreover, Robortello concedes that the situation of an error committed in ignorance by a middling character can, among the Greek tragedies, only be applied to the *Oedipus Tyrannus*. He observes that any other plot would be repulsive (μιαρόν) — according to Aristotle's theory, in fact, tragedy cannot represent a virtuous man falling into misfortune, as this would only arouse repulsion, nor can it represent an evil person falling into ruin as this would not elicit pity:[35]

> Non debent igitur omnes veterum tragoediae perpendi hoc examine, aut redigi ad hanc normam; nam praeter actionem, personamque Oedipodis, qualem expressit Sophocles, nescio, an aliam reperias apud ullum ex veteribus.

> Therefore, not all the tragedies of the ancients should undergo this enquiry, nor be composed according to this criterion; for besides Oedipus' action and character, as Sophocles represented them, I do not know whether you could find another tragedy [of this kind] among any of the ancients.[36]

Yet, Robortello goes beyond Aristotle: he argues that Aristotle prescribes a middling character as an ideal protagonist, since it is necessary to prevent human beings from feeling repulsion towards the gods to avoid any doubt about divine providence in the spectators:

> Maximum enim providentiae Deorum signum esse iudicant homines, si viros bonos praemiis afficiant, improbos autem ulciscantur, maleque perdant.

> In fact, men consider it to be the highest sign of divine providence if the gods reward virtuous men and punish and badly destroy the wicked.[37]

---

[33] Cf. Arist. *NE* III 1, 1110b24–1111a2.
[34] On *hamartia* in Robortello's commentary, see especially Leroux 2014; Brazeau 2018, 27–32.
[35] Cf. Arist. *Poet.* 13, 1452b31–37.
[36] Robortello 1548, 133. See Savettieri 2018, 159–161.
[37] Robortello 1548, 134.

Two elements, at least, are worth emphasising in these passages: first, the claim that Aristotle's theory of the middling character does not reflect the corpus of surviving ancient tragedies, but only the *Oedipus Tyrannus*; second, the misinterpretation of the concept of μιαρόν (repulsive). As for the latter, it ought to be considered that, whereas in Aristotle's *Poetics* the concept does not imply any specific link with religion, here Robortello explains that undeserved misfortunes could undermine religious devotion and cause a feeling of alienation from the gods. Interestingly, the idea put forward by Robortello — but absent in the *Poetics* — is that repulsion should be avoided in the audience to prevent any doubt about divine providence. The concept of 'divine justice' — that Thomas Rymer would properly identify in 1678 — will be deeply developed in the following decades, both in the theory and practice of tragedy, especially in France and England.[38]

Interpretations of *hamartia*, far from being limited to translations and commentaries on Aristotle's *Poetics*, played a key role in theoretical debates. In 1546, Sperone Speroni published a tragedy written in the vernacular, *Canace*, already known in 1542 in Padua within the Accademia degli Infiammati. *Canace* is a controversial tragedy, based on an epistle in Ovid's *Heroides* (XI), that retells the story of Aeolus' children, Canace and her brother Macareo, and their incestuous love that was provoked by Venus. Speroni's tragedy is the starting point of the most influential 16th-century literary quarrel over tragedy: an anonymous polemic dialogue entitled *Giudizio sopra la tragedia di Canace e Macareo* and attributed to Giraldi Cinzio, condemned Speroni for presenting Canace and Macareo because they were immoral characters who committed incest in full knowledge of their familial relationship, and thus transgressed the Aristotelian norms.[39] The meaning of the notion of *hamartia* and the moral stature of the middling character are some of the issues debated in the *Giudizio*. The crucial problem is not the incestuous relationship itself, but the element of willing behaviour.[40] A character in the *Giudizio*, Lodovico Boccadiferro, compares the plot with Sophocles' *Oedipus Tyrannus*, arguing that in the latter the theme of incest, since it is involuntary and the result of ignorance, reflects the moral condition of the middling character and arouses pity and fear:

---

38 See Savettieri 2014.
39 On the quarrel over Speroni's *Canace*, see Mastrocola 1998, 187–254; Maślanka-Soro 2010; Oberto 2017; Savettieri 2018, 152–159; Brazeau 2018, 25–27. The *Giudizio sopra la tragedia di Canace e Macareo* circulated in manuscript throughout the mid-16th-century and, published in 1550, was attributed to Giraldi Cinzio in Roaf 1959 e 1982.
40 See Oberto 2017, 77 and Brazeau 2018, 25.

> [Q]uello che potria essere di scelerato nella Tragedia non venne per scienza e volontà e consentimento o di Giocasta o di Edipo, ma per errore perché Giocasta non conosceva Edipo per figliuolo, né Edipo Giocasta per madre [...]. L'ignoranza del suo peccato ha levato da lui ogni sceleraggine e l'ha fatto degnissimo di compassione.

> Whatever act of wickedness there may be in the tragedy does not occur with the knowledge, will, or consent of either Jocasta or Oedipus, but rather due to *an error*. Jocasta did not know Oedipus was her son, nor did Oedipus know that Jocasta was his mother [...]. *The ignorance of his sin pardoned* him from any wickedness and made him very worthy of compassion.[41]

According to the author of the *Giudizio*, the incest portrayed in the *Canace* is a voluntary action — thus inappropriate for a tragic plot — as opposed to the involuntary error committed in ignorance by Oedipus and Jocasta. Ignorance is the key component used to define *hamartia*; the implicit reference is to both Robortello and the *Nicomachean Ethics*. The term *peccato* that occurs in this passage and refers to Oedipus' deed — as in the case of Robortello's commentary — coexists with the term *errore* and bears the same meaning: an involuntary error caused by ignorance and therefore worthy of pity and compassion.[42]

In defence of his *Canace*, Speroni wrote *Apologia* in 1554 and *Lezioni in difesa di Canace* in 1558.[43] According to Speroni, the incest of Canace and Macareo was an error resulting from an excess of love:

> Perché meglio due tali affetti si commovessero, non contento il poeta che i due fratelli fosser mezzo tra buoni e rei [...] volle imitarli il poeta nella età lor giovenile, nella quale è men vergogna il fallire, e la compassione è maggiore. E volle insieme che quello errore che fu cagion della lor miseria, fosse errore amoroso, con esso il quale rade volte adiviene che da pietade si discompagni.

> To best arouse those two emotions, the poet not only made the siblings middling between virtuous and wicked, [...] but represented them in their youth, where errors are less shameful and pity greater. And he also made it so that that *error which caused their misfortune be an error of love, which is rarely unaccompanied by pity*.[44]

In defending his *Canace*, Speroni, influenced by contemporary neo-Platonic philosophy, discusses the nature of love by referring to both Dante and Petrarch, distinguishing between three categories: a) the desire of beauty, b) an excess of

---

41 Giraldi, *Giudizio* in Roaf 1982, 100.
42 On the meaning of *errore* and *peccato* in the *Giudizio*, see Brazeau 2018, 25–27.
43 See Roaf 1982, XIV–LXI; Oberto 2017, 79–88. On Giraldi's and Speroni's understanding of tragic error, see Savettieri 2018, 154–159.
44 Speroni, in Roaf 1982, 191.

friendship, and c) an excess of love.[45] He argues that the case of Canace and Macareo should be included in the third category, excess of love, which he considers to be a 'human mistake' ('error...umano').[46] Speroni's digression about love is clearly aimed at comparing the definition of an excess of love as a 'human error' with the definition of *hamartia* contained in Aristotle's commentaries, as he explicitly points out:

> Gli *errori* de gli amanti non sono sceleratezze, ma si debbano chiamare *umani*, perché l'uomo ama come ragionevole e perciò *umanamente pecca*; e se così è che *l'error de gli inamorati sia umano*, adonque noi semo nella particula di Aristotele dove dice che persone tragiche sono quelle che *non per dedecus et pravitatem sed humano quodam errore in infelicitatem lapsi sunt*.

> The *lovers' errors* are not crimes and should be deemed *human*, because the human being loves as a reasonable creature and, as a human, commits sins; and if it is true that *the lovers' error is human*, then we agree with that paragraph in which Aristotle says that tragic characters are those who *non per dedecus et pravitatem sed humano quodam errore in infelicitatem lapsi sunt*.[47]

Speroni tries to justify the excess of love as *hamartia* by referring to the passage of Aristotle's *Poetics* 13 in the 1550 commentary of Vincenzo Maggi and Bartolomeo Lombardi on the *Poetics*.[48] As Savettieri points out, 'Speroni bypasses the relationship between the moral quality of the characters and the need for fear and pity to be elicited, and subordinates the former to the latter'.[49] However, it must be recalled that the relationship between human fallibility and an excess of passion was discussed by Aristotle not in the *Poetics*, but in the second book of his *Rhetoric*, where he affirms that most of the mistakes committed by the young are due to the latter.[50]

It is evident that Speroni, in defining the tragic error, is not referring here to Aristotle's *hamartia*, but rather to the error of incontinence: to discuss incontinence in such a way as to neutralise any criticism of immorality, though, he does not refer to the *Rhetoric* nor to the notion of *akrasia* (the 'weakness of will' discussed by Aristotle in book VII of the *Nicomachean Ethics*), but rather to the lovers Paolo and Francesca in Dante's *Inferno* (V, 103–105), as well as to Pet-

---

45 Roaf 1982, 227f.
46 Roaf 1982, 228.
47 Roaf 1982, 228.
48 Maggi/Lombardi 1550, 153.
49 Savettieri 2018, 157.
50 Arist. *Rh.* II 1389b2–8. Cf. Oberto 2017, 83.

rarch's *Canzoniere* (LXXI, 57–60).[51] Speroni focuses on the feelings of pity and compassion that Dante feels in telling the story of the two lovers, who are not at all presented as wicked, but just unable to control their passion.[52]

Pietro Vettori, in translating the passage on *hamartia* as part of his 1560 commentary on Aristotle's *Poetics*, introduces a new element. He does not emphasise the distinction between voluntary and involuntary actions as described in the *Nicomachean Ethics*, but instead he defines *hamartia* as 'doing what is worse', i.e., choosing the worse of two possible alternatives:

> *Inquit enim*: ἁμαρτία | δέ ἐστι τοῦ χείρονος πρᾶξις. *Cum igitur aliquis relicto eo, quod facere praestabat, propter imprudentiam id, quod est deterius gerit, tunc labitur ac peccat. Exempli causa. Oedipus lapsus est quia ira commotus interfecit Laium: nec cognovit eum patrem esse.*
>
> For he says: 'hamartia is doing what is worse.' Therefore, when someone leaves behind what he ought to have done on account of an imprudence for which he behaves wrongly, then he falls and sins. For example, *Oedipus acted wrongly because he killed Laius when moved by rage: he did not know him to be his father.*[53]

To explain the notion of *hamartia*, Vettori refers to a gloss from Aristotle's *Problemata* (919b24–25). In stressing the agent's responsibility, he takes the case of Sophocles' *Oedipus Tyrannus* as an example and argues that his *hamartia* results from a lack of control of his rage when he kills Laius at the crossroads. Vettori is certainly influenced by Robortello's commentary — as shown by his reference to both the notions of *imprudentia* and *ignorantia* (he says that Oedipus 'did not know Laius to be his father') — but Oedipus' *hamartia* is not considered to be an involuntary action worthy of pity and pardon as in earlier commentaries. His *hamartia* is explained as a moral failure caused by choosing wrongly and being dominated by rage. Oedipus should have controlled his anger; he *could* have acted differently.

As Brazeau convincingly suggests, it comes naturally to suppose that Vettori may be referring here to book VII of the *Nicomachean Ethics*, where Aristotle characterises anger resulting from *akrasia* (weakness of will) similarly to Vettori's description of Oedipus' murder of Laius.[54] What is most interesting is that the emphasis on Oedipus' responsibility that derives from the possibility that he could have chosen a different path adds the element of the protagonist's volition, thus proposing for the first time an interpretation of *hamartia* as a moral

---

51 Speroni, in Roaf 1982, 225–227.
52 Roaf 1982, 226.
53 Vettori 1560, 123.
54 Brazeau 2018, 34.

failure. This reading would influence 17th-century dramatic theory, especially in France.⁵⁵

To define Oedipus' moral failure, Vettori uses the verb *peccare* ('to sin'): *tunc labitur ac peccat* ('therefore he falls and sins'). It cannot be denied that Vettori's discussion underlines the personal responsibility of the tragic character; however, the increasingly frequent usage of *peccatum/peccato* instead of *error/errore* in the above-mentioned texts does not seem to be a sign of a theological interpretation influenced by a Counter-Reformation (mis)reading of *hamartia* as sin. Instead, *peccatum/peccato* and *error/errore* seem to be entirely interchangeable, with their use being integrated into the discussion on voluntary and involuntary actions and explained by reference to Aristotle's moral philosophy rather than a Christianisation of the *Poetics*.⁵⁶

The year 1570 was a turning point in the reception history of the *Poetics* with the publication of the first Italian commentary; indeed, the first in any European vernacular: Lodovico Castelvetro's *Poetica d'Aristotile vulgarizzata et sposta*. Differently from earlier commentators, Castelvetro not only vulgarises the *Poetics*, but he also explicitly declares his intention to develop his own theory, so that 'Aristotle [may be] used partly as a point of departure and partly as an opponent'.⁵⁷ His process of adaptation and refutation had a significant impact on the exegesis of the notion of *hamartia*:

> Ora, secondo Aristotele, se la persona santissima trapassa da felicità a miseria, presta cagione alla gente di mormorare contra Dio e di dolersi di lui che permette così fatto trapassamento; ma se la persona mezzana trapassa da felicità a miseria, non dà cagione alla gente di mormorare contra Dio né di dolersi di lui, perciochè sì come ci possiamo immaginare, è assai ragionevole che avenga questo così fatto trapassamento a quella persona per gli peccati suoi, avegna che non sieno de' più orribili del mondo e sieno mischiati tra alcune buone operazioni.
>
> Now, according to Aristotle, if a very holy person falls from happiness into misfortune, this gives the people reason to grumble against God and complain about him who allowed such a fall; but if a middling person falls from happiness into misfortune, this does not give the people any reason to grumble against God, nor to complain about him; thus, as we can imagine, it is quite reasonable that such a fall should happen to this person *on ac-*

---

55 Jean Racine translated and annotated part of Aristotle's *Poetics* using Vettori's text; in his translation, δι' ἁμαρτίαν τινά is rendered as 'par sa faute'. For the theory of passions in French neo-classical theory, see Walfard 2008; Zanin 2014a, 332–336.
56 On mid-16th-century readings of *hamartia* as *peccatum/peccato* and *error/errore*, see Brazeau 2018.
57 Weinberg 1961, 503. Cf. Zanin 2012a, 62f.

count of his sins, so long as they are not the worst in the world, and some other good acts are also mixed in.[58]

According to Castelvetro, Aristotle would forbid a plot about a virtuous character fallen into ruin, not because of its immorality or because of a lack of poetic efficacy, but exclusively because the downfall of 'very holy persons' ('persone santissime') might elicit resentment against God.[59] Nevertheless, Castelvetro ultimately states that, no matter what kind of configuration people witness in a tragic plot (whether the downfall of a virtuous or bad middling character), they will in any case believe that there is a greater and unknown plan following the rules of a God who is just and cares about human matters.[60] For the first time, the term *peccato*, used to define the notion of *hamartia* is clearly linked to Christian sin. According to Castelvetro, common people believe in the righteousness of God, who would not punish anyone undeservedly, so the downfall of the tragic character is always caused by his or her sins ('per gli peccati suoi'). This lexical choice is not only part of the process of the vulgarisation of pagan texts for a Christian audience, but, as we see for the first time in 16th-century poetics, also an instrument allowing for a broader discussion of Christian doctrine.[61]

3 Dramatising Oedipus' *Hamartia*

Alessandro Pazzi de' Medici is not only the author of *Aristotelis Poetica*, but also of the first vernacular translation of Sophocles' *Oedipus Tyrannus* (1525–26 ca.), the *Edipo Principe*. During the same years, he also translated the *Iphigenia in Tauris* into the vernacular, and the *Oedipus Tyrannus* and the *Electra* into Latin.[62]

---

58 Castelvetro 1570, 1: 370.
59 Castelvetro 1570, 1: 362.
60 Castelvetro 1570, 1: 361–364.
61 On Castelvetro's interpretation of the concept of *hamartia*, see Brazeau 2018, 35–40; Savettieri 2018, 162–164. Cf. also Zanin 2012a.
62 The text of Pazzi's *Edipo Principe* in the vernacular is preserved in two manuscripts: the first is in Florence (Biblioteca Nazionale Centrale, II, IV = *Magl.* VII, 972) and the second in Rome (Biblioteca Apostolica Vaticana, *Barb. Lat.* 4002). The Greek text is not included in either of the two manuscripts. The Latin translation of Pazzi's *Oedipus* is preserved (along with the translation of Sophocles' *Electra*) in two manuscripts: the first is in Florence (Biblioteca Nazionale Centrale, II, IV, 8 = *Magl.* VII, 950, bis.) and the second in Ravenna (Biblioteca Classense, cod. 372). Both the vernacular and Latin translations have recently been published in

Pazzi's *Edipo Principe* is a quite faithful translation of Sophocles' *Oedipus Tyrannus*, but there are additions to the original text that reveal the presence of a Christianising language.[63] Here are a few examples: the adjective 'sancto' (holy/saint) is frequently used throughout the play, occurring almost thirty times,[64] as well as the terms 'peccato'/'peccatore' (sin/sinner) referring to Creon, and 'martire' (martyr) referring to Oedipus. Moreover, the concept of 'being exiled' is referred to with the term 'scomunicato' (excommunicated), which derives from the 14th-century ecclesiastic Latin *excommunicare*.

The additions and omissions tend to avoid an explicit accusation of the gods and, hence, of the Christian God. In Sophocles' play, Oedipus, when he begins to suspect that he is the killer of Laius, desperately asks Zeus:

> Ὦ Ζεῦ, τί μου δρᾶσαι βεβούλευσαι πέρι;
>
> O Zeus, what have you decided to do with me?[65]

Pazzi translates this as follows:

> O Giove che far deggio in tal caso? Spirami.
>
> O Zeus, what should I do in this case? Inspire me.[66]

This involves an evident inversion of the subject, which aims at limiting Zeus' responsibility and stressing Oedipus' free will. In fact, as Patrick Finglass points out about the Sophoclean passage, 'the perfect βεβούλευσαι of Zeus suggests a fixed and irrevocable decision; the βουλή of Zeus could be associated with profound and unexplained human suffering'.[67] The downfall of Oedipus cannot be explained by Pazzi as the consequence of the will of Zeus exclusively, a consequence that clearly emerges in another passage in which Oedipus sees the working of a δαίμων as responsible for his sufferings:

Sorella 2013 together with Pazzi's preface to his tragedies (146–153). On Pazzi's works more generally, see Borza 2007, 167–204.

63 I am referring here to the text of the manuscript in Florence (Biblioteca Nazionale Centrale, II, IV = *Magl.* VII, 972), which I have personally consulted.

64 The adjective 'sancto' occurs as part of the following formulations: 'numi sancti', 'sancto augurio', 'sancto Apollo', 'sancto oracolo', 'sancta giustizia', 'sancti Dei', 'sancta leggi', 'sancto propheta'.

65 Soph. *OT* 738, translated by Finglass 2018, *ad l.*

66 Pazzi 1525–1526, f. 116ʳ.

67 Finglass 2018, 399.

> Ἆρ' οὐκ ἀπ' ὠμοῦ ταῦτα δαίμονός τις ἂν / κρίνων ἐπ' ἀνδρὶ τῷδ' ἂν ὀρθοίη λόγον;
>
> Would not someone who judged that this was the result of the action of an evil spirit be right in what he said in my case?[68]

Pazzi modifies the entire sentence, omitting the reference to a δαίμων acting against him:

> Per ch'io temo ch'el fato che mi discaccia / di qui non mi conduca a tai casi horrendi.
>
> Because I'm afraid that the fate that banishes me from here will cause me such horrible sufferings.[69]

The last example refers to the last scene in which Oedipus entrusts his daughters to Creon, rendered by Pazzi as follows:

> La colpa mia non imputando allor, prendati d'esse misericordia.
>
> Not blaming them for my fault, please offer mercy to them.[70]

Not only does Oedipus explicitly admit his culpability, but he also uses the term 'misericordia', which clearly refers to Christian pity.

Our previous observations might lead us to believe that Pazzi attempted a process of Christianisation of the Sophoclean text. Yet, throughout the translation, there are several references to pagan deities (followed by the adjective 'sancto') as well as to the concepts of fate and fortune (thus preserving the Sophoclean image of Oedipus as both a lucky 'child of *Tyche*' and the victim of an unlucky fate).[71] It is thus evident that Christian and pagan lexica coexist in the translation, which does not in fact purport to deliver a specifically religious message. Similarly to mid-16th-century scholars (e.g., Giraldi Cinzio, Robortello, Vettori), Christianising and moralising mistranslations seem to be part of a broader programme of cultural translation aimed at domesticating the texts for a Christian audience. Indeed, this process requires a limitation on divine agency in Oedipus' downfall so as to obtain the sympathy of the spectators. The case of Pazzi's *Edipo* should thus not be considered a Christianisation of the Sophocle-

---

68 Soph. *OT* 828–829, translated by Finglass 2018, *ad l.*
69 Pazzi 1525–1526, f. 119ʳ.
70 Pazzi 1525–1526, f. 134ʳ.
71 Cf. Soph. *OT* 1080. For the references to fate and fortune in Pazzi's *Edipo*, cf. (fato) ff. 106r, 199r, 130r, 133v, (fortuna) 99r, 101v, 109r, 117v, 122r, 123v, 127r, 130r, 135r.

an text: Pazzi's philological interest is preserved, and his additions and omissions testify to a cultural domestication of the Greek text.[72]

Completely different is the case of the *Edippo* written by Giovanni Andrea dell'Anguillara, one of the most criticised 16th-century adaptations.[73] Printed twice in 1565 in Padua and Venice, it was both the first printed vernacular edition of the *Oedipus Tyrannus* and the first to be performed in Italy.[74] Anguillara's contemporaries and modern scholars have agreed in condemning the additions to Sophocles' text. In his version he combines Sophocles' and Seneca's plays and adds a variety of ancient sources from Euripides' *Phoenician Women* and Statius' *Thebaid*. In 16th-century Italy, no one else redefined Oedipus entirely as did Anguillara.[75]

Anguillara's play focuses on a moral dilemma. As Tiresias reveals already in the first scene, the 'sin' committed by Oedipus and Jocasta is an involuntary action:

> Ciascun di lor la mente have innocente,
> e pecca, e nulla sa del suo peccato.
>
> They both have an innocent mind, / and they sin and don't know anything about their sin.[76]

Anguillara's play — which, according to Zanin, attempts to 'explain how it is possible to have an innocent conscience and yet to be a sinner'[77] — emphasises the ignorance of Oedipus, who convincingly claims his innocence:

> M'avete a perdonar, poi ch'ho peccato
> contra mia voglia: e l'animo innocente
> ho sempre avuto, e ben perdono io merto.
> Che se la man peccò, non peccò il core.

---

72 Di Maria 2002, 63f.
73 See D'Ovidio 1878, 276–293. The play/translation has recently been re-published in a critical edition (see Merola 2020).
74 The *Edippo* was first performed in Padua in 1556 or 1560, and then in Vicenza in 1561.
75 On Anguillara's *Edippo* and its ancient models (especially Sophocles' and Seneca's plays), see Paduano 1994, 266–270; Fabrizio 1995, Mastrocola 1996, 100–112; Di Maria 2005; Zanin 2008, 2011, 2012b and 2014a, 340–343; Guastella 2013, 260f.; Schironi 2016, 141–143; Lauriola 2017, 183–184; Fiore 2019, 16–20.
76 Anguillara 1565, I 1, 64f.
77 Zanin 2008, 70f.

Please, forgive me, as *I sinned / against my will, I have always had / an innocent conscience* and I deserve forgiveness. / Since it was my hand to sin, not my heart.[78]

Edippo is shown to be innocent; no one in the play considers him guilty of crimes. The messenger from Corinth, after Oedipus' recognition of the nature of his deed, justifies it:

> Peccaste non sapendo il fatto a pieno;
> non sete in questo degno di castigo.
> [...]
> Che l'error che si fa per ignoranza,
> non partorisce infamia.
>
> You sinned without knowing the whole truth; / you do not deserve any punishment. [...] / Since *a mistake made out of ignorance / does not bring disgrace*.[79]

Anguillara's emphasis on Oedipus' ignorance is also confirmed by several references to fate, which are aimed at stressing the fact that he was unaware of what he did and that he was a victim of a 'cruel fate' ('malvagia sorte').[80] In the opening scene, Tiresias and his daughter Manto (a character taken from Seneca's *Oedipus*) underline the impossibility of avoiding a predetermined fate through a number of rhetorical questions[81] that are eventually summarised in the last one: 'perché condanna il Fato un innocente?'.[82] Starting from the first scene, the moral paradox of the play is already clear. Oedipus is shown to be a good king, a loving father, a wise and judicious man who, despite his innocence, will suffer a terrible punishment: this is the 'cruel destiny' — being guilty of incest and parricide — that he will necessarily fulfil.[83] The question raised by Manto about a possible justification for undeserved suffering (I, 1, 191) remains unanswered, and the Chorus in the third act concludes that

---

[78] Anguillara 1565, III, 4, 93–99.
[79] Anguillara 1565, III, 5, 70–75.
[80] Anguillara 1565, III, 5, 107.
[81] Cf. Anguillara 1565, I, 1, 127, 'Edippo casto e pio nel suo pensiero, si governò da saggio e da prudente ma che val la prudenza contra il Fato?' (Edippo, having an innocent and pious conscience, acted as a wise and cautious man; yet how can prudence face Fate?); I, 1, 146, 'Chi può fuggir quel che destina il cielo' ('Who can escape what Heaven destines?').
[82] Anguillara 1565, I, 1, 191: 'Why does Fate condemn an innocent?'.
[83] Anguillara 1565, I, 1, 132f.: 'il suo destin crudel [...] avea disposto che fosse incestuoso e parricida' ('his cruel destiny fated him to be incestuous and parricide').

> da quel ch'al saggio nostro Edippo è occorso,
> si può veder come il giudizio humano
> scorge poco lontano
> contra il voler della malvagia sorte'.

> considering what happened to our wise Oedipus, / we can understand how human judgement / is unable to look far away / when it is hampered by the will of the cruel fate.[84]

It is clear that human judgement is limited in the face of a mysterious fate; although Oedipus acts according to strict moral rules, wisdom, knowledge and intelligence cannot guarantee happiness.[85] However, Anguillara's conception of fate should not be confused with the divine agency nor with the Christian deity; references to the latter are very common in the play, thus revealing a religious feeling 'that is more intense and more pious than the one expressed by their Greek and Roman counterparts'.[86] *Edippo*'s God is the Christian God and, unlike the 'malvagia sorte', has no responsibility for his fall into misfortune. The depth of the religious sentiment is also made evident by the choruses, who believe that 'sol chi si fonda in Dio / può dir d'avere un fin stabile e fermo'.[87] The reverential and devoted tone found in Anguillara's play contrasts with the hostile deity represented in both Sophocles' and Seneca's tragedies: this kind of representation, which in some way blames the gods' cruelty and lack of compassion, obviously has no place in 16th-century adaptations.[88] Although pious references to God do not imply religious belief, this specific case is not only part of a broader program of cultural domestication for a Christian audience (such as in Pazzi's *Edipo*), rather it seems to be a hermeneutical attempt at debating the moral paradox of Oedipus' innocence *within* a Christian context.

How does Anguillara solve the moral issue of Oedipus' innocent guilt? His innocence is contradicted by the terrible punishment he will eventually suffer, yet God cannot be considered responsible for his punishment. Zanin[89] has recently proposed a moral interpretation of Anguillara's Christianisation of the play: the author avoids the tragic ambiguity present in Sophocles' plot 'by presenting the hero's punishment as self-inflicted, as Oedipus claims after his final recognition' ('ma vo punirmi al tutto da me stesso / se non come vorrei , come

---

84 Anguillara 1565, III, 5, 104–107.
85 See Mastrocola 1996, 100–112.
86 Di Maria 2002, 64.
87 Anguillara 1565, III, 5, 167: 'Only those who act according to God can say that they have a stable and firm purpose'.
88 Cf. Soph. *OT* 1329f., 1360, 1519; Sen. *Oed.* 709–712. See Di Maria 2002 and 2005.
89 Zanin 2008, 69–71 and 2012b, 214–216.

potrò').[90] Anguillara thus stresses Oedipus' free will that leads the hero to blind himself as well as making him responsible for both his voluntary and involuntary actions. The last lines of the text, pronounced by the chorus, attempt to answer the above-mentioned question raised by Manto in the opening scene, 'perché condanna il Fato un innocente?':

> Quindi si può veder che'l sommo Dio
> Non sol dispon che i volontari eccessi
> Condannin l'huomo al debito castigo
> Ma quei peccati anchor ch'alcun commette
> Per ignoranza e contra il suo volere
> Vuol che condannin l'huomo a penitenza
> E la debita pena ne riporti.
>
> Thus we may see the great God / not only commanding that voluntary excesses / may condemn man to his due punishment, / but also ordering that *those sins committed / out of ignorance and unwillingly* / may condemn man to punishment / and exact due penalty.[91]

Anguillara emphasises the ignorance of Oedipus who, despite his innocence, will suffer a terrible punishment because he is *equally responsible* for both his voluntary and involuntary actions. It is God who condemns human beings to punishment even for those 'sins committed out of ignorance and unwillingly', a formulation that does not involve what will be later conceived of as 'poetic justice'. The excessive cruelty of Oedipus' punishment for 'unintentional sin' is justified by Zanin as stemming from Oedipus' refusal to receive grace.[92] A religious interpretation of the play would allow us to see in the scene of the sacrifice, inspired by Seneca's text, Oedipus' refusal of grace: the sacred ox is illuminated by a ray of light, but it refuses to look at it and rather throws itself onto the sword, which pierces its eye and kills it. According to this metaphorical reading, Oedipus' sin would be the original sin: 'Edippo might have overcome the original sin by accepting God's light, i.e., God's grace. But he refuses the light, and he receives eternal exile'.[93] However, Zanin argues that this moral explanation of the play, implying a conception of grace and redemption close to Protestant ideas of predestination and free will, is not wholly convincing. Oedi-

---

90 Anguillara 1565, III, 5, 91f.: 'I will punish myself thoroughly, if not as I wish, as I will be able to'. Cf. Soph. *OT* 1329–1333: in the Sophoclean tragedy, Oedipus' self-blinding is caused by Apollo, but at the same time by Oedipus himself. Cf. Cairns 2013; Fiore 2022.
91 Anguillara 1565, V, 3, 362–368.
92 Zanin 2008, 69–71.
93 Zanin 2008, 71.

pus' innocence and punishment continually question the justice of God. They can only be understood, Zanin says, 'behind the screen of the imitation', and — although accepting the Christianisation of several elements of the ancient plot — in the end leaving 'the question of evil unanswered'.[94]

Why does Anguillara tenaciously pursue the question of innocence? Edippo is portrayed as a good king[95] and father. His main concerns are dividing his kingdoms equally between his sons, arranging royal marriages for his daughters and giving them a good example of moral behaviour.[96] Francesca Schironi argues that Edippo's wise recommendations to his children ('siate cortesi e liberali')[97] 'echo Ottaviano Fregoso's discourse in Book 4 (esp. v–xliii) of Baldassar Castiglione's *Courtier* (1528) in which he claims that the courtier should teach the prince liberality, justice, and virtue'.[98] Personal honour and social reputation — even attempting to avoid shame through self-blinding — are the specific traits of Anguillara's *Edippo* as well as the 'leitmotiv in Renaissance ethical and political thought, beginning with Machiavelli's *Prince* and Castiglione's *Courtier*'.[99] Anguillara thus offers a religious, political and moral portrait of Oedipus that corresponds to the 'Renaissance man'[100] so that the contemporary audience is able to identify with the character on the stage. This is the main reason why Oedipus could not be culpable. From the beginning, Tiresias justifies Oedipus and Jocasta, clarifying that they are both unaware of what they did and believe in their innocence, as do all the other characters: 'credono ambi, quell che 'l mondo crede'.[101] As Valeria Merola suggests, Anguillara aims at identifying the contemporary audience of the court with the characters of the play: if the characters believe — as they do — in the innocence of Oedipus, who is an *exemplum* of morality, then the spectators will justify his actions as well. Oedipus' honour thus proves his innocence.[102]

---

94 Zanin 2008, 71. On imitation as the founding principle of 16th-century literary creation, see Di Martino in this volume.
95 Anguillara 1565, I, 1, 51f.: 'Il nostro saggio Edippo / il Re nostro prudente, invitto e giusto' (The wise Edippo, our prudent King, invincible and just).
96 Anguillara 1565, I, 2, 125–136.
97 Anguillara 1565, I, 2, 134 ('Be courteous and liberal').
98 Schironi 2016, 142.
99 Schironi 2016, 142.
100 Merola 2020, XXXIII.
101 Anguillara I, 1, 66: 'They both believe what the world believes'.
102 See Merola 2020, XXVII–XXXIV.

4 Conclusion

Our discussion of the case study of Oedipus' *hamartia* in 16th-century theoretical writings and dramatic adaptations has made evident the 'transformational processes' occurring in Italy between the 1520s and the 1570s, i.e., the complex relationship between change and continuity in the reception of the classics in this period. In fact, 'creative construction' as well as 'creative destruction' are the essential characteristics of the cultural changes that reciprocally occur between the 'reception sphere' and the 'reference sphere', both diachronically and synchronically.[103] How does this 'transformation' work? The aim of this study is to map the main trends — and different elements of 'transformation' — in the triangular relationship between dramatic theory and practice, the reception of ancient drama, and the reception of Aristotle's *Poetics* during the first decades following the rediscovery of the tragic genre.

Adopting the threefold partition of the Cinquecento proposed by Paola Mastrocola,[104] a few observations can be made about the relationship between dramatic theory and practice and about the ways in which the *Poetics* and the *Oedipus Tyrannus* have been interpreted. According to Mastrocola, the Cinquecento can be divided into three chronological periods: a) 1515–40, b) 1540–50, and c) 1550–1600.[105]

The first period (1515–40), which began, significantly, with the first 'regular' tragedy — Trissino's 1515 *Sofonisba* — is characterised by the earliest experimental dramatic writings without any theoretical counterpart: Pazzi's Latin translation of the *Poetics*, published in 1536, becomes an essential instrument for reading Aristotle's treatise, which will play a normative role starting from the 1540s. However, until then, it can be argued that the reception of Greek drama — as well as the resulting production of new tragedies — and the reception of the *Poetics* proceed on parallel tracks. Both Pazzi's *Poetica* (1536) and *Edipo Principe* (1525–26 ca.) aim at providing a first reliable translation — the former in Latin, the latter in the vernacular — without any specific intention of adding elements in an exercise of creative freedom. The Christianising additions, especially in the case of the vulgarisation of Sophocles' *Oedipus*, are part

---

103 On the terminology adopted by 'transformation theory', see Baker/Helmrath/Kallendorf 2019, 9–25.
104 Mastrocola 1998, 27–38.
105 Mastrocola 1998, 31f.

of a process of 'appropriation' that incorporates the ancient plot, largely preserved, into the receiving culture.[106]

According to Mastrocola, the second period (1540–50) corresponds to the moment of the greatest growth of both dramatic theory and practice. In the 1540s, translations of and commentaries on the *Poetics* (e.g., Robortello, Segni, Maggi-Lombardi) and dramatic treatises (e.g., Giraldi, Speroni, Trissino) gave rise to a new theory of tragedy characterised by a process of 'hybridization' between the reference and reception spheres. Both the theory and practice of tragedy — existing in a relationship of close interdependence (as shown in the *querelle* on the *Canace*) — reveal a form of syncretism between two ideological languages, pagan and Christian, thus leading to the coexistence of different semantic fields and a creative 'assimilation' of the reference sphere. The tendency to Christianise the notion of *hamartia* explicitly has been, more or less consciously, prevented by two different trends: a) an interpretation of the *Poetics* through the lens of the Aristotelian corpus (*Nicomachean Ethics*, *Rhetoric*, *Politics*); and b) the rise of modern theatrical practice and thus the need for a renewed theorisation of the tragic genre (also influenced by contemporary cultural, philosophical and literary thought). Moreover, in both dramatic theory and practice there is no space for the ambiguity that was a typical trait of Aristotelian *hamartia*: theoreticians and tragedians need to justify as much as possible the downfall of the middling character, driving their exegesis either towards Oedipus' innocence or his culpability, thus 'solving' the vagueness of the original concept — though not always successfully.

In the third period (1550–1600) the tragic genre is starting to lose its original form, which is occurring together with a loss of philological interest in the ancient sources.[107] Vettori's Latin commentary (1560) and — even more explicitly — Castelvetro's commentary (1570) propose a moralising reading of Oedipus' *hamartia* as a moral failure; in the case of Castelvetro, this reading has an explicitly religious intent. This process of 'disjunction' and 'hybridization'– inserting moral issues into the *Poetics* — integrates the concept of *hamartia* into a pattern of theodicy that will play a fundamental role, especially in 17th-century European dramatic theory and practice. Anguillara's *Edippo* is another case of 'hybridization' and 'disjunction': behind the Aristotelian choice of the subject, his play — a pastiche of Sophoclean and Senecan elements — is an excellent

---

106 Baker/Helmrath/Kallendorf 2019, 17.
107 The loss of philological interest by tragedians is counteracted by a growing philological interest into ancient texts from scholars such as Castelvetro and Piccolomini, for which see Cotugno 2006 and Di Martino in this volume.

example of the creative process of reciprocal production and destruction between the reference and reception spheres. Yet the value of this play — which allows the 21st-century reader to understand the extraordinary complexity of early modern culture — was not recognised by Anguillara's contemporaries, who preferred Giustiniani's *Edipo Tiranno*, as a more faithful translation of Sophocles' tragedy, for the opening night of the *Teatro Olimpico* in Vicenza.

Mid-16th-century classical reception is thus characterised by a precarious balance between conservation, rejection, and recombination of the ancient sources. Giraldi's admission of being 'guilty' of writing a play — *Didone* — that is in some way different from the ideal Aristotelian plot structure of the *Oedipus Tyrannus* seems to be nothing less than a proud statement of his creative assimilation of ancient drama and his adaptation of the Aristotelian rules to emerging dramatic theory. By exploring the reception history of the classical models and considering them independently from the ancient texts they refer to, the modern reader is given the opportunity to rediscover the cultural, philosophical and theological dynamism behind the revolution of early modern thought.

Coda: Dramaturgy and Translation

Giovanna Di Martino and Estelle Baudou
Early Modern Iphigenias and Practice Research

Abstract: The chapter presents the results of two performance workshops which explore parts of Euripides' *Iphigenia in Aulis* in three translations of the play: Thomas Sébillet's *Iphigénie* (1549), Lodovico Dolce's *Ifigenia* (1551), and Lady Jane Lumley's *The Tragedie of Euripides called Iphigeneia* (ca. 1557). The performing process herein designed relies on actors selecting turning points in the texts and matching words with bodily movements. The theatrical exercises proposed in the workshops serve to investigate the power dynamics between the characters and its evolution within the scene, the place and function of the chorus, and the situation — whether intimate or public — envisaged in the dramaturgy of each translation. Through investigating drama translation via performance practice, this chapter aims at widening the very meaning of drama translation, demonstrating that it is necessarily part of, and heavily relies on, a wider dramaturgical process.

1 Translation, Contamination, and Practice Research in 16th-Century Iphigenias

The present chapter proposes an analysis of ancient Greek tragedy and its early modern translation through performance practice; it also aims at exploring the process(es) entailed in the translation and embodiment of a dramatic text, thus inserting itself into the field of theatre translation studies. Indeed, whilst the theorization of the performance of Greek tragedy has recently benefited from successful collaborations between theatre and classical reception scholars,[1]

Section 1, paragraphs 5–7, 13, 15, 18–20, and 24 of section 2; paragraphs 1, 3–4, 6–7, 9–10 of section 3; and paragraphs 5, 7–8 of section 4 are by Giovanna Di Martino; paragraphs 1–4, 8–12, 14, 16, and 21–23 of section 2; paragraphs 2, 5, 8, 11–12 of section 3; and paragraphs 4 and 6 of section 4 are by Estelle Baudou; paragraphs 1–3 of section 4 are by both Giovanna Di Martino and Estelle Baudou. We would like to thank the other editors of this volume, Fiona Macintosh, Quentin Rioual, and Maria Wyke for reading earlier drafts of this chapter and for their invaluable suggestions.

1 See, amongst others, Hall and Harrop 2010; Dunbar and Harrop 2018.

little has been done on the translation of Greek tragedy that combines academic research with performance practice, or, more specifically, practice research.[2] This chapter will show the relevance of practice research for a deeper and fuller understanding of a dramatic text and its translation by presenting the results of two workshops on three 16th-century translations of Euripides' *Iphigenia at Aulis*: *L'Iphigène* by Thomas Sébillet (1549), *Ifigenia* by Lodovico Dolce (1551), and *The Tragedie of Euripides called Iphigenia* by Lady Jane Lumley (ca. 1557).[3]

Our understanding of translation rests on recent developments in translation and adaptation studies, which have shifted from a linear (source-to-target) and fidelity-based understanding of translation to intertextual analyses that privilege the role of the audience and readership in the meaning-making process of what Gérard Genette calls the 'hypertext'.[4] In this framework, there is little difference between translation and adaptation, as both are highly hypertextual processes and products.[5] Understanding any text as a 'hypertext' upsets linear and/or preconceived hierarchies between the source and target texts and channels attention onto the hypertext, which is explored as the creative site of the new forms of the hypotexts it reworks.

In addition to involving two linguistic systems and a reassessment of the contextual and cultural meanings of both the source and target texts, drama translation also encompasses a third language, that of the theatre.[6] As hyper-

---

[2] See Harrop and Wiles 2008, and Wiles 2007.
[3] The participants in the first workshop (28th–29th November 2019) were Marcus Bell, Fanny Bloc, Annaïg Briand, Giovanna Casali, Giovanna Di Martino, Cécile Dudouyt, Marie-Gabrielle Pelissie du Rausas and Marchella Ward. The participants in the second workshop (21st May 2021) were James Aldred, Claire Barnes, Giovanna Di Martino, Zoë Jennings, Lara Korach, Philippa Lang, Guia Mauri and Chuan Yue. Estelle Baudou directed both workshops, whereas Giovanna Di Martino directed work on Sébillet's translation in the second workshop and acted as a dramaturg for both workshops. The workshops were funded by the Leventis Foundation at University College London and the European Commission (Estelle Baudou's project has received funding from the European Union's Horizon 2020 research and innovation programme under the Marie Sklodowska-Curie grant agreement No 839770).
[4] Cf. Barnette 2018, 9–18 for a survey of the main shifts in adaptation studies, particularly within theatre and performance studies; on the use of Genette's 'hypertext' in adaptation studies, see, amongst others, Sanders 2006, 22. For more on Genette's theory, see the Introduction.
[5] On the interdependence of, and/or (im)possibility of distinguishing between, translation and adaptation in the theatrical process especially, see Link 1980; Bassnett 1985; Windle 2011; Krebs 2014; Laera 2014; and the introduction to this volume.
[6] Discussions about how to incorporate this third language in translation have multiplied since the 70s of the last century; for a recollection of the main developments in the field of theatre translation theory and practice, see, amongst others, Bigliazzi *et al.* 2013.

texts for the stage (if only ideally), translations of ancient Greek drama possess an inner dramaturgy: namely, the creative (re)arrangement of the dramatic meanings and structures that may be found in the hypotexts onto which the translation is grafted.[7] Research into such (re)arrangements not only illuminates the multiple (and infinite) possibilities of interpretation of any hypotext; it also brings to the fore the necessary cultural and theatrical recodifications implied in drama translation. By approaching the translations proposed in this chapter through practice we aim at exploring all the dramaturgical aspects inscribed within these texts, thus enriching as well as supplementing previous literary studies of them.

Our practice-research methodology is situated within both the theory and practice of dramaturgy;[8] it is informed by Di Martino's expertise in translation studies and the reception history of ancient Greek drama and by Baudou's professional training as a dramaturg. Since 2019, we have developed a methodology that builds on the conceptual and practical overlap between translation and dramaturgy in the theatrical process.[9] Prior to each workshop, we meet to explore the dramaturgy of the excerpt we will work on, first in the original, and then in the translations that we have decided to work on.[10] We start by investigating all the performance possibilities that the source text suggests. These are some of the dramaturgical questions that we ask of the source text and that guide us in the preparation of the workshop session: Who is onstage? What is the action comprised of? Who has the power? Who is in charge of the narrative? Who is speaking and what is the aim of the speech?

Once we have identified the main questions and problems that the excerpt raises in the original, we explore how these questions have been addressed in the different translations and plan the workshop accordingly. We design theatrical exercises aimed at comparing the various dramaturgical choices made by the translators and at testing the efficacy of such choices on the stage. Theatrical exercises range from building a story or a picture together to matching words with movements; building collective movement in the ensemble that responds to the main characters as they perform their lines to imagining the

---

[7] For recent (re)definitions of dramaturgy as a theory and practice, see, amongst others, Romanska 2014; Trencsényi and Cochrane 2014; Trencsényi 2015; Barnette 2018.
[8] On the productive relationship between theatre, translation, and dramaturgy, see, amongst others, Versényi 2014; Trencsényi 2015; and Barnette 2018.
[9] For more information on past workshops, see http://www.apgrd.ox.ac.uk/about/translating-ancient-drama/translating-ancient-drama-workshops (last accessed 01/09/2022).
[10] The excerpt is chosen on the basis of its relevance for the exploration of the dramaturgy of the translations taken into account.

setting by using the rehearsal space. Indeed, each translation undergoes a process of re-translation as it is physically embodied and pronounced by the actors onstage.

Prior to each workshop, the actors are asked to familiarise themselves in advance with the translations and the plot of the original play.[11] At the end of the workshop, there are several run-throughs of the whole scene in the different translations, after which we hold a 15/20-minute feedback session with the actors commenting on their experiences.

In the course of developing our methodology, the term 'contamination' has emerged as a particularly apt way to describe what is happening on stage when we embody and enact the various translations. 'Contamination' well captures the complex and mutual influence between the multiple stages and 'bodies' involved in translating for the stage; after all, the verb *contamino*[12] was famously employed in antiquity with reference to the translating process associated with the birth of Roman comedy and its derivation from, or indeed translation of, Greek New Comedy; more specifically, it referred to the blending of multiple sources together in the creation of new play-texts.[13]

In our own practice, we first used 'contamination' in a workshop that focused on 17th-century translations of Aeschylus' *Agamemnon* and *Choephoroi*, Sophocles' *Electra* and *Oedipus Tyrannus*, and Euripides' *Electra*, into English, Italian and French. More specifically, the term emerged from work on a particular scene in Sophocles' *Oedipus Tyrannus*, when Tiresias discloses to Oedipus that he is responsible for the outbreak of the plague in Thebes.[14] 'Contamina-

---

11 The actors are told very little of the translations' historical context; they have an idea of the different dramaturgies of the texts we are working on only through the director's explanation of the theatrical exercises they will be asked to perform during the workshop.
12 The dictionaries included in the *DLD* database related to antiquity feature the literary meaning of *contamino* as the merging of different sources together as first, before that of 'polluting'.
13 For a general introduction on the adaptation techniques employed in the poetic transposition of ancient Greek works into Latin literature in antiquity, see, amongst others, Traina 1970; on the translation of Greek drama into Latin by Plautus and Terence more specifically and the use of the term *contaminatio*, see, amongst others, Maurice 2013. On the modern use of the term 'contamination' for the process entailing the production of a translation for the stage, see, for example, Mark O'Thomas 2014, where he describes his own experience of translating a play by the Brazilian playwright Samir Yazbek for the National Theatre in 2012 as a complex process of contamination involving different kinds of contaminated bodies: the source text, the drafts of the translation, and the performers.
14 This workshop was co-directed by Giovanna Di Martino and Estelle Baudou and was presented in a joint paper at the conference titled *Translating Ancient Greek Drama in Europe*

tion' was therefore first suggested by the context of the plague, but was also heavily tied to the very context in which we were then working. The COVID-19 global pandemic strongly impacted our practice as we had to wear masks and socially distance ourselves in the rehearsal room.

We have since then been using 'contamination' as a tool to direct theatrical exercises and it has proved extremely useful in exploring the relationship between characters in different translations: How do one character's feelings, words, and reactions contaminate other characters and vice versa? And how does this contamination translate across the various scenes? It also provides us with a tool to investigate how contamination occurs between translations on the page and their embodiment on the stage: how the movements on stage are contaminated and influenced by the words in the texts and vice versa. Indeed, 'contamination' has become paradigmatic of the translating process that occurs between the hypo- and hypertexts and between the hypertexts themselves, but also the translating process that occurs between the page and the stage.

This chapter aims to combine the meanings that the term 'contamination' subsumed in our practice-research methodology with its theorisation in Jacques Derrida's works.[15] The first instance in which 'contamination' proves useful is in deconstructing the idea of the 'origin': by presupposing an *a priori* contamination inscribed within any utterance, Derrida replaces the idea of the 'origin' with an '*a priori* synthesis'. In his words, there exists 'an originary complication of the origin, of an initial contamination of the simple'.[16] The application of this statement to translation is of paramount importance. Not only is translation, as a product, a 'contaminated' hypertext; 'translation' and 'translating' also uncover the fragmentary and originary contaminated nature of the 'original' itself, which is revealed in its openness to multiple interpretations. Indeed, if only by dint of having been handed down for centuries, all classical literary texts can be seen as contaminated, a consideration that is especially true of *Iphigenia at Aulis*, which, in Susanna Philippo's words, is a text that is commonly understood

---

1600–1750, organised by Giovanna Di Martino, Cécile Dudouyt and Malika Bastin-Hammou in October 2020. The videos of the workshop are available here: https://www.youtube.com/watch?v=aGHh_MGNc-g. Participants in this workshop were: Claire Barnes, Fanny Bloc, Annaïg Briand, Simon D'Aquino, Cécile Dudouyt, Faye Lord, and Chris Mawson.
15 See Derrida 2003 and 2007 in particular.
16 Derrida 2003, xv.

to have undergone various degrees of 're-writing and editing (and possibly completion) by subsequent playwrights in antiquity'.[17]

But contamination, in Derridian terms, is also useful to deflect any exercise in mere *Quellenforschungen* ('source spotting') when conducting a comparative analysis of translations of the same play. Contamination, Derrida argues, surfaces as a 'necessity' rather than necessarily as the result of 'contact': the necessity is 'of tying together interruptions as such, in the very seriality of traces and the insistence of the ruptures'.[18] Indeed, it is in knotting the inevitable interruptions of any discourse (textual or non-textual), which has inherently been inhabited by others since its very inception, that creativity itself becomes possible: namely, the tying of these interruptions into new knots. These points of 'contact' before any actual contact are not clearly lodged in continuous lines, along which one can pinpoint archetypes and variants; rather, these are 'knots' on multiple threads, 'cut' and 'retie[d]', which simultaneously unveil the interrupted or contaminated nature of the 'original' itself, and also embody the creative response to the supposed 'original'.[19] Herein lies the affirmative nature of contamination, its creative and originally contaminated and contaminating potential.

The theoretical implications of this way of reading contamination in the translation process are multiple. On the one hand, the image of 'knots' on several threads directs focus onto the non-linearity of translation as a process and privileges the translation's cluster of contextual relations, which may have prompted it in the first place, either directly or indirectly. In this sense, similar features in the translations, whose authors may or may not have come in contact with one another, can be productively read as 'cultural symptoms'[20] of shared ways of understanding and/or (re)creating theatre, tragedy, and translation, despite regional and national differences. On the other hand, the act or process of contamination affords translation the possibility of existing as the (independently dependent) creative response to the (contaminated) original, as a new (textual) body, which, though anchored in its sources, takes on a life of its own.

---

17 Philippo 2013, 383 and fn. 12. Contamination was also employed specifically for works revolving around Euripides' play and the myth more generally in Jean-Michel Gliksohn's pioneering work on the reception of the myth from antiquity onwards (cf. Gliksohn 1985, 58ff.).
18 Derrida 2007, 167.
19 Derrida 2007, 166–167.
20 Cf. Panofsky 1955, 39.

The first interesting instance of contamination in a study on Euripides' *Iphigenia at Aulis* centres on the sudden proliferation of translations of the play in the 16th century. Erasmus's Latin version famously lit the fuse with its 22 editions between 1506 and 1546 in some of the most important printing centres of early modern Europe (Strasbourg, Lyon, Paris, Venice, Parma, Florence, Antwerp, Hertogenbosch, Basel, Cologne, Erfurt, and Vienna).[21] It not only represented the major reference point for subsequent translators of the same play; it also functioned as a model for early modern translators of Greek tragedy *tout court*.[22] By the middle of the century the Erasmian torch had already shared its light with many others.[23]

Over a little more than a decade (1545–1557), there emerged four vernacular translations: in France, the scholar and translator Jacques Amyot produced a translation of the play between 1545 and 1547[24] and the literary theorist and translator Thomas Sébillet published his *L'Iphigène* in 1549; in Italy, the scholar and tragedian Lodovico Dolce issued and performed his own *Ifigenia* in 1551;[25] and in England, a very young Jane Fitzalan, Lady Lumley, the daughter of the Earl of Arundel, Henry VIII's godson, composed the first translation of an ancient Greek play into English in the mid-1550s (ca. 1557), which was probably read, and possibly performed, before a private and selected audience, amongst whom may have figured Queen Elizabeth.[26]

The ancient play also variously contaminated similar Biblical tales and vice versa: the story of Iphigenia and Agamemnon mapped onto those of Abraham and Isaac, Jephtha and his daughter, God and Christ.[27] In his survey of early modern readings of Euripides' play, Robert Miola helpfully charts the commentaries and translations of the play; and a number of new tragedies further testifies to the prolific cross-pollination between these different stories. John Christopherson's *Jephthah* (ca. 1544) is an interesting case of contamination, with the Eng-

---

21 See appendix two in Pollard 2017, 242.
22 For further discussion, see Dedieu in this volume.
23 Pollard 2017, 260 mentions five translations into the vernacular in appendix three, to which one should add Giovanni Battista Capponi's *Ifigenia in Aulide*, quoted in Argelati 1766–1767.
24 Cf. Miola 2020, 15.
25 On the performance history of Dolce's *Ifigenia*, see Clerc 2016, 224.
26 Cf. Vedelago in this volume, fn. 58.
27 See, e.g., Gliksohn 1985, 62–30 and 54–60; Philippo 2013, 394; Pollard 2017, 49–60; Miola 2020, especially 9–15.

lish tragedy being written in ancient Greek and drawing on the ancient Greek tragedy, as is George Buchanan's Latin tragedy *Jephthes, Siue Votum* (1554).[28]

But its potentially Christian traits fused with another aspect of the play's appeal to an early modern audience: the interplay between religion, politics and power, whether domestic, royal, courtly, or of the church(es). In 1554, between the adjustments to the newly self-proclaimed Church of England and Mary I's return of the kingdom to Catholicism, there befell the execution (or sacrifice?) of a very young Lady Jane Grey, Mary I's protestant cousin and rival to the throne, a historical fact that may well have functioned as inspiration for Jane Lumley's translation of Euripides' play.[29]

In the same period, the Counter-Reformation movement responded to what had begun with Martin Luther in the first decades of the century with a series of measures, such as the Council of Trent (1545–1563) — at the end of which, incidentally, the church imprimatur extended to tragedies themselves —[30] and the creation of a *chambre ardente* by Henry II to prosecute heretics in the Parliament of Paris (1547–1550). There were various cultural, religious, and political conflicts, particularly those against the rising power of the Ottoman empire. The newly-crowned Holy Roman Emperor Charles V's crusades into Tunis (1535) and Algiers (1541), as has been suggested,[31] may lie behind the politically pregnant words of Dolce's priestly Calchas. Agamemnon's declaration of his natural filial love for his country and 'religion', Calchas argues, will prevent 'impious' and 'evil soldiers' from 'destroy[ing]' the Greeks' 'holy cities', 'beautiful palaces' and 'golden temples', and 'preying on' their 'kids' and 'wives'.[32] In perpetrating the sacrifice of his own daughter, Agamemnon would plead loyalty and subservience to 'religion' first and foremost: after all, no 'Kingdom would ever last long' without it, Dolce's Calchas concludes.[33]

---

28 Apparently Hans Sachs wrote a *Mordopffer der göttin Diane, mit der jungkfraw Ephigenie* ('Death sacrifice to the goddess Diana, with the virgin Iphigenia') which was mounted in 1555 in Nuremberg, on which cf. Gamel 2015, 18 and Miola 2020, 15; we could not track down the production's script and thus the relationship between this play and the ancient source is unknown to us.
29 Cf. Vedelago in this volume.
30 Cf. Clerc 2016, 222.
31 Giazzon 2012, 70, fn. 18.
32 Cf. '[…] i vostri alti nemici / Verriano in Grecia con armata mano / Distruggendo le nostre alme cittadi, / I bei palagi, et i dorati Tempi: / Et i nostri figliuoli, e le mogliere / O de la scelerata audacia preda / Diverrian dei soldati empi e malvagi; / O che del sangue lor vermiglie e brutte / Del barbarico stuol sarian le spade; / Cosa, che solo a imaginarla io tremo' (Dolce 1597, 10).
33 Cf. 'Perché vincendo il naturale affetto, / Vincete più che se vittoria havendo / Sopra i nemici, vi vedesse il mondo / Mille palme acquistar, mille trofei. / Apresso vi mostrate pari-

But religion, politics and power also intersected with another important sphere of early modern society: family, especially when royal, and its space within, and overlap with, the public domain. The ancient play is open to multiple and contrasting readings of how its main characters juggle family and politics, public and private. Agamemnon can shift from a Machiavellian, double-sided and ruthless ruler to a conflicted father and husband,[34] whilst Clytemnestra can change from able and rhetorically pungent judicial orator to compliant and supplicating mother and wife. Iphigenia is a dramaturgically pivotal character in unveiling the reasons behind Clytemnestra's and Agamemnon's words and actions and the relationship between such words and actions, one of the main themes running through the play (cf., above all, *IA* 1115). Her presence on stage regulates her parents' physical and conceptual operating space, whilst the chorus carefully constructs, limits and enables her own power as a character.

The scenes chosen for the workshops capture the complex relocation of the ancient play's interplay between religion, power and politics inside early modern royal families and societal roles. The first scene from the fourth episode of the tragedy (*IA* 1098–1208) retraces Clytemnestra's final confrontation with Agamemnon over his intention to kill Iphigenia after she has uncovered the truth; the second scene coincides with the last stasimon (*IA* 1510–1531) and retraces the chorus' words after Iphigenia's heroic resolution to engage in self-sacrifice.

Lines 1098–1208 function as a pivot point in the plotline; Clytemnestra finally confronts Agamemnon with the truth and fully unveils the underlying thematic threads on which the play has been hinging since the very beginning — the ethics of Agamemnon's choice. The tragedy is obsessed with finding a definition for what it means to be a 'good man' and whether a ruler can be one.[35] It is precisely on this point that Clytemnestra confronts her husband; and it is her way of questioning Agamemnon — or rather, her way of wielding power as she does so — that we have explored in the different dramaturgies of this scene in the three translations.

---

mente / A la religion servo et amico, / Senza la qual non si ritrova Regno, / Che durar possa lungamente in piede' (Dolce 1597, 9–10).

34 On the presence and influence of Machiavelli in Dolce's reading of the ancient play, see Giazzon 2012.

35 If Agamemnon's slave is by his own admission a 'good man' (ἄνδρ'ἀγαθὸν, 45), one whose life 'without risk, name or glory' (ἀκίνδυνον / βίον ἐξεπέρασ'ἀγνὼς ἀκλεής, 18–19), the king himself envies, Agamemnon, on the other hand, is prevented from becoming one: a man of 'noble birth' (τῷ γενναίῳ, 446) is not afforded the luxury of being open and truthful to one's own emotions, he suggests, but pretence and acceptance are key to rulership.

2 Clytemnestra, Agamemnon, and Iphigenia: *IA* 1098–1208

In the first workshop (28th–29th November 2019), we worked on Sébillet's and Lumley's translations and explored the uses of power, space, chorus, and Iphigenia's character therein. Informed by performance practice,[36] the questions we set out to investigate revolved around who was dominating the scene and when; whether it was felt that the characters were in a private or a public space; who the chorus were supporting and why; and how Iphigenia was informing the situation on the stage. As a way into answering these questions, we asked each participant in the workshop to identify individually a few words or an entire line in both translations that located a point of no return[37] for the characters in the scene. They were then asked to associate a bodily movement with that line and rehearse that movement in the room at the same time as everyone else. All participants chose the moment when Clytemnestra confronts Agamemnon about his intention to kill his daughter in both translations as they felt this represented the major shift for all of the characters in the scene:

> Clytemnestre: Donq, tu'réz-vous vottre filhe et la mienne?[38]
> (Sébillet 1549, 53)

> Clit. I heare saie that you goo aboute to sleye your owne childe.
> (Lumley 1557, 86)[39]

> Κλ. τὴν παῖδα τὴν σὴν, τήν τ'ἐμὴν μέλλεις κτανεῖν;[40]   1131

---

36 Drama is traditionally analysed in terms of conflict. Many acting theories and practices revolve around determining a character's objective within this conflict. Our dramaturgical practice is mainly informed by Michael Chekhov's techniques (cf. Chekhov 2002): we identify each character's 'main desire' and match 'psychological gestures' with it; we create and navigate 'atmospheres' and eventually determine where and when these 'atmospheres' shift.

37 The concept of 'point of no return' is a dramaturgical interpretation of Chekhov's notion of 'climax'. It refers to the main shift in a dramatic text, when the conflict starts moving towards the ending situation.

38 'So, will you kill your daughter and mine?'. Henceforth all translations from the French are by Estelle Baudou, and those from the Italian by Giovanna Di Martino.

39 Henceforth page numbers refer to the manuscript copy of Lumley's translation held at the British Library (ms Royal 15 A. IX. Holograph, folls 63–97).

40 Henceforth the Greek text is from the 1503 edition of Euripides' plays; page numbers are from the example held at the National Library of Florence and available at www.archive.org

The French Clytemnestra's pause ('donc'; 'so') and careful phrasing, with 'fille' ('daughter') between 'votre' ('yours') and 'mienne' ('mine'), contrast with Lumley's less confident queen, who softens the tremendous power of the question by introducing it as hearsay ('I heare saie').

These subtle differences emerged quite prominently in the two distinct sets of bodily movements designed for each translation. The francophone actors in charge of Sébillet's version resorted to clear-cut defence or attack gestures: Agamemnon's movement (Fanny Bloc) consisted of stepping towards Clytemnestra whilst inflating his chest, whereas Clytemnestra's (Annaïg Briand) turned her head away from Agamemnon, with her hand outstretched in his direction as though to stop him. The anglophone actors in charge of Lumley's version, on the other hand, designed movements that expressed painful incommunicability: Clytemnestra (Marchella Ward) hesitatingly stepped towards Agamemnon with her back bent, whereas Agamemnon (Marcus Bell) beat his chest and turned his seemingly unengaged gaze downwards. Once these movements had been perfected, we did two run-throughs of both versions where the other actors posing as chorus members were asked to respond to Agamemnon's and Clytemnestra's movements, physically and collectively. In the French version, the chorus ended up on the periphery of the rehearsal space, watching and following the power dynamics between Agamemnon and Clytemnestra by moving around them in a circular and fluid way; in the English version, instead, they were standing behind Clytemnestra, moving in fits and starts.

As it emerged from our bodily exploration of the language employed and the power dynamics between the characters on stage in the different versions, Sébillet's text was discovered to act 'circularly', built around Clytemnestra's political arguments. The actors felt as if they were in a public space, at whose centre stood Iphigenia, with the chorus members following the debate from the peripheries of this space and moving around the characters circumspectly. Lumley's text, on the other hand, seemed particularly stable and straightforward, with Agamemnon and Clytemnestra facing each other, whilst Iphigenia and the chorus stood behind Clytemnestra. The actors had formed an ideal line that cut across the stage horizontally and were tiptoeing around that line as if they had confined their bodies within an intimate, small and private space.

The first conclusion we were able to draw at the end of the workshop was that the French translation performed the spectacle of power, the scene's turning point clearly relying on Iphigenia's dramatic entrance, orchestrated by Cly-

---

(last accessed 01/09/22). The line-numbering employed throughout, however, agrees with Diggle 1994. The page number indicated for line 1131 is 228.

temnestra. In the English translation, on the other hand, the confrontation was treated as a family crisis: the accusation was directly addressed by the wife to the husband, and Iphigenia, as a child, had no part in her parent's fight, though her silent suffering was at the centre of the argument.

Some of these initial considerations are indeed reflected in the language employed in both translations throughout the scene. Sébillet's Clytemnestra has been throwing rhetorical shafts at her rival since the scene's inception, as if they were in a courtroom. Her manipulative skills are on display from the beginning, when, rather than the vague formulation of the Greek text about Agamemnon's impious plan being uncovered (1104–1105), Clytemnestra utters that Agamemnon:

> [...] ne se doutte pas
> d'éttre de moy comme il sera surpris
> villainement, en ce meurtre entrepris
> cruéllement par luy, contre raison,
> contra sa filhe, et moy, et sa maison.[41]
>
> (Sébillet 1549, 52)

> [...] ὃς ἐπὶ τοῖς αὑτοῦ τέκνοις
> ἀνόσια πράσσων αὐτίχ' εὑρεθήσεται.[42]   1105

She announces to the audience the leading role that she will assume ('de moi'; 'by myself') in the unmasking of her husband's plan, whose main target is emphatically translated into four phrases, the first being 'reason' ('raison'). To commit filicide is first and foremost an act against reason; i.e., against what society understands to be reasonable, acceptable, within reason's boundaries.

The contrast between Sébillet's and Lumley's Clytemnestras is patent in the translation of lines 1115–1116, a few lines after the above-mentioned passage; it is a pivotal turning point in the scene. Not only do these lines prompt Iphigenia's entrance onto the stage; they also capture the issue at the heart of this tragedy: the essential dichotomy between 'words' and 'actions' that affects almost every character in the play. The concise and contrite words of Lumley's Clytemnestra leading up to her final question regarding Agamemnon's plan are in stark contrast with those spoken by Sébillet's queen, a contorted phrasing

---

41 '[Agamemnon] does not suspect / That he will be revealed – by me – / In his villany, planning this murder, / In his cruelty, against reason, / Against his daughter, and me, and his house'.
42 Manuzio 1503, 227.

which seems more preoccupied with constructing an irrefutable argument than with retrieving the truth:

> You haue spoken well, thoughe in dede your doings do not agre with your words.
> (Lumley 1557, 86)

> Vous dittes bien, et d'assez bonne sorte,
> en tant au moins que vottre langue porte:
> mais si ie voeil voz méchans fais deduire,
> le seray fort empéchée a bien dire.[43]
> (Sébillet 1549, 53)

> Κλ. τοῖς ὀνόμασιν μὲν εὖ λέγεις· τὰ δ' ἔργα σου   1115
> οὐκ οἶδ' ὅπως χρή μ'ὀνομάσασαν εὖ λέγειν.[44]

Clytemnestra's reproach to Agamemnon's deceiving words in Sébillet's text is itself proof of how speech can be puzzling and manipulative when it employs a series of conditional clauses and convoluted phrasing.

To Lumley's more demure mother corresponds a distant Agamemnon, who replies to Clytemnestra's pressing nudges to tell the truth with imperative and impersonal phrases such as 'you ought to'[45] or 'it is not lawfull'.[46] Agamemnon

---

[43] 'Your words are fine, and you say them well, / As far as your language is concerned: / But if I want to deduce your misdemeanours, / I would be completely held back from using fine words'.

[44] Manuzio 1503, 227.

[45] For line 1132 (Αγ. ἔα· / τλήμονά γ' ἔλεξας, ὑπονοεῖς θ' ἃ μή σε χρή·; Manuzio 1503, 228), Lumley translates: 'What, you haue spoken thos thinges, whiche you oughte neither to saye, nor yet to thinke', which elaborates on the 'things' (ἃ) that Clytemnestra is suspecting (ὑπονεῖς); not only is she suspecting things she ought not to, as in the Greek: she should restrain herself from even thinking them. Erasmus here, whose translation seems to have played an important role in Lumley's translating process, translates χρή with *decet* (*AG. Hem, Misera elocutas es, quaeque neutiquam decet / Te suspieari, suspicaris improba*; Erasmus 1969b, 334).

[46] For line 1134 (Αγ. σὺ δ' ἤν γ' ἐρωτᾷς εἰκότ', εἰκότα κλύοις·; Manuzio 1503, 228), rather than reproducing Agamemnon's attempt to step out of the conversation by positing her words as unreasonable, Lumley has Agamemnon repeat his seemingly unchangeable veto over Clytemnestra's inquiry altogether: 'It is not lawfull for me to answer you to those thinges, which you oughte not to knowe'. Erasmus has *decet* again here (*at tu profecto, siquidem rogaueris / quae te decet rogare, quae decet audies*; Erasmus 1969b, 334); cf. Suthren 2020, 84–91, for an analysis of Lumley's engagement with Erasmus's theory and practice of translation, as well as Vedelago in this volume.

keeps up his game until the very end: whilst both Sébillet and Dolce corroborate his feelings of loss, defeat and misery in pathetic terms,[47] Lumley's king utters:

> I am constrained to holde my peace, because I haue tolde you so manifest a lye that I cannot denie it.
>
> (Lumley 1557, 87)

> Αγ. ἰδοὺ σιωπῶ· τὸ γὰρ ἀναίσχυντον με δεῖ
> ψευδῆ λέγοντα προσλαβεῖν τῇ συμφορᾷ.   1145

Whereas Euripides' Agamemnon admits that there is 'no need to tell more lies' or to 'add shameless to [his] misery', Lumley's Agamemnon calmly but helplessly realises that his lie is no longer sustainable within the bounds of reason.

The second workshop (21st May 2021) featured Dolce's translation in addition to the other two. Clytemnestra's power was further explored: the guiding questions pivoted around when, how, and if Clytemnestra gained power in the scene and how that affected and shaped Agamemnon's and Iphigenia's presence and space. The actors performing Clytemnestra and Agamemnon in each version were asked to pick two lines from the same scene and create two bodily movements associated with them. The first line-movement combination described the peak of the character (i.e., the moment when the character's power in the action was strongest); the second line-movement combination described the lowest point of the character (i.e., the moment when the character was weakest and most powerless). The lines chosen did not necessarily have to be lines assigned to the character they were embodying. For some time, the actors walked around in the rehearsal space, reciting the lines they had chosen whilst designing a movement that matched with the sounds, vibrations, and meanings of the words in their bodies. After considering various solutions, they refined the two sets of movements and were asked to include them in their performance of the whole scene whilst reciting the specific lines they had associated with them.

During the first run-through, chorus members were asked to side with Agamemnon or Clytemnestra and to adjust their movements to those of the character they had chosen to support. Each time we performed the English translation, Agamemnon (James Aldred) was isolated in corners of the room (figs. 3, 4) whilst Iphigenia (Philippa Lang) was standing in the centre, surrounded by a

---

[47] Whilst both Sébillet and Dolce translate line 1136 (Αγ. ὦ πότνια τύχη, καὶ μοῖρα, καὶ δαίμων γ' ἐμός·; Manuzio 1503, 228), where Agamemnon has realised that she knows his plan and thus revels in his misery, calling upon 'fate', Lumley cuts it altogether (cf. Lumley 1557, 87).

sympathetic chorus. As for Clytemnestra (Guia Mauri), during the first part of the sequence she occupied the whole space, standing sometimes close to Agamemnon, suggesting the same intimacy as in the first workshop, and sometimes hugging Iphigenia or circulating between the chorus members. During the second part of the dialogue, after the truth is disclosed, she stuck with Iphigenia, who was at this point surrounded by the chorus. The sympathy and physical proximity of the actors on stage confirmed that the English version focused on the family crisis, eclipsing the political potential of the situation.

Figs. 3 and 4: Agamemnon isolated in corners. Lumley's translation (4th episode). Iphigenia Workshop: 21/05/2021.

The exercise also highlighted the contrast between the characters. Agamemnon's peak was also Clytemnestra's lowest point; i.e., when he requested that the queen make preparations for their daughter's wedding day:

> Ag. [...] I have prepared all thinge redie for the sacrifice.
> (Lumley 1557, 86)

> ὡς χέρνιβες πάρεισιν εὐτρεπισμέναι,   1111
> προχύται τε βάλλειν πῦρ καθάρειον ἐκ χερῶν,
> μόχοιτε, πρὸ γάμων ἃς θεᾷ πεσεῖν χρεών [...][48]

The gesture associated with this line was a very open posture for Agamemnon (James Aldred), who was looking up, raising his arms above his head, and turning his palms towards the ceiling (fig. 5). His body language bespoke his intention to control the situation and his need to connect with the gods to do so.

Fig. 5: Agamemnon's peak point. Lumley's translation (4th episode). Iphigenia Workshop: 21/05/2021.

---

48 Manuzio 1503, 227.

In contrast, Clytemnestra (Guia Mauri) responded with a movement of protection, bending her shoulders and looking down, showing that, at that moment, she is powerless. Clytemnestra's peak then coincided with her first insinuation of falsehood in Agamemnon's words: 'You haue spoken well' (τοῖς ὀνόμασιν μὲν εὖ λέγεις; 1115). We found that this was the very first moment in which she felt like she was in control, because she knew more than he did. Her body language confirmed her power; the gesture associated with her peak was a movement of repulsion towards Agamemnon: a kick or a blow (fig. 6).[49] Agamemnon's lowest point was instead the translation 'so manifest a lye' (ψευδῆ; 1145), right after his lie had been discovered. The gesture associated with this line was a bending movement that, in some versions of the movement, ended in a fall on the floor.

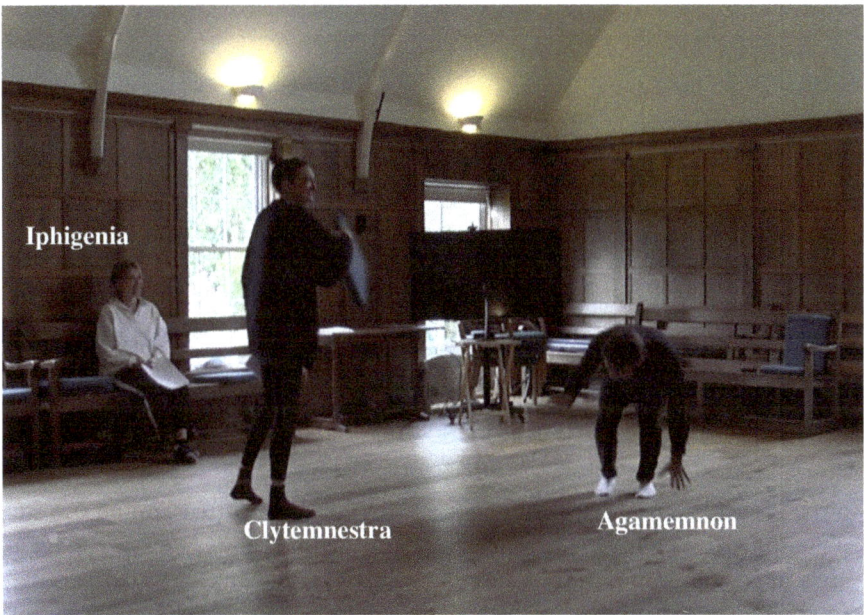

Fig. 6: Clytemnestra's peak point. Lumley's translation (4th episode). Iphigenia Workshop: 21/05/2021.

---

49 The movement the actors had to design and match with a line from the text underwent a number of different stages in the rehearsal process and throughout the various run-throughs of the whole scene; some actors never really settled on one single movement, but rather had a few versions which they alternated between.

Before the second run-through, we went back to the very first exercise done in the first workshop and asked Clytemnestra and Agamemnon to identify the point of no return for their character in the scene. Unsurprisingly, they both picked the announcement of Iphigenia's death: the blunt 'you goo aboute to slaye your owne childe' (1131). Emotionally speaking, the characters were in agreement about the location of the turning point in the dialogue: the dramaturgy here in fact is entirely based upon the character's individual and intimate reaction to the unbearable idea of the infanticide (fig. 7). According to the participants of both workshops, the progression of the whole scene felt chaotic, balancing between Agamemnon's helplessness and solitude and Clytemnestra's despair.

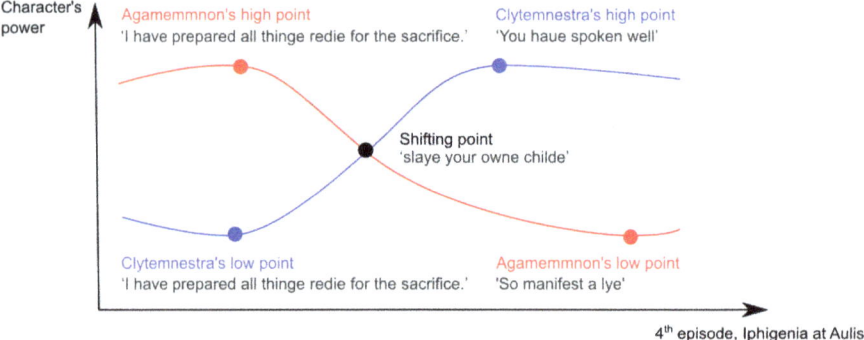

Fig. 7: Power balance between the characters. Lumley's translation (4th episode). Iphigenia Workshop: 21/05/2021.

In the French translation, the dialogue is logically structured around the confrontation between the two characters with Clytemnestra's (Estelle Baudou) direct question, 'Donq, tu'réz-vous vottre filhe et la mienne?' ('So, will you kill your daughter and mine?'), picked as the point of no return by all of the actors (fig. 8). The line chosen to describe Clytemnestra's lowest point was located in the first half of the scene, and indirectly refers to the upcoming sacrifice, which she knows is going to happen if she does not stop Agamemnon: 'Contre sa fille et moi et sa maison' ('Against his daughter and me and his house'), which elaborates on the second half of line 1104 (ἐπὶ τοῖς αὑτοῦ τέκνοις).[50] The strongly powerful combination of these three phrases in polysyndeton contrasted with

---

50 Sébillet 1549, 52; Manuzio 1503, 228.

what was chosen as Agamemnon's (James Aldred) highest point: 'Car ia l'offrande et la fouasse est prétte' ('For I have prepared the offerings and the bread is ready'),[51] loosely based on lines 1111–1113.[52] The sacrifice that Clytemnestra is referring to is patently different from, and ironically opposite to, the sacrifices that Agamemnon is hinting at here; the former concerning death and the latter celebrating a happy union.

The contrast portrayed through the actors' bodies was striking. The movement associated with Clytemnestra's lowest point consisted of a few steps backwards whilst she progressively bent her back with one hand on her belly. By contrast, Agamemnon's body language involved an overacting of the joy of the upcoming sacrifices: opening his arms and keeping his chin up, he accompanied the rhythm of his line with energetic hand movements.

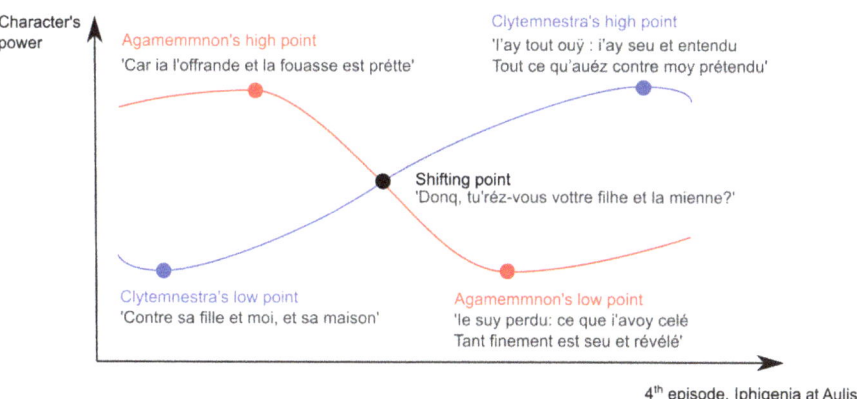

Fig. 8: Power balance between the characters. Sébillet's translation (4th episode). Iphigenia Workshop: 21/05/2021.

Indeed, Clytemnestra's words are already projected onto the future because they are based on a more complete understanding of the past, whilst Agamemnon's pronouncement seems obviously delusional, still anchored to a lie that Clytemnestra has already begun to dismantle. The portrayal of a delusional Agamemnon contrasting with a powerful Clytemnestra holding the reins of the

---

51 Sébillet 1549, 53.
52 Cf. ὡς χέρνιβες πάρεισιν εὐτρεπισμέναι, / προχύται τε βάλλειν πῦρ καθάρειον ἐκ χερῶν, / μόχοι τε, πρὸ γάμων, ἃς θεᾷ πεσεῖν χρεὼν / Ἀρτέμιδι, μέλανος αἵματος φυσήματα (Manuzio 1503, 228).

argument was further corroborated in the choice of Agamemnon's lowest and Clytemnestra's highest points:

> Agamemnon.
> Ie suy perdu, ce que i'auoy' celé
> Tant finement est seu et révélé.
> Clytemnestra
> I'ay tout ouÿ : i'ay seu et entendu
> Tout ce qu'auéz contre moy prétendu [...][53]
>
> (Sébillet 1549, 54)

> Αγ. ἀπωλόμεσθα· προδέδοται τὰ κρυπτά μου.   1140
> Κλ. πάντ'οἶδα, καὶ πεπύσμ'ἃ σὺ γε μέλλεις με δρᾶν.[54]

The surprise that accompanies the unveiling of his plan is most notable and in line with Sébillet's depiction of a delusional character: prior to Agamemnon's admission of guilt, Clytemnestra has openly demeaned his plan as most unrefined ('rien moins à fin tour ne ressemble'; 'nothing looks less like a subtle plan [than this]'); his speaking of it as a well-elaborated plan is in direct contrast with what he has just heard and with the reality he is facing. But the final blow comes from Clytemnestra's reply: her open confession about having full knowledge of the facts finally grants her sole power on stage.

At this point, Agamemnon raised his arms, joining his hands above his head, and stepped back, which contributed to expressing his helplessness. Immediately after, Clytemnestra walked towards him, whilst looking at him in the eye, and opened her arms with her palms facing him. Her posture was very open and illustrated the disclosure of the truth (fig. 9).

---

53 Agamemnon: 'I am lost, what I had concealed / Is now ingeniously known and revealed'. Clytemnestra: 'I have heard everything: I have known and understood / Everything that you have conspired against me'.
54 Manuzio 1503, 228.

Fig. 9: Agamemnon's lowest point and Clytemnestra's peak point. Sébillet's translation (4th episode). Iphigenia Workshop: 21/05/2021.

In the second and final run-through, the chorus members were asked to take part in the scene and to side with one character; unsurprisingly, they ended up on the periphery of the rehearsal space, as spectating witnesses of, perhaps even jurors at, Clytemnestra's conviction of Agamemnon through her extremely successful line of questioning (figs. 10, 11). The queen dominated the scene both verbally and physically. During the first part of the scene, until the truth is revealed, she stayed still, whereas Agamemnon moved around: her stillness highlighted that she was in control of the situation whilst he was trying to hide his lies behind his wasted energy. Her power was, then, confirmed during the second part of the scene: she stood close to the group whilst he was in a corner of the room; when she eventually walked up to him, Agamemnon fled to another corner. The use of Iphigenia's presence onstage was also notable: it was felt that Clytemnestra was using her for the sake of her own argument rather than her daughter's, which made Iphigenia's presence onstage awkwardly unnecessary. Each time we performed the scene, Iphigenia (Claire Barnes) eventually ended up close to the chorus, watching the argument unfold without being part of it in any way.

Figs. 10 and 11: Peripheral position of Iphigenia and the chorus. Sébillet's translation (4th episode). Iphigenia Workshop: 21/05/2021.

As is the case in Sébillet's translation, Clytemnestra seems to be the person in control in Dolce's version. Her main strength, however, lies less in her rhetorical strategies and more in the pathetic tone of her lines, which make careful, repeated, even mannered, use of key terms belonging to the domestic sphere: 'consorte' or 'sposo' ('husband'), 'padre' ('father'), 'madre' ('mother'), and 'figlia' ('daughter')[55] are frequently recurring terms in the speeches of both Clytemnestra and Iphigenia.

---

[55] In this scene alone: 'empio sposo' ('impious husband') is used as a translation of πόσιν at line 1098 (Dolce 1597, 33); as a long appendix to οἶσθα γὰρ πατρὸς / πάντως ἃ μέλλει γε (1117–1118; Manuzio 1503, 228), Clytemnestra insists on his duties as a father and again resorts to the repetition of key familial terms: 'Qual voi, che sete padre, ite facendo / a la figlia, a la madre, et a voi stesso?' ('What are you who are the father going about doing / to the daughter, mother,

But Dolce's Clytemnestra is aware of the fleeting power that words possess. She opens the fourth episode with the realisation that, as a woman, ('donna'), another recurring key term,[56] she has to resort to 'words' as her only weapon; this is a highly problematic statement, not least because words have been presented as potentially deceiving and manipulative since the beginning of the play:

> Ma poscia, ch'egli vien: ch'io'l veggio appresso:
> non sia, ch'io non isfoghi in qualche parte
> l'anima trista con parole, quando
> le femine a difesa altro non hanno.[57]
> (Dolce 1597, 33)

> μνήμην δ' ἄρ' εἶχον πλησίον βεβηκότος
> Ἀγαμέμνονος τοῦδ', ὃς ἐπὶ τοῖς αὑτοῦ τέκνοις
> ἀνόσια πράσσων αὐτίχ' εὑρεθήσεται.[58]   1105

Aware of the ephemeral power of words, Clytemnestra is nonetheless determined to employ speech as a means to unmask Agamemnon; it is this awareness that marks the main difference between her and Sébillet's character: whereas in the latter emotions are exploited as rhetorical weapons, in Dolce they maintain their pathetic appeal, facilitated by the co-opting presence of Iphigenia.

---

and yourself?'; Dolce 1597, 34), a triptych that resembles Sébillet's 'contre raison, contre sa fille, et moi, et sa maison'; in her confession to having full knowledge of the facts (1141 ff.), Clytemnestra makes recourse to both 'consorte' ('husband') and 'padre' ('father') to connote Agamemnon's actions as 'abominable' and 'cruel' (Dolce 1597, 34); 'padre' is repeated five times in Iphigenia's speech, which also features 'figlia' ('daughter'); as a translation of 1127–1128, Agamemnon once again is made to repeat those familial key terms: 'oime che dir vorrà? Donde procede / che la madre e la figlia, / veggio egualmente meste?' ('Oh, what will it mean? What might the reason be / that both mother and daughter / I see equally miserable?'; Dolce 1597, 34).

56 Clytemnestra identifies the term 'donne' ('women') with a category which she connotes as powerless and controlled by men; 'donna' is how Agamemnon refers to her at lines 1106 and 1108 in place of Λήδας γένεθλον ('offspring of Leida'; 1106) and τὰς γαμουμένας ('wives'; 1108); the maidens Clytemnestra orders to escort Iphigenia out onto the stage together with Orestes are 'donne gentili' ('gentle women'; Dolce 1597, 34).

57 'But here he comes: and I see him coming: / lest I shan't be able to unload / my sad soul with words in some way, when / women have nothing else to defend themselves with'.

58 Manuzio 1503, 227.

Indeed, Iphigenia's presence as a character on stage is powerfully employed in the dramaturgy of Dolce's translation. It is Clytemnestra herself who gives her the power to speak, deliberately overturning the Greek:

Ella favellerà per prima, e dapoi
Io fornirò di dir, quanto mi resta.[59]
(Dolce 1597, 34)

τὰ δ' ἄλλ' ἐγὼ πρὸ τῆσδε, κἀμαυτῆς φράσω.[60]

In place of lines 1123–1126, which in the Aldine edition of the play were assigned to Iphigenia rather than Clytemnestra,[61] an empowered Iphigenia makes the first pathetic appeal directly to Agamemnon, with 'padre' repeated five times in 19 lines. The passage elaborates on and amplifies the misfortunes (τῶν ... κακῶν; 1124) Iphigenia is suffering; it also shows Iphigenia making the first attack on Agamemnon.[62]

The different meaning of Iphigenia's presence in Dolce's dramaturgy was readily perceived in the workshop, even though the majority of the participants did not know the language. In the various run-throughs of the passage, the chorus always sided with Clytemnestra (Guia Mauri), encircling her and Iphigenia (Philippa Lang) whilst aggressively moving towards Agamemnon (Lara Korach) as one body (figs. 12, 13).

---

59 'She will speak first, and then / I will provide to say what is left'.
60 Manuzio 1503, 228.
61 Manuzio 1503, 228.
62 Sébillet's Iphigenia is given a contorted translation of these lines, which function more as an obscure side comment on the inscrutability of life matters (Sébillet 1549, 52–53); Lumley's Iphigenia very concisely retraces the Greek text and, like Sébillet, translates it into a general maxim on the unfortunate condition of humankind (Lumley 1557, 96).

Figs. 12 and 13: Chorus members siding with Clytemnestra. Dolce's translation (4th episode). Iphigenia Workshop: 21/05/2021.

Clytemnestra's and Agamemnon's lowest and highest points also revealed a slightly different interpretation of these two characters and their power dynamics in Dolce's translation. The peak point chosen for Clytemnestra was:

> V'apparecchiate voi scioglier di vita:
> di vita Ifigenia mia figlia e vostra?[63]
> (Dolce 1597, 35)

> Κλ. τὴν παῖδα τὴν σὴν, τήν τ'ἐμὴν μέλλεις κτανεῖν;   1131

Clytemnestra is at the height of her power: the translation's repetitions ('di vita') and emphatic phrasing ('mia figlia e vostra') add further weight to these already dense and powerful lines. Agamemnon's peak follows immediately after the line, 'Ah più questo non dir', which translates the exclamation in the Greek at line 1132 (ἔα). The peaks of both characters were thus linked, which emphasised the confrontational expression of their power on stage. Clytemnestra's movement consisted of stepping towards Agamemnon and pointing at him, which triggered a strong repelling movement in him.

The lowest point for Dolce's Clytemnestra was identified with what was her peak point in Sébillet's and Lumley's translations: 'e l'opra ho inteso abominosa e cruda' (1141). Confirmation of the truth of Clytemnestra's suspicions are cause for despair rather than empowerment; on stage, Clytemnestra expressed this despair by hugging Iphigenia. Agamemnon's downward path follows immediately after:

> Ecco ch'io tengo homai le labbra chiuse,
> da che s'aggiunge a la miseria mia,
> l'esser trovato ad un mendace, e crudo.[64]
> (Dolce 1597, 35)

> Αγ. ἰδοὺ σιωπῶ· τὸ γὰρ ἀναίσχυντον με δεῖ
> ψευδῆ λέγοντα προσλαβεῖν τῇ συμφορᾷ;   1145

'La miseria mia' was what Lara Korach (Agamemnon) identified as Agamemnon's lowest point: namely, the realisation that there was nothing he could do anymore, but also his appeal to an overall sympathetic evaluation of his story, already fraught with difficult decisions and inevitable tragedies, to which he

---

[63] 'Are you making preparations to loose the knot / of Iphigenia's life, my daughter and yours?'.
[64] 'Here, I shall keep my lips sealed now, / as to my misery is added / my being found mendacious, and cruel'.

added that of lying. Accompanying Agamemnon's line was a large circular arm movement from above his head towards the floor, ending in a fold of his whole body to express his helplessness. The characters' journeys were quite similar in the end: whilst both were at their peak at the beginning of the scene, by the end they shared the despair of losing their daughter (fig. 14). Although there was no clear shifting point in terms of balance of power in this version, it was felt that Clytemnestra's low point confirmed the dramaturgical importance of her disclosing the truth in the scene.

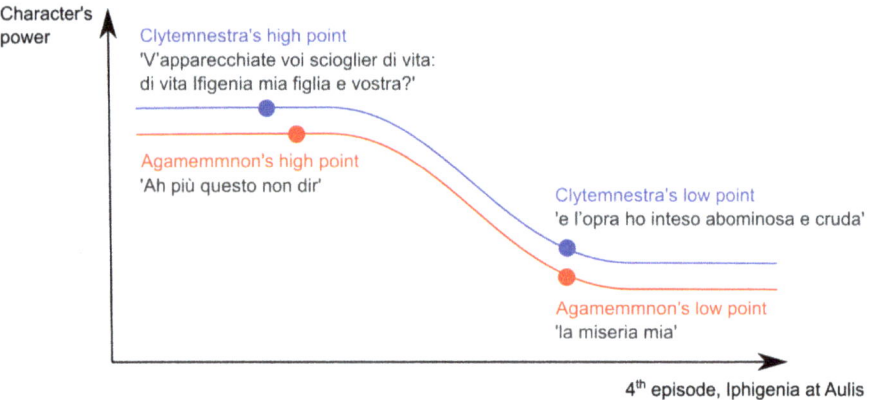

Fig. 14: Power balance between the characters. Dolce's translation (4th episode). Iphigenia Workshop: 21/05/2021.

In a way, Dolce presents a more subtly complicated set of characters: both Clytemnestra and Agamemnon seem emotionally drained and powerless at the end; even Iphigenia, despite her being fully part of the scene, is incapable of making a change for herself or anyone else. It may also be worth mentioning that Dolce's play ends with Iphigenia's sacrifice: the swap with a hind is related as an impossible alternative told to soothe those who did not watch; it is not to be trusted more than the eyewitness testimony of the messenger by the end of the tragedy.[65]

---

[65] Cf. Dolce 1597, 51.

3 Choruses and Chorality: *IA* 1510–1331

In both workshops, the chorus played a huge role in the construction of the scenes taken into account. In fact, we began both times with chorus-building exercises as a way of entering the story itself. In the first workshop, we were trying to construct a multilingual chorus that could incorporate the various dramaturgies of the translations whilst maintaining the different languages. In the second workshop, instead, we began by exploring the multiple possible dramaturgies of the chorus in the original first, before investigating their 'translation' into each text. The exercises designed to question the identity, power, and sympathy of the chorus provided us with an array of possible answers that helpfully guided us through our journey into each translation.

We started the second workshop with a preliminary exercise intended to construct the collective identity of the chorus as well as to build the scenery of the action. In *Iphigenia at Aulis*, chorus members are women from the city of Chalcis coming to the beach at Aulis to see the ships and the Greek soldiers. Whilst walking around the room, Baudou, who was directing the exercise, asked the actors to imagine that they were watching a series of scenes: soldiers training on the beach, ships anchored on the shore, Agamemnon taking notes, and a path leading to Aulis. They could individually decide where each scene was set in the room. Thus, though they were in the same situation and 'watching' the same landscape, each of them had their own representation of it. Baudou then asked them to react to each of the scenes they mentioned for the second time with a bodily movement. Everyone did something different; for example, whilst they were being asked to 'watch' the soldiers' training, some reactions were enthusiastic (light walking, generous waving), and others were more doubtful (standing still, hiding their eyes). In this exercise, the actors appeared as a community, experiencing the same situation and sharing a collective space, but because pictures and reactions were individually imagined and performed by each actor differently, the multiplicity of points of view was embedded in the experience of communality.

It was our experience of this multiplicity of points of view built into the dramaturgy of the tragic chorus that was particularly useful for approaching the very different ways in which each translator interpreted the chorus in the last stasimon of Euripides' tragedy (1510–1531). The choice of this choral ode over others was dictated by its strategic place at a pivotal point in the play, right after Iphigenia's last exit, and thus reacting to her voluntary self-sacrifice. The text's supposed inauthenticity made it even more interesting to us as it multiplied the chance of further contamination and dramaturgical possibilities.[66]

The French and the English versions were the texts we worked on the most as the Italian translation replaced the choral ode with a philosophical reflection on the inexorability of fate, which served the play's structure rather well given that Dolce's ending is much darker than Euripides'. Yet, even though Sébillet and Lumley followed the Greek text more closely, we soon realised how patently different their interpretations were.

We designed an exercise to explore the relationship between the chorus and Iphigenia. Everyone was part of the chorus apart from the actors interpreting Iphigenia (Philippa Lang in the English version and Claire Barnes in the French version) and the actor in charge of the text (James Aldred in both versions). Iphigenia had to leave the room whenever she felt it was the right moment, and chorus members were asked to respond physically to her departure, following each other's movements in order to build a collective body.

In the French version, although pitying the heroine throughout the ode with expressions such as 'pauure Vierge' ('poor virgin'), or 'la pauure' ('the poor [girl]'), the chorus function as a distant spectator describing the cruel realpolitik of the circumstances of her sacrifice:

> Hélas la pauure Vierge
> N'ira iamais en Arge.
> Regardéz-la aller,
> Las, elle va a Troie,
> Mettre la ville en proye,
> Faire téstes volér,
> Faire maisons brulér.
> Elle s'en va ornée,
> Et de fleurs couronnée'
> Comme allant épouser:
> Mais, o piteuse féste,
> La pauure va sa teste
> Dessus l'autel poser:
> Et de sand l'arroser.
> Sur la motte où se deesse
> L'autel de la dresse
> On la décollera :
> Lés fontaines sacrées
> Rougiront colorées
> Du sang qui coulera,

---

[66] For a general discussion of the ode's inauthenticity, see Collard/Morwood 2017, 621 ff.

Quant elle tombera.
Va, Pucelle constante
Satisfaire a l'attente
Dés Grés, tés citoiens :
Ta mort prompte ilz demandent,
Car par elle ilz s'attendent
D'aller voir lés Troyens,
Et n'hont autres moiens.[67]

(Sébillet 1549, 71)

The chorus confirm to their audience that Iphigenia will never make it back to Argos; the only action they suggest the audience can perform is to 'watch, spectate' ('regardéz'), as they are doing. Though by the end of the stasimon the chorus will speak of the 'victory' and the 'glory that will never die' ('victoire'; 'la gloire / qui jamais ne mourra'; Sébillet 1549, 72), which Iphigenia's sacrifice will make possible (cf. Eur. *IA* 1528–1531),[68] in the foreground there appear the horrors of warfare — 'hunt[ing] the city down' ('Mettre la ville en proye'), 'mak[ing] heads fly' ('téstes volér') and 'houses burn' ('maison brulér') — and the sacrifice of an innocent virgin.

Indeed, the description of Iphigenia's being 'crowned with flowers' (ἐπὶ κάρα στέφῃ, 1512)[69] as if she was going to 'get married' soon turns into the awful carnage the chorus know is going to happen: the oxymoron 'piteuse féste' ('piteous feast') well captures the contrast between the crude necessity of Iphigenia's sacrifice and the positive end result it is hoped it will bring about. In the following 11 lines, Sébillet elaborates on lines 1514–1516 of the Greek, where the chorus prefigure the heroine's slaughter by the goddess's altar, her neck being rescinded.[70] Sébillet fills the scene with horrific colours and pathetic tones, hinging the chorus' prefiguration of the heroine's death on the contrasting

---

[67] 'Alas poor Virgin / She will never go to Argos. / Look at her as she goes, / Alas, she is going to Troy, / Hunt the city down, / Make heads fly, / And houses burn. / Here she goes adorned, / And crowned with flowers / Like a bride: / But, o piteous feast, / The poor girl will her head / On the altar lay: / And pour it over with her blood. / On the mound where stands / The altar of the goddess / She will be beheaded: / The sacred springs / Will redden / With her flowing blood, / When she falls. / Go, steady Maiden / Satisfy the demands / Of the Greeks, your fellow citizens: / Your speedy death they require, / Because with it they expect / To go to see the Trojans, / Having no other way'.
[68] Cf. Ἀγαμέμνονά τε λόγχαις / Ἑλλάδι κλεινότατον στέφανον / δὸς ἀμφὶ κάρα τεὸν / κλέος ἀείμνηστον ἀμφιθεῖναι (Manuzio 1503, 235).
[69] Manuzio 1503, 235.
[70] Cf. Manuzio 1503, 235: βωμόν γε δαίμονος θεᾶς, / ῥανίσιν αἱματορρύτοις / θανοῦσαν, εὐφυῆ τε σώματος / δέρην σφαγεῖσαν.

tones between Iphigenia's necessary death and the cruelty of it. Though fully comprehending the atrocity of the sacrifice, the chorus are aware of its inevitability and thus spur Iphigenia on ('Va Pucelle constante'; 'Go, steady Maiden); she is performing her duty towards the 'Greek citizens', which they demand and wait for as their only way forward.

In the second workshop, Sébillet's chorus was felt to be direct and imperative. Claire Barnes (Iphigenia) spontaneously took the line 'Va, Pucelle constante' as a cue to leave the room. Chorus members stood still as a collective and sat behind the reader after her departure, thus expressing helplessness as well as detachment (fig. 15). According to the participants, it was the darkest version of the stasimon: one of the chorus members, James Aldred, said that it was awful to send Iphigenia to such a cruel death, knowingly and following a directive. Rather than 'feeling with' Iphigenia, the chorus were separating themselves from Iphigenia's body on stage whilst sending her off from a distance.

Fig. 15: Chorus members after Iphigenia's departure. Sébillet's translation (last stasimon). Iphigenia Workshop: 21/05/2021.

Lumley's chorus, on the other hand, seems much more sympathetic to, and emotionally invested in, Iphigenia's sacrifice. Heavily distancing her translation from Erasmums's rendering of this passage, whose translation is otherwise lurking behind some of Lumley's choices, she writes a choral ode that leaves little to no space for the horrific details of the sacrifice, which are translated in highly pathetic terms:

> Beholde yonder goethe the uirgine to be sacraficed withe a grete companye of souldiers after hir, whos bewtifull face and faire bodi anone shalbe defiled withe hir owne blode. Yet happie arte thou, O Iphigeneya, that withe thy deathe, thou shalte purchase unto the grecians a quiet passage, whiche I pray god may not only happen fortunatelie unto them, but also that they may returne [1325] againe prosperousely withe a glorious uictorie.
>
> (Lumley 1557, 95)

The interesting addition in this rendering is the 'grete companye of souldiers', which Lumley might have derived from Erasmums's *serta gestat frondea / iniecta militum manu* (2173–2174),[71] and which furthers the pathetic tone of the passage. The juxtaposition between the first sentence describing the sacrifice and the second one introducing the positive outcome is rather jarring, particularly so as the chorus diminish the glory deriving from it. And, in fact, in the scene where Iphigenia seals her final decision to self-sacrifice (1466–1499), part of which is repeated in the last stasimon,[72] Lumley uses the same formulation for the happy outcome, which loosely translates lines 1472–1473:

> [...] for withe my deathe I shall purchase unto them a glorious uictorie.
>
> (Lumley 1557, 95)

> [...] ὡς σωτηρίαν
> Ἕλλησι δώσουσ'ἔρχομαι νικηφόρον.[73]

Yet, in retracing Iphigenia's words, the chorus have now replaced that 'glorious uictorie' with 'quiet passage', an expression that stands as a translation of ἐπ' εὐτυχεῖ πότμῳ and strongly downplays (if not ridicules) its meaning (1523); as a loose translation of κλέος (1531), that 'glorious uictorie' has been moved to the end of the ode, now visually away from the immediate outcome of Iphigenia's death.

---

71 Erasmus 1969b, 353.
72 Cf. Collard/Morwood 2017, 621.
73 Manuzio 1503, 234.

The irony underlying this passage might be confirmed by the fact that the very same expression ('thoughe in dede I throughe my deathe shall purchase the grecians a glorious uictorie'; Lumley 1557, 90) was first employed by Iphigenia sarcastically during her lengthy outburst against Agamemnon's final decision to send her off as a sacrifice for Greece (*IA* 1279–1335).[74] The expression is added because the Greek does not suggest anything of the kind. It thus seems ironic that Iphigenia utters the same words, both when outraged at Agamemnon's order and once she has decided to sacrifice herself, leaving some space to think that Lumley's Iphigenia, or Lumley herself, is perhaps far from convinced of the goodness, or effectiveness, of the sacrifice.

On the stage, during the first run-through of Lumley's ode, Philippa Lang (Iphigenia) hesitated, looked around and exited only after the end of the text. Indeed, there is no cue in the text for Iphigenia to leave the room. The chorus members first stood in a semi-circle behind her holding out their hands as if they were about to cuddle her (fig. 16) and in the end they walked her to the exit, as if they were deploring her death and at the same time making it happen. In other words, the chorus acted in full empathy with her whilst acknowledging the inevitability of her death and thus accompanying her to the end.

After the first run-through, we did a second exercise to explore the paradox of the chorus' reaction. While James Aldred was reading the text, the rest of the actors were asked to physically respond to the words following the chorus leader's movements (Lara Korach). The bodies were performing an alternation of opposite feelings: bending postures showing the collective pain suggested by her forthcoming death alternated with wide gestures expressing the joy arising from Iphigenia's role in Greece's victory. In the feedback discussion, the actors as well as the spectators agreed on the ironic dynamic of the interpretation of this passage: the chorus and Iphigenia were behaving as they were supposed to; whilst they could not openly criticise the sacrifice, they expressed their disagreement with the political decisions through irony. One of the attendees at the workshop, Chuan Yue, also noticed that there was a communion between Iphigenia and the chorus which contrasted with the antagonistic atmosphere of the French version. Lumley's version of the chorus seemed to be able to bring out the complexity of the situation and develop the subtlety of the characters' psychology. Our practical experience of the text suggested an understanding of

---

74 Cf. Manuzio 1503, 231.

Lumley's translation as involving an empowering and liberating process, one which positioned female opposition at its very centre.[75]

Fig. 16: Chorus members around Iphigenia. Lumley's translation (last stasimon). Iphigenia Workshop: 21/05/2021.

4 Conclusions

The main discovery of these two workshops was the dramaturgical centrality of Iphigenia in both the fourth episode and in the last stasimon of the play. Her presence is pivotal for the way that other characters act and react to one anoth-

---

75 The 2013 production of Lumley's translation directed by Emma Rucastle with the Rose Company relied on the feminist dramaturgy of the text, on which see Emma Whipday 2015. Cf. Suthren 2020, 76–81, for situating this feminist reading within its historical European context.

er. Theatre productions have usually focused on Agamemnon's and Clytemnestra's powers and have neglected the dramaturgical importance of Iphigenia's presence in the play and particularly in the scene analysed in this chapter (1098–1208). However, our practice-research exploration of these scenes allowed us to understand Iphigenia's importance in the power dynamics of each translation.[76]

If this discovery was not contaminated by any previous literary analysis or production of *Iphigenia at Aulis*, it was indeed informed by the context in which we were practising. It was especially Lumley's dramaturgy of the Euripidean play that made us think of the timeliness of this story to a contemporary audience. Indeed, today's political and social protests about the global context, such as the #MeToo or the Young Climate movements, which hinge on women's bodies and rights as well as the teenagers' impact and voice, had informed and contaminated our own reception of these texts and the play. Contamination well described the reception process that saw us as protagonists inside and outside the rehearsal room.

But our dramaturgical exploration of the first scene was also pivotal in identifying some of the (contaminating) 'cultural symptoms' suggested at the beginning of this chapter and which emerged from these translations. Indeed, some of the considerations made on the translations echoed the political situation of the time in France, England, and Italy. In the first half of the 16th century; i.e., before the wars of religion, France's kingdom was aiming at stability and internal unity. As a consequence, François I had developed an all-controlling administration over the national territory, and notably over the Catholic Church. The royal power thus asserted its uncontested authority, relying especially on strong nationalist discourses. In his translation of *Iphigenia at Aulis*, Sébillet, who was also a lawyer in the Parliament of Paris, contributed to the national representation of politics as a rhetorical spectacle watched by the people.

Similarly, Dolce's translation, first performed around the same time as the Council of Trent, reflects on the dangers of religion colliding with politics and the terrible consequences this might lead to with the insertion of the figure of Calchas taking advantage of, and supporting, temporal power, as well as the looming sacrifice of Iphigenia, which, as mentioned, according to the messenger's final report, actually happened without the animal substitution. Dolce's tragedy is in line with the main themes addressed by Italian tragedy in the same

---

[76] Cf. amongst others, Ariane Mnouchkine, *Les Atrides* (1990–1992) and Katie Mitchell, *Iphigenia* (2004); for a more detailed discussion of Iphigenia's role in contemporary productions across the UK, France, and Germany, cf. Baudou 2021, 2852–2886, 396–397, 410–427.

period: namely, the complexity of political power and its human declinations. If, on the one hand, Italian tragedy was generally intended to unmask the 'hypocrisy of the courts', presented as places of conspiracy, as Sandra Clerc has argued, it was also genuinely interested in the human behaviour of the ruling figures.[77]

As for the English context,[78] one can glimpse the death of the young virgin Lady Jane Grey in 1554 in Lumley's reading of Iphigenia's sacrifice. Wanting a Protestant successor, Edward VI had named Lady Jane Grey as heir instead of his half-sister, the Catholic Mary. The 16-year-old was deposed by Mary and beheaded only nine days after becoming queen. The 17-year-old Lumley, too, grew up in an aristocratic family torn apart by religious issues: the choice of play and the translation itself may direct focus to the consequences of political moves made by individuals within a family.

Through the performance of these translations, we also discovered how much they resonated with famous later tragedies, a discovery that is corroborated by recent scholarship on these texts. The francophone participants at the workshop recognised in Sébillet a precursor to Racine, especially in the use of language and dramaturgy in his tragedies. Philippo demonstrates Sébillet's influence on Racine's own *Iphigénie*, notably via Jean Rotrou's version of the play, probably itself also influenced by Dolce's interpretation.[79] In the discussion ensuing the workshop performance,[80] some audience members also remarked upon the resonance between our staging of Lady Lumley's translation and Shakespeare's dramaturgy.[81] Indeed, our reception of these 16th-century translations had been inevitably contaminated by the neo-classical canons, just as these later plays had been contaminated by and showed some of the main 'cultural symptoms' of the translations taken into account in this chapter.

---

77 On the influence of Machiavelli on Dolce's tragedy, see Giazzon 2012 and Clerc 2016. This is also the period of the so-called 'horrendous wars of Italy', an expression borrowed from a collection of narrative and poetic compositions published in 1534 which was then employed to pinpoint the period between 1494 and 1559, resulting in the subjugation of nearly the entirety of the Italian territories to the Habsburgic influence.
78 For further discussion, see Vedelago in this volume.
79 Cf. 'Rotrou's creative input, in part at least sparked off by Erasmus's and Sébillet's translations, has provided material on which Racine's more complex dramatic imagination could set to work' (Philippo 2013, 397).
80 The results of the first workshop were performed on the 29th of November 2019 at the conference *On Translating Greek Drama in the Modern Period* co-organised by Malika Bastin-Hammou, Giovanna Di Martino, and Cécile Dudouyt at the Maison Française d'Oxford.
81 Cf. Craik and Pollard 2013, and Pollard 2017.

Whether or not Shakespeare and Racine actually came into contact with our texts, our experience of Sébillet's and Lumley's translations put them in the same (contaminated and contaminating) context.

Practice research proved to be essential in capturing the performance potential and dramaturgical meanings of this ancient text through, and within, its translations; it also further developed the conceptual and practical applicability of the term 'contamination' in order to pinpoint the many exchanges and influential contacts that occur between bodies, words, and concepts in the translation and embodiment of a dramatic text. By doing so, this chapter not only proposes a new way of exploring and analysing drama translation, whatever period it may belong to, but it also importantly contributes to widening the very meaning of 'translation', and of drama translation in particular, as the Introduction to this volume advocates. It proves that drama translation is necessarily part of, and heavily relies on, a wider dramaturgical process, and that its complex and multi-staged nature can only be fully understood when seen in its ideal and concrete medium, the stage.

Stuart Gillespie
Afterword: Prospects for Pan-European Translation History

With the rapid take-off of Classical Reception Studies in recent decades, the historical translation of ancient texts has become more frequently explored, especially within Classical Studies as a discipline. Translation is just one of 'the multiple ways in which early modern cultures, literatures, and languages interacted with, studied, appropriated, and recreated ancient Greek drama', as Giovanna Di Martino and Cécile Dudouyt's Introduction to the present volume puts it, but I would argue (with them) that it is the key one in terms of its ability to reveal what ancient Greek drama could mean to those early modern cultures. Classical Reception is not the only vantage point from which the phenomenon of translation may be regarded: it has an older, though until recent times usually very limited place in histories of individual vernacular literatures — individual literatures, that is, such as those belonging to English, French, and other European languages. But are there precedents for approaching the history of classical translation on a comparative basis across languages, or even on a pan-European basis? This is one of the most exciting directions in which the present volume beckons.

As far as the scholarly publication record is concerned, precedents for such an enterprise are few and far between. The furthest back anyone would think of looking today is probably R.R. Bolgar's *The Classical Heritage and its Beneficiaries*, 1954, conceived as a work of intellectual rather than purely literary history covering the period 700 CE to 1600. Translation is not, as it happens, particularly central to this sizeable study, but it concludes with a thirty-five-page Appendix in tabular form entitled 'The Translations of the Greek and Roman Authors before 1600'.[1] Here, two or three scholarly generations ago, may be found an attempt to itemize the earliest printed translations of individual works by ancient authors in each of five European languages. Robert Ralph Bolgar, a fellow in what was officially called 'Intellectual History' at King's College, Cambridge, sought in this way to list these translations in comparative fashion, with columns for English, French, German, Italian, and Spanish. The table is organized by ancient author, each row allowing us to read off and compare the dates of first (but not second or third) translations of individual works by Aristotle, or Ovid, or Plautus, across these five languages. The table proved to need correc-

---

[1] Bolgar 1954, 506–541.

tion in many details: Bolgar's information was often not first-hand but drawn from library catalogues and previous compilations.[2] Yet it was a start.

Bolgar's pan-European lead has been little followed. No doubt most literary scholarship will always tend to focus on individual works, but even where a group of works or a historical period is in view, studies have very rarely moved across more than one receiving language. Disciplinary boundaries and the structures of scholarly knowledge discourage this strongly, and in the present volume, too, individual contributions often restrict themselves to individual languages. But the volume is bookended by Part 1 on both Latin and Italian versions of Aristophanes, and a final contribution on a French, an Italian, and an English *Iphigenia at Aulis*. Between these points there are suggestive juxtapositions. This may prove a first step on a long and important road. Is the comparative study of reception possible? Can comparative translation history be envisaged? These are among the large questions this compilation raises, at least for this reader, and this Afterword is a suitable point at which to give them some attention.

A pan-European history of scholarship on ancient Greek literature in the early modern period does not seem too hard to imagine. We know that such scholarship was international, 'produced and theorised', as Giovanna Di Martino and Cécile Dudouyt note in their Introduction, 'by multilingual scholars, authors and printers who were reading each other's work'. I will shortly provide an example of how translators could take advantage of this international scholarship. Well, then: compile a history of translation for each European language, perhaps organized by genre, or perhaps (like Bolgar's table) by author. Then you'll have a chapter on, say, Euripides' translations in early modern England, another covering France, and so on. From here you can amalgamate these to form a pan-European history, right? Unfortunately, it is far from that simple.

Translation is not scholarship. Scholarship might be international (and the international currency of Latin sets that language apart in this connection), but translations into European vernaculars are in the nature of things tied to audiences in the schools and the colleges, in the studies and on the stages, of a circumscribed geographical area. These regions and nations each have their own cultural history. Direct translation of Greek tragedy into English is vanishingly scarce until the mid-17th century.[3] In France the narrative is quite otherwise: in

---

[2] For a list of corrections including numerous additions see Nørgaard 1958.
[3] How direct a translation Jane Lumley's *Iphigenia at Aulis* of *c*. 1555 was is still debated, and even then this rarity is a work of private study which did not reach print. Vedelago in this volume (p. 103) characterizes Lumley's translation as 'based on Erasmus's version and Euripi-

the 16th-century infancy of French tragedy, Greek authors are translated more often than Seneca; at least some of the time they are translated directly, and by figures of some stature; and the translations were in several cases printed.[4] One reason why an overarching history of vernacular translation of Euripides (let alone of Greek tragedy) is not easily imagined is that the histories of Europe's literary cultures, as defined by language, by region, or by nation, differ so radically from each other.

If a unified narrative is too much to ask, let us start by thinking about the other end of the scale, with the much more modest question of what we can do by looking beyond a single language. It might seem natural for historical scholarship to work within the parameters of a single language because this is very often how translation is done today. A translator might sit down to try his or her hand at a new translation of a Greek tragedy with little more than a parallel text presenting the Greek and one vernacular — for example, a Loeb Classical Library edition. But this contrasts strongly with the work of translators of the 16th or 17th century. For early modern translators, the edition of the Greek text would of course have its editorial material in Latin, with perhaps an interlinear gloss or marginal translation in Latin too (for an example see Figure 17). The edition's elaborate notes and interpretations would reflect decades of international scholarly effort. Cumulative rather than simultaneous effort, but still in a sense collaborative effort: many early modern editions set out to absorb all useful information and significant discussion from their predecessors, often presenting it explicitly as such, and then add to it. Translators availing themselves of such editions might also in many cases have knowledge of previous translations into their target language, or into other vernaculars, and might have copies of such translations in front of them as they proceeded. The worlds of scholar and translator overlapped heavily, and did not have limits set by national boundaries or by individual vernaculars. In this sense, the vernacular translator's work had international and plurilingual dimensions.

---

des' original'. *Pace* some recent speculation, there is no evidence that any readings or performances of it took place even in private.

4 For brief recent discussion of the general picture in the context of an edition of a 16th-century manuscript French translation of an Athenian playwright, see Alonge 2019, 249–250.

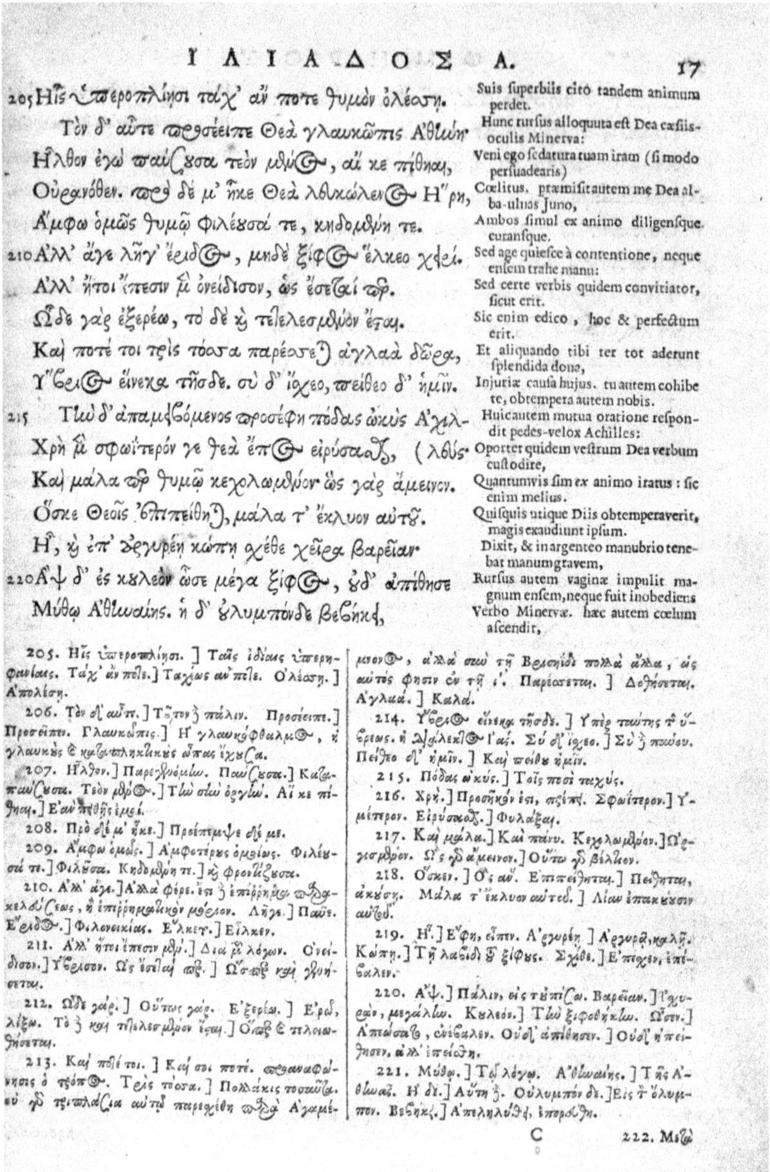

ΙΛΙΑΔΟΣ Α. 17

ᾗς ὑπεροπλίῃσι τάχ' ἄν ποτε θυμὸν ὀλέσσῃ.
Τὸν δ' αὖτε προσέειπε θεὰ γλαυκῶπις Ἀθήνη·
Ἦλθον ἐγὼ παύσουσα τὸ σὸν μένος, αἴ κε πίθηαι,
Οὐρανόθεν. πρὸ δέ μ' ἧκε θεὰ λευκώλενος Ἥρη,
Ἄμφω ὁμῶς θυμῷ φιλέουσά τε, κηδομένη τε.
Ἀλλ' ἄγε λῆγ' ἔριδος, μηδὲ ξίφος ἕλκεο χειρί.
Ἀλλ' ἤτοι ἔπεσιν μὲν ὀνείδισον, ὡς ἔσεταί περ.
Ὧδε γὰρ ἐξερέω, τὸ δὲ καὶ τετελεσμένον ἔσται.
Καί ποτέ τοι τρὶς τόσσα παρέσσεται ἀγλαὰ δῶρα,
Ὕβριος εἵνεκα τῆσδε. σὺ δ' ἴσχεο, πείθεο δ' ἡμῖν.
Τὴν δ' ἀπαμειβόμενος προσέφη πόδας ὠκὺς Ἀχιλλεύς·
Χρὴ μὲν σφωΐτερόν γε θεὰ ἔπος εἰρύσσασθαι,
Καὶ μάλα περ θυμῷ κεχολωμένον· ὣς γὰρ ἄμεινον.
Ὅς κε θεοῖς ἐπιπείθηται, μάλα τ' ἔκλυον αὐτοῦ.
Ἦ, καὶ ἐπ' ἀργυρέῃ κώπῃ σχέθε χεῖρα βαρεῖαν·
Ἂψ δ' ἐς κουλεὸν ὦσε μέγα ξίφος, οὐδ' ἀπίθησε
Μύθῳ Ἀθηναίης. ἡ δ' Οὔλυμπόνδε βεβήκει,

Suis superbiis citò tandem animum perdet.
Hunc rursus alloquuta est Dea cæsiis-oculis Minerva:
Veni ego sedatura tuam iram (si modo persuadearis)
Cœlitus. præmisit autem me Dea alba-ulnas Juno,
Ambos simul ex animo diligensque curansque.
Sed age quiesce à contentione, neque ensem trahe manu:
Sed certe verbis quidem conviciator, sicut erit.
Sic enim edico, hoc & perfectum erit.
Et aliquando tibi ter tot aderunt splendida dona,
Injuriæ causa hujus. tu autem cohibe te, obtempera autem nobis.
Huic autem mutua oratione respondit pedes-velox Achilles:
Oportet quidem vestrum Dea verbum custodire,
Quantumvis sim ex animo iratus: sic enim melius.
Quisquis utique Diis obtemperaverit, magis exaudiunt ipsum.
Dixit, & in argenteo manubrio tenebat manum gravem,
Rursus autem vaginæ impulit magnum ensem, neque fuit inobediens
Verbo Minervæ. hæc autem cœlum ascendit,

C 222. Μύθῳ

Fig. 17: A random page from *Ilias & Odyssea ... cum Latina versione accuratissima: et in easdem scholia, sive interpretatio Didymi : cum Latina versione accuratissima, indiceque Graeco locupletissimo rerum ac variantium lection / accurante Corn. Schrevelio* (Lugduni Batavorum, 1656).

These observations can be substantiated in detail from what has long been known of the working habits of individual early modern translators. Commentators were addressing this subject before Bolgar's time. In one example, J.M. Bottkol weighed the available evidence from which may be ascertained the 'actual working method' of John Dryden as a translator of ancient poetry in the last two decades of the 17th century. In this account Bottkol is thinking of Dryden's translations from such ancient authors as Juvenal, Persius, Ovid, Homer, and Vergil. All these observations are supported by the evidence of small decisions Dryden actually makes in his work as he chooses this interpretation, that English word, or a certain combination of rhyme words:

> He sat with a favourite edition open before him (Prateus, Ruaeus, Casaubon, or Cnipping), read the original carefully, often the Latin prose *Interpretatio*, and invariably studied the accompanying annotations. When he came to a difficult or disputed passage, he repeatedly turned to other editors, studied and compared their varying opinions, and then chose to follow one authority over another ... Also he had open before him on the table one or more earlier English translations, particularly those which were written in heroic couplets.[5]

This is only part of Bottkol's analysis. More recent scholarship has extended our knowledge of translations used by Dryden beyond Latin and English ones to other languages, in particular French.[6] With a figure like Dryden, it could hardly be clearer that we have a translator who is a thoroughly appreciative beneficiary of the European heritage of classical scholarship, and it's evident that the typical early modern translator's procedures resemble Dryden's much more closely than they reflect the norms of today's translators, some of whom are altogether unacquainted with both Greek and Latin.

Where vernacular translations are concerned, translators across early modern Europe stand in the same traditions of scholarship. While their contribution is to a national culture, it draws on an international one. This of course does not mean there is anything wrong with the study of translations within a single language, but it means that the work of early modern translators is closely linked across the languages of Europe, and that it seems to call for comparative study and analysis. How might this be carried out? The point of departure might be an ancient text, an ancient author, or, perhaps especially relevant in connec-

---

5 Bottkol 1942–1943, 243.
6 Scholars like Anne Dacier (1647–1720) were read and used in the Anglophone world, including by major verse translators like Dryden and, into the 18th century, Alexander Pope (see recently Taylor 2021). Dacier's published translations range from Anacreon and Sappho to complete versions of the *Iliad* and *Odyssey*.

tion with drama, a mythological or fictional character. I will next consider briefly examples of how each has been or could be addressed.

*

Individual Characters: If we think on the smallest scale just suggested, in terms of European 'versions' of one fictional character, one example has been set by Robert Miola, whose essay-length treatments of reception subjects have in recent years extended to the figures of Orestes, Antigone, and Iphigenia.[7] While centred on English-language treatments, these go at least some way beyond an individual language, so that, for instance, Miola attends to stage versions of Sophocles' *Antigone* by Robert Garnier in French and by Luigi Alamanni in Italian, as well as several Latin translations, in part as a context for the English reception. Can more concerted efforts be made? Some mythological and fictional characters have received so much attention from so many geographical and linguistic quarters that works of synthesis should now be feasible. Comparative studies of cross-European Medeas are an example of where such work might be appropriate.

Individual Plays: Here might be cited the pan-European range addressed in the essays devoted to reception in A.J. Boyle's ongoing editions of Senecan tragedies.[8] These admirable essays productively explore the European dramatic and literary tradition on each play, not circumscribing discussion by national or linguistic boundaries (translations, however, play a minor role). It must be admitted that Boyle, like Miola, is exceptional. Normally, attempts to trace a play's European or global reception single-handedly are heavily circumscribed by the limitations of the author's knowledge, including knowledge of languages. More typical, therefore, are the individual-play-focused 'Companions to Greek and Roman Tragedy' in the series published at various times by Duckworth, Bristol Classical Press, and Bloomsbury. Each volume includes a reception chapter which is, or may be, in principle pan-European. Within the bounds of any given example, however, breadth will lead to a sacrifice of depth or vice versa, translation will become at most a small part of the narrative, and the limits of the author's acquaintance with different languages will soon kick in.[9]

---

[7] Miola 2020; 2017; 2014.
[8] Boyle 2008 is followed to date by Boyle's *Oedipus* (2012), *Medea* (2014), *Thyestes* (2017), and *Agamemnon* (2019).
[9] One of the wider-ranging reception essays in this series appears in Ruffell 2012, briefly taking in German Romanticism and several 20th-century English-language poets' versions of Aeschylus' *Prometheus Bound*.

Individual Authors: As titles like *Seneca and his Influence* and *Homer in English* remind us, individual ancient authors have been the subjects of reception and translation study for a long time. But very little of this work has been comparative or supra-national. A short but well-populated catalogue of the earliest European translations and editions of Sophocles compiled by Elia Borza shows a history of translation at first into Spanish and Italian (from 1531–1532), then immediately afterwards Latin and French. I know of no follow-up to it, and the subtitle of Borza's short paper (Borza 1998), pointing to the obscurity of the history he is outlining, would not need to be any different today, a quarter-century on.

While I'm aware of very few similar studies from a single hand, some recent essay collections suggest a way forward might be to assemble multiple contributors. An example not from Greek but Latin is the 2018 volume *Virgil and his Translators*,[10] an essay collection taking in, among post-antique translations, half-a-dozen European languages, and beyond these, for example, Chinese, Russian, and Turkish. The timescale here extends from the 16th to the 21st century, and contributions do not concentrate on particular periods. However, all contributions making up the second and last section are in the nature of 'case studies' of individual works of translation, meaning that here once more we have juxtaposition rather than synthesis: although one or two contributions take in what are arguably different cultures, notably English and American, none deals with more than one language.

Might similar compilations with a 'global' outlook be assembled from contributions by several hands for ancient Greek playwrights? Arguably, this has in part been attempted already, in 'companion' volumes to an ancient author's reception. In the examples I have in mind, though, Brill's Companions to Classical Reception, it's understandable that translation is not central: these volumes are intended to provide 'a comprehensive account of the influence, reception and appropriation' of each author.[11] The comprehensiveness might be doubted, however, when there is usually no attempt to provide even brief overviews of the subject of translation, the contributors not, it seems, being expected to know much or find out much about it.[12]

As things currently stand, then, scholarship on translations which crosses national or linguistic boundaries is very limited, and there is no reason to antic-

---

10 Braund and Torleone 2018.
11 Publisher's description of Lauriola and Demetriou 2017.
12 The approach used to compile the Brill Companion volumes on Sophocles and Euripides is found wanting in a review by Jackson 2019.

ipate a sudden change. How could there be, when the basic resources to make it possible are not available? First we need the data on which to base the pan-European study of translations of ancient drama, by which I mean a reasonably complete record of historical translations.[13] This, at least, can be built up from individual languages, one at a time and even, if need be, one century at a time. There are few signs that this crucial resourcing of the field is on the horizon, or of much thinking about how it might be best to proceed. This is why I shall devote the last segment of this Afterword to this subject: to the prospects for databases of historical translations of pan-European scope, with particular reference to the early modern period.

For quite a few languages, existing databases could be used as a basis for a specialized record of translations. I cannot touch on them all here,[14] but for records of print publications the pace has been set in modern times in the Anglophone world, so let us begin there. Starting at the beginning of modern bibliography would mean beginning with the short-title catalogues of the mid-20th century,[15] assembled and expanded in 1987 into the English Short Title Catalogue (ESTC), a still growing but definitive union catalogue for British or English-language books printed before 1801, and freely available through the British Library's website. Designed as a bibliographic record, showing library locations, of every surviving copy of print publications including serials, it includes references, but not links, to free-to-view digital surrogates. The publications it catalogues are also digitally reproduced as page images in the standard commercial databases.[16] The ESTC (and its predecessor, 'STC': Pollard and Redgrave 1986–1991) has been important in providing a standard or model for other bibliographical databases, and records that use its fields and formats come with mutual compatibility built in.

ESTC is not a convenient starting point for a bibliography of translations, because it does not tag them or have a field for them, though its notes may iden-

---

13 As a minimum this would mean translations printed in their own time, but ideally the record would extend to translations printed later, as well as translations never printed and extant only in manuscript.
14 For Italian see Di Martino in this volume.
15 A short-title catalogue is a bibliographical resource listing printed items in an abbreviated fashion, early modern books commonly having long descriptive titles. Online 'short-title' catalogues actually tend to record complete title transcriptions.
16 Not every edition of every publication, but every 'significant' edition. STC records formed the basis for the large-scale microfilm series from which the page images of today's ECCO (Eighteenth-Century Collections Online) are taken, and ESTC is accordingly the best finding aid for ECCO.

tify them. The translators are listed as the authors. Thus a search for 'Euripides' in any field, or for 'Hippolytus' in the title field, gives a mixture of translations and imitations, Greek editions, and various other material which must be sifted. ESTC has, however, been used as the basis of an incomplete, but well developed and freely available database of translations into English in the early modern period. The Renaissance Cultural Crossroads Catalogue (RCCC) at www.dhi.ac.uk/rcc/index.php (last accessed 01/09/22) is a searchable list of (in principle but not yet in practice) all translations out of and into all languages in British and English-language books printed before 1641 (at the time of writing an extension to 1660 is awaited). It contains records for over 6,000 translations, keyed to ESTC record numbers, and annotated. The idea is in part that the manageable size of this resource enables its compilers to carry out the research required to confirm, where necessary, whether individual editions contain (or are) translations, and to supplement ESTC information on them, for example by noting the use of intermediate translations, and identifying which translations these were. The interface provides for searching of fields including original language, original author, target language, and intermediary language. But the helpful design is not, at the date of writing, fully supported by the database's content. No kind of search leads to the only pre-1641 English version of a Euripidean play, George Gascoigne and Francis Kinwelmersh's *Jocasta* (from Lodovico Dolce's Italian version of *Phoenissae*, performed 1566, printed 1573, 1575, 1587), because it is not present in RCCC. The relevant editions are present in ESTC, but, perhaps because the titles of the published volumes containing it make them look like collections of Gascoigne's poems (*A Hundreth Sundrie Flowers*, 1573, 1575; *Works*, 1587), RCCC has not (yet) absorbed it.

Although it, or some of its features, might suggest a model for a pan-European database of translations, only a small proportion of the materials RCCC includes is non-Anglophone. A similar linguistic concentration very understandably applies to the numerous other national bibliographies established since the mid-20th century. The Universal Short Title Catalogue (USTC; www.ustc.ac.uk – last accessed 01/09/22) is a resource with a much more cosmopolitan outlook which was first made available to the public as a whole in 2011. USTC began life as a bibliography of early modern French printings, which was then augmented mainly by absorbing and incorporating existing library catalogues and databases. Records currently extend down to the year 1650, covering 800,000 editions and 4,000,000 copies. An expansion to the year 1700 should bring the number of distinct items listed to around 1,400,000 in mid-2023. Searching can be carried out by keyword, printer, author/editor, or a combination, and can be filtered by language. Its limitations of coverage and accuracy reflect the catalogues on which it is based, and USTC records are unannotated.

USTC is oriented towards the recording of library holdings. If you are interested in, say, Dolce's Italian version of *Hecuba*, USTC will provide copious details of its publication history and diffusion. A Search for 'Hecuba' + 'Dolce' will turn up a total of six editions (some solo, some with other works of Dolce's) printed between 1543 and 1566. The library locations of multiple copies of each, and a link to at least one free-to-view surrogate in five of the six cases, are also here.

But only two of these six editions will be returned if you search for 'Euripides', because only two give his name in their titles; the rest are not in any way associated with the Greek playwright in the database. In other words, the 123 printings of 'Euripides' listed in USTC do not, in fact, contain all (or even most) of the Euripides translations in USTC. In effect, only translations of Euripides explicitly associated with Euripides on their title page are associated with the playwright in the database.[17] Although USTC is a resource which by its nature should include printed translations of ancient playwrights on a pan-European basis (i.e., into any language) for the period it covers, it is no easier to locate them than it is to locate English ones in ESTC. Using title instead of author is not a workable alternative approach: this would require separate searches for all variants in different languages (there are 41 entries for 'Medea', 20 for 'Medée') and it would not find any edition of Gascoigne's *Jocasta*, because this title is, of course, not among the thirteen results returned by a search for 'Phoenissae'.

The three databases mentioned so far use STC principles, but the only other relevant initiative of which I'm aware is not modelled on STC. As many readers of this volume will know, Oxford University's Archive for Performances of Greek and Roman Drama (apgrd.ox.ac.uk) has over time assembled a worldwide 'Productions Database', currently running to 13,000 entries for the period 1450-2020. 'Productions' are now extending to embrace printed translations, which, of course, are sometimes the texts used in theatrical productions. A pilot project has so far produced a database of 166 mainly French translations of ancient drama to 2020, searchable by title, playwright, or translator. These records are annotated, like RCCC's but differently and often more fully. In each record, bib-

---

[17] Gascoigne's *Jocasta* (or *Iocasta*) is associated with Euripides because his 1573 title goes on to make the connection: *A hundreth sundrie flowres bounde up in one small poesie Gathered partely (by translation) in the fyne outlandish gardins of Euripides, Ouid, Petrarke, Ariosto, and others*. But two 1587 printings of the play within editions of Gascoigne's *Whole Works* are not associated with Euripides.

liographical information is supplemented by notes and further references on the translation, its translator, and its publication history, and by cross-referencing to data indicating when and how a particular translation was used in performance. Here, too, links are provided to digital editions of the translations when they are available.

At the time of writing, the APGRD database of translations shows records of 26 printings before 1641, or a total 41 down to 1700. The bulk of its 166 records thus belong to later times. A start has been made on extending 'Translating Ancient Drama' to European vernaculars other than French. At its most ambitious it is conceived as potentially embracing all translations of ancient drama, in all languages, down to the present.[18]

To recap. I have very briefly described four databases. ESTC provides the raw material for an English translations database for the early modern period; RCCC is in the process of becoming that translations database, and could provide a model for others. Unlike these two, USTC is not restricted by nation or language, but it is not, and seems unlikely to become, a suitable basis for generating a translations database. It is, however, an excellent resource for checking independently-generated databases against, something from which APGRD's work could benefit. APGRD aims, in time, to provide a global translations database to cover ancient drama from the first days of printing down to the present, and is the only current prospect of this kind known to me. But that time, it is to be feared, will not be short.

---

18 For more details of future prospects see Macintosh and Di Martino 2021, 238–239.

List of Contributors

Thomas Baier (Universität Würzburg)

Malika Bastin-Hammou (Université Grenoble Alpes)

Estelle Baudou (Dramaturg, APGRD, University of Lincoln)

Simone Beta (Università di Siena)

Claudia Cuzzotti (Independent Researcher)

Alexia Dedieu (Université Grenoble Alpes-Università di Siena)

Giovanna Di Martino (University College London)

Cécile Dudouyt (Université Sorbonne Paris Nord)

Giulia Fiore (Università di Bologna)

Stuart Gillespie (University of Glasgow)

Lucy Jackson (Durham University)

Micol Muttini (Università di Siena)

Maria Luísa Resende (Universidade Católica Portuguesa)

Angelica Vedelago (Università degli Studi di Padova)

Bibliography

Adams, James (1981), 'Culus, Clunes and Their Synonyms in Latin', *Glotta* 59, 231–264.
Adams, James (1982), *The Latin Sexual Vocabulary*, Baltimore.
Adkins, Arthur W.H. (1966), 'Aristotle and the Best Kind of Tragedy', *The Classical Quarterly* n.s. 16, 78–102.
Alamanni, Luigi (1997), *Tragedia Di Antigone*, Francesco Spera (ed.), Turin.
Alciato, Andrea (1517 ca.), *Nubes*, cod. triv. 738 (f° 56r°-93r°), Biblioteca Trivulziana, Milan.
Alciato, Andrea (1523 ca.), *Philargyrus*, cod. triv. 738 (ff. 1r-41v), Biblioteca Trivulziana, Milan.
Allen, Percy Stafford (ed.) (1906), *Desiderius Erasmus: Opus Epistolarum Des. Erasmi Roterodami*, Vol. 1 (1484–1514), Oxford.
Alonge, Tristan (2016), '*Les Suppliantes* d'Euripide, une tragédie inédite de Jacques Amyot?', *Bibliothèque d'Humanisme et de Renaissance* 78/1, 109–126.
Alonge, Tristan (2019), '*Les Suppliantes* d'Euripide (*c.* 1540): A Lost Translation Recovered', *Translation and Literature*, 28, 249–316.
Alonge, Tristan (2019), 'Rethinking the Birth of French Tragedy', in: Giancarlo Abbamonte/ Stephen Harrison (eds.), *Making and Rethinking the Renaissance Between Greek and Latin in the 15th-16th Century Europe*, 143–156.
Anguillara, Giovanni Andrea Dell' (2020), *Edippo*, Valeria Merola (ed.), Avellino.
Anneau, Barthélémy (2001), 'Quintil Horacian [1551]', in: *Joachim Du Bellay, La Deffence et illustration de la langue françoyse (1549)*, Jean-Charles Monferran (ed.), Geneva, 304–361.
Ansino Domínguez, José Miguel (1999), 'El teatro de tema mitológico de Fernán Pérez de Oliva', *Florentia Iliberritana: Revista de Estudios de Antigüedad Clásica* 10, 11–27.
Aretino, Rinuccio (2011), *Penia*; a cura di Ludovica Radif, Florence.
Argelati, Filippo (1766–67), *Biblioteca degli volgarizzatori, opera postuma del segretario F. Argellati coll'addizioni di A.T. Villa*, vols. 4, Milan.
Artale, Elena/Guadagnini, Elisa (2018), 'Ci è bisognato servirci di molti volgarizzamenti e traslatamenti d'opere altrui. I testi di traduzione', in: Gino Belloni/Paolo Trovato (eds.), *La Crusca e i testi Lessicografia, tecniche editoriali e collezionismo librario intorno al Vocabolario del 1612*, 383–426.
Ascham, Roger (1865), *The Whole Works of Roger Ascham*, John Alles Giles (ed.), 3 vols., London.
Atkins, Jed W. (2014), 'Euripides's Orestes and the Concept of Conscience in Greek Philosophy', *Journal of the history of ideas* 75, 1–22.
Avezzù, Guido/Scattolin, Paolo (eds.) (2006), *I classici greci e i loro commentatori: dai papiri ai marginalia rinascimentali*, Rovereto.
Baier, Thomas (2015), 'Érasme traducteur', *Anabases* 21, 99–111.
Baier, Thomas/Hamm, Joachim/Schlegelmilch, Ulrich (eds.), *Opera Camerarii. Eine semantische Datenbank zu den gedruckten Werken von Joachim Camerarius d.Ä.*, http://wiki.camerarius.de (last accessed 08/06/2022).
Baïf, Jean-Antoine de (1966) [1573], *Euvres en rime*, Ch. Marty Laveaux (ed.), vol. 1, Geneva.
Baker, Patrick/Helmrath, Johannes/Kallendorf, Craig (eds.) (2019), *Beyond Reception. Renaissance Humanism and the Transformation of Classical Antiquity*, Berlin.
Baldassari, Stefano U. (2006), '*Il Discorso sopra la traduttione delle scienze e d'altre facultà* dell'umanista Girolamo Catena', *Per Leggere* 6. 11, 133–147.
Baldassarri, Stefano U. (2003), *Umanesimo e traduzione da Petrarca a Manetti*, Cassino.
Bandello, Matteo (1813), *Ecuba. Tragedia Di Euripide*, Guglielmo Manzi (ed.), Rome.

Bañuls Oller, José Vicente/Crespo Alcalá, Patricia/Morenilla Talens, Carmen (2006), *Electra de Sófocles y las Primeras Recreaciones Hispanas*, Bari.
Barbsy, John (ed.) (2002), *Greek and Roman Drama: Translation and Performance*, Lyon.
Barnette, Jane (2018), *Adapturgy: The Dramaturg's Art and Theatrical Adaptation*, Carbondale.
Barocchi, Paola (ed.) (1960), *Trattati d'arte del Cinquecento*, vol. 1, Bari.
Bassnett, Susan (1985), 'Ways through the labyrinth: strategies and methods for translating theatre texts', in: Theo Hermans (ed.), *The manipulation of literature: studies in literary translation*, London, 87–103.
Bastin-Hammou, Malika (2010), 'Anne Dacier et les premières traductions françaises d'Aristophane: l'invention du métier de femme philologue', *Littératures classiques* 72, 85–99.
Bastin-Hammou, Malika (2015), 'Les 'Traductions' d'Aristophane en français au XVIe siècle', in: Véronique Duché (ed.), *Histoire des Traductions en Langue Française - XVe - XVIe siècle (ANR HTLF)*, Paris, 1209–1216.
Bastin-Hammou, Malika (2015), 'Les traductions latines du théâtre grec. Introduction', *Anabases* 21, 41–44.
Bastin-Hammou, Malika (2019), 'Teaching Greek with Aristophanes in the French Renaissance', in: Constantinidou, Natasha/Lamers, Han (eds.), *Receptions of Hellenism in Early Modern Europe - 15th-17th Centuries*, Leiden/Boston, 72–93.
Baudou, Estelle (2021), *Créer le chœur tragique: Une archéologie du commun (Allemagne, France, Royaume-Uni; 1973–2010)*, Paris.
Belloni, Annalisa (2016), *L'Alciato e il diritto pubblico romano*, Vatican City.
Beltrami, Pietro (2011), *La metrica italiana*, Bologna.
Bembo, Pietro (1966) [1525], *Le Prose della Volgar Lingua*, Carlo Dionisotti (ed.), Turin.
Benjamin, Walter (2000), 'The Task of the Translator (1923)', in: Lawrence Venuti (ed.), *The Translation Studies Reader*, London, 15–25.
Bergk, Thomas (ed.) (1852), *Aristophanis comoediae*, vol. 1, Leipzig.
Berman, Antoine (2012), *Jacques Amyot, traducteur français: essai sur les origines de la traduction en France*, Paris.
Bernardi Perini, Giorgio (2004), *Il latino nell'età dell'Umanesimo. Atti del Convegno (Mantova, 26–27 ottobre 2001)*, Florence.
Bernard-Pradelle, Laurence (2016), 'La version latine du *Ploutos* d'Aristophane par Leonardo Bruni: un exemple de traduction expérimentale', in: *La Traduction: Pratiques d'hier et d'aujourd'hui*, 31–47.
Berschin, Walter (1989), *Medioevo greco-latino. Da Gerolamo a Niccolò Cusano*, Naples.
Bertalot, Ludwig (1929–30), 'Cincius Romanus und seine Briefe', *Quellen und Forschungen aus Italienischen Archiven und Bibliotheken* 21, 209–255.
Bertana, Emilio (1905), *La tragedia*, Milan.
Berthon, Guillaume (2020), 'Combattant marotique, traducteur humaniste, auteur évangélique. La trajectoire de Calvy de la Fontaine', *Cahiers de Recherches Médiévales et Humanistes* 40, -2, 163–182.
Berti, Ernesto (1988), 'Traduzioni oratorie fedeli', *MeR* 2, 245–266.
Berti, Ernesto (1998), 'Manuele Crisolora, Plutarco e l'avviamento delle traduzioni umanistiche', *Fontes* I, 81–99.
Bertolio, Johnny (ed.) (2020), *Il Trattato De Interpretatione Recta di Leonardo Bruni*, Rome.
Best, Thomas (1971), *Eccius dedolatus. A reformation satire*, Lexington.

Beta, Simone (2004), *Il linguaggio nelle commedie di Aristofane. Parola positiva e parola negativa nella commedia antica*, Rome.
Beta, Simone (2012), 'La prima traduzione latina della *Lisistrata*. Luci e ombre della versione di Andrea Divo', *Quaderni Urbinati di Cultura Classica* 129, 95–114.
Beta, Simone (2013), '*Aristophanes Venetus*: i fratelli Rositini e la prima traduzione italiana del poeta comico greco (1545)', *Cahiers d'études italiennes* 17, 57–70.
Beta, Simone (2017), 'Francesco Passi versipellis fra Aristofane e Plauto', in: Adriana Romaldo (ed.), *A Maurizio Bettini. Pagine stravaganti per un filologo stravagante*, Milan/Udine, 47–50.
Beta, Simone (2019), 'Adaptations (sixteenth to nineteenth centuries)', in: Alan Sommerstein (ed.), *The Encyclopedia of Greek Comedy*, vol. I, London, 10–12.
Bettini, Maurizio (2012), *Vertere: un'antropologia della traduzione nella cultura antica*, Turin.
Bevegni, Claudio (2017), 'Manoscritti greci in viaggio: Aristofane dall'Oriente all'Occidente nel XV secolo', in: Luisa Secchi Tarugi (ed.), *Viaggio e comunicazione nel Rinascimento. Atti del XXVII Convegno internazionale (Chianciano Terme-Pienza 16–18 luglio 2015)*, Florence, 135–144.
Biet, Christian/Triau, Christophe (2006), *Qu'est-ce que le théâtre?*, Paris.
Bigliazzi, Silvia/Kofler, Peter/Ambrosi, Paola (2013), 'Introduction', in: Silvia Bigliazzi/Peter Kofler/Paola Ambrosi (eds.), *Theatre translation in performance*, New York, 1–26.
Binet, Claude (1586), *Discours de la vie de Pierre de Ronsard*, Paris.
Black, Robert (1996), 'The Vernacular and the Teaching of Latin in Thirteenth and Fourteenth-Century Italy', *StudMed* 37, 703–751.
Black, Robert (2001), *Humanism and Education in Medieval and Renaissance Italy. Tradition and Innovation in Latin Schools from the Twelfth to the Fifteenth Century*, Cambridge.
Black, Robert (2010), 'Notes on Teaching Techniques in Medieval and Renaissance Italian Schools', in: Lucio Del Corso/Oronzo Pecere (eds.), *Libri di scuola e pratiche didattiche. Dall'Antichità al Rinascimento*. Atti del convegno internazionale di studi (Cassino, 7–10 maggio 2008), Cassino, 513–536.
Blackburn, Ruth H. (1971), *Biblical Drama Under the Tudors*, The Hague.
Blair, Ann (2008), 'Student Manuscripts and the Textbook', in: Emidio Campi *et al.* (eds.), *Scholarly Knowledge: Textbooks in early modern Europe*, Geneva, 39–73.
Blaydes, Frederick H.M. (ed.) (1875), *Aristophanis Equites*, London.
Bolgar, Robert Ralph (1954), *The Classical Heritage and its Beneficiaries*, Cambridge.
Borza, Elia (1998), 'Sofocle nel Rinascimento europeo: Una fortuna troppo sconosciuta', in: Rhona Schnur *et al.* (eds.), *Conventus Neo-Latini Bariensis, 1994*, Tempe, AZ, 169–75.
Borza, Elia (2003), 'Catalogue des travaux inédits d'humanistes consacrés à Sophocle jusqu'en 1600', *Humanistica Lovaniensia*, Leuven.
Borza, Elia (2007), *Sophocles redivivus: la survie de Sophocle en Italie au début du XVIe siècle: éditions grecques, traductions latines et vernaculaires*, Bari.
Borza, Elia (2013), 'La traduction de tragédies grecques', in: Philip Ford/Andrew Taylor (eds.), *The Early Modern Cultures of Neo-Latin Drama*, Leuven, 63–73.
Botley, Paul (2004), *Latin Translation in the Renaissance: The Theory and Practice of Leonardo Bruni, Giannozzo Manetti and Desiderius Erasmus*, Cambridge.
Botley, Paul (2010), 'Learning Greek in Western Europe, 1396–1529: Grammars, Lexica, and Classroom Texts', *TAPS* 100 n. 2.
Bottkol, Joseph McG. (1942–3), 'Dryden's Latin Scholarship', *Modern Philology* 40, 241–54.
Boyle, Anthony J. (ed.) (2008), *Octavia attributed to Seneca*, Oxford.

Braden, Gordon (2010), 'Translating Procedures in Theory and Practice', in: Gordon Braden/ Robert Cummings/Stuart Gillespie (eds.), *The Oxford History of Literary Translation in English, Volume 2: 1550–1660*, Oxford, 89–100.
Brammall, Sheldon (2015), *The English Aeneid: Translation of Virgil 1555–1646*, Edinburgh.
Brammall, Sheldon (2017), 'Laurence Humphrey, Gabriel Harvey, and the Place of Personality in Renaissance Translation', *The Review of English Studies* 69, 288, 56–75.
Brandão, Mário (1933), *O Colégio das Artes II: 1555–1580 (Livro I)*, Coimbra.
Braund, Susanna/Martirosova Torlone, Zara (eds.) (2018), *Virgil and his Translators*, Oxford.
Brazeau, Bryan (2018), 'My own worst enemy: translating *Hamartia* in sixteenth-century Italy', *Renaissance and Reformation* 41/4, 9–42.
Brazeau, Bryan (2020a), 'I Write Sins, Not Tragedies: Manuscript Translations of *Hamartia* in Late Sixteenth-Century Italy', in: Alessandra Petrina (ed.), *Acquisition Through Translation: The Rise of European Vernaculars*, Turnhout, 55–72.
Brazeau, Bryan (ed.) (2020b), *The Reception of Aristotle's Poetics in the Italian Renaissance and Beyond*, New Directions in Criticism, London.
Bremer, Jan M. (1971), *Hamartia. Tragic error in the Poetics of Aristotle and in Greek Tragedy*, Amsterdam.
Buchanan, George (1544), *Medea Euripidis tragoedia*, Paris.
Buchanan, George (1557), *Euripidis Poetae Tragici Alcestis Georgio Buchanano Interprete*, Paris.
Buchanan, George (1725), *Georgii Buchanani, Scoti, Poëtarum sui seculi facile Principis, Opera Omnia, Tomus Secundus*, Lyon.
Buck, August/Herding, Otto (1975), *Der Kommentar in der Renaissance*, Bonn.
Budé, Guillaume (1528), *Gulielmi Budaei Parisiensis, de contemptu rerum fortuitarum libri tres cum brevi et erudita eorundem expositione*, Paris.
Buonarroti, Michelangelo il giovane (1976), *La Tancia*, ed. by Luigi Fasso, Turin.
Buonarroti, Michelangelo il giovane (1984), *La Fiera: redazione originaria (1619)*, Uberto Limentani (ed.), Florence.
Buonarroti, Michelangelo il giovane (2003), *La Fiera: seconda redazione*, Olimpia Pelosi (ed.), Naples.
Buescu, Ana Isabel (2016). *A livraria renascentista de D. Teodósio I, duque de Bragança*, Lisbon.
Buonarroti, Michelangelo il giovane (2017), *Ecuba*, Claudia Cuzzotti (ed.), Lucca.
Burke, Peter (2007), 'Cultures of Translation in Early Modern Europe', in: Peter Burke/R. Pochia Hsia (eds.), *Cultural Translation in Early Modern Europe*, Cambridge, 7–38.
Burroghs, Catherine (2019), 'Introduction: 'Closet Drama Studies'', in: Catherine Burroghs (ed.), *Closet Drama: History, Theory, Form*, Abingdon, 3–31.
Bushnell, Rebecca W. (1990), *Tragedies of Tyrants. Political Thought and Theater in the English Renaissance*, Ithaca (NY).
Cairns, Douglas (2013), 'Divine and human action in the *Oedipus Tyrannus*', in: Douglas Cairns (ed.), *Tragedy and Archaic Greek Thought*, Swansea-London, 119–171.
Calderón Calderón (2011), 'La Venganza de Agamenón, de Pérez de Oliva', in: Anrique Aires Vitória (ed.), *Tragédia da Vingança que foi feita sobre a morte del rei Agaménom (Tragédia de Orestes)*, Lisbon, 25–29.
Camerarius, Joachim (1534), Σοφοκλέους τραγῳδίαι ἑπτά. *Sophoclis tragoediae septem cum commentariis interpretationum argumenti Thebaidos fabularum Sophoclis, authore Ioachimo Camerario Qu(aestore) iam recens natis atque aeditis*, I-II, Hagenau, VD16 S 7032.

Camerarius, Joachim (1546), *P. Terentii Comoediae sex, cum prioribus ferme castigationibus et plerisque explicationibus, et auctario insuper quodam, editae studio et cura Ioachimi Camerarii Pabergensis*, Leipzig, VD16 T 424.
Camerarius, Joachim (1554), *Tragoedia Hecuba, sapientissimi et elegantissimi poetae Euripidis, cum interpretatione, et explicatione (...) autore M. Matthaeo Heuslero*, Leipzig, VD16 E 4232.
Camerarius, Joachim (1556), *Commentatio explicationum omnium tragoediarum Sophoclis, cum exemplo duplicis conversionis Ioachimi Camerarii Pabepergensis (...)*, Basel, VD16 S 7043; VD16 S 7047.
Camerarius, Joachim (1568), *Σοφοκλέους αἱ ἑπτὰ τραγῳδίαι. Sophoclis Tragoediae septem*, Paris.
Collin, Rudolf (1541), *Euripidis Tragicorum omnium principis [...] Tragoediae XVIII [...] per Dorotheum Camillum [...] in lucem editae*, Basel.
Camões, José (ed.) (2011), 'Nota introdutória', in Anrique Aires Vitória. *Tragédia da Vingança que foi feita sobre a morte del rei Agaménom (Tragédia de Orestes)*, Lisbon, 7–11.
Campanelli, Maurizio/Pincelli, Maria Agata (2000), 'La lettura dei classici nello Studium Urbis tra Umanesimo e Rinascimento', in: Lidia Capo/Maria Rosa Di Simone (eds.), *Storia della Facoltà di Lettere e Filosofia de 'La Sapienza'*, Rome, 93–195.
Canosa, Romano (1991), *Storia di una grande paura: la sodomia a Firenze e a Venezia nel Quattrocento*, Milan.
Cantarella, Raffaele (ed.) (1949), *Aristofane. Gli Acarnesi, I Cavalieri*, vol. 1, Milan.
Canterus, Gulielmus (1571), *Euripidis tragoediae XIX [...] opera Gulielimi Canteri Ultraiectini*, Antwerp.
Cardillo, Angelo (2010), 'Lodovico Castelvetro: sul 'traslatare', *Misure critiche* ix.2, 5–21.
Carlson, Marvin (2001), *The Haunted Stage. Theatre as Memory Machine*, Ann Arbor.
Castelvetro, Lodovico (1570), *Poetica d' Aristotele Vulgarizzata e Sposta*, Vienna.
Castelvetro, Lodovico (1576), *Poetica d' Aristotele Vulgarizzata e Sposta per Lodovico Castelvetro. Riveduta, & ammendata secondo l'originale, & la mente dell'autore. Aggiuntovi nella fine un racconto delle cose più notabili, che nella spositione si contengono*, Basel.
Catena, Girolamo (1581), *Discorso Di Girolamo Catena, Fatto Nell'Academia De Gl'illustrissimi Affidati, Sopra La Traduttione Delle Scienze, & D'altre Facultà*, Venice.
Cave, Terence (2001), 'The Afterlife of the Poetics', in: Øivind Andersen and John Haarberg (eds.), *Making Sense of Aristotle. Essays in Poetics*, London.
Cecchini, Enzo/Cassio, Albio Cesare (1972), 'Due contributi sulla traduzione di Leonardo Bruni del Pluto di Aristofane', *GIF* 3, 472–482.
Cecchini, Maria/Cecchini, Enzo (1965), *Leonardo Bruni. Versione del Pluto di Aristofane (vv. 1–269)*, Florence.
Certon, Salomon (1615), *Les oeuvres d'Homère prince des poètes assavoir: l'Iliade, l'Odyssée, la Batrachomyomachie, les Hymnes et les épigrammes, le tout de la version de Salomon Certon conseiller, notaire et secretaire du Roy, Maison & couronne de France, & secretaire de la chambre de sa Majesté. L'Odyssée cy deuant imprimée, a esté de nouueau & exactement reueüe & corrigee par le Traducteur*, Paris.
Cesarini Martinelli, Lucia (2016), *Umanesimo e filologia*, Pisa.
Chamard, Henri (1939–40), *Histoire de la Pléiade*, Paris.
Chantry, Marcel (1994), 'Les emplois du mot ΘΗΛΙΑ dans les textes grecs anciens', *RPh* 8, 77–86.

Chantry, Marcel (1996), *Scholia in Aristophanem III 4b, Scholia recentiora in Aristophanis Plutum*, Groningen.
Chantry, Marcel (2009), *Scholies anciennes aux* Grenouilles *et au* Ploutos *d'Aristophane*, Paris.
Chardon, Henri (1970) [1905], *Robert Garnier, sa vie, ses poésies inédites*, Geneva.
Chavy, Paul (1981), 'Les Traductions humanistes au début de la Renaissance française: traductions médiévales, traductions modernes', *Revue Canadienne de Littérature Comparée*, 284–306.
Chekhov, Michael (2002), *To the Actor*, London.
Chiesa, Paolo (1987), 'Ad uerbum o ad sensum? Modelli e coscienza metodologica della traduzione tra tarda antichità e alto medioevo', *MeR* 1, 1–51.
Chirico, Maria Luisa (1991), *Aristofane in terra d'Otranto*, Naples.
Chirico, Maria Luisa (2014), 'Translations of Aristophanes in Italy in the 19th Century', in: S. Douglas Olson (ed.), *Ancient Comedy and Reception. Essays in Honor of Jeffrey Henderson*, Berlin/Boston, 727–746.
Ciccolella, Federica (2017), 'De utroque fonte bibere. Latin in the teaching of Greek grammar during the Renaissance', in: Eva Del Soldato/Andrea Rizzi (eds.), *City, Court, Academy: Language Choice in Early Modern Italy*, London, 137–157.
Ciccolella, Federica/Silvano, Luigi (eds.) (2017), *Teachers, Students, and Schools of Greek in the Renaissance*, Leiden/Boston.
Cinuzzi, Marcantonio (2006), *Il Prometeo del Duca. La prima traduzione italiana del* Prometeo *di Eschilo (VAT.URB.LAT. 789)*, Andrea Blasina (ed.), Amsterdam.
Cisterna, Domenica (2012), *I testimoni del XIV secolo del* Pluto *di Aristofane*, Florence.
Clerc, Sandra (2016), 'Verità e potere, ubbidienza e menzogna nella tragedia italiana del Cinquecento (1550–65)', *Annali d'Italianistica* 34, 219–242.
Cole, Janie (2005), '"Se di fuori è dorata, dentro è d'oro". Maffeo Barberini, Michelangelo il Giovane e Galileo', *Belfagor*, LX, 355, 1–26.
Cole, Janie (2007), *A muse of music in early baroque Florence: the poetry of Michelangelo Buonarroti il Giovane*, Florence.
Cole, Janie (2011), *Music, spectacle and cultural brokerage in Early Modern Italy: Michelangelo Buonarroti il giovane,* Florence.
Collard, C./Morwood, James (eds.) (2017), *Euripides. Iphigenia at Aulis*, Liverpool.
Conte, Adelheid (2002), 'La rinascita della Poetica nel Cinquecento Italiano', in: Diego Lanza (ed.), *La Poetica di Aristotele e la sua storia*, Pisa, 45–58.
Contini, Gianfranco (ed.) (1964), *Francesco Petrarca. Canzoniere*, Turin.
Copeland, Rita (2013), 'Horace's Ars poetica in the Medieval Classroom and Beyond: The Horizons of Ancient Precept', in: Andrew Galloway/Frank Grady (eds.), *Answerable style. The idea of the literary in medieval England*, Columbus, 15–33.
Corbett, Philip (1986), *The scurra*, Edinburgh.
Cornish, Alison (2011), *Vernacular Translation in Dante's Italy*, Cambridge.
Cortesi, Mariarosa (1979), 'Il Vocabularium di Giovanni Tortelli', *IMU* 22, 449–483.
Cortesi, Mariarosa (1995a), 'La tecnica del tradurre presso gli umanisti', in: Claudio Leonardi/Birger Munk Olsen (eds.), *The Classical Tradition in Middle Ages and in the Renaissance, Proceedings of the first European Science Foundation Workshop on The Reception of Classical Texts (Florence, Certosa del Galluzzo, 26–27 giugno 1992)*, Spoleto, 143–168.
Cortesi, Mariarosa (1995b), 'Umanesimo greco', in: Guglielmo Cavallo/Claudio Leonardi/Enrico Menestò (eds.), *Lo spazio letterario del Medioevo*, III *La ricezione del testo*, Rome, 457–507.

Cortesi, Mariarosa (2007), *Tradurre dal greco in età umanistica. Metodi e strumenti*, Atti del Seminario di studio (Firenze, Certosa del Galluzzo, 9 settembre 2005), Florence.
Cortesi, Mariarosa/Fiaschi, Silvia (eds.) (2008), *Repertorio delle traduzioni umanistiche a stampa- secoli XV-XVI*, Florence.
Cosentino, Paola (2003), *Cercando Melpomene: esperimenti tragici nella Firenze del primo Cinquecento*, Manziana.
Cosentino, Paola (2015), 'Pazzi de' Medici, Alessandro', in: *Dizionario Biografico degli Italiani*, vol. 82, 21–23.
Cotugno, Alessio (2006), 'Piccolomini e Castelvetro traduttori della Poetica (con un contributo sulle modalità dell'esegesi aristotelica nel Cinquecento)', *Studi di lessicografia italiana* 23, 113–219.
Coulon, Victor (ed.) (1923), *Aristophane. Les Acharniens, Les Cavaliers, Les Nuées*, vol. 1, Paris.
Craik, Katharine A./Pollard, Tanya (2013), *Shakespearean Sensations: Experiencing Literature in Early Modern England*, Cambridge.
Crastoni, Giovanni (1524), *Dictionarium Graecum*, Venice.
Cremante, Renzo (ed.) (1988), *Teatro del Cinquecento*, Milan.
Cronk, Nicholas (1999), 'Aristotle, Horace, and Longinus: the conception of reader response', in: Glyn P. Norton (ed.), *The Cambridge History of Literary Criticism*, vol. 3, 199–204.
D'Ovidio, Francesco (1878), *Saggi critici*, Naples, 276–293.
Da Falgano, Giovanni (1995), *Ippolito, Ecuba, Christus patiens. Volgarizzamenti inediti dal greco*, Lidia Caciolli (ed.), Florence.
Dacier, André (1693), *L'Œdipe et l'Electre de Sophocle. Tragédies Grecques. Traduites en François avec des remarques*, Paris.
Dacier, Anne, née Anne Le Févre (1684), *Le Plutus et les Nuées d'Aristophane. Comedies greques traduites en François. Avec des Remarques et un Examen de chaque piece selon les regles du theatre*, Paris.
Dacier, Anne, née Anne Le Févre (1712) [1699], *L'Iliade d'Homère traduite en françois avec des remarques par Madame Dacier nouvelle Edition revue & corrigée, où l'on a mis les remarques sous le Texte*, Amsterdam.
Daniello, Bernardino (1970) [1536], 'Della Poetica', in: Bernard Weinberg (ed.) (1970), *Trattati di Poetica e Retorica del Cinquecento*, Bari, vol. 1, 227–318.
Daskarolis, Anastasia (2000), *Die Wiedergeburt des Sophokles aus dem Geist des Humanismus. Studien zur Sophokles-Rezeption in Deutschland vom Beginn des 16. bis zur Mitte des 17. Jahrhunderts*, Tübingen.
De Andrés, Gregorio (1987), *Catálogo de los códices griegos de la Biblioteca Nacional*, Madrid.
De Cesare, Zeno (2005), *Le traduzioni latine del Pluto di Aristofane nel XV secolo: Rinuccio di Arezzo, Leonardo Bruni e Pietro da Montagnana*, (Tesi di Dottorato, Università degli Studi di Parma).
De Petris, Alfonso (1975), 'Le teorie umanistiche del tradurre e l'Apologeticus di Giannozzo Manetti', *BiblH&R* 37, 15–32.
Del Corso, Lucio/Pecere, Oronzo (2010), *Libri di scuola e pratiche didattiche. Dall'Antichità al Rinascimento. Atti del Convegno Internazionale di Studi (Cassino, 7–10 maggio 2008)*, Cassino.
Delcourt, Marie (1925), *Études sur les traductions des tragiques grecs et latins depuis la Renaissance*, Bruxelles.
Deligiannis, Ioannis (2017), 'Investigating the Translation's Process in Humanistic Latin Translations of Greek Texts', *Mediterranean Chronicle* 7.

Deloince-Louette, Christiane (2017), 'Entre rhétorique et dramaturgie: la lecture de Térence par Mélanchthon', *Exercices de rhétorique 10*: 'Sur Térence', 1–31, https://doi.org/10.4000/rhetorique.564 (last accessed 08/06/2022).

Demetriu, Tania/Pollard, Tanya (eds.) (2017), 'Homer and Greek tragedy in early modern England's theatres. An Introduction', *Classical Receptions Journal* 9 (1), 1–35.

Derrida, Jacques (1985), *The Ear of the Other: Otobiography, Transference, Translation*, New York.

Derrida, Jacques (2003) [1990], *The Problem of Genesis in Husserl's Philosophy*, transl. Marian Hobson, Chicago.

Derrida, Jacques (2007), 'At This Very Moment in This Work Here I Am', in: Jacques Derrida, *Psyche: Inventions of the Other*, vol. 1, Peggy Kamuf/Elizabeth Rottenberg (eds.), Stanford, 143–190.

Di Blasi, Maria Rosa (1997), 'Studi sulla tradizione manoscritta del Pluto di Aristofane. Parte II: i codices recentiores', *Maia* 49, 367–380.

Diggle, James (1984), *Euripidis Fabulae*, vol. I, Oxford.

Diggle, James (1994), '*Iphigenia Aulidensis*', *Euripides Fabulae*, vol. III, Oxford, 357–425.

Di Maria, Salvatore (2002), *The Italian Tragedy in the Renaissance: Cultural Realities and Theatrical Innovations*, London.

Di Maria, Salvatore (2005), 'Italian Reception of Greek Tragedy', in: Justina Gregory (ed.), *A Companion to Greek Tragedy*, Oxford, 428–443.

Di Martino, Giovanna (2019), 'The Reception of Aeschylus in sixteenth-century Italy: the case of Coriolano Martirano's Prometheus Bound (1556)', in: Stephen Harrison/Giancarlo Abbamonte (eds.), *Making and Rethinking Renaissance. Between Greek and Latin in 15th-16th-century Europe*, Berlin, 125–142.

Di Martino, Giovanna (2019a), 'Vittorio Alfieri's tormented relationship with Aeschylus: *Agamennone* between Tradition and Innovation', *Anabases* 29, 121–133.

Di Martino, Giovanna (forthcoming), 'Tradurre il teatro per il teatro: presenza e assenza di dialoghi in due adattamenti cinquecenteschi del *Prometeo incatenato* di Eschilo', *Le Dialogue de l'Antiquité à l'âge humaniste. Péripéties d'un genre dramatique et philosophique*.

Di Martino, Giovanna/Fiore, Giulia (in preparation), 'Cataloguing Volgarizzamenti/Tragedie between 1450 and 1600 in Italy'.

Diggle, James (1991), *The Textual Tradition of Euripides' Orestes*, Oxford.

Dionisotti, Carlo (1967), 'Tradizione classica e volgarizzamenti', in: Carlo Dionisotti, *Geografia e storia della letteratura italiana*, Turin, 103–144.

Dionisotti, Carlo (1968), *Gli umanisti e il volgare fra Quattro e Cinquecento*, Florence.

Dionisotti, Carlo (1984–1985), 'From Stephanus to Du Cange: Glossary stories', *RHT* 14–15, 303–336.

Dolce, Lodovico (1543), *La Hecuba, tragedia di M. Lodovico Dolce, tratta da Euripide*, Venice.

Dolce, Lodovico (1549), *La Giocasta, tragedia di M. Lodovico Dolce*, Venice.

Dolce, Lodovico (1557), *La Medea, tragedia di M. Lodovico Dolce, tratta da Euripide*, Venice.

Dolce, Lodovico (1560), *Le Tragedie di M. Lodovico Dolce*, Venice.

Dolce, Lodovico (1566), *Le Troiane, tragedia di M. Lodovico Dolce recitata in Vinegia l'anno 1566, con privilegio*, Venice.

Dolce, Lodovico (1597) [1551], *Ifigenia. Nuovamente con diligenza ristampata*, Venice.

Dolce, Lodovico (2005), *Medea*, Ottavio Saviano and Francesco Spera (eds.), Turin.

Dolce, Lodovico (2010), *Tieste*, Stefano Giazzon (ed.), Turin.

Dolet, Etienne (1540), *Manière de bien traduire d'une langue en autre*, Lyon.

Donini, Pierluigi (2004), *La tragedia e la vita. Saggi sulla Poetica di Aristotele*, Alessandria.
Dover, Kenneth (ed.) (1970), *Aristophanes. Clouds*, Oxford.
Du Cange, Charles (1883–1887), *Glossarium mediae et infimae Latinitatis*, Niort.
Du Verdier, Antoine (1585), *Catalogue de tous ceux qui ont escrit, ou traduict en françois, & autres Dialectes de ce Royaume*, Lyon.
Duché, Véronique (ed.) (2015), *Histoire des traductions en langue française*, vol. 3, Paris.
Dudouyt, Cécile (2016), 'Aristophanes in Early-Modern Fragments: Le Loyer's La Néphélococugie (1579) and Racine's Les Plaideurs (1668)', in: Philip Walsh (ed.), *Brill's Companion to the Reception of Aristophanes*, 175–194.
Dutton, Elizabeth (2020), 'Protestant place, Protestant props in the plays of Nicholas Grimald', in: Chanita Goodblatt/Eva von Contzen (eds.), *Enacting the Bible in medieval and early modern drama*, Manchester, 157–174.
Earle, Thomas F. (2008), 'Classical Mythology and Portuguese Renaissance Poetry', in: Catarina Fouto/Inês Mendes (eds.), *From Renaissance to Post-Modernism: Rewritings of myths in Britain and Portugal. Proceedings of a Conference held at the University of Oxford*, https://www.mod-langs.ox.ac.uk/files/myths_08/thomas_earle.pdf (last accessed 01/09/2022).
Earle, Thomas F. (2012), 'António Ferreira's *Castro*: Tragedy at the Cross-Roads', in: Maria Berbara/Karl A.E. Enenkel (eds.), *Portuguese Humanism and the Republic of Letters,* Leiden, 279–318.
Eco, Umberto (2003), *Dire quasi la stessa cosa. Esperienze di traduzione*, Milan.
Edwards, Kurt A. (2004), 'John the Baptist: Protestant Character in Tudor Drama', *OAH Proceedings*, 9–17.
Eleuteri, Paolo/Canart, Paul (1991), *Scrittura greca nell'Umanesimo italiano*, Milan.
Enenkel, Karl/Nellen, Henk (eds.) (2013), *Neo-Latin Commentaries and the Management of Knowledge in the late Middle Ages and the Early Modern Period (1400–1700)*, Supplementa Humanistica Lovaniensia 23.
Erasmus, Desiderius (1506), '*Reuerendo in Christo Patri Gulielmo Archiepiscopo Cantuariensi Primati Angliae Erasmus Roterdamus S.P.D. 'Euripidis Tragoediae duae, Hecuba, et Iphigenia in Aulide, latine factae, Des. Erasmo Roterodamo interprete*', Paris, A2r.-A3v.
Erasmus, Desiderius (1507), *Tragoediae duae Hecuba et Iphigenia in Aulide, Latinae factae, Erasmo Roterodamo interprete*, Venice.
Erasmus, Desiderius (1906), *Opus epistolarium Des. Erasmi Roterodami,* vol. 1, 1484–1514, P.S. Allen (ed.), Oxford.
Erasmus, Desiderius (1947), 'Ornatissimo viro Ioanni Cholero [...]', in: H.M. Allen/H.W. Garrod (eds.), *Opus epistolarum Des. Erasmi Roterodami, Tom XI 1534–1536,* Oxford, 172–186.
Erasmus, Desiderius (1969), 'Reverendo in Christo Patri Nicolao Ruterio Episcopo [...]', R.A.B. Mynors (ed.), in: *Opera omnia Desiderii Erasmi [...], ordinis primi tomus primus*, Amsterdam, 181–184.
Erasmus, Desiderius (1969a), 'Guilielmo Archiepiscopo Cantuariensi [...]', Jan Hendrik Waszink (ed.), in: *Opera omnia Desiderii Erasmi [...], ordinis primi tomus primus*, Amsterdam, 216–219.
Erasmus, Desiderius (1969b), '*Euripidis Hecuba et Iphigenia*', Jan Hendrik Waszink (ed.), in: *Opera omnia Desiderii Erasmi [...], ordinis primi tomus primus*, Amsterdam, 193–359.
Erasmus, Desiderius (1969c), 'Ad lectorem', Jan Hendrik Waszink (ed.), in: *Opera omnia Desiderii Erasmi [...], ordinis primi tomus primus*, Amsterdam, 220–21.

Erasmus, Desiderius (1975), *Collected works of Erasmus: Letters 142 to 297, 1501 to 1514*, R.A.B. Mynors, D.F.S. Thomson, W.K. Ferguson (eds.), Toronto-Canada.

Erasmus, Desiderius (1988), *De copia uerborum ac rerum*, B.I. Knott (ed.), in: *Opera omnia Desiderii Erasmi Roterdami [...] ordinis primi tomus sextus*, Amsterdam.

Erasmus, Desiderius (1989), '1341A/To Johann von Botzheim', in: R.A.B. Mynors/James M. Estes (eds.), *The Correspondence of Erasmus, Letters 1252 to 1355*, Toronto, 291–364.

Erasmus, Desiderius (2000), *Tragedie di Euripide (Hecuba, Iphigenia in Aulide)*, Giovanni Barberi Squarotti (ed.), Turin.

Estienne, Henry (1567) (ed.), 'ΣΟΠΗΟΚΛΕΟΥΣ ΑΝΤΙΓΟΝΕ', in: Henry Estienne, *Tragoediae selectae Aeschyli, Sophoclis, Euripidis*, Geneva, 738–850.

Even-Zohar, Itamar (1990), 'The Position of Translated Literature within the Literary Polysystem', in: *Polysystem Studies*, Durham, 45–51.

Fabrizio Richard (1995), 'The Two Oedipuses: Sophocles, Anguillara, and the Renaissance Treatment of Myth', *MLN* 110/1 178–91.

Fairclough, Henry R./Goold, George P. (1999), *Virgil*, Cambridge (Massachusetts).

Fauconnier, Denis (2001), *La Pléiade*, Paris.

Fausto Da Longiano, Sebastiano (1990) [1556], 'Dialogo del modo de lo tradurre d'una in altra lingua secondo le regole mostrate da Cicerone', *Quaderni Veneti* 12 (1990), 57–152.

Fera, Vincenzo/Ferraù, Giacomo/Rizzo, Silvia (eds.) (2002), *Talking to the Text: Marginalia from Papyri to Print*, in: *Proceedings of a Conference held at Erice (26 september-3 october 1998), as the 12th Course of International School for the Study of Written Records*, Messina.

Ferguson, George (1961), *Signs and Symbols of Christian Art*, Oxford.

Finglass, Patrick J. (2017), 'Electra', in: Lauriola, Rosanna/Demetriou, Kyriakos N. (eds.), *Brill's Companion to the Reception of Sophocles*, Leiden/Boston, 475–511.

Finglass, Patrick J. (2018), *Sophocles: Oedipus the King*, Cambridge.

Fiore, Giulia (2019), 'L'Œdipe moralisé. Éthique et culpabilité dans les réécritures de la première modernité', in: Ricci, Maria T. (ed.), *Savoir-vivre, normes et transgression*, Cahiers d'Histoire Culturelle 30, Tours, 11–34.

Fiore, Giulia (2022), '"Religion is dying". Doubting the Divine in Sophocles' *Oedipus Tyrannus*', in: Nicole Hartmann/Franziska Naether (eds.), *The Benefit of the Doubt*, Archiv für Religionsgeschichte, Berlin/New York (23:1), 61–78.

Flegès, Amaury (2000), *Les Tombeaux littéraires en France à la Renaissance* (Thèses de doctorat), Tours.

Folena, Gianfranco (1991), *Volgarizzare e tradurre*, Turin.

Ford, Philip J./Green, Roger (2009), 'George Buchanan: Poet and Dramatist', *Classical Press of Wales* (accessed 26/01/2021).

Fouto, Catarina (2015), 'The Reinvention of Classical Comedy and Tragedy in Portugal. Defining Drama in the Work of Sá de Miranda, António Ferreira and Diogo de Teive', in: T.F. Earle/Catarina Fouto (eds.), *The Reinvention of Theatre in Sixteenth-Century Europe. Traditions, Texts and Performance*, London, 89–111.

François, Ide (2015), 'Towards a Critical Edition of Francesco Filelfo's 'Consolatio ad Iacobum Antonium Marcellum de obitum Valerii filii'', *Aevum* 89, 2, 393–407.

Fubini, Riccardo (1961), 'La coscienza del latino negli umanisti. An latina lingua Romanorum esset peculiare idioma', *StudMed* 2, 505–550.

Furno, Martine (ed.) (2017), *Traductions vers le latin au XVIe siècle*, *Astérion* (16).

Gabia, Giovan Battista (ed.) (1543), '*Antigone*', in: Giovan Battista Gabia, *Sophoclis tragoediae omnes, nunc primum Latinae ad uerbum factae, ac scholijs quibusdam illustratae, Ioanne Baptista Gabia Veronensi interprete*, Venice, 82–105.

Galladei, Maffeo (1558), *Medea tragedia di M. Maffeo Galladei*, Venice.

Gamba, Eleonora (2016), *Pietro da Montagnana: la vita, gli studi, la biblioteca di un* homo trilinguis, (Tesi di Dottorato, Università degli Studi di Padova).

Gargiulo, Marco (2009), 'Per Una Nuova Edizione *Degli Avvertimenti Della Lingua Sopra 'l Decamerone* Di Leonardo Salviati', *Heliotropia* 6.1–2, 15–41.

Garin, Eugenio (1949), *L'educazione umanistica in Italia*, Bari.

Garin, Eugenio (1957), *L'educazione in Europa. 1400–1600*, Bari.

Garin, Eugenio (1958), *Il pensiero pedagogico dell'Umanesimo*, Florence.

Garnier, Bruno (1999), *Pour une poétique de la traduction: l'Hécube d'Euripide en France, de la traduction humaniste à la tragédie classique*, Paris.

Garnier, Bruno (2009), 'Maîtres serviles et disciples ingrats à la Renaissance', in: Valérie-Angélique Deshoulières/Constantinescu Muguraş (eds.), *Les Funambules de l'affection, maîtres et disciples*, 165–186.

Gelous, Sigismond (1551), *Euripidis Orestes Tragoedia cum primis elegans, Latino carmine longe doctissime expressa, nuncque primum in lucem edita*, Basel.

Genette, Gérard (1997), *Palimpsests, Literature in the Second Degree* [1982], trans. C. Newman/C. Doubinsky, Nebraska.

Giannopoulou, Vasiliki (2007), 'Aristophanes in Translation before 1920', in: Edith Hall/Amanda Wrigley (eds.), *Aristophanes in Performance, 421 BC- AD 2007: Peace, Birds and Frogs*, London, 309–342.

Giazzon, Stefano (2011), *Venezia in coturno*, Rome.

Giazzon, Stefano (2012), 'Il Manierismo a Teatro: *L'Ifigenia* Di Lodovico Dolce', *Forum Italicum* 46.1, 53–81.

Giazzon, Stefano (2014), 'La maschera dell'ambiguità. Sull'*Ifigenia* di Lodovico Dolce', *Per Leggere* 26.1, 63–90.

Giazzon, Stefano (2016), 'Note sul teatro tragico di Lodovico Dolce', in: Paolo Marini/Paolo Procaccioli (eds.), *Per Lodovico Dolce. Miscellanea di studi, I. Passioni e competenze del letterato*, Rome, 217–243.

Giles, John A. (ed.), (1864), *The Whole Works of Roger Ascham* (3 vols.), London.

Gillespie, Stuart (2011), *English Translation and Classical Reception*, Oxford.

Gindhart, Marion, 'P(ublii) Terentii comoediae sex', in: OC, http://wiki.camerarius.de/OC_0487 (last accessed 04/02/2020).

Gindhart, Marion, 'Terenz 1546', in: OC, http://wiki.camerarius.de/Terenz,_Comoediae_sex,_1546 (last accessed 05/10/2021).

Giraldi Cinzio, Giovan Battista (2002) [1554], 'Discorso sulle commedie e sulle tragedie', in: Giovan Battista Giraldi Cinthio (2002), *Discorsi intorno al comporre rivisti dall'autore nell'esemplare Cl. I 90*, Susanna Villari (ed.), Messina, 205–318.

Giraldi Cinzio, Giovan Battista (1970) [1543], 'Lettera sulla tragedia', in: Bernard Weinberg (ed.), *Trattati di Poetica e Retorica del Cinquecento*, Bari, vol. 1, 469–486.

Giraldi Cinzio, Giovan Battista (1988) [1543], *Orbecche*, in: Renzo Cremante (ed.) (1988), *Teatro del Cinquecento. Tomo I. La Tragedia*, Milan/Naples, 283–448.

Giraldi Cinzio, Giovan Battista (1970a) [1543], 'Prologo all''Altile', in: Bernard Weinberg (ed.), *Trattati di Poetica e Retorica del Cinquecento*, Bari, vol. 1, 487–492.

Giraldi Cinzio, Giovanbattista (1554), *Discorsi intorno al comporre dei romanzi, delle comedie e delle tragedie, e di altre maniere di poesie*, Venice.
Gliksohn, Jean-Michel (1985), *Iphigenie de la Grèce antique à l'Europe des Lumières*, Paris.
Grafton, Anthony (1985), 'Renaissance Readers and Ancient Texts: Comments on Some Commentaries', *RenQ* 38, 615–649.
Grafton, Anthony (1997), *Commerce with the Classics: Ancient Books and Renaissance Readers*, Ann Arbor.
Grafton, Anthony/Jardine, Lisa (1986), *From Humanism to the Humanities*, Cambridge.
Gratarolo, Bongianni (1589), *Astianatte tragedia di M. Bongianni Gratarolo*, Venice.
Green, William C. (ed.) (1870), *Aristophanes. The Acharnians, The Knights*, London/Oxford/Cambridge.
Greene, Thomas M. (1982), *The Light in Troy: Imitation and Discovery in Renaissance*, London.
Greenwood, David (1964), 'The Staging of Neo-Latin Plays in Sixteenth Century England', *Educational Theatre Journal*, 16 (4), 311–23.
Grendler, Paul (1989), *Schooling in Renaissance Italy. Literacy and Learning, 1300–1600*, Baltimore/London.
Grendler, Paul (2002), *The Universities of the Italian Renaissance*, Baltimore/London.
Gresy, Eugène (ed.) (1848), *Vie de J. Amyot, tirée des mémoires concernant l'histoire civile et ecclésiastique d'Auxerre, par l'abbé Lebeuf*, Melun.
Gualdo Rosa, Lucia (1985), 'Le traduzioni dal greco nella prima metà del '400: alle radici del classicismo europeo', in: Marcel Renard/Pierre Laurens (eds.), *Hommages à Henry Bardon*, Bruxelles, 177–193.
Guastella, Giovanni (2013), '*Edipo re* nel teatro italiano del Cinquecento', in: *Dyonisus ex machina* IV, 258–266.
Guastella, Giovanni (ed.) (2006), *Le rinascite della tragedia: origini classiche e tradizioni europee*, Rome.
Guillerm, Luce (1988), *Sujet de l'écriture et traduction autour de 1540*, Lille.
Guthmüller, Bodo (1990), 'Fausto da Longiano e il problema del tradurre', *Quaderni Veneti* 12, 9–56.
Guthmüller, Bodo (1993), 'Letteratura nazionale e traduzione dei classici nel Cinquecento', *Lettere Italiane* 45, 501–518.
Hall, Edith (2005), 'Aeschylus' Clytemnestra versus her Senecan Tradition', in: Fiona Macintosh/Pantelis Michelakis/Edith Hall/Oliver Taplin (eds.), *Agamemnon in Performance 458 BC to AD 2004*, Oxford, 53–75.
Hall, Frederick W./Geldart, William M. (eds.) (1906), *Aristophanis comoediae*, vol. 1, Oxford.
Halliwell, Stephen (1987), *The Poetics of Aristotle. Translation and Commentary*, London.
Hamm, Joachim (2011), 'Camerarius (Kammermeister), Joachim d.Ä.', in: Wilhelm Kühlmann et al. (eds.), *Frühe Neuzeit in Deutschland 1520–1620. Literaturwissenschaftliches Verfasserlexikon*, vol. 1, Berlin/Boston, 425–438.
Hankins, James (1994), 'Translation Practice in the Renaissance: the Case of Leonardo Bruni', in: Charles Marie Ternes (ed.), *Études classiques IV. Actes du colloque «Méthodologie de la traduction: de l'Antiquité à la Renaissance»*, Luxembourg, 154–175.
Hardison, O.B. (1989), *Prosody and Purpose in the English Renaissance*, Baltimore.
Hardwick, Lorna (2007), 'Translating Greek Tragedy to the Modern Stage', *Theatre Journal* 59, 358–361.
Hardwick, Lorna (2010), 'Negotiating Translation for the Stage', in: Edith Hall/Stephe Harrop (eds.), *Theorising Performance*, London, 192–207.

Hardwick, Lorna (2021), 'Translation and/as Adaptation', in: Vaios Liapies/Avra Sidiropoulou (eds.), *Adapting Greek Tragedy Contemporary Contexts for Ancient Texts*, Cambridge, 110–130.
Harington, John (1591), 'A Preface, or Rather a Briefe Apologie of Poetrie and of the Author and Translator of this Poem', in: Lodovico Ariosto, *Orlando Furioso*, London, ¶iiv-¶viiiv.
Harsh, Philip (1945), '*Hamartia* Again', *TAPhA* 76, 47–58.
Hartmann, Alfred (1957), 'Collinus, Rudolfus', in: *Neue Deutsche Biographie*, 3:325. Bayerische Staatsbibliothek. https://www.deutsche-biographie.de/pnd119605562.html#ndbcontent (last accessed 01/09/2022).
Hartmann, Alfred (ed.) (1943), *Die Amerbachkorrespondenz*, vol. II (1514–1524), Basel.
Hathaway, Baxter (1962), *The Age of Criticism: The Late Renaissance in Italy*, Westport.
Hausmann, Frank-Rutger (1980), 'Carmina Priapea', in: Edward Cranz/Paul Oskar Kristeller (eds.), *Catalogus translationum et commentariorum*, vol. 4, Washington, 423–450.
Heath, Malcom (1987), '"Jure principem locum tenet": Euripides' *Hecuba*', *Bulletin of the Institute of Classical Studies* 34, 40–68.
Heavey, Katherine (2015), *The early modern Medea: Medea in English literature, 1558–1688*, Hampshire, New York.
Henderson, Jeffrey (1975), *The Maculate Muse: Obscene Language in Attic Comedy*, Oxford.
Henderson, Jeffrey (ed.) (1998), *Aristophanes. Acharnians and Knights*, Cambridge/London.
Hermans, Theo (2014) [1985], 'Images of Translation: Metaphor and Imagery in the Renaissance Discourse on Translation', in: Theo Hermans (ed.), *The Manipulation of Literature: Studies in Literary Translation*, Abingdon, 103–135.
Hernández López, Araceli (2019), *Edición crítica de la obra dramática de Hernán Pérez de Oliva: sus tragédias La vengança de Agamenón y Hécuba triste*, (doctoral tesis), Madrid.
Herrick, Marvin T. (1946), *The Fusion of Horatian and Aristotelian Literary Criticism*, Urbana.
Hervet, Gentien (1541), *Sophoclis Antigone. Tragoedia a Gentiano Herveto Aurelio traducta e Graeco in Latinum*, Lyon.
Herzog-Hauser, Gertrud (1938), 'Ennius imitateur d'Euripide', *Latomus* 2/4, 1938, 225–232.
Hodgson-Wright, Stephanie (1998), 'Jane Lumley's *Iphigenia at Aulis*: Multum in parvo, or, less is more', in: Susan P. Cerasano/Marion Wynne-Davies (eds.), *Readings in Renaissance Women's Drama: Criticism, History, Performance 1594–1998*, London, 129–141.
Holmes, Lorna Marie (1990), *Character Naming in Aristophanes*, Harvard.
Holtz, Louis (1995), 'Glosse e commenti', in: *Lo spazio letterario del Medioevo*, vol. 3, Rome, 59–111.
Holtz, Louis (1996), 'Glossaires et grammaire dans l'Antiquité', in: Jacqueline Hamesse (ed.), *Les manuscrits des lexiques et glossaires de l'Antiquité tardive à la fin du Moyen Âge*, Leuven, 1–21.
Holzberg, Niklas/Brunner, Horst (eds.) (2020), *Hans Sachs. Ein Handbuch*, Berlin/Boston.
Hosington, Brenda (2014), 'Translation and Neo-Latin', in: Craig Kallendorf (ed.), *Brill's Encyclopaedia of the Neo-Latin World*, http://dx.doi.org/10.1163/9789004271296_enlo_B9789004271012_0011 (last accessed 01/02/2021).
Hösle, Vittorio (2008), 'Cicero's Plato', in: *Wiener Studien* 121, 145–170.
Hubert, Alexander/Huth, Manuel, 'Camerarius an Turnèbe', 1556, *OCEp*, http://wiki.camerarius. de/OCEp_0376 (last accessed 27/11/2019).
Huet, Pierre-Daniel (1683), *Petri Danielis Huetii De Interpretatione Libri Duo: Quorum Prior Est, De Optimo Genere Interpretandi: Alter De Claris Interpretibus. His Accessit De Fabularum Romanensium Origine Diatriba*, The Hague.

Jackson, Lucy (2019), 'Review of *Brill's Companion to the Reception of Sophocles* and *Brill's Companion to the Reception of Aeschylus*', *Translation and Literature*, 28, 317–23.

Jackson, Lucy (2020), 'Proximate Translation: Buchanan's 'Greek' Biblical Plays and Sixteenth-Century English Drama', *Translation and Literature* 29, 85–100.

Jamyn, Amadis (1605), *Les XXIIII livres de l'Iliade d'Homere prince des poetes grecs traduit du Grec en ver François les Xi premiers par M Hugues Salel abbé de saint cheron et les XIII derniers par amadis Iamyn, secretaire de la chambre de Toy : tous les XXIIII reveus et corrigez par ledit Am. Iamyn avec les trois premiers livres de l'Odyssée d'Homère plus une Table bien ample sur l'Iliade d'Homère*. Rouen.

Javitch, Daniel (1999), 'The assimilation of Aristotle's Poetics in sixteenth-century Italy', in: Glyn P. Norton (ed.), *The Cambridge History of Literary Criticism*, vol. 3, 53–65.

Javitch, Daniel (2001), 'On the Rise of Genre-Specific Poetics in the Sixteenth Century', in: Øivind Andersen/John Haarberg (eds.), *Making Sense of Aristotle. Essays in Poetics*, London, 127–144.

Jayne, Sears/Johnson, Francis R. (eds.) (1956), *The Lumley Library: The Catalogue of 1609*, London.

Jebb, Richard Claverhouse (ed.) (1896), *Sophocles, The Plays and Fragments, With Critical Notes, Commentary and Translation in English Prose*, Vol. 7: *The Ajax*, Cambridge.

Kappl, Brigitte (2006), *Die Poetik des Aristoteles in der Dichtungstheorie des Cinquecento*, Berlin/New York.

Kappl, Brigitte (2016), 'Profit, Pleasure, and Purgation: *Catharsis* in Aristotle, Paolo Beni and Italian Late Renaissance Poetics', in: *Skenè Journal of Theatre and Drama Studies* 2/1, 105–132.

Kelly, Henry A. (1993), *Ideas and Forms of Tragedy from Aristotle to the Middle Ages*, Cambridge.

Kim, Ho (2010), 'Aristotle's hamartia reconsidered', in: *Harvard Studies in Classical Philology* 105, 33–52.

Kraus, Christina S./Stray, Christopher (eds.) (2016), *Classical commentaries. Explorations in a Scholarly Genre*, Oxford.

Krebs, Katja (2014), 'Introduction: Collisions, Diversions, and Meeting Points', in: Katja Krebs (ed.), *Translation and Adaptation in Theatre and Film*, New York, 1–10.

Kristeva, Julia (1969), *Recherches pour une sémanalyse, Essais*, Paris.

Laera, Margherita (2014), 'Introduction: Return, Rewrite, Repeat: The Theatricality of Adaptation', in: Margherita Laera (ed.), *Theatre and adaptation: return, rewrite, repeat*, London, 1–17.

Lalemant, Jean (1557), *Sophoclis Tragicorum veterum facile principis Tragoediae, quotquot extant, septem*, Paris.

Lanson, Gustave (1920), *Esquisse d'une histoire de la tragédie française*, New York.

Lateiner, Donald (2007), *Obscenity in Catullus*, Oxford.

Lauriola, Rosanna (2016), 'Still on Aristophanes and Euripides: from *Hippolytus* 345 to *Knights* 16–18', in: *Prometheus* 42, 71–95.

Lauriola, Rosanna (2017), 'Oedipus the King', in: Rosanna Lauriola/Kyriakos N. Demetriou (eds.), *Brill's companion to the reception of Sophocles*, Leiden/Boston, 147–325.

Lauriola, Rosanna/Demetriou, Kyriakos N. (eds.) (2017), *Brill's Companion to the Reception of Sophocles*, Leiden.

Lazarus, Micha (2015), 'Greek literacy in sixteenth-century England', *Renaissance Studies* 29 (3), 433–458.

Lazarus, Micha (2020), 'Tragedy at Wittenberg: Sophocles in Reformation Europe', *Renaissance Quarterly* 73, 33–77.
Le Loyer, Pierre (2004), *La Néphélococugie ou la Nuée des Cocus*, M. Doe and K. Cameron (eds.), Paris.
Lebègue, Raymond (1977), *Etudes sur le théâtre français*, Paris.
Lechevalier, Claire (2007), *L'Invention d'une origine: Traduire Eschyle en France*, Paris.
Leo, Russ (2019), 'Herod and the Furies: Daniel Heinsius and the Representation of Affect in Tragedy', *Journal of Medieval and Early Modern Studies* 49 (1), 137–167.
Leonardi, Domenico Felice (1747), *Tragedie trasportate dalla greca nell'italiana favella da monsignor Cristoforo Guidiccioni lucchese vescovo d'Ajace in Corsica*, Lucca.
Leroux, Virginie (2012), 'Tragique et tragédie : la réception de l'héritage aristotélicien dans les poétiques néo-latines de la Renaissance', *Atti dell'Accademia Pontaniana*, Supplemento, n.s. 61, 309–336.
Leroux, Virginie (2014), 'Commentaire et cadrage du sens : l'error tragique selon Francesco Robortello et Martin Antoine Del Rio', in: Laurence Boulègue (ed.), *Commenter et philosopher à la Renaissance: Tradition universitaire, tradition humaniste*, Villeneuve d'Ascq, 225–238.
Leroux, Virginie (2017), 'Les premières traductions de l'Iphigénie à Aulis d'Euripide, d'Érasme à Thomas Sébillet', *Renaiss. Reform. Renaiss. Réforme* 40/3, 2017, 243–264.
Lianeri, Alexandra (2019), 'Translation and Classical Reception', Oxford Bibliographies, https://ezproxy-prd.bodleian.ox.ac.uk:3144/view/document/obo-9780195389661/obo-9780195389661-0335.xml?rskey=lX9jr3&result=358 (last accessed 04/03/2022).
Link, Franz H. (1980), 'Translation, Adaptation and Interpretation of Dramatic Texts', in: Ortun Zuber-Skerritt (ed.), *The Languages of Theatre: Problems in the Translation and Transposition of Drama*, Oxford, 24–50.
Lloyd-Jones, Hugh (ed.) (1994), *Sophocles. Ajax, Electra, Oedipus Tyrannus*, Cambridge/London.
Lo Monaco, Francesco (1992), 'Alcune osservazioni sul commento ai classici del secondo Quattrocento', in: Ottavio Besomi/Claudio Caruso (eds.), *Il commento ai testi. Atti del seminario di Ascona (2–9 ottobre 1989)*, Basel/Boston/Berlin, 103–149.
Lockwood, Dean (1909), 'Aristophanes in the Fifteenth Century', *TAPA* 40, lvi–lvii.
Lockwood, Dean (1913), 'Aretino Graecarum Litterarum Interprete', *HSCP* 24, 51–109.
Lockwood, Dean (1913), 'De Rinucio Aretino graecarum litterarum interprete', *HSPh* 24, 51–109.
Lockwood, Dean (1931), 'Leonardo Bruni's Translation of act I of the Plutus of Aristophanes', *Classical Studies in Honor of. J.C. Rolfe*, Philadelphia, 163–172.
Lockwood, Dean (1967), 'Leonardo Bruni's Translation of Act I of the *Plutus* of Aristophanes', in: G.D. Hadzsits (ed.), *Classical Studies in Honor of John Carew Rolfe*, Philadelphia, 163–172.
López, Pociña/José, Andrés (2016), 'A Antiguidade Clássica no teatro de Gil Vicente', in: Maria de Fátima Silva/Maria do Céu Fialho/José Luís Brandão (eds.), *O Livro do Tempo: Escritas e reescritas. Teatro Greco-Latino e sua recepção II*, Coimbra, 15–27.
Lowry, Martin (1994), 'Aristotle's *Poetics* and the Rise of Vernacular Literary Theory', *Viator* 25, 411–425.
Lucan (1993), 'Hercule Gaulois', trans. J. Bompaire, in: *Oeuvres, Opuscules 1–10*, Paris, 59–62.
Ludwig, Walther (1975), *Die Fabula Penia des Rinucius Aretinus; herausgegeben, eingeleitet und kommentiert von Walther Ludwig*, Munich.
Lumley, Jane (1998), 'The Tragedie of Iphigeneia', in: Diane Purkiss (ed.), *Three Tragedies by Renaissance Women*, London, 3–35.

Lumley, Lady Jane (1557 ca.), *The Tragedie of Euripides called Iphigeneia translated out of the Greake into Englisshe*, ms Royal 15 A. IX. Holograph, folls 63–97, British Library.

Lurie, Michael (2004), *Die Suche nach der Schuld. Sophokles' Oedipus Rex, Aristoteles' Poetik und das Tragödienverständnis der Neuzeit*, München/Leipzig.

Lurie, Michael (2012), 'Facing up to tragedy: towards an intellectual history of Sophocles in Europe from Camerarius to Nietzsche', in: Kirk Ormand (ed.), *A companion to Sophocles*, Oxford, 440–461.

Lurje, Michael (2004), *Die Suche nach der Schuld. Sophokles' Oedipus Rex, Aristoteles' Poetik und das Tragödienverständnis der Neuzeit* (BzA 209), Leipzig.

Heath, M. (2010), "Iure principem locum tenet': Euripides' *Hecuba*', *Bull. Inst. Class. Stud.* 34, 2010, 40–68.

Macintosh, Fiona (2009), 'The Rediscovery of Aeschylus for the modern stage', *Entretiens sur l'Antiquité classique* 55, Zürich, 435–468. http://doi.org/10.5169/seals-661023 (last accessed 07/04/2022).

Macintosh, Fiona (2013), 'Theatre Translation and Performance', in: Georgios Giannakis (ed.), *Encyclopaedia of Ancient Greek Language and Linguistics*, Leiden, 1–4.

Macintosh, Fiona/Di Martino, Giovanna (2021), 'Archiving and Interpreting Greek and Roman Theatre: The Archive as Engine Room and Digital Hub', *Futuro Classico* 7, 233–254.

Mack, Peter (2011), *A History of Renaissance Rhetoric 1380–1620*, Oxford.

Maffei, Scipione (ed.) (1723), 'L'Oreste tragedia di Giovanni Rucellai non più stampata', in: *Teatro italiano o sia scelta di tragedie per l'uso della scena tomo I*, Verona, 89–193.

Maggi, Vincenzo/Lombardi, Bartolomeo (1550), *In Aristotelis librum de poetica comune explanationes, Madii vero in eundem librum propriae annotationes*, Venice.

Maino, Paolo M.G. (2012), 'L'uso dei testimoni del 'Decameron' nella rassettatura di Lionardo Salviati', *Aevum* 86.3, 1005–1030.

Maisano, Riccardo/Rollo, Antonio (eds.) (2002), *Manuele Crisolora e il ritorno del greco in Occidente*. Atti del Convegno Internazionale (Napoli, 26–29 giugno 1997), Naples.

Manuzio, Aldo (ed.) (1502), 'ΣΟΠΗΟΚΛΕΟΥΣ ΑΝΤΙΓΟΝΕ', in: Aldo Manuzio (ed.), *Σοφοκλέους τραγωδίαι*, Paris, vr-oviiv.

Manuzio, Aldo (ed.) (1503), *Euripidou tragodiai heptakaideka on eniai met'exegeseon eisi de autai. Ekabe Orestes Phoinissai ... Euripidis tragoediae septendecim, ex quib. quaedam habent commentaria. & sunt hae. Hecuba Orestes Phoenissae Medea Hippolytus Alcestis Andromache Supplices Iphigenia in Aulide Iphigenia in Tauris Rhesus Troades Bacchae Cyclops Heraclidae Helena Ion.*, Venice.

Manuzio, Aldo/Grigoropoulos, Ioannis (1503), *Euripidis tragoediae septendecim*, Venice.

Marrou, Henri-Irénée (1965), *Histoire de l'education dans l'antiquité*, Paris.

Martindale, Charles (1993), *Redeeming the Text*, Cambridge.

Martyn, John R.C. (1986), 'The Tragedies of Buchanan, Teive and Ferreira', in: McFarlane (ed.), *Acta Conventus Neo-Latini Sanctandreani* (Binghamton), 85–98.

Martyn, John R.C. (ed.) (1987), *The Tragedy of Inês de Castro by António Ferreira*, Coimbra.

Maslanka-Soro, Maria (2010), 'Il mito di Eolo e il problema del tragico nella tragedia *Canace* di Sperone Speroni', *Rivista di Letteratura italiana* 28/3, 35–44.

Mastrocola, Paola (1996), *Nimica Fortuna. Edipo e Antigone nella tragedia italiana del Cinquecento*, Turin.

Mastrocola, Paola (1998), *L'idea del tragico. Teorie della tragedia nel Cinquecento*, Soveria Mannelli.

Mastromarco, Giuseppe (1983), 'Due casi di aprosdoketon scenico in Aristofane (Acarnesi 393–413, Vespe 526–538)', *Vichiana* 12, 249–254.
Mastromarco, Giuseppe (1997), Aristofane, *Commedie*, vol. 1, Turin.
Mattioda, Emilio (1994), *Teorie della tragedia nel Settecento*, Modena.
Maurice, Luisa (2013), "'Contaminatio' and Adaptation: The Modern Reception of Ancient Drama as an Aid to Understanding Roman Comedy', in: *Bulletin of the Institute of Classical Studies. Supplement* 126, 445–465.
Mazouer, Charles (2010), 'Censure religieuse et théâtre du Moyen Âge à la fin du XVIIe siècle', *Cahiers de l'Association internationale des études françaises* 62, 291–307.
Mazzoni, Guido (ed.) (1887), *Giovanni Rucellai. Le opere*, Bologna.
McCallum-Barry, Carmel (2004), 'Why Did Erasmus Translate Greek Tragedy?', *Erasmus of Rotterdam Society yearbook* 24, 1, 52–70.
McLaughlin, Martin (1995), *Literary Imitation in the Italian Renaissance: The Theory and Practice of Literary Imitation in Italy from Dante to Bembo*, Oxford.
Meineke, August (ed.) (1860), *Aristophanis comoediae*, vol. 1, Leipzig.
Melanchton, Philip, and Veit Winsheim (1546), '*Antigone*', in: *Interpretatio tragoediarum Sophoclis: ad utilitatem iuventutis*, Frankfurt, Or-R4r.
Melanchthon, Philipp (1570), *Declamationum omnium, quae ab ipso, & alijs, in Academia Vuitebergensi recitatae ac editae sunt, nunc primum [...] in tres tomos, distinctae, opera & studio M. Iohannis Richardij [...], Tomus I Philosophicus*, Strasbourg, VD16 M 3578.
Merrill, Le Roy (1925), *The life and poems of Nicholas Grimald*, Yale.
Mervyn Jones, David/Wilson, Nigel G. (1969), *Prolegomena de comedia. Scholia in Acharnenses, Equites, Nubes*, fasc. II continens *Scholia vetera in Aristophanis Equites*, D. Mervyn Jones (ed.), *Scholia tricliniana in Aristophani Equites*, Nigel G. Wilson (ed.), Groningen/Amsterdam.
Minturno, Antonio (1559), *De Poeta*, Venice.
Minturno, Antonio (1564), *L'arte poetica*, Venice.
Miola, Robert (2014), 'Aristophanes in England, 1500–1660', in: S. Douglas Olson (ed.), *Ancient Comedy and Reception. Essays in honor of Jeffrey Henderson*, 479–502.
Miola, Robert (2020), 'Early Modern Reception of *Iphigenia at Aulis*', *Classical Reception Journal* 12, 3, 279–298.
Miola, Robert S. (2014), 'Early Modern Antigones: Receptions, Refractions, Replays', *Classical Receptions Journal* 6, 221–244.
Miola, Robert S. (2017), 'Representing Orestes' Revenge', *Classical Receptions Journal* 9, 144–165.
Miola, Robert S. (2020), 'Early Modern Receptions of Iphigenia at Aulis', *Classical Receptions Journal* 12, 279–298.
Montorfani, Pietro (2006), '*Giocasta*. Un Volgarizzamento Euripideo di Lodovico Dolce (1549)', *Aevum* 80.3, 717–739.
Morani, Moreno (2003), 'Sensum de sensu, uerbum de uerbo. Riflessioni su teoria e storia della traduzione in margine a uno scritto di Eugenio Coseriu', in: Vincenzo Orioles (ed.), *Studi in memoria di Eugenio Coseriu*, Udine, 317–336.
Morini, Massimiliano (2017) [2006], *Tudor Translation in Theory and Practice*, Abingdon.
Moss, Jessica (2007), 'What Is Imitative Poetry and Why Is It Bad?', in: Giovanni R.F. Ferrari (ed.), *The Cambridge Companion to Plato's Republic*, Cambridge/New York, 415–444.
Most, Glenn W. (2003), 'Violets in Crucibles: Translating, Traducing, Transmuting', *Transactions of the American Philological Association* 133, 2, 381–390.

Mounin, Georges (1965), *Teoria e storia della traduzione*, Turin.
Mund-Dopchie, Monique (1984), *La survie d'Eschyle à la Renaissance*, Leuven.
Mundt, Lothar (ed. unter Mitwirkung von Eckart Schäfer und Christian Orth) (2008), *Joachim Camerarius, Eclogae/Die Eklogen. Mit Übersetzung und Kommentar* (NeoLatina 6), Tübingen.
Mousouros, Markos (ed.) (1498), *Aristophanis Comoediae novem*, Venice.
Muttini, Micol (2019a), 'Appunti sulla circolazione del Pluto di Aristofane in età umanistica (I). Gli apografi dei vetustiores e delle recensioni bizantine', *RHT* 14, 1–40.
Muttini, Micol (2019b), 'Appunti sulla circolazione del Pluto di Aristofane in età umanistica (II). I codici misti', *S&T* 17, 305–363.
Mynors, Roger A.B./Thomson, Douglas F.S./Ferguson, Will K. (1975), *Collected works of Erasmus: Letters 142 to 297, 1501 to 1514*, Toronto.
Naogeorgus, Thomas (1558), *Sophoclis Tragoediae Septem Latino Carmine redditae et Annotationibus illustratae*, Basel, VD16 S 7040.
Nassichuk, John (2013), '"Strepsiades" Latin Voice: Two Renaissance Translations of Aristophanes' *Clouds*', in: S. Douglas Olson (ed.), *Ancient Comedy and Reception. Essays in Honor of Jeffrey Henderson*, Berlin/Boston, 427–446.
Neil, Robert A. (ed.) (1901), *The Knights of Aristophanes*, Cambridge.
Nergaard, Siri (1995), *Teorie contemporanee della traduzione*, Milan.
Nergaard, Siri (2002), *La teoria della traduzione nella storia*, Milan.
Neri, Ferdinando (1904), *La tragedia italiana del Cinquecento*, Florence.
Nicosia, Salvatore (1991), *La traduzione dei testi classici. Teoria, prassi, storia. Atti del Convegno di Palermo 6–9 aprile 1988*, Naples.
Nogara, Antonio (2016), 'Gli otia di un giurista filologo: il Philargyrus di Andrea Alciato', *Laboratoire italien*, 17.
Noo, Hendrik de (1927), *Thomas Sebillet et son Art poétique françoys rapproché de* La deffence et illustration de la langue françoyse *de Joachim du Bellay*, Utrecht.
Nørgaard, Holger (1958), 'Translations of the Classics into English before 1600', *Review of English Studies* 9, 164–172.
Norland, Howard B. (1995), *Drama in Early Tudor Britain 1485–1558*, Lincoln, Nebraska.
Norton, Glyn P. (1974), 'Translation Theory in Renaissance France: Etienne Dolet and the Rhetorical Tradition', *Renaissance and Reformation* 10.1, 1–13.
Norton, Glyn P. (1984), *The Ideology and Language of Translation in Renaissance France and their Humanist Antecedents*, Geneva.
Nürnberger, Richard (ed.) (1961), *Melanchthon Werke, III. Band. Humanistische Schriften*, Gütersloh.
O'Thomas, Mark (2014), 'Stages of the Loss, Translation as Contamination: How *The Ritual* Made It to the Royal National Theatre, London', *Theatre Research International* 39 (2), 120–32.
Oberto, Simona (2017), 'What happens to Aristotle in practice? Sperone Speroni's Canace before the background of the Accademia degli Infiammati and Elevati', *Horizonte* n.s. 2, 59–97.
Okàl, M. (1974), *La vie et l'oeuvre de Sigismond Gelous Torda* VI, Bratislava.
Olson, Douglas (1992), 'Names and naming in Aristophanic comedy', *CQ* 42, 304–319.
Paduano, Guido (1994), *Lunga storia di Edipo Re. Freud, Sofocle e il teatro occidentale*, Turin.
Panofsky, Erin (1955), *Meaning in the Visual Arts*, Garden City, NY.
Paratore, Ettore (ed.) (1978–1983), *Virgilio, Eneide*, trans. Luca Canali, Milan.

Parisotti, Giovanni Battista (1735), 'L'Alceste tragedia d'Euripide tradotta di greco in verso toscano, e dedicata all'eminentiss. e reverendiss. principe Lodovico Pico della Mirandola, cardinale di S. Chiesa', in: *Raccolta d'opuscoli scientifici e filologici* vol. 12, Venice, 1–139.
Passius, Franciscus (1501), *Plutus antiqua comoedia ex Aristophane quae nuper in linguam latinam translata est, apud Angelum Ugoletum*, Parma.
Pazzi de' Medici, Alessandro (2013) [1525–1526 ca.], 'Edipo Principe', in: Antonio Sorella (ed.), *Alessandro de' Pazzi e il Rinascimento fiorentino. Dalle posizioni machiavelliane ai Medici e a Bembo*, Chieti, 409–625.
Pazzi de' Medici, Alessandro (1536), *Aristotelis Poetica, per Alexandrum Paccium, patritium Florentinum, in Latinum conuersa*, Venice.
Pelletier, Jacques du Mans (1545), *L'Art poétique d'Horace, traduit en vers françois*, Paris.
Pelletier, Jacques du Mans (1555), *L'Art poétique de Jacques Peletier du Mans*, Lyon.
Penguilly, Thomas (2014), 'Une éducation grecque. André Alciat et l'hellénisme à Milan au début du XVIe siècle', in: *Société internationale Leon Battista Alberti* XVII, 163–191.
Penguilly, Thomas (2019), 'Huiusmodi, hercle, Aristophanes si cerneret... La première traduction latine des *Nuées* d'Aristophane par André Alciat', in: Gauvin, B./Jacquemard, C., *Rire et sourire dans la littérature latine au Moyen Âge et à la Renaissance*, Dijon, 183–199.
Pereira, Francisco M.E. (ed.) (1918), *A Vingança de Agamenom. Tragédia de Anrrique Ayres Victoria conforme a impressão de 1555, publicada por ordem da Academia das Sciências de Lisboa*, Lisbon.
Pereira, Maria Helena da Rocha (2008), *Temas clássicos na poesia portuguesa*, Lisbon.
Pérez de Oliva, Hernán (2019), 'La vengança de Agamenón. Tragedia que hizo Hernán Pérez de Oliva, maestro, cuyo argumento es de Sófocles, poeta griego', in: Hernández López, Araceli (2019), *Edición crítica de la obra dramática de Hernán Pérez de Oliva: sus tragédias* La vengança de Agamenón *y* Hécuba triste, (doctoral tesis), Madrid, 169–248.
Pertusi, Agostino (1960), 'La scoperta di Euripide nel primo Umanesimo', *IMU* 3, 101–152.
Pertusi, Agostino (1966), 'Il ritorno alle fonti del teatro greco classico: Euripide nell'Umanesimo e nel Rinascimento', in: Agostino Pertusi (ed.), *Venezia e l'Oriente fra tardo Medioevo e Rinascimento*, Florence, 205–224.
Petrina, Alessandra/Masiero, Federica (eds.) (2020), *Acquisition through Translation: Towards a Definition of Renaissance Translation*, Belgium.
Petrina, Giovanni (1999), 'Euripide nel Cinquecento: l'edizione di Willem Canter (1571)', in: *DIDASKALIAI, Tradizione e interpretazione del dramma attico*, Padua, 211–242.
Petrocchi, Giorgio (ed.) (1966–67), *La Commedia secondo l'antica vulgata*, Milan.
Philippo, Susanna (2013), '"Accidental Creativity": Scribes, Scholars, Translators and the 'Iphigenia' dramas of seventeenth-century France', *Bulletin of the Institute of Classical Studies. Supplement 126, Dialogues with the past 2: Classical Reception Theory and Practice*, 381–399.
Piccolomini, Alessandro (1575), *Annotationi di M. Alessandro Piccolomini, nel libro della Poetica d'Aristotele, con la traduttione del medesimo libro, in lingua volgare*, Venice.
Pieri, Marzia (2006), 'La tragedia in Italia', in: Gianni Guastella (ed.), *Le rinascite della tragedia*, Rome, 167–197.
Pigman, G.W. (1980), 'Versions of Imitation in the Renaissance', *Renaissance Quarterly* 33, 1, 1–32.
Pillola, Maria Pasqualina (1994), 'Plauto in Esopo. Echi comici in una traduzione del Quattrocento', *Maia* 46, 301–313.

Pincelli, Maria Agata (1993), 'In principio lectionis Aristophanis praeludia. La prolusione al corso su Aristofane', *RR* (Inedita - 6), Rome.
Pincelli, Maria Agata (2008), 'Un profilo dell'interpres nel primo Rinascimento: l'orazione In ingressu di Pierio Valeriano nello Studio di Roma', in: Paolo Pellegrini (ed.), *Bellunesi e Feltrini tra Umanesimo e Rinascimento: filologia, erudizione e biblioteche. Atti del Convegno di Belluno (4 aprile 2003)*, Rome/Padua, 179–217.
Pinho, Sebastião Tavares de (2006), 'Humanismo e Helenismo: Estudos Gregos na Universidade de Coimbra no séc. XVI', *Humanismo em Portugal*, 2 vols., Lisbon, 297–322.
Plett, Heinrich F. (2012), *Enargeia in Classical Antiquity and the Early Modern Age: The Aesthetics of Evidence*, Leiden.
Pollard, Alfred W./Redgrave, Gilbert R. (eds.) (1986–1991), *Short-Title Catalogue of Books Printed in England, Scotland, and Ireland and of English Books Printed Abroad 1475–1640*; 3 vols.; second edition, revised and enlarged; begun by W.A. Jackson and F.S. Ferguson, completed by Katharine F. Pantzer, 1991.
Pollard, Tanya (2012), 'What's Hecuba to Shakespeare?', *Renaissance Quarterly* 65, 1060–1093.
Pollard, Tanya (2017), *Greek Tragic Women on Shakespearean Stages*, Oxford.
Pollock, Sheldon (2000), 'Cosmopolitan and Vernacular in History', *Public Culture* (12.3), 591–625.
Porro, Antonietta (1981), 'Volgarizzamenti e volgarizzatori di drammi euripidei a Firenze nel Cinquecento', *Aevum* 60, 481–508.
Porro, Antonietta (1992), 'Dotti bizantini e libri greci nell'Italia del secolo XV', in: *Atti del Convegno internazionale. 23 and 24 October 1990*, Trento, 343–362.
Porto, Emilio/Canter, Willem (1597), *Euripidis tragoediae XIX [...] Latinam interpretationem M. Aemilius Portus [...] Carminum ratio Gul. Cantero diligenter obseruata, additis eiusdem in totum Euripidem notis*, Heidelberg.
Purkiss, Diane (1998), 'Introduction', in: Diane Purkiss (ed.), *Three Tragedies by Renaissance Women*, London, xi–xliii.
Purkiss, Diane (1999), 'Blood, Sacrifice, Marriage: Why Iphigeneia and Mariam Have to Die', *Women's Writing* 6, 1, 27–45.
Puttenham, George (1589), *The Arte of English Poesie*, London.
Quaglia, Riccardo (2006), 'Su alcune traduzioni italiane di Aristofane: azzecca garbugliando tra i secc. XVI e XIX', *Maia* 57, 349–357.
Quondam, Amedeo (ed.) (1999), *Rinascimento e Classicismo. Materiali per l'analisi del sistema culturale di Antico regime*, Rome.
Quondam, Amedeo (2002), 'Per un'archeologia del Canone e della Biblioteca del Classicismo di Antico Regime', in: Amedeo Quondam (ed.), *Il Canone e la Biblioteca. Costruzioni e decostruzioni della tradizione letteraria italiana. Atti del V Congresso ADI, Roma 26–29 settembre 2001*, vol. 1, Rome, 39–63.
Radif, Ludovica (2011), *Rinuccio Aretino. Penia*, Florence.
Radif, Ludovica (2014), 'Aristofane mascherato: un secolo (1415–1504) di fortuna e sfortuna', in: Douglas Olson (ed.), *Ancient Comedy and Reception. Essays in Honor of Jeffrey Henderson*, Berlin/Boston, 397–409.
Rataller, George (1550), 'Antigone', in: George Rataller, *Sophoclis Aiax Flagellifer, et Antigone. eiusdem Electra*, Lyon, 92–157.
Rataller, George (1570), 'Antigone', in: George Rataller, *Tragodiae Sophoclis quotquot extant*, Antwerp, 63–119.

Refini, Eugenio (2009), *Per via d'annotationi. Le glosse inedite di Alessandro Piccolomini all'Ars Poetica di Orazio*, Lucca
Refini, Eugenio (2020), *The Vernacular Aristotle: Translation as Reception in Medieval and Renaissance Italy*, Cambridge.
Reiss, Timothy J. (1999), 'Renaissance theatre and the theory of tragedy', in: G.P. Norton (ed.), *The Cambridge History of Literary Criticism*, vol. 3, 229–247.
Rener, Frederick M. (1989), *Interpretatio: Language and Translation from Cicero and Tytler*, Amsterdam.
Resende, Maria Luísa (2020), 'A tradução portuguesa da *Ilíada* atribuída a D. Jerónimo Osório: considerações sobre a sua datação e autoria', in: Cristina Pimentel/Sebastiao Tavares de Pinho/Maria Luísa Resende (eds.), *O Humanismo Português e Europeu: no 5º Centenário do* Cicero Lusitanus*: Dom Jerónimo Osório (1515–1580)*, Coimbra, 355–366.
Resende, Maria Luísa (forthcoming), *A Transmissão de Luciano de Samósata em Portugal no século XVI*, Lisbon.
Rhodes, Neil (2018), *Common: the development of literary culture in sixteenth-century England*, Oxford.
Rhodes, Neil/Kendal, Gordon/Wilson, Louise (eds.) (2013), *English Renaissance Translation Theory*, London.
Richardson, Brian (1994), *Print Culture in Renaissance Italy. The Editor and the Vernacular text, 1470–1600*, Cambridge.
Rizzo, Silvia (1996), 'L'insegnamento del latino nelle scuole umanistiche', in: Mirko Tavoni (ed.), *Italia ed Europa nella linguistica del Rinascimento: confronti e relazioni. Atti del convegno internazionale (Ferrara, Palazzo Paradiso, 20–24 marzo 1991)*, Modena, 3–39.
Rizzo, Silvia (2002), *Ricerche sul latino umanistico*, I, Rome.
Roaf, Christina (1959), 'A Sixteenth Century Anonimo: the Author of the *Giuditio Sopra la Tragedia di Canace e Macareo*', *Italian Studies* 14, 49–74.
Roaf, Christina (ed.) (1982), *Canace, e scritti in sua difesa; Giudizio ed Epistola latina*, Bologna.
Robortello, Francesco (1548), *In Librum Aristotelis de arte poetica explicationes*, Florence.
Rocke, Michael (1996), *Forbidden Friendship: Homosexuality and Male Culture in Renaissance Florence*, New York.
Rollo, Antonio (2016), 'Maestri di greco nell'Umanesimo: libri e metodi', *IMU* 57, 165–186.
Rollo, Antonio (2019), 'Lettura degli auctores e costruzione dei lessici nella scuola di greco del primo Umanesimo', in: Stefano Martinelli Tempesta/David Speranzi/Federico Gallo (eds.), *Libri e biblioteche di umanisti tra Oriente e Occidente*, Milan, 269–286.
Romanini, Fabio (2007), 'Volgarizzamenti dall'Europa all'Italia', in: Gino Belloni/Riccardo Drusi (eds.), *Il rinascimento Italiano e l'Europa*, vol. 2, *Umanesimo ed educazione*, Treviso-Vicenza, 381–405.
Romanska, Magda (2014), 'Introduction', in: Magda Romanska (ed.), *The Routledge Companion to Dramaturgy*, New York, 1–16.
Ronsard, Pierre de (1967) [1617], 'Recueil des sonnets, odes, hymnes, élégies et autres pièces retranchées aux éditions précédentes des œuvres de Ronsard gentilhomme Vandomois', in: Paul Laumonier (ed.), *Œuvres complètes* XVIII, Paris, 358–359.
Rossi, Niccolò (1970) [1590], 'Discorsi intorno alla tragedia', in: Bernard Weinberg (ed.), *Trattati di Poetica e Retorica del Cinquecento*, Bari, vol. 4, 59–120.
Ruffell, Ian (ed.) (2012), *Aeschylus: Prometheus Bound*, London.
Rummel, Erika (1985), *Erasmus as a translator of the classics*, Toronto.

Ryan, Cressida (2017), 'Camerarius and Sophocles', in: Thomas Baier (ed.), *Camerarius Polyhistor. Wissensvermittlung im deutschen Humansimus* (NeoLatina 27), Tübingen, 147–167.
Sabbadini, Remigio (1922), *Il metodo degli umanisti*, Florence.
Saïd, Suzanne (1978), *La faute tragique*, Paris.
Salliot, Natacha/Schweitzer, Zoé (eds.) (2012), *Maffeo Galladei, Médée*, Saint-Étienne.
Samxon, Jehan (1530), *Les Iliades d'Homère, poète grec et gant historiographe, avecques les premisses et commencements de Guyon de Coulonne, souverain historiographe; addition et séquences de Dares Phrygius et de Dictys de Crète*, Paris.
Sanders, Julie (2006), *Adaptation and Appropriation*, London.
Savettieri, Cristina (2014), 'Una genealogia per il tragico', *Moderna* 16/1–2, 29–47.
Savettieri, Cristina (2017), 'Il disagio dell'innocenza: tragedia, teoria e romanzo moderno', *Between* 7/14, http://www.betweenjournal.it (last accessed 01/09/2022).
Savettieri, Cristina (2018), 'The Agency of Errors: *Hamartia* and its (Mis)interpretations in the Italian *Cinquecento*', in: Toni Bernhart/Jaša Drnovšek/Sven Thorsten Kilian/Joachim Küppeer (eds.), *Poetics and Politics: Net Structures and Agencies in Early Modern Drama*, Berlin, 149–167.
Scheible, Heinz (1993), 'Philipp Melanchthon (1497–1560). Melanchthons Werdegang', in: Paul Gerhardt Schmidt (ed.), *Humanismus im deutschen Südwesten. Biographische Profile*, Sigmaringen, 221–238.
Scheible, Heinz (ed.) (1977ff.), *Melanchthons Briefwechsel. Kritische und kommentierte Gesamtausgabe, im Auftrag der Heidelberger Akademie der Wissenschaften*, Stuttgart/Bad Cannstatt.
Schironi, Francesca (2016), 'The Reception of Ancient Drama in Renaissance Italy', in: Betine van Zyl Smit (ed.), *A Handbook to the Reception of Greek Drama*, Chichester, 131–153.
Schmitt, Arbogast (2002), 'La *Poetica* di Aristotele e la sua reinterpretazione nella teoria poetica del secondo Cinquecento', in: Diego Lanza (ed.), *La poetica di Aristotele e la sua storia*, Pisa, 31–43.
Schoeck, Richard J. (1985), *Acta conventus neo-latini Bononiensis: proceedings of the Fourth International Congress of Neo-Latin Studies*, Binghamton-N.Y.
Schultheiß, Jochen, 'Commentatio explicationum omnium tragoediarum Sophoclis', http://wiki.camerarius.de/OC_0631 (last accessed 03/02/2020).
Schultheiß, Jochen, 'Camerarius 1534', *OC*, http://wiki.camerarius.de/Sophokles,_Τραγῳδίαι_ἑπτά,_1534 (last accessed 05/01/2021).
Schultheiß, Jochen, 'Eclogae 1568', *OC*, http://wiki.camerarius.de/Camerarius,_Eclogae,_1568 (last accessed 05/01/2021).
Schultheiß, Jochen, 'Winsheim 1546', *OC*, http://wiki.camerarius.de/Winsheim,_Interpretatio_tragoediarum_Sophoclis_(Druck),_1546 (last accessed 10/11/2019).
Schultheiß, Jochen, 'Camerarius an Burchart, 13.03.1534', *OCEp*, http://wiki.camerarius.de/OCEp_1401 (last accessed 17/12/2019).
Schultheiß, Jochen, 'Camerarius an Heusler, 13.04.1554', *OCEp*, http://wiki.camerarius.de/OCEp_1457 (last accessed 17/12/2019).
Schultheiß, Jochen, 'Camerarius an Oporinus, 15.03.1556', *OCEp*, http://wiki.camerarius.de/OCEp_1406 (last accessed 17/12/2019).
Schütrumpf, Eckart (1989), 'Traditional Elements in the Concept of *Hamartia* in Aristotle's *Poetics*', *Harvard Studies in Classical Philology* 92, 137–156.

Schweitzer, Zoé (2013), 'Buchanan, helléniste et dramaturge, interprète d'Euripide (Medea et Alcestis)', *Etudes Épistémè*, 23, https://doi.org/10.4000/episteme.258 (last accessed 11/11/2022).
Schweitzer, Zoé (2015), 'La traduction d'Alceste par Buchanan, l'imago retrouvée ?', *Anabases Tradit. Récept. L'Antiquité* 21, 2015, 113–124.
Sébillet, Thomas (1549), *L'Iphigenie d'Euripide Poète Tragique tourné de Grec en François*, Paris.
Sébillet, Thomas (1910) [1549], *Art Poétique françoys*, Félix Gaiffe (ed.), Paris.
Segni, Bernardo (1549), *Rettorica et poetica d'Aristotile, tradotte di greco in lingua vulgare fiorentina da Bernardo Segni Gentil' huomo & Accademico Fiorentino*, Florence.
Segni, Bernardo (1811) [1551], *Edipo principe tragedia di Sofocle*, Florence.
Serra, José P. (2011), 'A *Tragédia da Vingança que foi feita sobre a morte del Rei Agaménom (Tragédia de Orestes)* e a *Electra* de Sófocles', in: Anrique Aires Vitória, *Tragédia da Vingança que foi feita sobre a morte del rei Agaménom (Tragédia de Orestes)*, Lisbon, 13–24.
Serra, José P. (2015), 'Electra, The Voice of Hades', in: A. Raquel Fernandes/José P. Serra/Rui C. Fonseca, (eds.), *The Power of Form. Recycling Myths*, Cambridge, 90–103.
Sessa, Riccardo (ed.) (2014), *Tragedie: Altea, Astianatte, Polissena/Bongianni Grattarolo*, Brescia.
Sgarbi, Marco (2019), 'What was meant by vulgarizing in the Italian Renaissance?', *Intellectual History Review* 29:3, 389–416.
Sharrat, P./Walsh, P.G. (1983), 'Introduction', in: George Buchanan, *Tragedies*, P. Sharrat and P.G. Walsh (eds.), Edinburgh, 1–20.
Sherman, Nancy (1992), 'Hamartia and Virtue', in: Amélie Oksenberg-Rorty (ed.), *Essays on Aristotle's Poetics*, Princeton, 177–196.
Sicherl, Martin (1997), *Griechische Erstausgaben des Aldus Manutius. Druckvorlagen, Stellenwert, kulturell Hintergrund*, Paderborn.
Silvano, Luigi (2019), 'Étudier le grec au Studium de Florence: observations sur quelques cahiers d'élèves et de maîtres (fin XVe - début XVIe siècle)', in: Christine Bénévent/Xavier Bisaro/Laurent Naas (eds.), *Cahiers d'écoliers à la Renaissance*, Tours, 45–71.
Soares, Nair de Nazaré Castro (1996), *Teatro Clássico no Século XVI. A Castro de António Ferreira. Fontes – Originalidade*, Coimbra.
Soares, Nair de Nazaré Castro (1999), *Tragédia do Príncipe João de Diogo de Teive. Introdução, texto latino, tradução e notas*, Lisbon.
Soares, Nair de Nazaré Castro (2006), 'A Tragédia do Príncipe João (1554) de Diogo de Teive, primeiro dramaturgo neolatino português', in: Pinho, Sebastião Tavares de (ed.), *O Teatro Neolatino em Portugal no contexto da Europa. 450 anos de Diogo de Teive*, Coimbra, 183–214.
Solerti, Angelo (ed.) (1887), *Le tragedie metriche di Alessandro Pazzi de' Medici*, Bologna.
Sommerstein, Alan (ed.) (2001), *Aristophanes. Knights*, Warminster.
Sommerstein, Alan (ed.) (2001), *Aristophanes. Plutus*, Warminster.
Sommerstein, Alan (2010), 'The history of the text of Aristophanes', in: Gregory Dobrov (ed.), *Brill's Companion to the Study of Greek Comedy*, Leiden, 399–422.
Sommerstein, Alan (2019), *The Encyclopedia of Greek Comedy*, Hoboken.
Sonnino, Maurizio (2017), *Michel'Angelo Giacomelli. Aristofane. I. Un capitolo ignoto di storia degli studi classici nella Roma del Settecento*, Rome.
Sorella, Antonio (2013), *Alessandro de' Pazzi e il Rinascimento fiorentino. Dalle posizioni machiavelliane ai Medici e a Bembo*, Chieti.

Spera, Francesco (1995), 'Il modello tragico dell'*Orazia*', in: *Pietro Aretino nel cinquecentenario della nascita, Atti del Convegno di Roma-Viterbo-Arezzo (28 settembre–1 ottobre 1992), Toronto (23–24 ottobre), Los Angeles (27–29 ottobre 1992)*, Rome, 787–801.
Stählin, Friedrich (1936), *Humanismus und Reformation im bürgerlichen Raum. Eine Untersuchung der biographischen Schriften des Joachim Camerarius*, Leipzig.
Stefani, Luigina (1986), *Tre commedie fiorentine del primo 500; edizione critica e introduzione di Luigina Stefani*, Ferrara.
Steggle, Matthew (2007), 'Aristophanes in Early Modern England', in: Edith Hall/Amanda Wrigley (eds.), *Aristophanes in Performance 421 BC-AD 2007. Peace, Birds, and Frogs*, London, 52–65.
Steiner, George (1998), *After Babel: Aspects of Language and Translation*, Oxford.
Stevens, Linton C. (1950), 'How the French Humanists of the Renaissance Learned Greek', *PMLA* 65 (2), 240–248.
Stiblin, Caspar (1562), *Euripides poeta tragicorum princeps, in Latinum sermonem conuersus […] autore Gasparo Stiblino*, Basel.
Stinton, T.C. (1975), '*Hamartia* in Aristotle and Greek Tragedy', *The Classical Quarterly* 25/2, 221–254.
Strozzi, Giovan Battista (1970) [1599], 'Dell'unità della favola', in: Bernard Weinberg (ed.), *Trattati di Poetica e Retorica del Cinquecento*, Bari, vol. 4, 333–44.
Sturel, René (1913), 'Essai sur les traductions du théâtre grec en français avant 1550', *Revue d'histoire littéraire de la France*, 269–296, 637–652.
Süß, Wilhelm (1911), *Aristophanes und die Nachwelt*, Leipzig.
Suthern, Carla (2020), 'Iphigenia in English: Reading Euripides with Jane Lumley', in: Alessandra Petrina/Federica Masiero (eds.), *Acquisition Through Translation: Towards a Definition of Renaissance Translation*, TMT 18, 73–92.
Tarrío, Ana María Sánchez (2015), *Leitores dos Clássicos. Portugal e Itália, séculos XV e XVI. Uma Geografia do Primeiro Humanismo em Portugal (com uma nota de Vincenzo Fera)*, Lisbon.
Tateo, Francesco (2006), *Sul latino degli umanisti*, Bari.
Tavoni, Mirko (1984), *Latino, grammatica, volgare. Storia di una questione umanistica*, Padua.
Taylor, Helena (2021), 'Polemical Translation, Translating Polemic: Anne Dacier's Rhetoric in the Homer Quarrel', *Modern Language Review*, 116, 21–41.
Tesi, Riccardo (1997), *Aristotele in italiano. I grecismi nelle traduzioni rinascimentali della 'Poetica'*, Florence.
Tigerstedt, Eugène (1968), 'Observations on the Reception of the Aristotelian Poetics in the Latin West', *Studies in the Renaissance* XV, 7–24.
Toscanella, Orazio (1575), *Discorsi cinque*, Venice.
Totaro, Piero (2017), 'Sul testo del Pluto di Aristofane', in: Giuseppe Mastromarco/Piero Totaro/Bernhard Zimmermann (eds.), *La commedia attica antica. Forme e contenuti*, Lecce-Brescia, 173–194.
Traina, Alfonso (1970), *Vortit Barbare: Le Traduzioni Poetiche Da Livio Andronico a Cicerone*, Rome.
Tramontana, Alessandra (ed.) (2016), *Giovan Battista Gelli, Ecuba,* Turin.
Trencsényi, Katalin/Cochrane, Bernadette (2014), *New Dramaturgy: International Perspectives on Theory and Practice*, London.
Trencsényi, Katalin, (2015), *Dramaturgy in the Making: A User's Guide for Theatre Practitioners*, London.

Trisoglio, Francesco (1996), 'Giovanni da Falgano traduttore della tragedia greca', *Rinascimento* XXXVI, 393–406.
Trissino, Gian Giorgio (1970) [1562], 'La quinta e la sesta divisione della poetica del Trissino', in: Bernard Weinberg (ed.), *Trattati di Poetica e Retorica del Cinquecento*, Bari, vol. 2, 5–90.
Trissino, Giovan Giorgio (1977), '*Sofonisba*', in: Marco Ariani, *La tragedia nel Cinquecento*, vol. 1, Turin, 26–162.
Tuilier, André (1962), 'Euripide et Ennius', *Bull. Assoc. Guillaume Budé* 21/4, 1962, 379–398.
Turyn, Anne (1957), *The byzantine manuscript tradition of the tragedies of Euripides*, Urbana (IL).
Valla, Giorgio (1498), *Giorgio Valla Placentino interprete, in hoc volumine continentur Nicephori Logica [...] Aristotelis ars poetica*, Venice.
Valla, Laurentius (1526), *Elegantiarum linguae Latinae libri sex [...]*, Colonia, VD16 V 239.
Van Kerchove, Dirk (1974), 'The Latin Translation of Aristophanes' *Plutus* by Hadrianus Chilius 1533', *HumLov* 23, 42–127.
Vanautgaerden, Alexandre (2012), *Érasme typographe: humanisme et imprimerie au début du XVIe siècle*, Genève.
Van Leeuwen, Jan (ed.) (1900), *Aristophanes. Equites*, Leiden.
Vedelago, Angelica (2021), '*Ex variis metri generibus*: Two 'Metrical' Neo-Latin Translators of Greek Tragedy across the English Channel', *Skenè. Journal of Theatre and Drama Studies* 7, 2, 81–116.
Venuti, Lawrence (1995), *The Translator's Invisibility. A History of Translation*, London/New York.
Versényi, Adam (2014), 'The dissemination of theatrical translation', in: Magda Romanska (ed.), *The Routledge Companion to Dramaturgy*, New York, 288–293.
Vettori, Pietro (1545), *Euripidou Elektra. Euripidis Electra. Nunc primum in lucem edita*, Rome.
Vettori, Pietro (1560), *Commentarii in primum Librum Aristotelis de Arte Poetarum*, Florence.
Vieillefond, Jean René (1935), 'Complemento al catalogo de manuscritos griegos de la Biblioteca Nacional de Madrid', *Emerita* III 2, 193–213.
Villari, Susanna (2016), 'Esegesi aristotelica e drammaturgia. Postilla a due progetti di censimento', *Studi Giraldiani* 2, 75–92.
Vioque, Guillermo Galán (2011), 'A new manuscript of classical authors in Spain', *HSCPh* 106, 97–123.
Vitale, Maurizio (1953), 'Le origini del volgare nelle discussioni dei filologi del '400', *Lingua Nostra* 14, 64–69.
Viti, Paolo (2004), L. Bruni, *Sulla perfetta traduzione*, Naples.
Vitória, Anrique Aires (2011), *Tragédia da Vingança que foi feita sobre a morte del rei Agaménom (Tragédia de Orestes)*, José Camões (ed.), Lisbon.
Vives, Juan Luis (2018) [1532], *De Ratione Dicendi*, David Walker (ed.), Leiden.
Wagniart, Anne (2015), 'Feindbild oder Identifikationsfigur? Zur Rezeption von Sophokles' 'Ajax' im Umkreis Melanchthons (1534–1558)', in: Peter Andersen Vinilandicus/Barbara Lafond-Kettlitz (eds.), *Die Bedeutung der Rezeptionsliteratur für Bildung und Kultur der Frühen Neuzeit (1400–1750). Beiträge zur dritten Arbeitstagung in Wissembourg/Weißenburg (March 2014)*, Bern, 409–445.
Walfard, Adrien (2008), 'Justice et passions tragiques. Lectures d'Aristote aux xvie et xviie siècles', *Poétique* 155/3, 259–281.
Warner, J. Christopher (2013), *The Making and Marketing of Tottel's Miscellany, 1557*, London.

Waszink, J. Hendrik (1969), 'Introduction to Erasmus's *Euripidis Hecuba et Iphigenia*', in: *Opera omnia Desiderii Erasmi [...], ordinis primi tomus primus*, 195–212.
Waszink, J. Hendrik (1971), 'Einige Betrachtungen über die Euripidesübersetzungen des Erasmus und ihre historische Situation', *Antike Abendl.* 17/1, 1971, 70–90.
Watson, Thomas (1581), *Sophoclis Antigone*, London.
Way, Arthur S. (1958), *Euripides: With an English Translation*, Cambridge/London/Harvard.
Weinberg, Bernard (1961), *A History of Literary Criticism in the Italian Renaissance*, Chicago, 2 vols.
Weinberg, Bernard (1970–1974), *Trattati di Poetica e Retorica del Cinquecento*, Rome.
Weinberg, Bernard (1971), 'ps. Longinus, Dionysus Cassius', in: P.O. Kristeller/F.E. Cranz/Virginia Brown, *Catalogus Translationum et Commentariorum: Medieval and Renaissance Latin Translations and Commentaries*, vol. 2, Washington, 193–198.
Whipday, Emma (2015), 'Iphigenia at Aulis. Lady Jane Lumley. Emma Rucastle, dir. With the Rose Company', *Early Modern Women* 9 (2), 144–148.
White, John Williams (1906), '*The manuscripts of Aristophanes*', *CPh* 1, 1–20, 255–278.
Wilamowitz-Moellendorff, Ulrich V. (1899), 'Excurse zum Oedipus des Sophokles', *Hermes* 34/1, 55–80.
Willi, Andreas (2003), 'New language for a New Comedy: A linguistic approach to Aristophanes' Plutus', *PCPhS* 49, 40–73.
Williams, C.H. (ed.) (1967), *English Historical Documents, 1458–1558*, Oxford.
Wilson, Nigel G. (1973), 'Erasmus as a translator of Euripides: supplementary notes', *Antike und Abendland* 18, 87–88.
Wilson, Nigel G. (1992), *From Byzantium to Italy: Greek Studies in the Italian Renaissance*, London.
Wilson, Nigel G. (2007), Aristophanea: *studies on the text of Aristophanes*, Oxford.
Wilson, Nigel G. (ed.) (2007), *Aristophanis Fabulae*, vol. 1, Oxford.
Wilson, Nigel G. (2014), 'The Transmission of Aristophanes', in: Michael Fontaine/Adele Scafuro (eds.), *The Oxford Handbook of Greek and Roman Comedy*, Oxford, 655–666.
Wilson, Nigel G. (2016), *Aldus Manutius. The Greek Classics. Edited and translated by N.G. Wilson*, Cambridge (MA).
Windle, Kevin (2011), 'The Translation of Drama', in: Kirsten Malmkjær/Kevin Windle (eds.), *The Oxford Handbook of Translation Studies*, Oxford, 154–168.
Winsheim, Veit (1546), *Interpretatio tragoediarum Sophoclis, ad utililtatem iuventutis, quae studiosa est Graecae linguae, edita a Vito Winshemio*, Frankfurt am Main, VD16 ZV14511.
Witt, Charlotte (2005), 'Tragic error and agent responsibility', in: *Philosophic Exchange*, 35/1, article 4.
Worth-Stylianou, Valerie (1999), '*Translatio* and Translation in the Renaissance: From Italy to France', in: *The Cambridge History of Literary Criticism*, vol. 3, Cambridge, 127–135.
Wright, Matthew (2008), *Euripides: Orestes*, London.
Wynne-Davies, Marion (2008), 'The Good Lady Lumley's Desire: *Iphigeneia* and the Nonsuch Banqueting House', in: Rina Walthaus/Marguérite Corporaal (eds.), *Heroines of the Golden Stage*, Kassel, 111–128.
Xylander, Wilhelm (1558), *Euripidis Tragoediae, quae hodie extant: omnes, Latine soluta oratione redditae, ita ut uersus uersui respondeat*, Basel.
Xylander, Wilhelm (1562), *Euripidis Tragoediae, quae hodie extant omnes Latine soluta oratione redditae, ita ut uersus uersui respondeat*, Frankfurt.

Xylander, Wilhelm (1562a), *Evripides Poeta Tragicorum princeps, in Latinum sermonem conuersus*, Basel.
Zacher, Konrad (ed.) (1897), *Aristophanis* Equites, Leipzig.
Zanin, Enrica (2008), 'Early Modern Oedipus: A Literary Approach to Christian Tragedy', in: Arthur Cools (ed.), *The Locus of Tragedy*, Leiden/Boston, 65–80.
Zanin, Enrica (2011), 'The Moral of the Story: on Narrative and Ethics', *AJCN* 6 http://cf.hum.uva.nl/narratology/a11_zanin.htm (last accessed 08/06/2022).
Zanin, Enrica (2012a), 'Les commentaires modernes de la *Poétique* d'Aristote', *Études littéraires* 43/2, 55–83.
Zanin, Enrica (2012b), 'Le théâtre pré-moderne comme quête herméneutique: le cas d'Œdipe', in: Véronique Lochert/Zoé Schweitzer (eds.), *Philologie et théâtre. Traduire, commenter, interpréter le théâtre antique en Europe (XVe-XVIIIe siècles)*, Amsterdam, 209–226.
Zanin, Enrica (2014a), *Fins tragiques. Poétique et éthique du dénouement dans la tragédie prémoderne en Italie, en France et en Espagne*, Geneva.
Zanin, Enrica (2014b), 'Paratexte et théorie dramatique dans la tragédie italienne (1540–1640)', *Littératures classiques*, 83/1, 273–291.
Zanin, Enrica (2017a), 'Tragedy ends unhappily – the concealed influence of medieval poetics in early modern theory of tragedy', *Horizonte* 2, 23–37.
Zanin, Enrica (2017b), 'Il tragico prima del tragico', *Between* 7/14 http://www.betweenjournal.it (last accessed 01/09/2022).
Zinano, Gabriele (1970) [1590], 'Discorso della tragedia', in: Bernard Weinberg (ed.), *Trattati di Poetica e Retorica del Cinquecento*, Bari, 121–140.
Zyl Smit, Betine van (ed.) (2016), *A Handbook to the Reception of Greek Drama*, Chichester.

Index Nominum et Rerum

Accademia della Crusca 155
Accademia Fiorentina 145, 159
Ad uerbum 3, 9–10, 29, 37–39, 41, 44–46, 52, 54 n.5, 74, 78, 83, 125–127, 146, 210, 216
Ad uersum 3, 9, 37–39, 42, 45
Adaptation 3, 39, 51–52, 143, 164 n.18, 168, 175–176, 241, 252, 256, 258 n.13
Aemulatio 100, 101, 102
Agon 61, 63
Akrasia 239–240
Alboin 162–163 n.11
Alciato, Andrea 37–38, 42–52
Aldo Manuzio 7, 10, 38, 53, 57, 65, 74 n.7, 75, 110, 122 n.33, 161 n.6–7, 266 n.42, 267 nn.44–46, 268 n.47, 270 n.48, 272 n.50, 273 n.52, 274 n.54, 277 n.55, 278 n.58, 279 nn.60–61, 285 nn.68–70, 287 n.73, 288 n.74
Alessandro Pazzi de' Medici 12, 15, 110, 144, 146, 151 n.44, 163, 168, 170–171, 227, 234, 242–244
Alexander of Otranto 22, 25, 27 n.23, 28 nn.24–25, 32 n.39 and 41
Ammonius Hermiae/Ammonius of Alexandria 65–66
Amplificatio 12, 164–165, 167, 170 n.35, 173, 197
Ancient comedy 20, 37, 43, 47–48, 50–52, 192
Ancient Regime 143 n.21, 157 n.71
Ancient tragedy 128, 137, 143
Andreas Divo 26 n.19, 32 n.39, 54 n.5, 67 n.35
Anguillara, Giovanni Andrea Dell' 151 n.44, 245–249
António Ferreira 175 n.1, 177–178
Arabic 60
Archaeology of translation 76

Argument IX, 48, 191, 204, 266–267, 274, 276
Art poétique françois 7, 101
Athens 32 n.41, 36, 50 n.33, 67
Atkins, Jed 222
Authority 10, 76, 79, 143 n.21, 290, 297
Baghdad 65 n.30
Balcianelli, Giovanni 12, 162
Bandello, Matteo 12, 146, 162, 167–168, 170 n.35
Barberini, Maffeo 13, 160, 168–169, 171–173
Barthélémy Aneau 195, 199, 204
Bartolomeo and Pietro Rositini 32 nn.39 and 41, 53–64, 66–67
Basel 44 n.20, 54, 57 n.12, 77–78, 80, 99, 130, 261
Boccaccio, Giovanni 149, 154–155, 157, 161
Bono Giamboni 153 n.52
Book of Revelation 105 n.66
Brasenose College, Oxford 214
Brescia 54, 60, 66 n.33
Brisset, Ronald 190–191
Brunetto Latini 153 n.52
Budé, Guillaume VIII n.2
Buonarroti Archive 160, 168 n.32
Buonarroti, Michelangelo il Giovane 12, 151 n.44, 159, 162, 164, 170
Byzantine triad 19, 42, 80, 94, 161
Caccini, Francesca 159
Calvy de la Fontaine 191–193
Camerarius 10–11, 80, 115, 119–130, 132
Canter, Willem 161 nn.6–7, 164 n.20
Canzone 12, 170–173
Capodistria 54
Carlson, Marvin 209–210
Castelvetro, Lodovico 6 n.16, 142–144, 152 n.48, 241–242, 251

Names of ancient authors and titles of their works (for which see the Index locorum) and names of literary characters (except for some famous mythical figures) are not indexed

Castiglione, Baldassarre 39
Chambre ardente 262
Charles Toutain 190–191
Chattering 61
Chorus 10, 13, 15, 46, 51–52, 83–86, 95, 97, 103–104, 110–111, 131, 147, 168 n.29, 177–179, 187, 216–217, 220, 246–248, 255, 263–265, 268–269, 275–277, 279–280, 283–289
Christ Church College, Oxford 211
Christian morality 175, 177, 183
Christianity 230
Christopherson 214, 261
Christ's College, Cambridge 214
Cleon 55
Coin, currency 6–7, 60, 294
Collaboration IX, 22 n.9, 75, 91, 103, 106 n.73, 113
Collin, Rudolf 78, 161 n.7
Colloquial 29, 61
Commentary glosses 35
Compassion 148, 238, 240, 247
Competition 91–93, 95, 97–99, 101–102, 106–107, 111, 113
Compound words 29
Contamination 15, 255, 258–261, 284, 290, 292
Coriolano Martirano 25 n.18, 32 n.39
Cornaro, Caterina 66 n.32
Cornaro, Federico 66 n.32
Corpus Christi College, Oxford 212
Council of Trent 67, 262, 290
Counter-Reformation 210, 232, 241, 262
Crasis 54
Cremona 54, 66 n.32
Crusca Academy 159
Cyclops 162, 168 n.31
Cyprus 66 n.32
Da Falgano, Giovanni 12, 151 n.45, 162, 167–168, 170
Dante 13, 154–155, 157, 166, 170, 172–173, 238, 240
Dedicatory letter 47–48, 64–66, 73, 79–80, 84–86, 89, 94 n.10, 118–119, 124–125, 131, 146, 212
Delphic sanctuary 61
Demagogues 63

Demos 61 n.22, 63
Desiderius Erasmus of Rotterdam 5, 10, 73–80, 82–98, 103–106, 110–113, 121–122, 132–133, 161, 169, 213, 267 nn.45–46, 287 n.71
Diogenes Laertius 64
Diogo de Teive 176, 178
Dolce, Lodovico 12, 141, 146–149, 151 n.45, 161–164, 167–168, 256, 261–263, 268 n.47, 277–279, 281–282, 302
Dramatis personae 63
Dramaturgy 8, 15, 255, 257, 272, 279, 283, 289–291
Ecuba Barberini 160, 168–169, 172–173
Enargeia 112
Etienne Dolet 92
Etienne Jodelle 189 n.3
Euidentia 112–113
Explanatory glosses 32–33
Fear 81, 109, 180–181, 184 n.34, 186 n.39, 221, 229, 237, 239
Florence 20–21, 41, 54 n.2, 158–160, 164, 213, 235, 242–243, 261, 264 n.40
Francesco De Sanctis 157 n.70
Francesco Passi 32 n.39
Galilei, Galileo 159
Garnier, Robert 77, 80, 191, 194, 298
Gelli, Giovan Battista 12, 145–146, 161–162, 167, 169–170
Gelous 76, 80–83, 87–88
Genealogy 167
George Buchanan 10, 76–80, 82–83, 85–86, 89–90, 111, 222
Giambattista Giraldi Cinzio 140, 146–150, 171 n.38, 178, 227–228, 237–238, 244, 251
Gian Giorgio Trissino 147–148, 164, 170, 172–173, 234 n.30, 251
Giocasta 163–164, 238
Giovanni Battista Capponi 262 n.23
Giovanni Rucellai 164, 170
Giovanni Tortelli 22 n.9
Giraldi Cinzio, Giovan Battista 140, 147, 149, 171 n.38, 178, 227, 237, 244
Giustiniani, Orsatto 140 n.10, 252
Gorboduc 105 n.70
Grammatical glosses 34

Gratarolo, Bongianni 163
Greci 138 n.3, 148 n.40, 150 n.43, 152 nn.49–50, 154 n.60, 156 n.67, 167
Greek drama V, VII, X, 1–2, 4–5, 7, 13, 37, 44, 52, 73, 75–76, 78–79, 87, 89–90, 95 n.16, 103, 146, 156, 164, 189–195, 197, 210–211, 213–214, 225, 233 n.20, 250, 257–258, 291 n.80, 293
Greek tragedy V, 1–2, 10, 12–15, 37–38, 73–75, 85, 91–93, 102–103, 106, 113, 115–116, 122, 124, 133, 137, 141, 143–144, 146, 156, 175, 177 n.11, 187, 192–193, 209–211, 213–215, 217–218, 220, 222, 225, 227, 230–231, 255–256, 261–262, 294–295
Grimald, Nicholas 14, 209, 211–216, 219–220, 223–225
Guarino Veronese 32 n.39
Guidiccioni, Cristoforo 168
Guidotto da Bologna 153 n.52
Hamartia 14–15, 227, 229–231, 233–242, 250–251
Hans Sachs 262 n.28
Hapax 55–56
Hendecasyllables 12, 170–173, 218
Hendiadys 58, 153
Heptasyllabic verses 170
Herod 14, 211, 215–216, 219–220, 222–225
Herodias 215, 217, 220–225
Hippocrates 64
Hippolytos 54 n.7, 162
Huet, Pierre-Daniel Huet 6 n.16
Hugues Salel 101, 196, 198
Hypallage 109
Imitatio 33, 99–100
Imitatio auctorum 33
Imitation 4–7, 10, 12, 30 n.35, 38, 47 n.25, 51, 91–93, 98–103, 105–106, 113, 122–123, 127, 137–139, 141–145, 148, 150–151, 157, 190, 196, 199–200, 202, 204–205, 249
Infinitive 54
Interjections 29
Interlinear translation 9, 19, 21, 40, 126
Interpretatio linguarum 11, 93, 99
Ippolito 151 n.45

Jacques Amyot 75, 191–193, 197, 261
Jacques Peletier du Mans 189 n.3, 195 n.14, 200
Jane FitzAlan, Lady Lumley 103–104, 261
Jean Racine 241 n.55, 291–292
Jean Rotrou 291
Jean-Antoine de Baïf 186, 189, 191–194
Jehan Samxon 195
Jerusalem 66 n.32
Joachim Du Bellay 13, 189–190, 202–205
John Christopherson 214, 261
John Mesue/*Giovanni* Mesue, Yūhannā ibn Māsawaih 65
John the Baptist 14, 211–212, 214–215, 217–218, 224
Kingdom of Sardinia 67
Kisseus 167
Lalemant 86, 106 n.75, 111 n.92
Latin lexicon 30
Latinization 30
Lazarus, Micha 82 n.51, 91, 95 n.15, 212–213
Le Fenisse 162
Leonardo Bruni 7–8, 22 n.9, 24–26, 28, 30, 39–41, 44, 46, 92
Lombardi, Bartolomeo 140 n.9, 239, 251
Lombardia 60
Louis-François Le Duchat 190–191
Lodovico da Puppi 8, 15, 19–23, 25–26, 28–33, 35–36, 39–40
Lyon 53 n.1, 65 n.28, 233 n.20, 261
Maffei, Scipione 171
Maggi, Vincenzo 239, 251
Malingri, Coriolano/Count of Bagnolo 67
Matrit. gr. 4697 19–22, 33–34
Mazzoni, Guido 171
Medical wording 61
Melanchthon 10, 42, 80–81, 90, 108 n.83, 115–122, 126, 132
Merrill, L.R. 212 nn.10–11, 214–215, 217 n.33, 221, 221–222
Metaphors 60, 98, 129, 178
Meters 170–171
Method of translation 78 n.31, 126
Minturno, Antonio Sebastiano 138–141, 147 n.35, 234 n.30
Misinterpretations 28–29, 231

Monodies 170
Moschus 175 n.1
Myth 165, 183, 187, 260 n.17
Mythology 111, 118, 167, 183 n.30
Naogeorgus 5, 85 n.67, 106–113, 115, 130–132
National Library of Spain 19–21
Negative 55, 67 n.34, 102, 200, 224
Neologism 60
Niccolò Machiavelli 41–42, 263 n.34, 291 n.77
Nicias 55
Obscene language 7, 25
Orbecche 146, 148–149, 151, 171, 227
Order of the Knights of St. John of Jerusalem 66 n.32
Orti Oricellari 164
Panegyricus 94
Paphlagonian 55, 59–60, 63
Paraphrase 31, 34, 209
Parataxis 60
Paratext 11, 33, 35, 47, 49, 94, 122 n.30
Parisotti, Giovanni Battista 162 n.11
Parma University 66 n.33
Parodos 110–111, 170–171, 173, 178
Passion Play of Oberammergau 224
Patronymics 167
Pazzi de' Medici, Alessandro 12, 15, 110, 144, 151 n.44, 163, 168, 170–171, 227, 234, 242
Pèrez De Oliva 13, 178–180, 182–187
Petrarch 12–13, 92, 154, 157, 170, 172–173, 238
Phaedra 149 n.41, 223
Phalaecian Hendecasyllables 218
Pierre de Ronsard 189, 190, 194
Pierre Le Loyer 37 n.2, 191, 194
Pietro Aretino 22 n.9
Pietro de Montagnana 22, 27–28, 32 nn.39 and 41, 39–40, 44–45, 95 n.16, 96–97
Pilato, Leonzio 161
Pity 183–185, 229, 235–240, 244, 284
Planudean Anthology 98
Pnyx 59, 63
Po Valley 54
Poetic justice 248

Poetics 7, 13, 31, 78 n.32, 139, 141–142, 190, 195–196, 231–232, 242
Poinsinet de Sivry 54 n.6
Politicians 59, 61, 63
Polydorus 165, 167
Polyxena 163 n.11, 165, 168
Pope Urban VIII 13, 159–160
Porphyry of Tyre 65
Porto, Emilio 161 n.7, 164 n.20, 169, 173, 176 n.8
Pralboino 54, 60, 66
Priam/Priamus 165, 183
Prologue/Prologus 20 n.6, 39–42, 46–52, 55, 60, 95–96, 121, 127, 129, 146, 148–149, 165, 169, 178, 183, 187, 189, 191, 228 n.3
Proper nouns 27–28
Proprietas 100
Prose 3, 8–9, 11, 13, 41, 45, 54 nn.4 and 6, 61, 96 n.24, 100 n.47, 103, 105, 122, 125, 129, 154–155, 160 n.2, 162 n.11, 177–178, 195–198, 297
Pylades 164, 178
Quintilian/Marcus Fabius Quintilianus 216, 231
Rabelaisian 67
Realia 28, 45–46
Recognition/*anagnorisis* 140, 195, 229, 246–247
Redondilha maior 13, 177, 187
Reformation 80 n.42, 116, 192, 224
Respublica litteraria 93, 105, 113
Reversal/*peripeteia* 140, 200–201, 229
Rhetorical figure 58
Rinuccio Aretino 22 n.9
Robortello, Francesco 140 n.9, 220 n.44, 235–238, 240, 244, 251
Rosmunda 140 n.10, 149, 151, 161–164
Rymer, Thomas 237
Sausage-seller 61
Schmalkaldic War 116
Scholium/scholia 55–57, 82, 85, 123, 131, 298
Segni, Bernardo 228–229, 234 n.30, 251
Serafini, Michelangelo 162
Serenissima 60
Sertini, Alessandro 168 n.32

Sexual and scatological language 26
Siena 20, 59 n.16, 145
Slang word 60
Sofonisba 140, 149, 162 n.11, 164, 170–173, 250
Solerti, Angelo 163 n.13, 170 n.36
Soothsayer 57
Sperone Speroni 149 n.41, 237–240, 251
St John's College, Cambridge 212
Stanza 170, 172
Stasimon 15, 109–111, 165, 170, 172, 263, 283, 285–287, 289
Statius 218 n.35, 245
Stiblin, Caspar 81–82, 161
Surgery 65
Syphilis 64
Syria 219 n.39
Theology 94, 99
Theory of translation 78 n.31
Thomas Sébillet 7 n.18, 13, 92, 101, 106 n.74, 189, 191–199, 202, 204, 256, 261, 264, 266–268, 272–274, 279 n.62, 284–285, 290–291
Tragic chorus 10, 83, 283
Transformation theory 233 n.24, 250 n.103
Translation Studies 1, 15, 157, 205, 255, 257
Translation techniques 33, 45

Transliteration 28, 31
Trissino, Giovan Giorgio 147–148, 164, 170, 172–173, 234 n.30, 251
Tyrannicida 97
Unrhymed verses 170
Valla, Lorenzo 117
Valla, Giorgio 234 n.28
Vatican Library 160
Venice 7, 10, 38, 45, 53–54, 60, 64–66, 83, 122 n.33, 138, 146, 161 n.7, 193, 213, 233 n.21, 245, 261
Uerbum de uerbo 58, 62, 66, 119
Verona 1 n.1, 91
Vettori, Pietro 77–78, 161 n.6, 240–241, 244
Volgarizzamento 12, 137–138, 151–153, 155, 158
Watson, Thomas 91, 93, 106–113
Weinberg, Bernard 109 n.87, 139 nn.4–5, 142 n.15, 228 n.2, 231, 234 nn.25–26, 241 n.57
William Shakespeare 157, 292
Winsheim, Veit 11, 108 n.83, 115–120, 126, 130, 132
Word-for-word translation 6, 22–23, 45
Wordplay 26 n.22, 32, 56
Xenophon 175 n.1
Zeuxis 142–143, 146

Index Locorum

Aeschylus
Ag.
1078–9	220
1107–1128	219 n.41

Apollonius Rhodius
Argon.
8	79

Apollonius
Bibl.
3.7.5	215 n.27

Aristophanes
Nub.
14	46

Plut.
84–85	28 n.25
149–156	24
174–180	27, 28
176	26
279	31
293	30
295	32
325	32
383	31
386	29
427	34
431	28
521	34
529	30
541	31
545	35
546	32
560	30
575	32
606	35
639	29
660	29
661	29 n.27
663	35
674	30
688	30
699	26 n.21
703	26 n.21
706	26
720	31
729	34
768	31
797	32
937	30
999	28
1011	29 n.27
1013	36
1016	30
1024	30
1037	32 n.39
1061	26 n.22
1065	35
1067	30
1082–1083	26
1093	30 n.34
1095	30
1096	26, 35
1097	32
1123	32
1128	29 n.27
1129	32
1139	30
1146	36
1193	32
1206	29 n.27, 30 n.33

Aristotle
Eth. Nic.
III 1, 1110b24–1111a2	236 n.33

Poet.
1447a.14–17	142 n.16
1452a32–34	229 n.6
1452b31–37	236 n.35
1453a7–14	15
1454.b10	142 n.16
1460b.20	142 n.16
1451b.1–19	142 n.16
1448b.5–10	143 n.20
1461b.9ff	142
1461b.13	142 n.19
1451b–52a	147

Rh.
II 12, 1389b2–8 239 n.50

Cicero
Acad.
5 121
Fin.
I, 2 79 n.34
I, II, 4 79 n.37
Inv. rhet.
II.I.3 142 n.18
II.I.4 142 n.18
Off.
I, 16, 51 79 n.34

Euripides
Hec.
46 165 n.21
68 166
70 166
71 166
151–152 169
450 169
592 167 n.24
714–715 167 n.24
950–951 165 n.22
1127 168
444–483 172
629–656 172
767 169 n.34
905–951 172
1024–1034 172
IA
10–13
16–33 162 n.11
18–19 263 n.35
45 263 n.35
446 263 n.35
1098–1208 15, 263–264, 290
1103–1105 278
1104–05 266, 272
1106 278 n.56
1111–13 270, 273
1115–16 263, 266–267
1117–18 277 n.55
1123–26 279
1127–28 278 n.55
1131 264, 272, 281
1132 267 n.45
1134 267 n.46
1136 268 n.47
1140–1 274
1144–45 268
1278–1335 288
1466–99 287
1472–73 287
1512 285
1514–17 285
1523 287
1510–31 15, 283
1528–31 285
1587 104
Or.
34–51 216
88–90 216
153–210 216
211–236 216
253–315 216
255–57 216 n.30
264–65 216 n.30
396 221
1107 219 n.40
1199 219 n.40
1368–79 219 n.38
1455–56 219 n.37

Horatius
Ars P.
189–90 147
322 83 n.58
Sat.
I, 4, 1–5 50 n.34
I, 8, 46 26 n.21
II, 8, 91 25

Josephus
Antiquities of the Jews
18.109 223 n.52

Livy
Ab urb. cond.
1.25ff. 149

[Longinus]
On the Sublime
1.8	216 n.28
15.2	216 n.30
15.8	216 n.30

Ovid
Her.
9	237

Met.
1.568–746	145

Pindar
Ol.
2.38–42	215 n.27

Pyh.
4	120

Plato
Resp.
VI	123
X 595a–608b	231 n.12

Plautus
Amph.
50–54	214 n.24
50–63	149
711	46 n.24

Aul.
396	46 n.24
270	30

Bacch.
1006	30
1138a	30

Capt. 214 n.24

Mostell.
275	30

Pseud.
180	30
1118	30

Rud.
662	30

Trin.
199–202	31

Plutarch
Mor.
465d (*Tranquility of Mind*)	216 n.28
501c (*Affections*)	216 n.28

Seneca
Ag.
1012	216 n.29

Med.
488	222 n.50

Tro.
861	223 n.51

Oed.
709–712	247 n.88

Sophocles
Aj.
10	127

Ant.
1–3	107
11–14	107
100	111
420	112
475	111
505	109
727	112
1115–1117	109

El.
53–58	182 n.25
406	181 n.24
416–423	179 n.16
453–477	180 n.19

OT
738	243 n.65
828–29	244 n.68
1080	244 n.71
1329–1333	247 n.88
1360	247 n.88
1519	247 n.88

Terentius
An.
324	30

Eun.
298	30

Virgil
Aen.
1.50–80	149
4.471–3	216
6.37	217 n.33
6.570–72	215 n.27
7.324–26	215 n.27
10.905–6	221 n.45
12.666–8	221
12.845–48	215 n.27

Vulgate
1 *Corinthians*
4.4	222 n.46

1 *Kings*
2.44	222 n.46

Leviticus
5.1	222 n.46

www.ingramcontent.com/pod-product-compliance
Lightning Source LLC
Chambersburg PA
CBHW050513170426
43201CB00013B/1938